# The
# NEWPORT &
# NARRAGANSETT BAY
# Book
## *A Complete Guide*

Craig Hammell

# THE
# NEWPORT &
# NARRAGANSETT BAY
# BOOK

## *A Complete Guide*

### With Block Island

SECOND EDITION

Pamela Petro

Photography by
Craig Hammell

Berkshire House Publishers
Lee, Massachusetts

On the cover and frontispiece: Photography by Craig Hammell
Front cover: *Newport is famous for its Gilded Age "cottages."*
Frontispiece: *Newport Harbor at sunset.*
Back cover: *Church fairs—a way of life in the Narragansett Bay area; the Newport International Tennis Hall of Fame; harborside dining in Newport.*

The Newport & Narrangansett Bay Book: A Complete Guide
Copyright © 1994, 1998 by Berkshire House Publishers
Cover and interior photographs by Craig Hammell and other credited sources

Library of Congress Cataloging-in-Publication Data
Petro, Pamela, 1960–
    The Newport & Narragansett Bay book : a complete guide with Block Island / Pamela Petro : photography by Craig Hammell. — 2nd ed.
        p.    cm. — (The great destinations series, ISSN 1056-7968)
    Includes bibliographical references (p.    ) and indexes.
    ISBN 0-936399-93-7
    1. Newport (R.I.)—Guidebooks. 2. Narragansett Bay Region (R.I.)—Guidebooks. I. Title. II. Series.
F89.N5P46                                        1998
917.45'60443—dc21                        97-32467
                                                      CIP

ISBN  0-936399-93-7
ISSN  1056-7968 (series)

Editor: Constance Lee Oxley. Managing Editor: Philip Rich. Original design for Great Destinations™ series: Janice Lindstom. Page layout and typeset by Dianne Pinkowitz. Cover design: Jane McWhorter.

Berkshire House books are available at substantial discounts for bulk purchases by corporations and other organizations' promotions and premiums. Special personalized editions can also be produced in large quantities. For more information, contact:

Berkshire House Publishers
480 Pleasant St., Suite 5; Lee, Massachusetts 01238
800-321-8526
E-mail: info@berkshirehouse.com
Web: www.berkshirehouse.com

Manufactured in the United States of America

First printing 1998
10 9 8 7 6 5 4 3 2 1

*No complimentary meals or lodgings were accepted by the author and reviewers in gathering information for this work.*

# The <u>Great Destinations</u>™ Series

**The Berkshire Book: A Complete Guide**
**The Santa Fe & Taos Book: A Complete Guide**
**The Napa & Sonoma Book: A Complete Guide**
**The Chesapeake Bay Book: A Complete Guide**
**The Coast of Maine Book: A Complete Guide**
**The Adirondack Book: A Complete Guide**
**The Aspen Book: A Complete Guide**
**The Charleston, Savannah & Coastal Islands Book:**
  **A Complete Guide**
**The Gulf Coast of Florida Book: A Complete Guide**
**The Central Coast of California Book: A Complete Guide**
**The Newport & Narragansett Bay Book: A Complete Guide**
**The Hamptons Book: A Complete Guide**
**Wineries of the Eastern States**

*The Great Destinations™ series features regions in the United States rich in natural beauty and culture. Each Great Destinations™ guidebook reviews an extensive selection of lodgings, restaurants, cultural events, historic sites, shops, and recreational opportunities, and outlines the region's natural and social history. Written by resident authors, the guides are a resource for visitor and resident alike. The books feature maps, photographs, directions to and around the region, lists of helpful phone numbers and addresses, and indexes.*

# Acknowlegments

The second edition of *The Newport & Narragansett Bay Book* owes its publication to the heroic work of many people. For their discriminating palates, under-the-table espionage, and extensive memories, I'd like to thank Nelson and Nancy Vieira, Marcus Freitas, Renata Campos, Luiz Valente, Katherine Berg, Patricia Sobral, Alejandro Mier-Langner, Isabel Ferreira, Paul Garfinkel, Dick Newman, Mary Beveridge, Susan Saccoccia, Beatrice Parker, Jackie and Bill McGrath, and especially Bill Rae, Lora Urbanelli, and Paula and Casey Knynenburg. Much gratitude and thanks also go to my parents, Patricia and Stephen Petro, and my aunt and uncle, June and Morton Snowhite, for braving Newport on the soggiest, wettest Monday in memory.

Special recognition is due to Nelson Vieira for his invaluable help with the Newport Chapter, to Joe Diaz, who not only got up before 5:30 a.m. but skulked around the shops of Block Island taking notes on my behalf, and to Bill McGrath, who tirelessly and with kindness and good humor lent his eyes, ears, and legs to assist me with Newport lodging — a wonderful gift. More thanks are due to the talented Kristen McGrath, fact-checker extraordinaire, who is one of the most thorough, persistent, and fearless people I know. I'd also like to mention Elva of the Block Island Chamber of Commerce, whose knowledge and cheerful assistance have made an essential contribution to this book.

Then there is the exceptional trio of Philip Rich, the epitome of a gentlemanly and patient editor, Craig Hammell, the photographer who once again provided striking images to accompany the text, and editor Constance Oxley, whose attention to detail has saved me from myself on more than one occasion. Heartfelt thanks to you all.

Lastly, my gratitude goes out to my friend and research companion, Marguerite Harrison, who not only warned me to take a break now and then but made research jaunts much more fun. In fact, to the whole research crew — Tenby, the backseat-driving puppy, and the new 1990 Toyota wagon — my thanks.

# Contents

CHAPTER ONE
*Of Rhodes & Rogues*
**HISTORY**
1

CHAPTER TWO
*Between the Bridges*
**TRANSPORTATION**
19

CHAPTER THREE
*The City by the Sea*
**NEWPORT**
29

CHAPTER FOUR
*Rocky Shores & Rolling Fields*
**NARRAGANSETT BAY**
125

CHAPTER FIVE
*A Last Great Place*
**BLOCK ISLAND**
243

CHAPTER SIX
*The Nitty-Gritty*
**INFORMATION**
284

# Introduction

In 1997, Newport was ranked the top tourist destination on the East Coast. I don't know how such rankings are determined, but if the number of new shops, inns, restaurants, and recreational centers that have sprouted throughout Rhode Island's waterfront communities are any indication, then Newport's most-visited status must be true. Since the original edition of *The Newport & Narragansett Bay Book* was published in 1994 (based on material researched in 1993), a kind of adrenaline of confidence has run rampant not only in Newport proper, but also throughout the small towns that cluster on either side of Rhode Island's own, intimate ocean, called Narragansett Bay.

The second edition of *The Newport & Narragansett Bay Book* embraces all that is new on the bay and updates original material in Chapters Three, Four, and Five, with sections on Lodging, Dining, Culture, Recreation, and Shopping. In Chapter One, *History*, historical depth is provided to the communities that you'll find on the bay today. Chapter Two, *Transportation* still tells how to get from there to here, and Chapter Six, *Information* continues to contain nitty-gritty details, such as emergency telephone numbers and weather hot lines. There is one significant difference between the first and second editions, however, and that involves format: in this edition, all information on Newport, for example, is grouped together in Chapter Three, *Newport* for easier reference, with sections on Newport Lodging, Newport Dining, Newport Culture, etc. The same is true for Chapter Four, *Narragansett Bay*, which covers all Narragansett Bay communities (grouped under East Bay and West Bay headings), and for Chapter Five, *Block Island*, which deals exclusively with Block Island.

May the new organization make for improved access to information about the islands and shores of Narragansett Bay: together, one of the most historic, scenic, and vibrant smorgasbords of earth and sea ever to carve a niche out of the eastern seaboard.

Pamela Petro
Providence, Rhode Island

## THE WAY THIS BOOK WORKS

This book is divided into six chapters, each with its own introduction. There are three geographically based chapters dedicated to Newport, Narragansett Bay, and Block Island. The other three chapters, History, Transportation, and Information are thematic and concern all three regions.

Some entries, most notably those in the Lodging and Dining sections of the regional chapters, include specific information (telephone, address, hours, etc.)

organized for easy reference in blocks in the left-hand column. The information here, as well as the telephone numbers and addresses in the descriptions, were checked as close to publication as possible. Even so, details change with frustrating frequency. It's best to call ahead.

## PRICES

**B**ecause prices are subject to constant change, we've avoided listing specific rates and have instead indicated a price range. Lodging price codes are based on a per-room rate, double occupancy, in high season (roughly Memorial Day to Labor Day); I've noted only when breakfast and private bath are *not* included. Low-season rates are likely to be twenty to forty percent less. Again, it's best to call. Remember that lodging prices do not include tax.

Restaurant prices indicate the cost of an individual meal, including appetizer, entrée, and dessert, but not including cocktails, wine, tax, or tip. Restaurants with a prix fixe menu are noted accordingly.

A final word about prices. Like the Gilded Age, the penchant for conspicuous consumption that went with it has long since disappeared. Today's visitors to the area — and their hosts — appreciate the importance of frugality. Even the finest and most formal of establishments consciously seek to offer patrons a good value for their money. Therefore, the use of the word "Expensive" here, in connection with some establishments, is intended for comparative purposes only — not as a value judgement.

## PRICE CODES

|  | Lodging | Dining |
|---|---|---|
| Inexpensive | Up to $60 | Up to $15 |
| Moderate | $60 to $120 | $15 to $25 |
| Expensive | $120 to $200 | $25 to $35 |
| Very Expensive | Over $200 | Over $35 |

**Credit Cards** are abbreviated as follows:

| | |
|---|---|
| AE — American Express | T — Transmedia |
| CB — Carte Blanche | MC — MasterCard |
| D — Discover | V — Visa |
| DC — Diner's Club | |

# The
# NEWPORT &
# NARRAGANSETT BAY
# Book

## A Complete Guide

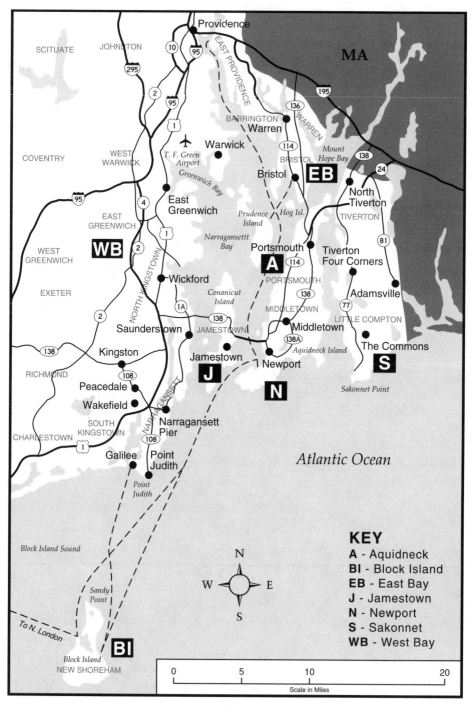

**Newport and Narragansett Bay with Block Island**

# CHAPTER ONE
## *Of Rhodes & Rogues*
### HISTORY

*Most of the big shore places were closed now, and there were hardly any lights except the shadowy, moving glow of a ferryboat across the Sound. And as the moon rose higher, the inessential houses began to melt away until gradually I became aware of the old island here that flowered once for Dutch sailor's eyes — a fresh green breast of the new world.*

F. Scott Fitzgerald, *The Great Gatsby*, 1925

It was no accident that *The Great Gatsby* was filmed in Newport, Rhode Island. Even though the novel was set in New York, nowhere else in the country better embodies Fitzgerald's fable of the American Dream than the City by the Sea.

Newport occupies the southern tip of Aquidneck, a long, slender island that rises from the water like the great backbone of Narragansett Bay. The city is famous as the show-place of all that money can buy, in particular

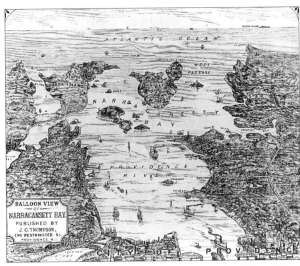

Courtesy Rhode Island Historical Society

*A "Balloon View" of Narragansett Bay from 1882.*

the "summer cottages" of Gilded Age millionaires — aptly described as crosses between Grand Central Station and the Palace of Versailles. Yet despite the grandeur of the built environment, it doesn't require a leap of imagination by moonlight to envision Aquidneck and neighboring islands as they were when Verrazzano sailed into the bay in 1524. Pockets of that old New World, still fresh and green, remain just a car or boat ride away from the mansions, those famous new copies of Old World splendor.

Mrs. Oyster once decreed that it took money three generations to "cool off."

One simply wasn't welcome in turn-of-the-century Newport society without at least a lukewarm pocketbook. Yet ironically, the host city of the nation's most byzantine social caste system — it was a faux pas, for instance, to overtake someone of higher status in one's coach — was one of four original Rhode Island towns founded by freethinking radicals in the name of equality, religious tolerance, and freedom of speech; Providence, Warwick, and Portsmouth were the other towns. From the first, these Rhode Island towns were havens for icon-oclasts unacceptable elsewhere — *rogues*, according to proper Puritans. Today, that policy seems courageous and forward-thinking, but at the time, Cotton Mather called Rhode Island "the sewer of New England." Newport not only welcomed the first Jewish congregation in the country (Touro Synagogue is the oldest on the continent), but also hosted other then-suspect groups as well, including Quakers, French Huguenots, and Baptists.

High-minded principals did not preclude the fact that Newport, and to a lesser degree other cities on Narragansett Bay, including Bristol, Warren, and Providence, reaped a fortune from the colonial slave trade. Such wealth made Newport one of the supreme cultural and economic centers in the colonies. In 1989, a desk crafted in the city's famous eighteenth-century Townsend-Goddard furniture workshop fetched eleven million at auction: one of the highest prices ever paid for a work of art other than a painting.

When nouveau riche New York millionaires began to arrive in Newport in the 1870s, they hoped some of this high-toned colonial culture would rub off on them. Few realized that the cobbled streets and stately public buildings of the old city had been paid for by a tax slapped on the slave ships. Like Fitzgerald's great American novel, Newport's history is laced with ironies, not the least of which is that many "beach cottages" are celebrating their centen-nial birthdays under the scrutiny of public tour groups. What Thornton Wilder called "the warming satisfaction of exclusion" that gently toasted the man-sions' builders has long cooled. The City by the Sea now warms itself by other means, from hot music and zesty meals to temperate sea breezes and the pro-tective embrace of Narragansett Bay.

## NATURAL HISTORY

### DEEP FREEZE

Like glaciers and the woolly mammoth, Narragansett Bay ultimately derives from the last great Ice Age — or rather from its demise. About 250 million years ago, a chain of high mountains rose along what is now the southern expanse of the bay. By the time the glaciers arrived at the beginning of the Pleistocene era, some 600,000 years ago, the region had eroded to a landscape of rolling hills. When the glaciers retreated, the whole region sank, creating a basin that would become Narragansett Bay; the highest peaks became islands.

Between 8000 and 6000 B.C., the ice that remained began to melt, causing the sea level to rise as much as fifty feet and inundating the sunken basin and its extensions, which today include the saltwater bodies of Greenwich Bay in the west, Mount Hope Bay in the east, and the Providence River estuary in the north. By 2000 B.C., the geography was essentially the same as that encountered by Roger Williams and his followers when they arrived as dissidents from Massachusetts in 1636.

When the bay was young, its shores were heavily forested and home to herds of mastodon, caribou, moose, and giant beavers. The western region especially was dotted with immense boulders, unceremoniously dumped there by retreating glaciers.

## THE OCEAN STATE

Rhode Island wasn't dubbed the Ocean State on a whim. Over one-fifth of its total area is taken up by Narragansett Bay, the state's premier physical feature and natural resource. The bay is twenty-eight miles long from its mouth at Newport to its head in Providence, roughly two-thirds of the distance from the sea to Rhode Island's northern border with Massachusetts. At its southernmost, Narragansett Bay stretches twelve miles from the town of Narragansett in the west to that of Little Compton in the east; its width narrows to about three miles in the north. Though the bay is full of dozens of small islets, three major islands congregate in the center: Aquidneck, Conanicut (better known as Jamestown), and Prudence. They have the effect of splitting the bay into two unequal halves, with the bulk on the western side and a slender filament two or three miles wide on the eastern side, known as the Sakonnet River.

What Rhode Island lacks in landmass — it's been said that two hundred Rhode Islands could fill the state of Texas — the bay reclaims in nearly 400 miles of irregular shoreline. Its coastal lowlands include sandy beaches, marsh flats, brackish pools, and dramatic, rocky promontories where the wind never quits. For the past several decades, watchdog groups like Save the Bay have helped to reduce pollution dramatically in Upper Bay waters and to protect the integrity of the Lower Bay.

In January 1996, however, the barge *North Cape* grounded off the western bay shore near Moonstone Beach (a seabird sanctuary), releasing 828,000 gallons of home-heating fuel into Narragansett Bay. The spill was devastating not only to wildlife, but also to Rhode Island fishermen who had to endure a months-long closure of 254 square miles of bay fishing grounds. Lobsters, which are the mainstay of the state's small commercial fishing fleet based in Galilee and Point Judith, were particularly hard-hit. Today, however, lobsters, as well as scallops, soft-shell clams, quahogs, blue crabs, and mussels have made a comeback and are once again being harvested in bay waters.

## CLIMATE CONTROL

On February 23, 1934, Professor Ellsworth Huntington made a dramatic announcement at Yale University: He had discovered that Newport, Rhode Island, has the best weather in America and proposed making it the nation's official summer capital. Rhode Island leaders were so pleased by this discovery that after World War II, they cited it in a petition to the United Nations to establish its permanent headquarters in Newport.

Alas, the U.N. took its business elsewhere, but Huntington may have been on to something. One of the results of a large body of water sitting in the midst of a small landmass is that it regulates temperature extremes. The bay retains warmth in the winter and coolness in the summer, casting a kind of weather force field over the areas covered in this book. When it snows in Providence, it rains in Newport; when it reaches 90° F in Providence, it's invariably only 80° F in Newport, though there are exceptions: In 1799, the ice was so thick on Narragansett Bay that farmers were able to run oxen teams over the ice from Newport to Fall River.

Despite the fact that "variability" is cited as the state's chief weather characteristic, temperatures around the bay tend to be so equitable that the area supports several thriving vineyards, including Sakonnet, the largest winery in New England. The moderate microclimate allows the grape vines a long, slow growing season. As Sakonnet's owner says, "All great vineyards are near water."

Of course, the bay is occasionally less than benign. At least three times in recorded history, it has served as a funnel for floodwaters that have pummeled Providence to bits: the Great Gale of 1815 and the hurricanes of 1938 and of 1954 (a concrete hurricane barrier now protects Providence). The 1938 hurricane was the worst disaster ever to hit the Narragansett Bay area, with winds clocked at 120 miles per hour and with the deaths of 311 people; homes demolished on the western shore were later found washed up on eastern beaches.

# SOCIAL HISTORY

## ISLE OF PEACE

As the Massachusetts Bay colony governor John Winthrop noted in 1634, "The country on the west of the bay of Narragansett is all champain for many miles, but very stony and full of Indians." (Champain is flat, open country suitable for farming.) Winthrop's findings may have been news to European settlers, but not to Native Americans, who had inhabited the shores of Narragansett Bay for at least ten thousand years before Winthrop made his report. They were on hand to witness the end of the Ice Age, to hunt mastodon and harvest shellfish. While sites from the Paleo-Native American period are rare — inhabitants were few and made only seasonal encampments, fishing coastal waters by summer and hunting interior forests by winter — archaeologists on Block Island recently unearthed the oldest year-round settlement in southern New England, dating back to 500 B.C. It was a stunning discovery that extended anthropologists' knowledge of permanent Native American villages by almost a millennium.

By the sixteenth century, the territory surrounding Narragansett Bay was inhabited by several tribes of Algonquins, a network of related nations that lived up and down the Eastern Seaboard from Canada to North Carolina. In Rhode Island, the Narragansetts were the largest Algonquin tribe at about 7,000 strong. They occupied the western shore of the bay, while their rivals, the Wampanoags, held the eastern side, including the principal islands; a third tribe, the Nipmucks, were pawns of these two stronger groups. (It was the Wampanoags who gave the name "Aquidneck," or "Isle of Peace," to the bay's largest island, home to present-day Newport, Middletown, and Portsmouth.) Block Island, meanwhile, was the stronghold of the Manisseeans, who called their home Manisses, or "The Isle of the Little God." John Greenleaf Whittier borrowed the name for his poem *The Palatine* (1867) about a famous wreck off Block Island.

> *Circled by waters that never freeze,*
> *Beaten by billow and swept by breeze*
> *Lieth the island of Manisees . . .*

When Verrazzano arrived in 1524, searching for a passageway to China for the king of France, it was Block Island that he described as being "in the form of a triangle, distant from the mainland ten leagues, about the bigness of the Island of the Rhodes." Verrazzano dubbed it "Luisa" after the queen mother of France, heralding the first in a train of European names. In 1614, Dutch navigator Adriaen Block renamed it "Adriaen's Eyland," though it was his surname that eventually stuck. Several decades later Roger Williams and his cohorts mistakenly thought Aquidneck was the island that Verrazzano had compared to Rhodes and so duly named *it* Rhode Island. Eventually the name outgrew its seventy-five-square-mile territory and took over the entire state, the official title of which is Rhode Island and Providence Plantations. Today, the Isle of Peace is once again known as Aquidneck.

Whether or not Verrazzano was the first European to comb the bay is an open question, but he was certainly the first to leave a record of his findings. Portuguese navigator Miguel Corte-Real, who left Lisbon in 1502 never to return, may have been the one to carve his name, the Portuguese coat of arms, and the date 1511 on a sandstone boulder (the Dighton Writing-Rock) in the Taunton River, which flows into an eastern arm of the bay. Historians are split on the authenticity of the inscription, though the legend of a "Viking Tower" in Newport (once thought to have been built by Norse explorers) has since been debunked; the tower is actually the foundation of a colonial windmill, built ca. 1670. Whether or not the Vikings sailed their longboats into Narragansett Bay will remain forever a mystery.

The "Viking Tower" in Touro Park in Newport. Legend had it that this massive structure was constructed by Vikings in the eleventh century, but the real story is that English colonists built it around 1600.

Craig Hammell

## EARLY SETTLERS, EARLY TROUBLES

Roger Williams founded Providence in 1636. While the Puritans in Massachusetts Bay may be famous for having sought religious freedom, once they got it they applied it only to themselves. Williams was more inclusive (incurring the wrath of folks like Cotton Mather) and opened his settlement to one and all, and in the process he secured the trust of Native Americans whose right to the land he recognized over that of the King of England. Williams later wrote, "It was not price nor money that could have purchased Rhode Island. Rhode Island was purchased with love." Though scorn followed from Puritan founding fathers, so, literally, did a host of fellow nonconformists eager to establish communities of their own: "humble and unwanted folk . . . at war with the orthodox and conventional in life."

Two of these who joined Williams in what he called his "lively experiment" were Anne and William Hutchinson, who founded Portsmouth on the northern tip of Aquidneck in 1638. Anne has the distinction of being the first woman to found a town in North America; her party's Portsmouth Contract is one of the first documents in the world to decree a truly democratic form of government.

The Hutchinsons' wealthiest follower was William Coddington, who moved on to establish Newport in 1639. Coddington tried to prevent Aquidneck and neighboring Conanicut from merging with Williams's Providence Plantations — despite his freethinking associations, he had feudal ambitions — but was thwarted by Williams and Dr. John Clarke, a physician from Newport. It was Clarke who wangled Rhode Island's famous royal charter from King Charles II. The charter secured "full liberty in religious concernments" and gave Rhode Island the greatest degree of self-government in the colonies. It was a document so ahead of its time that it lasted until 1843, long after other states had drafted new constitutions.

Other pioneers included the first white woman born in New England, Betty Pabodie, daughter of Priscilla Mullens and John Alden (the Mayflower's most famous couple). Pabodie and her family settled the Sakonnet region, also known as S'cunnet, Seaconnet, and Saykonate, all of which derive from the Sogkonate tribe, whose name means "haunt of the wild goose." At the time of her death in 1717 at the age of ninety-two, Pabodie had an astounding eighty-two grandchildren and 556 great-grandchildren; her tombstone is in the Commons Burial Ground in Little Compton. More astounding than Betty Pabodie's fecundity is that the sixteen families who purchased Block Island in 1660, taking up residence a year later, still have descendants well represented in the island's current telephone directory.

On the western side of the bay, early seventeenth-century trading posts soon evolved into a plantation system of rambling, prosperous estates based on a slave-holding economy. The oldest of these, Cocumscussoc in Wickford (known as Smith's Castle) was destroyed in King Philip's War; it was rebuilt in 1678 and is now open to the public. Four decades of living cheek by jowl with white settlers accomplished what many centuries never could: it united the Wampanoags and Narragansetts, in this case, against the English. The result was King Philip's War (1675–1676), a brutal, guerrilla-style conflict in which over 600 colonists and several thousand Native Americans died. After the Wampanoag chief King Philip was killed, what few natives remained joined together under the aggregate name Narragansett.

## A GOLDEN AGE, SLIGHTLY TARNISHED

Providence burned to the ground in King Philip's War. Roger Williams, then an old man, watched the town perish, though the Narragansetts spared his own home out of respect. Throughout the fighting, Newport remained unscathed, poised to enter its most successful century prosperous and intact.

By 1730, Newport was the fifth largest and wealthiest city in America, preceded only by New York, Boston, Philadelphia, and Charleston. Shipping and commerce were the cornerstones of its economy. The most lucrative aspect of which was the infamous triangle trade: rum distilled in Rhode Island was exchanged for slaves in Africa, who were sold to West Indian sugar planters, who paid in molasses to make rum. From a colony founded on the principles of freedom and tolerance, Rhode Island became the foremost conveyor of slaves to the New World, with the city of Newport leading the way. Men like Simeon Potter of nearby Bristol had few scruples; Potter swore he would "plough the sea into pea-porridge" to make money. Godfrey Malbone of Newport became so wealthy that he threw feasts for his returning sea captains and then let them smash all of the china and crystal on the table. Aaron Lopez of Newport, James De Wolf of Bristol, and John Brown of Providence all reaped millions in the slave trade, pumping some of their money into the glorious architecture that even today sets these towns apart; Bristol's town plan is even accredited to Sir Christopher Wren.

*Rhode Island sea captains live it up in Surinam in an eighteenth-century painting.*

According to historian William McLoughlin, "Only Boston equaled the stylish grace and urban sophistication of Newport in the decades prior to the Revolution." Much of Newport's architectural riches remain in evidence; the City by the Sea retains more buildings from the Colonial and early Federal period than any other city in the country. Some civic and ecclesiastical standouts in the Historic District include Trinity Church (1725–1726), also designed by Christopher Wren; the Colony House (1739), site of Rhode Island's annual General Assembly meeting until Providence became the state's only capital in 1900; the Redwood Library (1748–1750), which is the oldest library in the country to remain in its original building; Brick Market (1762) built at the head of seventeenth-century Long Wharf; and Touro Synagogue (1763). Although it closed in 1791, the synagogue reopened for regular services in 1883 and has been holding services ever since.

Newport's most illustrious visitor from the early part of the colonial period was Irish clergyman, essayist, and philosopher George Berkeley, who said the following about Aquidneck and his host city in his *Letter to Lord Percival* (1729).

> *The climate is like that of Italy north of Rome . . . . The land is pleasantly diversified with hills, vales, and rising grounds. Here are also some amusing rocky scenes. There are not wanting several fine rivulets and groves. The sea, too, mixed with capes and adjacent islands, makes very delightful prospects . . . . The town is prettily built, contains about five thousand souls, and hath a very fine harbour. The people are industrious, and though less orthodox, I cannot say have less virtue . . . than those I left in Europe. They are indeed a strange medley of different persuasions, which nevertheless all agree in one point, viz, that the Church of England is the second best.*

## FIRST IN WAR, LAST IN PEACE

R hode Island's tradition of dissent and wariness of external authority —
codified in its liberal charter — gave the colony the most to fear from a
meddlesome central government, be it in London or Washington. It was no
surprise, then, that on May 4, 1776, Rhode Island became the first of the thirteen colonies to renounce the crown; nor was it surprising that on May 29,
1790, it became the last state to ratify the Constitution, of which Rhode
Islanders were deeply suspicious. The following poem by a Connecticut
author refers to the state's ratification stalling.

> *Hail, realm of rogues, renowned for fraud and guile,*
> *All hail, the knaveries of yon little isle . . .*
> *Look through the state, the unhallowed ground appears*
> *A nest of dragons and a cave for bears . . .*
> *The wiser race, the snare of law to shun,*
> *Like Lot from Sodom, from Rhode Island run.*

During the War of Independence, the town of Portsmouth put up the first
African-American regiment ever to fight under the American flag, members of
which took part in the Battle of Rhode Island in August 1778. Though they
fought for the new union, African-Americans were not yet privileged to full
rights under Rhode Island law. It was not until 1784 that state legislators passed
an emancipation statute freeing all children born of slave mothers, and not until
1787 that antislavery forces, led by John Brown's brother Moses, succeeded in
passing a law prohibiting Rhode Islanders from participating in the slave trade.

The Battle of Rhode Island came at the end of a long siege designed to pry
the British out of Newport, which they had occupied since 1776. The city's
exposed position, combined with the loyalist leanings of many prominent
Newporters, had made it a sitting duck. While the redcoats didn't budge, the
battle marked the first joint expedition of American and French forces; when
the British voluntarily gave up the city in 1779, French troops made Newport
their home base. All of this upheaval did little for the city. In fact, Newport
never truly recovered from the Revolution, and the nineteenth century saw the
ascendancy of Providence as Rhode Island's chief city.

## OF CHICKENS AND COSMOPOLITES

T he first three-quarters of the nineteenth century were fairly quiet years for
Newport and the southern Narragansett Bay towns. (Block Island, though,
had been in its own agrarian cocoon since 1661, neither initiating nor welcoming much contact from the mainland.) While northern Rhode Island,
Providence especially, was becoming urbanized and industrialized, with an
influx of new immigrants to work the growing cotton, wool, and metal industries, the Narragansett Bay area remained an essentially rural backwater, its
chief milestone the breeding of the Rhode Island Red chicken. Between 1854

and 1896, a Little Compton farmer, William Tripp, worked with scientists and other area farmers to crossbreed the revolutionary fowl; it even has a monument, in the village of Adamsville.

Nearby Bristol, which had been burned by the British in 1775, rebounded by 1820 to become a little gem of urbanity on the bay. Its prosperity was closely linked to that of the De Wolf family — the wealth of both can be gauged from Linden Place, George De Wolf's elaborate mansion at 500 Hope Street. Due to overspeculation, De Wolf's financial empire collapsed in 1825; he and his family skipped town literally under cover of darkness for their Cuban estate, leaving Bristol reeling. Virtually the entire town went bankrupt overnight, and like Newport, never fully recovered.

While the western bay communities of Narragansett and North Kingstown remained ensconced in the rural plantation system that encompassed much of "South County" (the southwesternmost area of Rhode Island officially, but *never* in conversation, called Washington County), "real" plantation owners from the antebellum South were already coming to Newport for "the season." As early as 1784, a group of planters from Charleston had begun to summer in the City by the Sea, fleeing southern heat and malaria. By 1830, wealthy families from Virginia and South Carolina were returning year after year to spend the summer on rented farms or in big new boardinghouses. Ironically, one of the most luxurious of the latter was the Sea Girt House, built in 1855 by George T. Downing, a distinguished African-American businessman, who in 1866 almost single-handedly persuaded the Rhode Island legislature to outlaw racial segregation in public schools.

During the Civil War, the U.S. Navy transferred its academy from Annapolis to Newport. Though the Academy returned south after hostilities were over, Newport was compensated in 1884 by being chosen as home for the prestigious Naval War College. The city remains the Navy's premier educational center, with adjuncts to the War College, such as the Naval Justice School.

The U.S. Navy was not the only one beginning to pay attention to Newport; while few southerners had the means to summer on Narragansett Bay after the Civil War, a new crowd of "slightly disenchanted cosmopolites," as Henry James called them, began to arrive from Boston. These were the people Newporters dubbed "the nice millionaires." Luminaries like Henry James, Edith Wharton, Henry Wadsworth Longfellow, Oliver Wendell Holmes, John Singer Sargent, John LeFarge, and Julia Ward Howe headed a group of artists and intellectuals who descended for the summer to think deeply beside the sea. James gently parodied the young men of the group, himself included. "The gentlemen, indeed, look wonderfully prosperous and well conditioned," he wrote. "They gallop on shining horses or recline in a sort of coaxing Herculean submission beside the lovely mistress of a curricle."

But they weren't to recline for long. By the last quarter of the nineteenth century, the New York City crowd had began to arrive in droves, and the Brahmins beat a quick retreat. Of the reasons for their departure, Edith Wharton simply said, "I did not care for watering-place mundanities."

## THE PLAYGROUND OF THE GREAT ONES OF THE EARTH

"**A**void Newport like the plague until you are certain you will be acceptable there. If you don't, it will be your Waterloo."

By the time Harry Lehr uttered this advice to would-be social climbers, Gilded Age Newport had already become what William McLoughlin called "the most palatial, extravagant, and expensive summer resort that the world had seen since the days of the Roman Empire." Credit for transplanting New York society to Newport for the summer generally goes to Samuel Ward McAllister, known behind his back as "Mr. Make-a-lister." McAllister is the one who came up with the term "The Four Hundred," referring to the number of people in New York society worth knowing. There were, according to his calculations, "about four hundred people in fashionable New York society. If you go outside that number, you strike people who are either not at ease in a ballroom or make other people not at ease."

The real arbiters of this crowd were women. Shut out of the business world in which their husbands were kings (or robber barons to the press), wealthy wives set themselves up as queens in a seaside court of their own devising. The rules of entry were ruthless. According to one socialite, "Newport was the very Holy of Holies, the playground of the great ones of the earth from which all intruders were ruthlessly excluded by a set of cast-iron rules." If you got in at all, it usually took at least two seasons. Neophytes were advised to spend a summer at Bar Harbor first, honing their skills. Once in town, however, there was protocol to learn: don't build a "cottage" immediately, rent first; never out-jewel or out-dress your hostess; never actually enter the home of a lady upon whom you've called — just leave your card. Above all, try to be as idle as possible in the city where, according to Oscar Wilde, "idleness ranks among the virtues."

However frivolous, such a lifestyle required an immense amount of managerial skill. Again in McLoughlin's words, these women "were not brainless big spenders, but talented, shrewd, and forceful administrators." To live out a life of "conspicuous consumption" — a term Thorstein Veblen coined in his 1899 work *The Theory of the Leisure Class* — one needed vast amounts of capital and the bravado to spend it. The average "cottage" was more like a private resort hotel, had between fifty to seventy rooms and up to 100 servants — with twice that number hired for special occasions. (The servant and craftsmen corps that served the mansions was so large that its members' own cottages in Newport's Fifth Ward, often detailed in wonderful carpentry work, now constitute a separate historic district.) Ten-course dinners with solid gold service were held nightly, unimaginably consumed by women in corsets. One ball could cost as much as $200,000 and that was when money was worth more; one 1890 dollar equals $100 today.

All of this took stamina as well. Bessie Drexel, who was unhappily married to the court jester of Newport society, Harry Lehr, wrote in her autobiography *King Lehr and the Gilded Age* (1935), "Every summer Harry and I went to

*In their finery: Miss Minnie Stevens, later Lady Paget, and Perry Belmont, who built Belcourt Castle on Bellevue Avenue in Newport, outfitted for a Gilded Age costume ball. Both photographs Courtesy Newport Historical Society*

Newport like everyone else in our world, for in those days so much prestige was attached to spending July and August at the most exclusive resort in America that to have neglected to do so would have exposed a definite gap in one's social armor." Some were better at the game than others. Some were terrifying. Alice "of the Breakers" Vanderbilt used to don immaculate white gloves every morning and run her fingers over the tops of picture frames and stair railings. Heads rolled if they came away less than white. Yet Alice had her kinder and gentler moments as well. In the middle of dinner, she once ordered a pair of scissors and cut off a third of her pearls, then worth $200,000. She handed them to her pearlless daughter-in-law, mother of "Little Gloria," and said, "Here, take them. All Vanderbilt women have pearls."

The "Great Triumvirate" who ruled Newport society in the 1890s were Alva Vanderbilt Belmont, Tessie Oelrichs, and Mamie Fish. (Corresponding mansions include Marble House and Belcourt Castle for Alva, Rosecliff for Tessie, and Crossways for Mamie.) Tessie's greatest coup was simply getting to Newport at all. From birth in a mining camp — her father unearthed the Comstock Lode — she wound up not only on Bellevue Avenue (*the* Newport address), but also in Rosecliff, arguably the most elegant mansion of all. Mamie was considered the best party giver of the lot. It was she, with encouragement from Harry Lehr, who threw the "Dogs Dinner," to which 100 society dogs were invited to dine on stewed liver, rice, and fricassee of bones. News of this hit the newspapers during the countrywide recession of the mid-1890s and did not fair well on editorial pages.

Alva's greatest achievement came in marriage brokering. That many dabbled in this pastime is evident from the spreadsheets: by 1909, 500 American heiresses were married to titled Europeans (the chief catch) with dowries totaling $220 million. But Alva engineered society's greatest coup, persuading the Duke of Marlborough to marry her daughter Consuela in 1895 for a price of ten million. (The marriage proved so unhappy that Alva, now a staunch supporter of women's rights, confessed to coercion and had the marriage annulled.) Some men brokered for themselves, with less efficiency. John Jacob Astor VI finally let the courts decide to whom he was legally married (since there were so many contenders); the prize, though, goes to William Budlong, who divorced a total of twenty-one wives.

Newport men were decidedly less flamboyant than Newport women. Often they came only on weekends and then tended to be uncomfortable and ill at ease at teas and dinner parties. One notable exception was James Gordon Bennett, the New York publisher who famously sent Stanley to Africa to find Livingstone. Bennett not only had a yacht equipped with a full Turkish bath and a miniature dairy, and another bedecked with a full-sized pipe organ, but also used to drive his coach stark naked at midnight through the streets of Newport — "to breathe," he said. Bennett was also the driving force behind the Newport Casino, which he commissioned Stanford White to design in 1879. Then the first country club in America, the Casino was the original home of the U.S. Lawn Tennis Tournament and today houses the Tennis Hall of Fame.

In his book *The Barons of Newport* (1988), Terence Gavan suggests that the excesses of the summer crowd stemmed from their "collective insecurities" in having become too rich too fast. There was a rush to create an aura of refinement and good taste with money that hadn't quite "cooled off," which is why Newport, with its understated colonial elegance and patrician architecture, became the resort of choice. More often than not this rush took the form of one-upmanship in jewels, yachts, clothes, and coaches, but more than anything else, in houses. The lasting legacy of the Great Ones of the Earth are their "cottages" on Bellevue Avenue and Ochre Point Road, many of which back up to the famous Cliff Walk, and along Ocean Drive (for more on architectural features of the mansions, see the section Culture in Chapter Three, *Newport*). The mansions are still, to use McLoughlin's term, "wondrous to behold," and thanks to organizations like the Preservation Society of Newport and Doris Duke's Newport Restoration Foundation, many are now restored and open for tours (held in several languages). Most were conceived as "improvements" of Italian palazzos, Elizabethan country houses, and French châteaux — in a word, private, New World theme parks with running water, electricity, and central heating, built to the specifications of wealthy New World vacationers.

Yet Newport society looked to Europe for more than architectural models. Its social cult of idleness and frivolity was not only ahead of its time, prefiguring "the vacation" that would eventually become sacred to middle-class Americans as well, but also seemed even then to be a vaguely foreign, decidedly unAmerican concept borrowed from European royalty. Henry James, writing twenty years before the Gilded Age entered full swing in the 1890s, precisely envisioned the world for which Newport was on the threshold of becoming famous.

> *The villas and "cottages," the beautiful idle women, the beautiful idle men, the brilliant pleasure-fraught days and evenings, impart, perhaps, to Newport life a faintly European expression, in so far as they suggest the somewhat alien presence of leisure . . . Nothing, it seems to me, . . . can take place in America without straightway seeming very American; and, after a week at Newport, you begin to fancy that to live for amusement simply, beyond the noise of commerce or of care, is a distinctively national trait. Nowhere else in this country . . . does business seem so remote, so vague, and unreal. It is the only place in America in which enjoyment is organized.*

> Collected Travel Writings, Great Britain and America, 1876

## AMERICA'S FIRST RESORT

Fittingly, one of Rhode Island's nicknames for itself is "America's First Resort." In the early twentieth century, while the state's northern cities were becoming rich on the fruits of industry, towns along Narragansett Bay and the south coast were capitalizing on the latest popular fashion: the summer vacation. What began in Newport as a trend among the elite was not taking hold of all strata of society, and Rhode Island was one of the first states to respond by offering a niche for just about everyone. The general rule was that the Upper Bay, around Providence, was the in-state playground (more downscale), and the Lower Bay was the out-of-state playground (more upscale). The following thumbnail histories of how tourism has shaped or bypassed the towns covered in *The Newport & Narragansett Bay Book* will also give an overview of their character today. (Newport is treated separately in Chapter Three.)

## A JOURNEY AROUND THE BAY

### WEST BAY

In addition to Block Island, Narragansett Pier was Newport's only serious rival as a Gilded Age resort. It even had its own Stanford White-designed casino, built in 1886, but destroyed by fire in 1900. Today only the casino's decorative towers still stand astride Ocean Road as a memorial to swankiness past. "Narragansett Pier" is really the oceanside village center of the sprawling municipality of Narragansett, which also includes the commercial fishing villages of Point Judith and Galilee.

To the north, the village of Wickford in North Kingstown maintains an ele-

Courtesy Rhode Island Historical Society

*The famous Narragansett Casino was a landmark on the coast at Narragansett Pier for only fourteen years; it burned down in 1900. Today only The Towers, on the left, remain.*

gant little harbor and fine shops, also a legacy of popularity with a sportier and less ostentatious Gilded Age crowd. East Greenwich was never developed as a resort and retains the quiet air of a fine old countryseat. Like Wickford, it is full of eighteenth- and nineteenth-century homes, quietly kept in decent shape over the years rather than lavishly and recently restored.

The village of Jamestown on Conanicut Island has come to describe the whole island, which is just called "Jamestown" these days. While the Astors and the Vanderbilts were living it up in Newport, Jamestown was popular with a fashionable, but "quietly rich" crowd who wanted to get away from it all. Their modest, mostly shingle-style estates cluster on Beaver Tail, the island's rock-ringed southern peninsula. Much of Jamestown remains rural and undeveloped — a small, well-kept secret between two bridges (the Newport Bridge to the east and the Jamestown-Verrazzano Bridge to the west).

## EAST BAY

The East Bay towns of Bristol and Warren generally proved immune to turn-of-the-century resort fever. Only one mansion was erected in Bristol by a renegade millionaire: the elegant Blithewold, built by Augustus Van Wickle in 1908 on thirty-three acres now maintained as a park and arboretum. It was Bristol's good fortune to be home to the Haffenreffer family, who donated 500 acres known as Mount Hope to Brown University and thus spared the town further development. (Mount Hope is the anglicized version of "Montaup," the Wampanoags' name for this land.)

It has been said, accurately, "He who would live in a dream of fair houses should go to Bristol and pitch his tent there." Bristol's fair houses — a collection of magnificent, templelike Greek Revivals — have always been occupied year-round, so that over the decades there has been virtually no room in town for summer people to pitch their tents. They did stop by, however, between 1863 and 1946 to commission yachts from the world famous Herreshoff Boatyard on Bristol Harbor. Herreshoff-designed yachts dominated America's Cup competition in the days when contenders were enormous racing machines up to 144 feet long, sailed by sixty-six-man crews.

Warren has always been a little overshadowed by its somewhat fancier southern neighbor. Its homes are slightly more modest if equally old (in Warren, Federal-style clapboards outnumber Greek Revival temples) and are often hidden beneath asphalt shingles and aluminum siding. But Warren still offers something that few other bay towns retain — the charm of discovery. An evening stroll on Water Street in the summer is akin to putting away one's guidebook in a small, European city and wandering into an uncharted neighborhood. It's where the locals go, where no one minds that the sidewalk café is just a few blocks down from the seafood plant. Adding to this impression is the fact that many townspeople still speak Portuguese. From the 1850s throughout the early twentieth century, large numbers of Portuguese and Azorean fishermen settled in both Warren and Bristol; the latter still retains a small fishing fleet run by descendants of Portuguese-speaking immigrants.

## AQUIDNECK

Except for consumer-strip stretches along Aquidneck's two north-south axes (Routes 138 and 114), much of Portsmouth and Middletown still offers a quiet contrast to the exuberance of Newport. In fact, these two northern communities have no real town centers; instead they're loose aggregations of vineyards, nurseries, orchards, and potato and berry farms, ringed by stone walls that arch over the island and meander down to both eastern and western shores; these walls are so handsome and so old that they're protected by the National Trust. Privacy is highly esteemed: country estates in this area are hidden at the end of narrow lanes, far from public view; one such estate is Green Animals, which boasts perhaps the best topiary gardens in the country.

Quietest of all are the inner bay islands of Hog and Prudence, administered by the town of Portsmouth. Hog is tiny — only one-and-a-half-square miles — and is accessible by a seasonal ferry that covers the two-mile span from Bristol Harbor. Its 200 summer residents make do with no public electricity.

Prudence, though much bigger at about five-square miles, with a year-round ferry from Bristol (only a twenty-minute ride), has no hotel and just one general store. Prudence Island was a thriving farming community before the Revolution, but was burned by the British during the war; like Bristol and Newport, it never really recovered. Today the island is threaded with abandoned stone walls that make a latticework of once-tilled fields, long overtaken by dense woodlands.

## SAKONNET

The fact that Rhode Island is the smallest and second most densely populated state in the union only makes the Sakonnet area more remarkable. There are no pockets of strip malls in Tiverton or Little Compton, no supermarkets nor resorts, no movie theaters nor convenience stores. Little Compton's historic village center, called The Commons, however, is the loveliest in the state. This thin peel of land between the eastern arm of the bay and the Massachusetts border was deeded to Rhode Island in 1747 (along with Warren and Bristol) as part of a land settlement with Massachusetts Bay. It's an area blessed by a rich partnership between farmlands and the sea, and it's not much of an exaggeration to say that it probably doesn't look much different than it did when Tiverton and Little Compton first became part of Rhode Island over 200 years ago.

Little Compton has had its own summer colony for ages, but it was never part of the resort network. Today's "summer people" are more on the order of the southern families who first came to Newport in the late eighteenth and early nineteenth centuries — quiet country lovers who rent or own old colonial farmhouses. A clue to both the charm and aloofness of this area is that its best beach, Goosewing, not only has no parking, but also no access by car.

## BLOCK ISLAND

Block Island — former home of the Manisseeans' "little god," nicknamed "the stumbling block" by sailors — is just three miles wide by seven miles long, located ten miles off the coast of Point Judith and marooned in the open ocean. It boasts Mohegan Bluffs, claimed to be the highest sea cliffs in New England, and a distinctly Old World feel, as if the island just recently broke off the Irish coast and floated to this side of the Atlantic.

*The Spring House in the late nineteenth century.*

Courtesy Block Island Historical Society

*The clapboard grandeur of
The National Hotel
dominates Block Island's
Old Harbor.*

Craig Hammell

Block Island first emerged from its two-century cocoon in the 1870s when the islanders finally persuaded the government to build a breakwater now known as Old Harbor; before that, no natural harbor existed. The project effectively issued an invitation for "off-islanders" to come and visit.

And they did. By 1900, Block Island was in full swing as an elite resort, with thirty hotels and over two thousand summer visitors a day. Families interested in sporty pursuits like sailing, fishing, and "taking the waters" at The Spring House, rather than in conspicuous consumption, came here instead of Newport. More than any other resort in the state, Block Island epitomized a kind of national romance with the past that attended the 1876 Centennial. People bewildered by incomprehensible new technologies and rapidly changing cities sought places that filtered out modern life and preserved "the good old days." Thanks to its isolation, Block Island was such a place par excellance.

Around Old and New Harbors, the result was a four-decade boom of houses and hotels of shingle and clapboard, bedecked with mansard roofs, wraparound porches, and gingerbread trim. After World War I, however, Block Island fell in a Sleeping Beauty-like phase from which it didn't awaken until the 1970s. During that time, the island was decimated by the 1938 hurricane, after which virtually all of its cultivated fields were left to overgrowths of wild bayberry, exactly as they remain today. When Block Island awoke, visitors were again treated to a rare glimpse of the past, this time as an archive of Victorian architecture perfectly preserved in rambling hotels and the shingled turrets of beach cottages.

Today Block Island is once again a hopping place to be, with visitors in pursuit of a latter-day version of the nostalgia that their ancestors sought a century ago. Thanks to a recent zoning law designed to protect the island's open space, new construction is limited to sizable lots, on which big postmodern beach houses are being built — the legacy to the next century.

# CHAPTER TWO
# *Between the Bridges*
## TRANSPORTATION

*When we moved to Prudence Island, we made the decision to commute to school each day in our own boat. Matt and I are both teachers (on the mainland). Since then, each year in the season when the harvest is ready, the vacationers are going home, the birds are on the move, we prepare for our own migration.*

Grace Hall McEntee, *Where Storms Are Beautiful*, 1993

Craig Hammell

*Masts and cables — Newport Harbor and the Newport Bridge.*

Whether or not you choose to live on Prudence Island and commute to work everyday by sea, a quick check of Rhode Island geography proves that the best way to get around Narragansett Bay and Block Island Sound is by boat. The waters have long accommodated commuters, in everything from canoes, a form favored by both Native Americans and early settlers (the settlers used them to commute to what amounted to seventeenth-century business meetings) to Fall River steamships that carried businessmen to and from Newport when "the season" was in swing. Ships of trade, on which many a passenger hitched a ride, have plied the bay as well, most romantically the great, square-rigged China clippers of the nineteenth century.

Ever since the commodores of the Gilded Age made Newport the yachting capital of the world, most of the craft afloat on the bay have been pleasure boats, participating in the scores of races and regattas held throughout the summer.

For the boatless, the bay can be bit trickier to navigate. To get from Narragansett Pier to Sakonnet Point in Little Compton, for example, a distance of only twelve miles, you must cross the Jamestown-Verrazzano Bridge, traverse Conanicut Island, cross the Newport Bridge, drive the length of Aquidneck from south to north, cross the Sakonnet Bridge, then drive the length of Rhode Island's eastern shore from north to south, finally arriving in Little Compton about an hour later. It seems easier to swim, but then you'd miss out on the rolling landscape, historic homes, pastures, roadside vegetable stands, and classic bayside seafood shacks that make the landward journey such a pleasure.

# GETTING TO THE NARRAGANSETT BAY AREA

*Sunset on the bay.*

Craig Hammell

## BY CAR

From the **south and west** (New Jersey, New York, Connecticut): Take I-95 to RI exit 3; pick up Route 138 East to Jamestown Bridge, cross Conanicut Island, and continue to Newport (still on Route 138) via the Newport Bridge (toll $2.00).

From the **north** (through Providence): Get to Newport by heading down either the eastern or western sides of Narragansett Bay. The eastern route is slightly faster.

*Eastern route:* Take I-95 to I-195 East into Massachusetts; take MA exit 2 and follow Route 136 South, which will lead you back into Rhode Island and eventually to the Mount Hope Bridge (toll $.30) Before reaching the bridge, if you wish to drive through the town centers of Warren and Bristol, bear right at the sign labeled "Warren," which puts you onto Market Street. This will lead to a T-junction on Route 114 in Warren center. Turn left. Route 114 parallels Route 136 and also brings you to the Mount Hope Bridge.

Once on Aquidneck, continue on either Route 114 or Route 138 South to Newport. Route 138 has less traffic; take it to a left turn onto 138A, also known as Aquidneck Avenue; follow this until it becomes Memorial Boulevard at the Newport/Middletown line. Easton Beach will be on your left. At the top of the hill, Memorial Boulevard intersects Bellevue Avenue; the mansions are to the left.

An alternative eastern route is to remain on I-195 until MA exit 6; take Route 24 South across the Sakonnet River and pick up either Routes 138 or 114 once on Aquidneck. Some say this is faster.

*Western route:* Take I-95 South from Providence to exit 9 where the highway splits; bear left onto Route 4 South, which feeds directly into Route 1 South. Take Route 138 East to the Jamestown Bridge and across Conanicut Island, over the Newport Bridge (toll $2.00) to Newport. If you wish to head south to Narragansett instead of east to Newport, continue on Route 1 to Bridgetown Road, which leads to Scenic Route 1A South. This will take you directly to Narragansett Pier.

From the **north and east** (through Boston and Fall River): From the Boston area, follow Route 24 South through Fall River, over the Sakonnet River bridge (at which point you'll be in Rhode Island), and onto Aquidneck. Then see *Eastern route* directions above, under From the **north** (through Providence), beginning at "Once on Aquidneck . . . ." If you're arriving from the east, take I-195 West until MA exit 6, which puts you onto Route 24 South.

## BY BUS

R hode Island Public Transit Authority **(RIPTA)** runs several direct buses between Providence and Newport from 5:30 a.m.–11:05 p.m. daily. Call 401-781-9400 (in Providence), 401-847-0209 (in Newport), or 800-662-5088 for schedule information and for other destinations throughout the Narragansett Bay area.

**RIPTA** arrives in Newport at the **Newport Gateway Convention & Visitors' Bureau** at 23 America's Cup Avenue, as does **Bonanza Bus Lines** (401-846-1820 in Newport; 401-751-8800 in Providence; 800-556-3815). Bonanza has direct daily service to or from Boston and connections to and from all points in New England, including Cape Cod and New York City.

## BY FERRY

T he **Viking Fleet** (516-668-5709) out of Montauk, New York, offers three scheduled trips from the tip of Long Island, New York, to Newport, Rhode Island, each summer. Ferries depart from the Montauk dock at 7:00 a.m. and leave Newport at 5:00 p.m.; the trip takes two hours each way. Bicycles and pets are welcome.

## BY PLANE

T o travel to the Narragansett Bay area by plane, the best bet by far is to fly into the brand new T.F. Green State Airport in Warwick, Rhode Island (Post

Road, Route 1, 401-737-4000). The airport was entirely updated and enlarged in 1996, but compared to Logan Airport in Boston remains negotiable and ultraefficient, with inexpensive and ample parking. Best of all, when you leave the airport, you don't sit in traffic (leaving Logan, you are immediately confronted with the Sumner Tunnel), but have immediate access to a traffic-free stretch of I-95. If after all this, you'd still prefer to fly into Logan Airport, call 617-542-6700 (Logan is about two hours from Newport, one hour from Providence).

The following airlines serve T.F. Green State Airport:

**American** (800-433-7300).
**American Eagle** (800-433-7300).
**Business Express** (800-345-3400).
**Cape Air** (800-352-0714; offers 7 flights a day to Nantucket).
**Continental** (800-525-0280).
**Continental Express** (800-523-3273).
**Delta** (800-221-1212).
**Delta Express** (800-325-5205; flies nonstop to Orlando, FL).
**Northwest** (800-225-2525).
**Southwest** (800-435-9792).
**United** (800-241-6522).
**United Express** (800-241-6522).
**US Airways** (800-428-4322).
**US Airways Express** (800-428-4322).

**Airport transfer services** to and from T.F. Green State Airport include the following private companies, as well as **Bonanza Bus** and **RIPTA:**

**Airport Taxi and Limo** (401-737-2868).
**Airport Van Shuttle** (401-763-1900).
**Cozy Cab Newport Shuttle** (401-738-1504).
**Private Chauffeur Service** (401-783-9369).
**Viking Tours & Transportation** (401-847-6921).

**Rental car** companies at T.F. Green State Airport include the following:

**Alamo** (800-327-9633).
**Avis** (401-736-7500; 800-831-2874).
**Budget** (401-739-8900; 800-527-0700).
**Dollar** (401-739-8450; 800-800-4000).
**Enterprise** (800-736-8222).
**Hertz** (401-738-7500; 800-654-3131).
**National** (401-737-4800; 800-227-7368).
**Thrifty** (401-732-2000; 800-367-2277).

There are several other small, state-run airports throughout Rhode Island. There are no scheduled flights arriving at the **Newport State Airport** in Middletown, Rhode Island (401-846-2200), but it does serve charters and private aircraft. The **Quonset State Airport** in North Kingstown, Rhode Island (401-294-4504) also serves some corporate and private planes, though principally naval craft. (See the section Block Island below for information about flights to and from the island.)

## BY TRAIN

There are three **Amtrak** (800-872-7245) stations in Rhode Island, at Westerly, Kingston (the best bet for those en route to Newport), and Providence. Newport-based **Cozy Cab Newport Shuttle, Private Chauffeur Service,** and **Viking Tours & Transportation** (see **Airport transfer services** above for telephone numbers) all provide limousine service to and from both Kingston and Providence stations. RIPTA also runs regularly scheduled buses from Kingston to Newport. See information in **By Bus** above.

## GETTING AROUND NARRAGANSETT BAY

## BY CAR & PARKING

There's no way around it: the car, for all its faults, is the best nonaquatic way to explore the Narragansett Bay area. Unfortunately, however, cars eventually need to be parked, and therein lies the rub.

Seasoned travelers who claim that Newport is one of their favorite places on earth nevertheless single out parking as the city's number one nightmare. The Newport Gateway Convention & Visitors' Bureau recommends the lot directly behind their center at 23 America's Cup Avenue, which has a capacity of 1,000+ cars. All-day parking costs only $10, but it's a substantial hike from there to the Cliff Walk. There are several wharf lots nearby in the heart of the Thames Street and Newport Harbor shopping district, but these are smaller and fill up fast; the same goes for the lot in front of the Newport Creamery on Bellevue Avenue, directly opposite the International Tennis Hall of Fame (it's great for mansion touring, if you can get in).

Be careful parking on the street; many areas require a residential permit, and others are limited to one or two hours, all strictly enforced. A new breed of digitalized parking meter has spawned all over the city. Rates are $.25 per fifteen minutes; be sure to read the fine print regarding hours of operation. Also watch your speed on Memorial Boulevard; it was voted Best Place to Get a Ticket by readers of *Newport Life Magazine*.

A tip: keep calm if you get lost in the Sakonnet region. The town of Little Compton seems to have an aversion to road signs, but the area is so beautiful that it's fun to prowl a little bit, even if you don't know where you're going.

For additional advice on getting around the bay on land, or for roadside assistance, try the **AAA** offices in the following towns.

# NARRAGANSETT BAY ACCESS

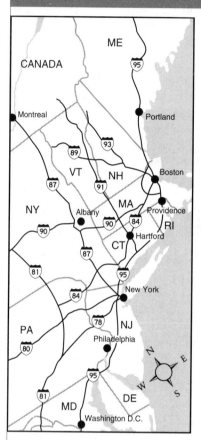

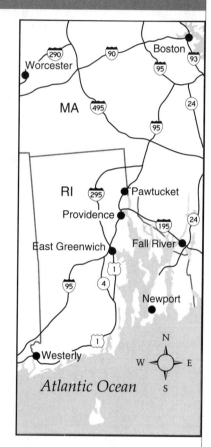

The chart below gives approximate miles and driving times between Newport and the following cities:

| City | Time | Miles |
|------|------|-------|
| Albany | 3.5 hours | 185 |
| Boston | 1.25 hours | 65 |
| Hartford | 1.5 hours | 85 |
| Hyannis | 2 hours | 105 |
| Montreal | 7 hours | 365 |
| New York | 3.5 hours | 175 |
| Philadelphia | 5 hours | 270 |
| Portland | 3 hours | 175 |
| Providence | 45 minutes | 35 |
| Washington, D.C. | 7.5 hours | 400 |

**Middletown, RI** (401-841-5000).
**Narragansett, RI** (401-789-3000).
**Providence, RI** (401-272-6353).
**Warwick, RI** (401-732-5100).

## BY FERRY

Ferries to **Prudence and Hog Islands** leave from Church Street Wharf in Bristol, Rhode Island. Call 401-253-9808 for schedule information. Ferries run year-round to and from the village of Homestead on Prudence Island; the Prudence crossing takes twenty minutes. On select days in-season, the ferry also makes stops at Hog Island; the Hog crossing takes ten minutes.

The original Jamestown Ferry was retired in 1969, but a new **Jamestown-Newport Ferry** was launched in 1993. The twenty-six-foot boat sails on weekends from Memorial Day through the end of June, daily from July 1-Labor Day, and on weekends from early September-October 15. It leaves from Conanicut Mooring on Jamestown and stops in Newport at Fort Adams, the New York Yacht Club, and Rose Island on request, in addition to scheduled stops at Bowen's Landing, Long Wharf, and Goat Island. Call 401-423-9900 for schedule information.

The **Oldport Marine Harbor Ferry** (401-847-9190) plies Newport Harbor daily from 10:00 a.m.–8:00 p.m. (Memorial Day-Labor Day; weekends until the Newport International Boat Show in mid-September) back and forth between Goat Island Marina and Bowen's Wharf. For $1.75 one-way, it's a real foot saver.

## BY PRIVATE BOAT

For information on state guest moorings and rental slips, see Marinas, under the heading Sailing & Boating in the Recreation sections in Chapter Three, *Newport* and Chapter Four, *Narragansett Bay.*

## BLOCK ISLAND

### BY CAR TO THE GALILEE FERRY

Coming from north or south, it's about a thirty-minute drive from I-95 to the Block Island boat at Galilee. Be sure to arrive *at least* thirty minutes before departure time; there is often a line at both the parking lot (across the street from the dock) and the ticket window. If seasickness depends on where you sit on the ferry, arrive one hour in advance to get choice locations.

From the **north:** When I-95 South splits at RI exit 9, bear left onto Route 4 South, which leads directly into Route 1 South; from there, take the exit for Route 108 South; continue approximately three miles to the right-hand turn for the Block Island ferry.

## Narragansett Bay Bridges

Scenario: two figures walking along the beach. The outline of a bridge looms in the distance, its silhouette like the skeleton of a great dinosaur. One bends to pose a question to the other. A romantic moment? Possibly, but more probably the query was, "Now, which one is that?"

This refrain — Which bridge did you say that was? — can be heard up and down Narragansett Bay. Bridges divide the bay into a network of fascinating, related, yet diverse components. But with four principal bridges, telling them apart can sometimes be difficult. Here's a short guide.

**The Newport Bridge** connects Newport (the southwestern peninsula of Aquidneck) with the eastern shore of Jamestown. It is just over two miles long and is considered "Narragansett Bay's Most Spectacular Man-Made Sight." When the bridge was opened in June 1969, it retired the Jamestown Ferry, which had provided the oldest continuous ferry service in the country. The same family (the Carrs) had participated in the running of the ferry for almost 300 years. The real name of the Newport Bridge is the Claiborne Pell Bridge; 1,654,675 vehicles crossed its span during July and August 1996.

**The Jamestown-Verrazzano Bridge** connects the western shore of Jamestown to the eastern shore of the Rhode Island mainland, about three miles south of Wickford. This newer bridge, which has a span of about 650 feet, opened in 1992. It replaced the old Jamestown Bridge, which had been built in 1940 (Rhode Islanders also call the new one the Jamestown Bridge). Ask locals about the near mythical snafu over how long it took to build the J-V Bridge — it's a classic Rhode Island saga.

**The Mount Hope Bridge** connects the Rhode Island mainland at the Bristol peninsula to the northern tip of Aquidneck. The precipitous Mount Hope Bridge was built in 1929, replacing a ferry that had run between Bristol and Portsmouth since 1698. At the time, its main span of 1,200 feet made it the eighth largest suspension bridge in the world (and also the first ever to be painted — it's green). In 1930, the bridge received an American Institute of Steel Construction Award as the most beautiful bridge in its class. Note the wonderful gas-style street lamps.

**The Sakonnet Bridge** connects the northeastern tip of Aquidneck (an area called The Hummocks in Portsmouth) to the town of Tiverton on the easternmost strip of Rhode Island. The bridge, built in 1956, is short but has a long history. Three previous drawbridges existed in its place between 1794 and 1957, all called Stone Bridge. The stretch of the Sakonnet River that they spanned has always been known as Howland's Ferry, in honor of the previous form of river crossing.

From the **south:** Take CT exit 92 from I-95 and bear right onto Route 2 (North Stonington Road); take a right-hand turn onto Route 78; at the end of Route 78, take a left onto Route 1 North and continue until exit for Route 108 South; continue three miles to the right-hand turn for the Block Island ferry.

## BY FERRY

There are several options for arriving on Block Island by ferry; they present a fair range of embarkation ports and travel times.

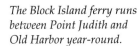

*The Block Island ferry runs between Point Judith and Old Harbor year-round.*

Craig Hammell

**Interstate Navigation Company** (in New London, CT, 203-442-7891; 203-442-9553; in Galilee, RI, 401-783-4613) Runs seasonal ferries from Providence (four hours), Newport (two hours), and New London (two hours), plus a year-round boat from Galilee State Pier (one hour, ten minutes). Cars are allowed only on the Galilee and New London boats, and reservations are absolutely necessary. All ferries arrive/depart Old Harbor, Block Is.

**Jigger III** (in NY, 516-668-2214) Runs seasonal service mid-Jun.–Sept. The boat leaves Montauk Point, Long Is. at 8:45 a.m. daily and returns from New Harbor, Block Is., at 4:30 p.m. Crossing time is two hours.

**Viking Fleet** (in NY, 516-668-5709) Seasonal daily service from Jun. 13–Sept. 1, weekend service from Apr.–Jun. and Sept.–Oct. Boats leave Montauk Point, Long Is. at 9:00 a.m. and arrive one hour, forty-five minutes later in New Harbor, Block Is.; leave New Harbor at 4:30 p.m.

Note that the Montauk ferries are for passengers only (no cars), though they do accept bicycles and pets.

For passengers arriving at T.F. Green State Airport bound for the Galilee ferry, there is daily, nondirect Rhode Island Public Transit Authority (RIPTA) service from the airport to the Galilee dock (take a bus from the airport to the University of Rhode Island (URI) in Kingston, then transfer to a Galilee bus). RIPTA also serves ferry-bound folk arriving on Amtrak at the Kingston station. Call RIPTA at 401-781-9400 in Providence or 800-662-5088 for schedule information.

**Private Chauffeur Service** (401-783-9369) Also offers transportation to the Galilee dock.

## BY PLANE

There are both regularly scheduled flights and charter service between Block Island and airports in Rhode Island, Connecticut, and New York.

**Action Airlines** (203-448-1646; 800-243-8623) Has both scheduled and charter service year-round to Block Is. from Groton, CT, and La Guardia Airport in NYC. Call for information.

**New England Airlines** (401-596-2460 in Westerly; 401-466-5881 on Block Is.; 800-243-2460) Flies hourly to Block Is. from the Westerly State Airport (401-596-2357; 401-596-6312). Passengers may also arrange to be picked up at T.F. Green State Airport in Warwick, RI.

Charter service only is provided by **Long Island Airways** (516-537-1010) between Block Island and East Hampton, Long Island.

For information on flights and weather conditions, contact the **Block Island State Airport** at 401-466-5511.

### BY PRIVATE BOAT

For public docking facilities on Block Island, see Marinas, under the heading Sailing & Boating in the section Recreation in Chapter Five, *Block Island*.

## ONCE ON BLOCK ISLAND

At first it may seem like an inconvenience, but believe me, you'll soon be glad there are virtually no cars for rent on Block Island. It's too small and too full of people (and of rare species unique to the island, such as the small, furry creature called the Block Island vole) to warrant a lot of cars and exhaust fumes. Islanders stridently complain that motor traffic is dangerous and frightens the wildlife, and they're right. By far the best way to see Block Island is by bicycle or on foot. Some of the hills are tough, but the pleasures of smelling and hearing the island, as opposed to catching a quick glimpse of it, far outweigh the extra exertion.

True to Block Island's nickname "The Bermuda of the North," there are mopeds available for rent, as well as bicycles and taxis. For bicycle, moped, and water sport rentals, see the section Recreation in Chapter Five, *Block Island*. Note that roads are often sand covered, and moped tires have a tendency to skid (I speak from personal experience).

There are always a small pack of cabs awaiting scheduled ferry arrivals. For taxi service on Block Island, try the following:

**The Colonel** (401-842-4391; 401-466-5546).
**Hot Fudge Taxi** (401-742-0000).
**Kirb's Taxi** (401-788-4749).
**Lady Bird Taxi** (401-466-3133).
**OJ's Taxi** (401-782-5826).
**Uncle Lou's Cab** (401-788-4181).
**Wolfie's Taxi** (401-466-5550).

# CHAPTER THREE
## The City by the Sea
### NEWPORT

Craig Hammell

*Yacht Racing is one of Newport's favorite pastimes.*

Like the never-still sea that surrounds it, Newport, Rhode Island, is a city of countless moods and colors, catching the eye and ear from every angle, ever-shifting, never dull. It is a city of mansions, the "summer cottages" of Gilded Age millionaires, cottages that Henry James likened to a tribe of "white elephants." It is a party city, famous — or infamous — for the harborside revelry that spreads like wildfire along Thames Street on summer Saturday nights. It is a yachting city, former home of the America's Cup, its natives as comfortable on the currents of Narragansett Bay as they are on paved — or cobblestoned — streets. It's an old city, with a higher concentration of restored colonial and early Federal homes than any other place in America, save Williamsburg, Virginia.

Newport has always had many personalities. In his fondly comic portrayal of the town in the novel *Theophilus North*, Thornton Wilder compared Newport in the 1920s to the archaeological site of ancient Troy. He said that like Troy, Newport is really nine cities superimposed on one another, all visible to some

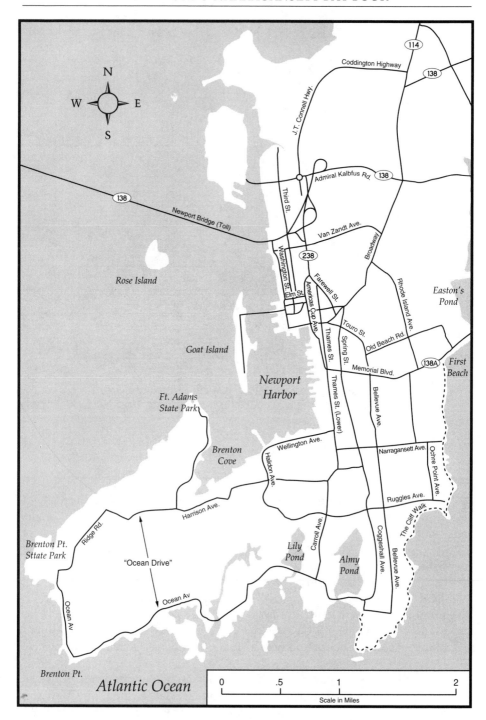

**Newport**

degree and all coexisting, if with very little relation to each other. The first he ascribed to the original seventeenth-century village; the second to Newport's glory days in the eighteenth-century; the third was the wharf world of chandleries, drying nets, and fishermen's bars; the fourth belonged to the naval base; the fifth was inhabited by nineteenth-century intellectuals like Henry James and Edith Wharton; the sixth flexed the glittering muscles of the Gilded Age rich; the seventh city existed to serve the sixth; in the eighth Wilder included himself, a city of voyeurs, protégés and hangers-on; and the ninth, finally, was the middle-class town that held all of the other squalid and glittering fragments together.

To a degree, Wilder's excavation holds true. The wharves are no longer glamorously seedy, but teeming with shops and boats and visitors — otherwise, traces of all of the other cities remain. Within this fractured image, however, one fact persists: Newport, above all else, is *home*. Unlike many resorts and reconstructed colonial towns, Newport is a living place. To borrow an image from the surrounding sea, Newport is anchored; anchored to its multifaceted past and present. As ever, Henry James captured this vision in his memoir, *Notes of A Son and Brother*.

> *Newport was and still is a unique place. One of the most beautiful towns in America, it is a tone and the same time a colonial city of singular distinction and a well-known summer resort of long standing; to walk through Newport is to walk through three hundred years of American architecture, much of which is beautifully preserved, used, and lived in still.*

*Lived in still.* This is the secret to Newport's success.

# LODGING

In 1945, the city of Newport petitioned a brand new organization, called the United Nations, to locate its headquarters in the City by the Sea. Although the U.N. regretfully declined, one of the reasons Newport's petition was considered at all was the city's impressive possession of *seven* resort hotels. Times have changed. In addition to hotels, motels, inns, time-shares, and guest houses, Newport now has more "Bed & Breakfast" establishments than any other city in the country. San Francisco, a much bigger town, comes in second.

Which brings up an issue. "Bed & Breakfast" in this book refers to European-style lodging in a home; in other words, the home came first, the business came later. Many larger inns may call themselves B&Bs — doubtless imagining guests flocking to the cozy image — but if I consider an establishment to be an inn at heart, I've listed it here as such.

A word about location: the more convenient a spot, the more noisy it may be at night. If quietude and calm are your thing, seek out a colonial or Victorian B&B in the historic, residential Point Section; if you like to party, a harbor location (generally on Thames Street) is a must.

One final note of caution: as I researched the second edition of this book (in 1997), Rhode Island newspapers repeatedly congratulated the state on its best summer of tourism ever, and on the fact that on many weekends every room in the state was booked. My advice: reserve early. The Newport Gateway Convention & Visitors' Bureau (23 America's Cup Avenue) posts nightly room availability.

## LODGING NOTES

**Tax.** Most prices are quoted without the seven percent Rhode Island sales tax; to that, alas, add another five percent room (also called bed) tax. If the full twelve percent tax is included in the price, this is noted.

**Parking.** When making a reservation in Newport, be sure to ask about free off-street parking. Most lodgings do offer parking spaces, but it is crucial to check in advance.

**Minimum stay.** Many establishments, large and small, have minimum-stay requirements (though they tend to be flexible if it's been raining all summer). Check first; it's usually two nights in-season, three on holiday or festival weekends.

**When to book.** It's always a good idea to reserve early; to procrastinate when making reservations for Jazz or Folk Festival Weekend is holiday suicide. Those weekends in mid-August are Newport's busiest, with many inns fully booked a year in advance. Call at least six months early to reserve a room for either festival.

**Reservation services.** The following services are free to folks trying to hunt down a room in Newport. They represent scores of small B&Bs that deal exclusively through the service (and therefore are not included here), as well as many that are in these listings.

*Anna's Victorian Connection* (401-849-2489; 800-884-4288; fax 401-847-7309; E-mail: Annas@wsii.com; 5 Fowler Ave., Newport, RI 02840) Anna's offers reservations for rental properties and self-catering apartments, as well as inns, hotels, and B&Bs. Concierge service is also a plus.

*Bed & Breakfast Newport* (401-846-5408; 800-800-8765; fax 401-846-1828; 33 Russell Ave., Newport, RI 02840) Offers a choice of 400 rooms in over eighty homes in the Newport area.

*Bed & Breakfast of Rhode Island* (401-849-1298; 800-828-0000; fax 401-849-1306; PO Box 3291, Newport, RI 02840) A unique service that places guests in hotels, condos, apartments, and B&Bs all over RI, as well as throughout New England, Great Britian, Southern Ireland, and Arizona. Go figure.

*Bed & Breakfast Society* (401-846-2130; 800-227-2130) A small service that specializes in B&Bs on Ocean Dr. and near the mansions on and around Bellevue Ave.

***Taylor-Made Reservations of Newport*** (401-848-0300; 800-848-8848; 16 Mary St., Newport, RI 02840) A lodging and concierge service for Newport, the rest of Aquidneck, and Block Is. Handles mainly larger B&Bs, inns, hotels, and time-shares.

*800 842 0202*

### Rates

Rates are based on one night, double occupancy (most rooms are doubles), and reflect high-season prices (generally from Memorial Day to Labor Day). Off-season prices are often substantially lower. I've noted the few cases in which breakfast is not included or rooms do *not* have private baths.

### Lodging Price Code

| | |
|---|---|
| Inexpensive | Under $60 |
| Moderate | $60 to $120 |
| Expensive | $120 to $200 |
| Very Expensive | Over $200 |

### Credit Cards

| | |
|---|---|
| AE — American Express | DC — Diners Club |
| CB — Carte Blanche | MC — MasterCard |
| D — Discover | V — Visa |

## HOTELS

**DOUBLETREE NEWPORT ISLANDER HOTEL**
Manager: Mark Fallon. 401-849-2600; 800-222-TREE; fax 401-846-7210. Goat Island, Newport, RI 02840.
Open: Year-round.
Price: Expensive to Very Expensive.
Credit Cards: AE, D, DC, MC, V.
Smoking: Nonsmoking rooms available.
Handicap Access: Rooms available.
Restrictions: No pets.

The Doubletree has a prime spot all by itself on tiny Goat Is. in Newport Harbor — drive over the causeway or take a water shuttle from Bowen's Wharf. The 265 rooms offer a choice between harbor or bay views; both views are exquisite, possibly the best in town. This big, deluxe hotel has a fine restaurant (see the section Dining for the Windward Grille), a health club, and indoor/outdoor pool. Breakfast isn't included unless you choose a B&B package. The location here can't be beat, but you pay for it (or rather corporations do; this is a big meeting and convention center).

**THE HOTEL VIKING**
Manager: Scott Alemany. 401-847-3300; 800-556-7126; fax 401-848-4864. 1 Bellevue Ave., Newport, RI 02840.

Newport's summer folk built the Viking for their guests (to get them out of the mansions, no doubt) at Newport's most exclusive address: 1 Bellevue Ave. When it was new in 1926, the biggest, grandest rooms faced the avenue, the

Open: Year-round.
Price: Moderate to Very
  Expensive.
Credit Cards: AE, D, DC,
  MC, V.
Smoking: Smoking rooms
  available.
Handicap Access: Yes.
Restrictions: No pets.
Special Features: Banquet
  facilities, pool, sauna,
  whirlpool, exercise room,
  restaurant and pub;
  excellent off-season
  packages.

**INN ON LONG WHARF**
Manager: Thomas
  O'Gorman.
401-847-7800; 800-225-3522;
  fax 401-846-3888.
142 Long Wharf, Newport,
  RI 02840.
Open: Year-round.
Price: Expensive to Very
  Expensive.
Credit Cards: AE, CB, D,
  DC, MC, V.
Smoking: Yes.
Handicap Access: Yes.
Restrictions: No pets.
Special Features:
  Restaurant.

**THE INNTOWNE**
Owner: Carmella Gardner.
401-846-9200; 800-457-7803.
Thames and Mary Sts.,
  Newport, RI 02840.
Open: Year-round.
Price: Expensive to Very
  Expensive.
Credit Cards: AE, MC, V.
Smoking: Yes.
Handicap Access: One
  room.
Restrictions: No pets.

smaller ones, reserved for children and servants, overlooked Newport Harbor. Today the hotel has been renovated to accommodate contemporary tastes, and a motel-style west wing was added. The lobby retains an aura of grandeur, but the standardized bedrooms lack character. Unless specified, breakfast is not included. Don't miss the Top of Newport, a rooftop bar that is not only the highest spot in town, but also is the best for watching the sunset over the harbor. Also on the top floor are five shared bath "Bed & Breakfast" rooms; significantly lower priced than the hotel's other 178 rooms, they're a hidden treasure.

Though primarily geared to time-share customers, the forty suites at Inn on Long Wharf are also availble for nightly or weekly rentals. The weathered-shingle inn — really more of an all-suite hotel — is surrounded by water on three sides; it's literally *in* Newport Harbor. Some units look west onto a fleet of fishing boats, others look south toward the harbor basin (sunsets are legendary). Compact, one-bedroom suites have contemporary furnishings, including queen bed, pull-out sofa, cable TV, and minikitchen. Bathrooms add a touch of elegance with marble tiles and whirlpool tubs. Just down Thames St., the Inn on the Harbor (401-849-6789; 800-225-3522), also owned by Eastern Resorts, has similar units as well as an exercise room and rooftop deck. See the section Dining for comments on Long Wharf Steakhouse.

This small, independent, midtown hotel is convenient, possibly a little noisy (in the heart of the wharf shopping area), well run and maintained, with twenty-six attractive rooms. The lobby is warm and appealing; spacious guest rooms have matching bedspreads and wallpaper and are furnished with wicker and fine colonial reproductions (a few have antiques). All have telephones and air-conditioning and include continental breakfast and afternoon tea, served in a pleasant dining room. The lack of free parking (it's $15 per day) is made up for by complimentary use of the Marriott's swimming pool and health club. Don't miss the rooftop deck.

**MILL STREET INN**
Owner: Tom Petot.
401-849-9500;
 fax 401-848-5131.
75 Mill St., Newport, RI
 02840.
Open: Year-round.
Price: Very Expensive.
Credit Cards: AE, CB, DC,
 MC, V.
Smoking: Nonsmoking
 rooms available.
Handicap Access: One
 suite.
Restrictions: No pets.

Originally a nineteenth-century sawmill (where the window and door frames of many Newport homes were made), this National Register property has been converted into an all-suite hotel. The rooms are contemporary and bright, with exposed beams and brick walls. Some offer private decks overlooking Newport Harbor — just a block away — and all come with a queen or king bed, plus queen pull-out sofa. The extensive continental breakfast and complimentary afternoon tea, served on the rooftop deck in-season, make this a nice combination that offers the amenities of a hotel with the self-sufficiency of a time-share.

**NEWPORT HARBOR**
 **HOTEL & MARINA**
Manager: Patricia Joseph.
401-847-9000; out-of-state
 800-955-2558;
 fax 401-849-1380.
49 America's Cup Ave.,
 Newport, RI 02840.
Open: Year-round.
Price: Expensive to Very
 Expensive.
Credit Cards: AE, CB, D,
 DC, MC, V.
Smoking: Nonsmoking
 rooms.
Handicap Access: One
 harbor view room.
Restrictions: No pets.
Special Features: Ballroom,
 sauna, sundeck, indoor
 pool, restaurant.

Smack in the heart of Newport's bustling harbor area, this four-floor hotel offers 133 guest rooms, standardized but attractive, bright with sealight off the water. Waverley's, the hotel restaurant, serves from morning until late at night and offers outdoor dining in-season. For those arriving by boat, there's also a sixty-slip marina. If you like to stay where things are happening late into the night yet wake up to a peaceful marine view, this is the hotel for you. Beware: I've heard reports that public spaces (such as rest rooms) aren't cleaned as often as they should be. Breakfast is only included with certain rates packages.

**NEWPORT MARRIOTT**
Manager: Robert Schmeck.
401-849-1000; 800-228-9290;
 fax 401-849-3422.
25 America's Cup Ave.,
 Newport, RI 02840.
Open: Year-round.
Price: Very Expensive.
Credit Cards: AE, CB, D,
 DC, MC, V.

This is Newport's contemporary luxury hotel, with full amenities (see the section Dining for more on JW's Sea Grille and Oyster Bar in the Marriott), shops, and an impressive open atrium hung with yachting flags. There are 317 rooms, all of which offer either harbor, bridge, city, or atrium views. Seventh-floor rooms are the most lavish, with seasonal concierge service and "honor bar"

Smoking: Nonsmoking
rooms available.
Handicap Access: Rooms
available.
Restrictions: No pets.
Special Features: Full
health club,
indoor/outdoor pool
with bar, racquetball,
restaurant.

with complimentary hors d'oeuvres and dessert, plus a private observation deck. Special touches, including valet service and in-room irons, ironing boards, and coffeemakers, make the Marriott worth the expense. There's a fee for overnight parking.

**NEWPORT ONSHORE
RESORT**
Manager: Lewis Gordon.
401-849-1500; 800-225-3522;
fax 401-846-3888.
405 Thames St., Newport,
RI 02840.
Open: Year-round.
Price: Very Expensive.
Credit Cards: AE, CB, D,
DC, MC, V.
Smoking: Yes.
Handicap Access: Yes.
Restrictions: No pets.
Special Features:
Indoor/outdoor pool,
exercise room, sauna.

Like the Inn On Long Wharf, Newport Onshore Resort is principally a time-share establishment, though its lavish apartments accommodate overnight guests as well. The horseshoe-shaped resort is composed of four shingled buildings surrounding a double indoor/outdoor pool, all overlooking the harbor. Most of the sixty-two units have two bedrooms, a handful have one or three. For privacy and comfort, all bedrooms have their own baths and decks, separated by a vast living room decorated in gracious, traditional style. Extras include fireplace with complimentary wood bundle, cable TV with VCR (the resort has a video library), additional TV in the master bedroom, and stackable washer and dryer. Well-equipped kitchens have standard-sized refrigerators, microwaves, and dishwashers. A great, all-inclusive family resort.

**OCEANCLIFF**
General Manager: Patricia
Joseph.
401-841-8868;
fax 401-849-3927.
Ocean Dr., Newport, RI
02840.
Price: Moderate to Very
Expensive.
Credit Cards: AE, MC, V.
Smoking: Bar only.
Handicap Access: Possible.
Restrictions: No pets, or
children under 9.
Special Features:
Spectacular glass-walled
pool overlooking the sea,
tennis courts, live jazz on
sea view patio Sun. and
Mon.

Some confusion attends Oceancliff: turn off Ocean Dr. at the sign and you'll find not one but three structures. Ignore the modern shingled buildings on either side of a grand, betowered, red sandstone mansion — they're modern time-share resorts of the same name. Concentrate on the mansion hotel itself, and you won't go wrong. This elegant spot was built in 1896 as a private residence in a secluded location overlooking Narragansett Bay. Now a twenty-five-room hotel, guest rooms vary greatly in size and price but have similiar understated, champagne-hued color schemes and antique reproduction furnishings. All rooms have marble baths, air-conditioning, cable TV, and telephones; many include Jacuzzis, stone fireplaces, and panoramic bay views. Note that tucked under the eaves, third-floor rooms are especially cozy, and each room has a corresponding bathroom down the hall.

**VANDERBILT HALL**
Manager: Grant Howlett.
401-846-6200; 888-VAN-
HALL; fax 401-846-0701.
41 Mary St., Newport, RI
02840.
Open: Year-round.
Price: Very Expensive.
Credit Cards: AE, D, DC,
MC, V.
Smoking: All bedrooms
nonsmoking; some
common rooms available
for smokers.
Handicap Access: Rooms
available.
Restrictions: No pets, or
children under 12.

Newport's new "Mansion House Hotel" is based on Britain's country house hotels: palpable luxury, gourmet dining, no reception desk to mar the imposing, clubby atmosphere. The problem is that Vanderbilt Hall is as austere within as it appears without — a massive brick structure hemmed onto a side street near Washington Sq., it has no plantings to soften its severity. The renovated interior of this 1909 Colonial Revival mansion is so new that it lacks a comfortable patina; the public rooms feel a little slick, a little forced. The facilities, however, are impressive, from an in-house masseuse to fitness rooms, sauna, billiards room, and a variety of dining rooms. Fifty bedrooms and suites are individually decorated with period reproductions, fine linens, and wallpapers; breakfast is served on Wedgewood china.

## INNS

**ADMIRAL BENBOW INN**
Manager: Cathy Darigan.
401-846-4256; 800-343-2863;
fax 401-848-8006; E-mail:
5*admiralsinns.com.
91 Pelham St., Newport, RI
02840.
Open: Year-round, except
one month in winter.
Price: Moderate to
Expensive.
Credit Cards: AE, CB, D,
DC, MC, V.
Smoking: No.
Handicap Access: No.
Restrictions: No pets, or
children under 12.

The Admiral Benbow Inn, on quiet Pelham St. in Newport's historic hill district, was built in 1855 as a seafarers inn and is now listed on the National Register. Polished pine floorboards, tall, arched windows, and a variety of antiques and colonial reproductions, including handsome four-poster beds, give the fifteen guest rooms a refined but easy, livable air (one third-floor bedroom has a private deck with a harbor view). An extensive continental breakfast is served in the light, bright common room, and guests are welcome to use the TV parlor (closes after 8:00 p.m.). All around, a very friendly place to stay. *Note:* There are three Admiral Inns of Newport: Benbow, Fitzroy, and Farragut. All are distincitve and maintain a high standard of service. Space permits only two to be reviewed here; the Admiral Farragut, in a colonial home on Clarke Street, is just as pleasant.

**ADMIRAL FITZROY INN**
Manager: Sharon Gavia.
401-848-8204; 800-343-2863;

This former convent was moved to bustling Thames St. in 1986; now it's a midrange, eighteen-room inn (an elevator serves five floors). The

*The Admiral Fitzroy is one of Newport's three admirable Admiral inns.*

Craig Hammell

fax 401-848-8006; E-mail:
5*admiralsinns.com.
398 Thames St., Newport,
RI 02840.
Open: Year-round.
Price: Moderate to
   Expensive.
Credit Cards: AE, CB, D,
   DC, MC, V.
Smoking: No.
Handicap Access: One
   room.
Restrictions: No pets.

atmosphere is relaxed, and the furnishings are pretty and appealing, including sleigh beds, lace curtains, and hand-painted border designs. All rooms include air-conditioning, TV, telephone, and refrigerator. A communal third-floor deck overlooks the harbor; two guest rooms also have private back decks. The bright, cheerful breakfast room, where guests are treated to a full meal, sets the tone for the rest of the inn. Despite the busy location, the rooms are quiet, and the service is amiable.

**ARTFUL LODGER**
Owners: Rose & Rick
   Ranucci.
401-847-3132; 800-503-1850;
   E-mail: artfullodger@
   ids.net; Web: www.
   artfullodger.com.
503 Spring St., Newport, RI
   02840.
Open: Year-round.
Price: Moderate to
   Expensive.
Credit Cards: AE, MC, V.
Smoking: No.
Handicap Access: No.
Restrictions: No pets; call
   first about children.

A bright, third-floor conservatory with splendid views of Newport Harbor (you can even spy Ft. Adams) is the highlight of this laid-back, moderately priced inn on Spring St. (located just behind The Elms mansion). Four bedrooms and a two-room suite are furnished in comfortable, unflashy style: some nice pieces, some worn, as you'd find in a family beach house. Most rooms have separate sinks as well as private baths. Guests are welcome to use two parlors (both with music stands), an upper screened porch, small wet bar, and outdoor garden furniture. Happy hour with music in the conservatory is the real draw, however. Full breakfast is also served here in the morning (caramel French toast is a favorite).

## BANNISTER'S WHARF GUEST ROOMS
Manager: Jan Buchner.
401-846-4500.
Bannister's Wharf,
   Newport, RI 02840.
Open: Year-round.
Price: Moderate to
   Expensive.
Credit Cards: AE, D, MC, V.
Smoking: Yes.
Handicap Access: No.

**B**annister's Wharf isn't an inn or a hotel — it's a pier alive with shoppers, ice-cream slurpers, and three of the best restaurants in town (see the section Dining for more on the Clarke Cooke House, Le Bistro, and The Black Pearl). Above all this, overlooking nothing but water and yachts, are eight guest rooms that are little known and ideally located. The office is smack at the end of the wharf, accessible to those who arrive by boat or on foot. Choose from five doubles and three suites, all of which include air-conditioning, telephone, TV, refrigerator, two double beds, and private harbor-front patios. The decor of varnished wood and wicker furniture is simple, clean, and attractive — a very nautical look. You're on your own for breakfast.

## BEECH TREE INN
Owners: Ed & Kathy
   Wudyka.
401-847-9794; 800-748-6565;
   fax 401-847-6824.
34 Rhode Island Ave.,
   Newport, RI 02840.
Open: Year-round.
Price: Moderate to Very
   Expensive.
Credit Cards: AE, D, MC,
   V.
Smoking: Deck and
   common rooms only.
Handicap Access: No.
Restrictions: No pets.

**O**n the eastern side of Bellevue Ave., the Beech Tree Inn occupies an extensively renovated 1887 home in a quiet neighborhood. The owners have gone to great pains to think of everything: rooms have both air-conditioning and ceiling fans, cable TV, telephones, and laptop jacks. All five B&B rooms and two apartments are individually decorated in a variety of styles and color schemes from floral pastels to fire-engine red walls; six rooms have fireplaces. The rear third-floor bedroom is especially nice, with a water view, Jacuzzi, fireplace, and mustard-and-aubergine color scheme. In addition to offering what the owner calls "the biggest breakfast in Newport," the inn has lovely grounds with patio and barbecue equipment and two decks with views of First Beach. Despite the age of the house, there's a contemporary feel to this inn, which is high on amenities and comfort, low on Gilded Age atmosphere.

## BRINLEY VICTORIAN INN
Owners: John & Jennifer
   Sweetman.
401-849-7645; 800-999-8523;
   fax 401-845-9634.
23 Brinley St., Newport, RI
   02840.
Open: Year-round.
Price: Moderate to
   Expensive.

**W**hen I included this inn in the first edition, I did so because the new owners were likeable and their renovation plans showed promise; my hunch paid off in spades. Since then most of the Brinley's fifteen bedrooms and one suite have been completely renovated and appointed with antiques and comfortable Victorian furniture. All but two rooms now have private baths; the suite features a Jacuzzi and working fireplace. My favorite is the Colonial Room, dominated by a massive brick fire-

Credit Cards: AE, MC, V.
Smoking: No.
Handicap Access: No.
Restrictions: No pets, or children under 8.

place. John wants the inn to be relaxed and pleasing without "looking like a movie set." He's more than accomplished his goal. Breakfast is continental style. Note that the inn is conveniently located, but not in a touristy or ultrafashionable neighborhood.

*The patio at the Castle Hill Inn is an ideal spot from which to survey the bay.*

Craig Hammell

**CASTLE HILL INN AND RESORT**
Owner: Paul MacEnroe.
401-849-3800.
Ocean Dr., Newport, RI 02840.
Open: Year-round.
Price: Very Expensive.
Credit Cards: AE, MC, V.
Smoking: Yes.
Handicap Access: No.
Restrictions: No pets, or children under 12.

This cedar-shingled mansion sits in majesty at the end of a long drive, with the mouth of Narragansett Bay as its backyard. Alexander Agassiz, a world traveler and biologist, built Castle Hill in 1874 and filled it with carved woodwork and antiques from the Far East, many of which still grace the dining rooms and sitting areas on the first floor (see the section Dining). The ten guest rooms in the main inn aren't quite as grand, but each is attractively decorated and architecturally unique (the most famous is the pentagonal suite on the third floor, mentioned in Thornton Wilder's *Theopholis North*). Basic, beachfront cottages are available for weekly rental in the summer, and a year-round, five-room chalet shares the same magnficient views as the rooms in the main inn. For location and wildly romantic atmosphere, you can't do better.

**THE CLARKESTON**
Owner: Rick Farrick.
401-849-7397.
28 Clarke St., Newport, RI 02840.

On the National Register as the Joseph Burrill House, The Clarkeston was built around 1705 and has the wide floorboards and fireplaces to prove it. Its nine rooms, many with working fireplaces, have been sumptuously decorated with

Open: Year-round.
Price: Moderate to Very
  Expensive.
Credit Cards: MC, V.
Smoking: No.
Handicap Access: One
  room.
Restrictions: No pets; call
  first about children.

antiques and four-poster feather beds, matched by modern conveniences, such as air-conditioning, TVs, and soundproofing (an important feature in an old house). Bathrooms also have received lavish attention; all are appointed with marble and some have Jacuzzis. Rick now serves a full breakfast. Note that while it's just moments from the harbor, the Clarkeston is on a quiet, one-block street, as is Rick's new venture, the neighboring Cleveland House. Check into midweek discounts.

**CLIFFSIDE INN**
Innkeeper: Stephan
  Nicolas.
401-847-1811; 800-845-1811;
  fax 401-848-5850.
2 Seaview Ave., Newport,
  RI 02840.
Open: Year-round.
Price: Expensive to Very
  Expensive.
Credit Cards: AE, CB, D,
  DC, MC, V.
Smoking: On porch only.
Handicap Access: No.
Restrictions: No pets, or
  children under 13.

One of a handful of Newport's truly top-drawer inns, this glorious 1880 clapboard cottage is on a one-block street that ends at the Cliff Walk — the beach and mansions are just moments away. Eleven of the thirteen guest rooms have Jacuzzis and air-conditioning, twelve have fireplaces, and all have telephones and cable TV with VCR. But these aren't the only reasons to indulge in a night at the Cliffside. The exceptional antique furnishings, including towering, polished armoires and carved bed frames, are more reasons, as are the Laura Ashley fabrics and unique touches like a washstand made from an old phonograph. Full breakfast is served in a very handsome dining room. Cliffside was once the home of artist Beatrice Turner; of her 1,000 self-portraits only seventy were saved from a bonfire after her death. A few originals and several laser copies hang throughout the inn.

**THE 1855 MARSHALL
  SLOCUM GUEST
  HOUSE**
Owners: Joan & Julie
  Wilson.
401-841-5120; 800-372-5120;
  fax 401-846-3787.
29 Kay St., Newport, RI
  02840.
Open: Year-round.
Price: Moderate.
Credit Cards: AE.
Smoking: Deck only.
Handicap Access: No.
Restrictions: No pets, or
  children under 12.

A gracious, generously proportioned home on a shady side street off Bellevue Ave., the Marshall Slocum has lace curtains in the windows, wicker chairs on the front porch, and a big deck out back. Tall trees keep the parlor and dining room a bit shaded, but the six guest rooms upstairs are sunny and pleasant (the three third-floor rooms have air-conditioning). Furnishings are simple as befits an old summerhouse, with touches like sturdy beds covered by handcrafted quilts. Two rooms have private half-baths, otherwise all share. A full breakfast is served in the dining room, and a lobster dinner is served with every three-night, midweek stay. This is a genteel, mother-daughter enterprise.

**ELM STREET INN**
Innkeeper: Rick Farrick.
401-849-7397; 800-524-1386;
fax 401-847-6071.
36 Elm St., Newport, RI
   02840.
Open: Year-round.
Price: Moderate to Very
   Expensive.
Credit Cards: MC, V.
Smoking: No.
Handicap Access: No.
Restrictions: No pets.

Two suites and two guest bedrooms cluster into this turn-of-the-century home on a residential street in the Point Section of town. All are comfortably and attractively furnished; antiques provide the atmosphere, and air conditioners keep it cool (TVs and telephone jacks are also present). The third-floor suite is a secluded haven with eccentric eaves and a ladder — painted white with flower garlands along the sides — that leads through a trapdoor to the rooftop deck and a view of Newport Harbor. A continental breakfast of fresh fruit and baked goods is served in the kitchen, and there's a microwave and refrigerator for guests' use.

**FRANCIS MALBONE HOUSE**
Managers: Will Dewey &
   Mary Frances Mahaffey.
401-846-0392; 800-846-0392;
   fax 401-848-5956; E-mail:
   innkeeper@malbone.com.
392 Thames St., Newport,
   RI 02840.
Open: Year-round.
Price: Expensive to Very
   Expensive.
Credit Cards: AE, MC, V.
Smoking: No.
Handicap Access: One room.
Restrictions: No pets, or
   children under 12.

Don't let the busy location on Thames St. fool you, this is a very patrician spot. Legend has it that the first home of slave trader Francis Malbone caught fire while he was hosting a dinner party. Rather than have his meal ruined, Malbone ordered his servants to move the table to the front lawn where guests dined by the light of burning timbers. In 1760, he built this brick house, now on the National Register, as a replacement. Each of the four common rooms, sixteen bedrooms, and two suites is exquisitely furnished with period antiques and artwork; fifteen guest rooms have working fireplaces, eleven have Jacuzzis (half of the rooms are in a carriage house that was added in 1996). The Counting House Suite on the first floor has its own entrance and garden exit. Front rooms offer a harbor view, while the backyard shelters a quiet courtyard garden, where breakfast is served in-season.

**HAMMETT HOUSE INN**
Manager: Marianne
   Spaziano.
401-848-0593; 800-548-9417.
505 Thames St., Newport,
   RI 02840.
Open: Year-round.
Price: Moderate to
   Expensive.
Credit Cards: AE, CB, D,
   DC, MC, V.
Smoking: No.

On busy Lower Thames St., the Hammett House Inn occupies a three-story Georgian home; Restaurant Bouchard is on the first floor. A steep staircase leads to five guest rooms, all of which have plush carpeting, air-conditioning, cable TV, and queen-sized bed (the largest has two beds). Pleasant furnishings range from Victorian wicker to French Regency, canopy beds to floral wallpaper. Continental breakfast arrives at each guest room at 7:30 a.m.; hinged trays are provided

Handicap Access: No.
Restrictions: No pets.

in the corridor for this purpose. Some rooms have harbor views. Note that the innkeeper doesn't arrive until 2:00 p.m.; guests register via an answering machine at the reception desk.

**HARBORSIDE INN**
Innkeeper: Carol Bamberry.
401-846-6600; 800-427-9444.
Christie's Landing,
   Newport, RI 02840.
Open: Year-round.
Price: Expensive to Very
   Expensive.
Credit Cards: AE, DC, MC,
   V.
Smoking: Yes.
Handicap Access: No.
Restrictions: No pets.

As a friend of mine put it, you have to *want* to stay at the Harborside Inn; not because it isn't a nice place, but because it's located next to Christie's restaurant, a popular twenty-something bar that erupts with live music late into the night. What you may lose in sleep, however, you make up for in convenience — the Thames St. tourist throng is close at hand — and the view is top-notch. Fifteen suites are decorated in contemporary nautical style; all include air-conditioning, cable TV with HBO, refrigerator, wet bar, and sleeping loft. A continental breakfast and afternoon refreshments are served in the comfortable Harbor Room. *The* spot for partyers.

**HYDRANGEA HOUSE INN**
Owners: Dennis Blair &
   Grant Edmondson.
401-846-4435; 800-945-4667;
   fax 401-846-6602; Web:
   www.bestinns.net/usa/r
   i/hydr.html.
16 Bellevue Ave., Newport,
   RI 02840.
Open: Year-round.
Price: Expensive to Very
   Expensive.
Credit Cards: MC, V.
Smoking: No.
Handicap Access: No.
Restrictions: No pets, or
   children under 12.

Attention to detail, a flair for sumptuous Victorian decoration, and creativity contribute to the appeal of the small, owner-operated Hydrangea House Inn. Upstairs are five guest rooms and one suite; downstairs is the owners' contemporary art gallery (see the section Culture, under the heading Fine Art Galleries) where guests are served a full buffet breakfast, including such items as homemade granola, Venetian eggs, or raspberry pancakes. A journal in each uniquely decorated room records the impressions and recommendations of guests. In the evening, the proprietors serve milk and homemade chocolate chip cookies, plus snacks on the second-floor veranda in the afternoon. The Inn is a very fine, elegantly appointed place to stay that's too deliberately low profile to be splashy and well known.

**INN AT OLD BEACH**
Owners: Cyndi & Luke
   Murray.
401-849-3479; 888-303-5033;
   fax 401-847-1236.
19 Old Beach Rd., Newport,
   RI 02840.

A gem tucked into a residential Victorian neighborhood behind the northern end of Bellevue Ave., this 1879 Gothic Revival home and its lovely garden and gazebo are extremely neat and well kept. Common rooms (with TV) are cozy and well

Open: Year-round.
Price: Moderate to
  Expensive.
Credit Cards: AE, MC, V.
Smoking: On porches only.
Handicap Access: No.
Restrictions: No pets, or
  children under 12.

appointed — in the summer, they're full of fresh flowers, in the winter, logs burn in the fireplaces. Note the fabulous "Four Seasons" stained-glass window in the stairway. Five guest rooms in the main house are gracefully decorated in flower motifs; one has a Victorian wood-burning stove, the others have fireplaces. Two more guest rooms are in the Carriage House out back. There's also a handy guest pantry on the second floor. Each morning Cyndi serves a generous, homemade continental breakfast; Luke manages the famous Black Pearl restaurant (see the section Dining) so be sure to ask for dining tips.

### THE IVY LODGE

Owners: Maggie & Terry
  Moy.
401-849-6865.
12 Clay St., Newport, RI
  02840.
Open: Year-round.
Price: Moderate to
  Expensive.
Credit Cards: AE, D, MC,
  V.
Smoking: No.
Handicap Access: No.
Restrictions: No pets.

Easily one of Newport's finest inns, The Ivy Lodge is in a big, rambling 1886 home, designed by Stanford White, off Bellevue Ave. The well-kept yard and dreamy veranda, lovely as they are, are only a prelude to the magnificent entrance hall, a Gothic extravaganza of carved English oak paneling. Hosts Maggie and Terry are friendly and down-to-earth and will make you feel at home in this shingle-style palace. There are eight guest rooms with air-conditioning, all decorated with flair and elegance. Nineteenth-century features abound — fireplaces, stained glass, and a wonderful turret — and are updated with contemporary colors and bright fabrics. The common rooms are delightful; the dining room table, where Maggie serves a full breakfast (including Scotch eggs) seats sixteen. Light refreshments are served in the afternoon.

### JAMES B. FINCH HOUSE

Owner: Bill Brulotte.
401-848-9700; 800-235-1274;
  fax 401-848-9311; E-mail:
  jbfinch@wsii.com.
102 Touro St., Newport, RI
  02840.
Open: Year-round.
Price: Expensive.
Credit Cards: MC, V.
Smoking: No.
Handicap Access: No.
Restrictions: No pets.

This stately mid-Victorian is superbly located on Touro St., right next to the Newport Historical Society and Touro Synagogue, very near both Bellevue Ave. and the harbor. The well-kept grounds and immense, first-floor windows are inviting, and the inside doesn't disappoint. Each of the six bedrooms has its own character: some have sleigh beds, others four-posters, two have Jacuzzis, all have air-conditioning. Furnishings range from Oriental rugs and bookcases to floral print schemes. A full gourmet breakfast is served in the dining room. Above all, this is a family-oriented, friendly spot where the owners take time to cater to guests' individual needs.

**LA FORGE COTTAGE**
Owners: Louis & Margot
  Droual.
401-847-4400; E-mail:
  margotd@laforgecottage.
  com.
96 Pelham St., Newport, RI
  02840.
Open: Year-round.
Price: Inexpensive to
  Expensive.
Credit Cards: AE, D, MC, V.
Smoking: Yes.
Handicap Access: No.
Restrictions: No pets;
  children welcome (cribs
  available).
Special Features: French,
  German, and Spanish
  also spoken.

**PILGRIM HOUSE**
Owners: Donna Messerlian,
  Pam & Bruce Bayuk.
401-846-0040; 800-525-8373;
  fax 401-848-0357.
123 Spring St., Newport, RI
  02840.
Open: Year-round.
Price: Moderate to
  Expensive.
Credit Cards: MC, V.
Smoking: On deck only.
Handicap Access: No.
Restrictions: No pets, or
  children under 12.

**RHODE ISLAND HOUSE**
Owner: Michael Dupre.
401-848-7787.
77 Rhode Island Ave.,
  Newport, RI 02840.
Open: Year-round.
Price: Expensive.
Credit Cards: AE, MC, V.
Smoking: No.
Handicap Access: No.

Since 1889, there have been only two sets of owners/innkeepers at La Forge Cottage; the current house, a gabled clapboard with green awnings and window boxes on the delightful front porch, was built in 1913. The Drouals have held up their end of the century very admirably — the house and grounds are delightfully maintained. There are six guest rooms and four suites, all with queen bed, air-conditioning, TV, telephone, and refrigerator. Furnishings are old-fashioned but not antique and range from brass beds to sturdy bedroom furniture of cherry and mahogany. The in-house French chef prepares either a continental or full breakfast, which arrives at your bedside each morning via room service.

Even though Spring St. is two long blocks from the water, the ca. 1837 Pilgrim House has a rear deck with a drop-dead view of Newport Harbor. This is where breakfast is served in-season and guests come for evening cocktails — the steeple of Trinity Church seems close enough to touch. But the deck isn't the only fine spot. Each evening sherry and shortbread are served in the living room, which features a wonderful fireplace mantel that the owners found during restoration. The eleven guest rooms (two are shared bath, all have air-conditioning), are equally charming, with lace curtains, antiques, and floral wallpaper. The atmosphere, like the decor, is pleasantly informal. Rooms seem quiet despite the central location. Note that street parking is only available from 5:30 p.m.–8:30 p.m.

The aroma of fresh baking is so enticing that it may take a few moments to notice the graceful, warm surroundings of this marvelous inn. Michael Dupre has a reputation as one of the best young chefs in Newport, and as part of a winter weekend package, he offers cooking classes in which guests prepare a five-course meal. Year-round, his full breakfast is superb. The inn offers five guest rooms, each with a character all its own, achieved through

Restrictions: No pets, or children under 14.

masterful combinations of printed fabrics, antiques, and painted highlights; two have Jacuzzis and one a private deck overlooking the back garden. The windows throughout this venerable 1882 home are magnificent, especially in the downstairs common rooms, one of which is a library with a fine collection of books and CDs.

**SANFORD-COVELL VILLA MARINA**
Owner: Ann Ramsey Cuvelier.
401-847-0206.
72 Washington St., Newport, RI 02840.
Open: Year-round.
Price: Expensive to Very Expensive.
Credit Cards: No.
Smoking: No.
Handicap Access: Possible.
Restrictions: Pets "frowned upon."

This National Register villa, which boasts a thirty-five-foot entrance tower accented with stenciling and five kinds of wood, was built in 1869 in the Point Section on Newport Harbor, just before the frenzy of the Gilded Age. I unashamedly confess that it's my favorite Newport inn. Perhaps because the Sanford-Covell retains many of its original furnishings, it preserves an air of authentic, affluent relaxation that harks back to the last century; by comparison most other inns, despite their antiques and hit-you-over-the-head luxury, feel *modern*. A wraparound porch overlooks the harbor, Newport Bridge, and the villa's private wharf (with a restored gazebo at the end), plus a heated saltwater swimming pool and Jacuzzi. Six guest rooms (with both shared and private baths) include fireplaces, window seats, lace curtains, slightly worn Oriental rugs, and original wainscoting — the former nursery even has a big built-in chalkboard. Two rooms may be rented as a suite, with kitchenette and king-sized Murphy bed. Complimentary sherry and port are served in the magnificent music room. Breakfast is continental style. This is the real thing.

**STELLA MARIS INN**
Owners: Dorothy & Ed Madden.
401-849-2862.
91 Washington St., Newport, RI 02840.
Open: Year-round.
Price: Moderate to Expensive.
Credit Cards: No.
Smoking: No.
Handicap Access: Possible.
Restrictions: No pets or children.

This big, handsome, mansard-roofed brownstone in Newport's quiet Point Section was built as a convent in 1861. Of the eight guest rooms and cottage, five overlook the harbor and four have grand old fireplaces. All have soaring ceilings and are impressively decorated in floral prints, Victorian antiques, and bright colors. Everything is spacious here, from the hallways, majestic parlors, and dining room to the grounds, which include a back patio and front veranda where guests may watch the boats, while polishing off items from the homemade breakfast buffet. Note that the brochure-cluttered entrance hall gives the inn an impersonal feel that the grounds and bedrooms happily belie.

**VICTORIAN LADIES**
Owners: Donald & Hélène O'Neill.
401-849-9960;
  fax 401-849-9960
  (fax 8:00 a.m.–8:00 p.m. only).
63 Memorial Blvd., Newport, RI 02840.
Open: Year-round, except Jan.
Price: Expensive.
Credit Cards: MC, V.
Smoking: No.
Handicap Access: No.
Restrictions: No pets; welcomes children over 10.

"**H**ave you seen the Victorian Ladies?" is a frequent refrain around Newport. On busy Memorial Blvd., between the Cliff Walk and Bellevue Ave., it's easy to spot — just look for all of the flowers, frequent winners of the Newport in Bloom competition. The front parlor looks exactly as if it had been decorated by a discriminating Victorian lady; the guest rooms are elegant, quiet, and comfortable, individually decorated with antiques and fine reproductions. Three buildings house eleven rooms, all with air-conditioning and TV. A full breakfast buffet may be enjoyed on the flower-laden back patio.

**VILLA LIBERTE**
Owner: Leigh Anne Mosco.
401-846-7444; 800-392-3717;
  fax 401-849-6429.
22 Liberty St., Newport, RI 02840.
Open: Mar.–mid-Nov.
Price: Moderate to Very Expensive.
Credit Cards: AE, MC, V.
Smoking: No.
Handicap Access: No.
Restrictions: No pets, or children under 12 (in main inn).

**A** flat roof, an unusual second-floor porch perched over the arched entryway, and a Mediterranean color scheme give the Villa Liberte a distinctive look. Built in 1910 as a "House of the Evening," this is more a small hotel than an inn. The fifteen guest rooms, including three housekeeping suites in the annex next door, share the same contemporary pastel decor and feature dramatic black-and-white tiled baths tucked under arched alcoves. All include air-conditioning, telephone, and cable TV. Continental breakfast is set up buffet style; guests may take a tray to the airy sundeck out back, to one of the sitting areas throughout the villa, or to their rooms.

**THE WILLOWS OF NEWPORT**
Owner: Pattie Murphy.
401-846-5486; Web: www.newporttri.com/users/willows.
8 Willow St., Newport, RI 02840.
Open: Apr.-Nov.
Price: Moderate to Very Expensive.
Smoking: In garden only.
Credit Cards: No.
Handicap Access: No.
Restrictions: No pets; children inappropriate.

**P**atti Murphy has found a niche with The Willows, and her niche is romance. Recommended by the "Best Places to Kiss" guide, her seven guest rooms and two suites (the latter feature "hourglass" Jacuzzis for two) are fantasies of sybaritic luxury. Murphy's "Silk and Chandelier Collection" (the two suites in her annex across the street) have elaborate Italianate furniture, lights on dimmer switches, and billowing swathes of organza draped over canopy beds. Rooms in her original inn — two joined town houses built 100 years apart (1740 and 1840) — currently have a pink color scheme, though everything's being redone in white, cream, and fuchsia. Extras include breakfast in bed, which is delivered by Pattie in black tie and top hat, fresh flowers, morning wake-up call through a central intercom, wet bar, and a fabulous garden out back that's featured on Newport's Secret Garden tour (check out the heart-shaped fish-pond). A real plus is complimentary concierge service; two weeks before your arrival, Pattie will help you plan your entire itinerary.

## BED & BREAKFASTS

There are scores upon scores of B&Bs in Newport. The handful that I've listed offer a representative sampling, but only graze the tip of the B&B iceberg.

**BLUESTONE B&B**
Owners: Cindy & Roger
  Roberts.
401-846-5408; 800-800-8765;
  fax 401-846-1828.
33 Russell Ave., Newport,
  RI 02840.
Open: Year-round.
Price: Moderate.
Credit Cards: AE, D, MC,
  V; no personal checks.
Smoking: No.
Handicap Access: No.
Restrictions: No pets or
  children.

If you're looking for a friendly atmosphere and helpful hosts, want to save a little money, and don't mind snug surroundings nor a short hike to the mansions or harbor, this quiet, residential spot is for you. The Bluestone is furnished in country Victorian style and offers a full breakfast; its two comfortable guest bedrooms have air-conditioning, telephone, TV, refrigerator, and queen beds. Cindy and Roger are good cooks and ideal hosts; they've even been known to lend ties to guests who needed them for restaurant-going. As small B&Bs go, the Bluestone is a charmer. Cindy also operates the comprehensive reservation service Bed & Breakfast Newport.

**THE BURBANK ROSE
  B&B**
Owners: Bonnie & John
  McNeely.
401-849-9457; 888-297-5800.
111 Memorial Blvd. W,
  Newport, RI 02840.
Open: Year-round.
Price: Inexpensive to
  Expensive.
Credit Cards: AE, D.
Smoking: No.
Handicap Access: No.
Restrictions: No pets, or
  children under 12.

The Burbank Rose was named for American horticulturist Luther Burbank, who developed a miniature, thornless rose. He'd doubtless be pleased to stay in his namesake, as a guest of the charming, soft-spoken McNeelys. This 1850s home, across the street from St. Mary's Church, also incorporates John and Bonnie's antique and collectibles shop of the same name. Three guest rooms, all with air-conditioning and cable TV, are decorated in a pleasant, plain style that highlights the hardwood floors and freshly painted walls. A buffet breakfast, featuring John's omelettes and pancakes, is set up in the salmon pink dining room. There's also a parlor with TV, telephone, and games.

**CULPEPER HOUSE B&B**
Owner: Ann Wiley.
401-846-4011.

For a faithfully restored colonial home (ca. 1771), Shaker-style decoration, original artwork, a full

30 Second St., Newport, RI 02840.
Open: Year-round.
Price: Moderate to
Expensive.
Credit Cards: No.
Smoking: No.
Handicap Access: No.
Restrictions: No pets; call
first about children.
Special Features: Access to
the Marriott's pool and
health club.

## ELLIOTT BOSS HOUSE
Owners: Tom & Loretta
Goldrick.
401-849-9425.
20 Second St., Newport, RI
02840.
Open: Year-round, except
Nov.
Price: Expensive.
Credit Cards: No.
Smoking: No.
Handicap Access: No.
Restrictions: No pets, or
toddlers.

## ELM TREE COTTAGE
Owners: Priscilla & Thomas
Malone.
401-849-1610; 888-ELM-
TREE; fax 401-849-2084;
Web: wwwelmtreebnb.
com.
336 Gibbs Ave., Newport,
RI 02840.
Open: Year-round, except
Jan.
Price: Expensive to Very
Expensive.
Credit Cards: AE, MC, V.
Smoking: No.
Handicap Access: One
room partially handicap
accessible.

library with everything from cookery books to English mysteries, afternoon wine and conversation with the articulate owner, and — getting down to basics — terrific mattresses, stay at the Culpeper. When a B&B is frequently recommended by other innkeepers, you know that it's good, and that's the case here. The two guest rooms both have fireplaces. In the summer, a full breakfast is served in the garden, which has so many trees it's practically a bird sanctuary; in the winter — when European down quilts warm the beds — it is served in the library. Culpeper House is in the exceptionally quiet, historic Point Section just one block from Newport Harbor. You'll know it by the roses out front.

From its enclosed "secret garden" to the cool calm of its early nineteenth-century decor, the Elliott Boss House (built in 1820) conjures an otherwise vanished world of taste, care, and serenity. This intimate, exquisitely decorated B&B smells of wood fire, boasts wide, gleaming floorboards, antiques and nautical artwork, and offers two guest rooms: one with a king or two twin beds, for which the bath is just down the hall, the other with a queen canopy with private bath. Owners Loretta and Tom are charming, knowledgable about Newport, and cook up a delicious, full breakfast.

One of the truly outstanding B&Bs in Newport — *anywhere*, for that matter — the Elm Tree Cottage is a fetching spot, owned and run by a friendly young couple who also design and make stained glass. It occupies an 1882 shingle-style mansion in a Gilded Age neighborhood north of Memorial Blvd. Lavish and stately without being overpowering, the front parlor ends in a bay of windows overlooking Easton's Pond; a brilliantly sunny morning room and paneled pub area (BYOB) are off to one side. Five guest rooms and the Windsor suite are magnificently appointed with fine linens, French and English provincial antiques (highlights are the Louis XV beds), and special touches like a washstand with Austrian

Restrictions: No pets, or children under 14.

crystal legs. All rooms have fireplaces, only one of which doesn't work. A continental breakfast, featuring one cooked entrée, is served in the delightful dining room. Even the the magazines here are top-notch.

**LONG WHARF YACHT CHARTERS**
Proprietor: Carl Bolender.
401-849-2210.
168 Long Wharf Marina, PO Box 366, Newport, RI 02840.
Open: Jun.–Oct.
Price: Moderate.
Credit Cards: MC, V.
Smoking: No.
Handicap Access: No.
Special Features: Provides litter boxes for pets.

Since Newport is the City by the Sea, why not sleep on a boat? Carl's "Boat and Breakfast" offers overnight accommodations on one of several yachts docked in Newport Harbor. Guests may reserve ahead, or take a chance that one of the boats may be available. Board around 5:00 p.m., disembark at 11:00 a.m. Carl's boats sleep up to six, and most have onboard TV and showers. Continental breakfast includes coffee and Danish. Be sure to pet Carl's dog Brutus, a fierce-looking but gentle beast.

*The Melville House on quiet Clarke Street was built ca. 1750.*

Craig Hammell

**THE MELVILLE HOUSE**
Owners: Vincent DeRico & David Horan.
401-847-0640.
39 Clarke St., Newport, RI 02840.
Open: Year-round.
Price: Expensive.
Credit Cards: AE, D, MC, V.
Smoking: No.
Handicap Access: One room.

Quiet Clarke Street is a dream: one block, one way, near the harbor, on the Hill, and a moment's walk to a favorite restaurant (The Place at Yesterday's, see the section Dining). The Melville House, built ca. 1750, is a winner, too. The front parlor is a study in understated colonial charm, with a wonderful collection of old kitchen appliances. Of seven rooms, five have private baths. Look for gleaming hardwood floors, armoires, George Washington spreads, handsome area rugs,

Restrictions: No pets, or children under 12.

and lace curtains. All rooms include fluffy robes and journals. Full breakfast features such items as quiche, stuffed French toast, and jonnycakes. Don't leave without trying Vincent's delicious home-made biscotti.

**MERRITT HOUSE B&B**
Owners: Angela & Joseph Vars.
401-847-4289.
57 Second St., Newport, RI 02840.
Open: Year-round.
Price: Moderate.
Credit Cards: No.
Smoking: No.
Handicap Access: No.
Restrictions: No pets, or children under 13.

Such a warm, welcoming atmosphere pervades this ca. 1850 home in Newport's Point Section that people often spontaneously hug one another here. The parlor is old-fashioned and cozy; the dining room, where a full breakfast is served each morning (Angela's recipes have appeared in print), harbors a pretty collection of amethyst glass. There are two double rooms on the second floor, one with private bath; the other shares a downstairs bath with the family. Both have charming colonial furnishings, including a small library of old books. A room brimming with gifts that guests have brought or sent from all over the world is the best recommendation for this relaxed, considerate B&B, named one of the 100 best in the country.

**ROSE ISLAND LIGHTHOUSE**
Owner: City of Newport.
401-847-4242.
Rose Island, Newport, RI 02840.
(Office: Newport Harbor Center, 365 Thames St., Newport, RI 02840)
Open: Year-round.
Price: Expensive.
Credit Cards: AE, MC, V.
Smoking: No.
Handicap Access: No.
Restrictions: No pets.
Special Features: This is a working lighthouse!

Tiny Rose Island is situated in the middle of Narragansett Bay between Jamestown and Newport; the lighthouse, built in 1869 and relit in 1993, is a mansard-roofed landmark. Staying here is not an experience for everyone, but adventurous sorts will love it. During the day the first floor of the lighthouse is a museum; by night it becomes a two-room B&B. There's limited electricity, which is produced by a wind generator, but most guests bring candles. Other amenities include a gas hot plate, no running water (the pantry and shared WC, which features a clear, ecologically sound toilet, are outfitted with hand pumps), and an outdoor solar shower and gas grill for use in-season. Bedrooms are tiny, and overnight visitors are expected to change the sheets in the morning, but the duties are a small exchange for the natural joys of Rose Island. Explore on your own or take a guided tour. In the summer, seabirds and wild roses abound; in the winter, harbor seals take over. The fifteen-minute launch to the island costs $10 round-trip per person. Note that there's also a four-person, second-floor keeper's apartment that rents weekly; guests must be willing to do light maintenance and recordkeeping.

**SARAH KENDALL HOUSE**
Owners: Fran & Bryan Babcock.
401-846-7976; 800-758-9578.
47 Washington St.,
  Newport, RI 02840.
Open: Year-round.
Price: Expensive to Very Expensive.
Credit Cards: AE, CB, D, DC, MC, V.
Smoking: No.
Handicap Access: No.
Restrictions: No pets; call first about children.

Think of the Sarah Kendall House as a B&B, but with privacy, or as a small, unusually intimate hotel. This 1871 Victorian in the Point Section has stately proportions, a generous, wraparound porch, well-tended garden, and a stately dining room where a full breakfast is served; check out the owner's great-grandfather's Civil War medals. Four guest rooms in the original house, plus an apartment in a 1980 addition (notable for harbor views), are individually decorated and sport hotel-style amenities: robes, hair dryers, air-conditioning, cable TVs, telephones, refrigerators, radios, etc. One room has a private deck off the bathroom. Especially nifty are the moose head in the stairwell and the plans to reaffix an immense rooftop tower, blown off the house in the 1938 hurricane.

**WAYSIDE B&B**
Owners: Dorothy & Al Post.
401-847-0302;
  fax 401-848-9374.
406 Bellevue Ave.,
  Newport, RI 02840.
Open: Year-round.
Price: Expensive (rates include tax).
Credit Cards: No.
Smoking: Yes.
Handicap Access: No.
Restrictions: No pets.
Special Features: Heated in-ground pool.

The Wayside is a stately mansion, enlarged to its present size in 1896. Despite the austere, yellow brick grandeur of the facade, the interior is relaxed and comfortable. There are ten guest rooms in this twenty-two-room house, all with ceiling fans; four also have air-conditioning, plus there is a six-person apartment in the carriage house. Everything here is on a grand scale; the Library Room has a fourteen-foot ceiling and a huge fireplace. Continental breakfast is served in a lovely dining room.

**WEATHERLY COTTAGE**
Owner: Patti Toppa.
401-849-8371.
30 Weatherly Ave.,
  Newport, RI 02840.
Open: Apr. 15–Oct.
Price: Moderate.
Credit Cards: No.
Smoking: Deck only.
Handicap Access: Possible.
Restrictions: No pets.

This unprepossessing, shingled bungalow is about a twenty-minute walk from the harbor fray, in a very quiet, residential neighborhood at the southern end of town between Bellevue Ave. and Ocean Dr. With only two bedrooms (one has a private bath, the other shares), it's like staying in a tasteful relative's home. The furnishings are traditional but not antique, and the bedrooms are comfortable rather than ornate. There's a wonderful backyard overseen by a second-floor deck, and a big family room that guests are welcome to use. Patti draws on family recipes to cook up a full breakfast, and as a native Newporter is a great guide to the town.

# DINING

Newport, Rhode Island, is a city with so much taste that it's chosen an edible symbol to represent itself — the pineapple. Legend holds that in the eighteenth century, when Yankee sea captains returned home from long voyages to the West Indies, they stuck a pineapple on their gatepost or front door to proclaim their return and to invite neighbors over for a visit. That's how the pineapple came to be known as a symbol of Newport hospitality. The custom hasn't entirely vanished; check out the number of bronze pineapple door knockers gracing Newport homes.

Newport actually seems to have a way with fruit. It was also here that some reckless soul in the eighteenth century ventured to bite into a tomato; before that they were considered to be poisonous. Such bravery suggests an adventerous civic palate, which the city retains to this day. It also retains the White Horse Tavern, the oldest continuously operated tavern in the United States, built in 1673.

*Bowen's Wharf is equally home to ships and shoppers.*

Craig Hammell

You can have an elegant meal in an eighteenth-century clapboard home, wash down seafood-in-the-rough with draft beer on the wharf, or dine late in a hip bistro. Newport's top restaurants rank with the country's best. Expect meals to be fresh, innovative, and sophisticated and expect to pay for culinary trendiness. A word of advice: make reservations whenever possible. A genteel feeding frenzy takes hold of the town on summer weekends, and waits can be long. Also be advised that the BYOB designation that you see in the listings below means Bring Your Own Booze.

The following restaurant listing is a generous cross section of Newport's many and varied eateries. The Food & Beverage Purveyors section lists the best spots for provisions for everything from gourmet picnics to those essential ice-cream stops.

The price range reflects the cost of a single dinner meal, including appetizer, entrée, dessert, and coffee or tea. Alcoholic beverages, tax, and tip are not included in the price scale.

### Dining Price Code

| | |
|---|---|
| Inexpensive | Under $15 |
| Moderate | $15 to $25 |
| Expensive | $25 to $35 |
| Very Expensive | Over $35 |

### Credit Cards

| | |
|---|---|
| AE — American Express | MC — MasterCard |
| CB — Carte Blanche | T  — Transmedia |
| D — Discover | V — Visa |
| DC — Diner's Club | |

**ANNIE'S**
401-849-6731.
176 Bellevue Ave.,
   Newport, RI 02840.
Open: Daily.
Price: Inexpensive.
Cuisine: American.
Serving: B, L.
Credit Cards: No.
Smoking: Yes.
Handicap Access: No.

This exceptionally attractive coffeehouse next to the Newport Casino serves breakfast all day long (7:00 a.m.–6:00 p.m.), but get there either early or late, because it gets terrifically crowded. Omelettes, eggs Benedict, and special pancakes are all excellent breakfast bets; lunch ventures into quiches, salads, sandwiches, and soups, with a range of desserts and pastries. The fresh fruit salad is a winner.

**ANTHONY'S SHORE
   DINNER HALL**
401-848-5058.
Waites's Wharf, Newport,
   RI 02840.
Open: D weekdays,
   Fri.–Sun. from noon,
   May–Oct.
Price: Mostly Inexpensive.
Cuisine: Seafood.
Serving: L, D.
Credit Cards: MC, V.
Reservations: No.
Smoking: Yes.
Handicap Access: Yes.

For seafood-in-the-rough, Anthony's is *the* place. They have their own retail fish market, so the clams, lobster, and fish catches are fresh daily. Order your clam cakes and chowder combo, or the immense Newport lobster boil, or even honey-dipped chicken, get a tray, queue up for drinks (beer and wine), find a spot at a free picnic table, then watch boats come and go in the harbor until your number is called. Go to Anthony's when you don't feel like changing for dinner or challenging your palate with fancy sauces, but just want a good, simple, seafood meal without any hype. Chowders, available in Manhattan, New England, clear, and catch-of-the-day varieties, are all distinct, flavorful, and full of clams.

**ASTERIX & OBELIX**
401-841-8833.

I'm not sure what this restaurant's namesakes — French cartoon characters from ancient Gaul —

599 Thames St., Newport,
RI 02840.
Open: Daily.
Price: Expensive to Very
Expensive.
Cuisine: Eclectic.
Serving: L, D.
Credit Cards: AE, D, DC,
MC, V.
Reservations:
Recommended.
Smoking: Smoking section
("cigar friendly").
Handicap Access: Yes.

have to do with food, but never mind. Asterix & Obelix is one of Newport's hippest eateries. From the seared earth tones of the decor to the strong flavors of the menu, this is a spot that enjoys creative, unexpected pairings and jazzy presentations. Monkfish is coated in potato flakes and served with bacon confit; pork chops come with apples, prunes, and apricots; influences range from German (Wiener schnitzel) to Thai (my curried shrimp and scallops on basmati rice with coconut milk and lemon grass looked like a rain forest but was almost too spicy-hot to eat). Other entrées range from salmon, tuna, chicken, and steak to ostrich. Note, however, that imagination is reserved for entrées, special touches (vegetable purees for dipping bread), and atmosphere — desserts are rather ordinary. A creative spot, if unduly serious about itself given its fun name.

**THE BLACK PEARL**
401-846-5264.
Bannister's Wharf,
Newport, RI 02840.
Open: Daily.
Price: Very Expensive.
Cuisine: Continental.
Serving: L, D.
Credit Cards: AE, MC, V.
Reservations: Necessary for
Commodore Room.
Smoking: Yes.
Handicap Access: One step.

You can sit wharfside at the outdoor café (enjoy the raw bar) or inside in the Tavern, which offers a lighter fare menu, or even go to the Black Pearl hot dog annex. To splurge, go to the Commodore Room. The low, long ceiling is spanned by one glossy, black beam; walls are a deep green with more black trim, tablecloths are crisply white. The essentials — menu and wine list — are first rate, as are the small details: piping hot French rolls, fresh flowers, elegant presentation. Roast duckling in a black mushroom and truffle sauce was outstanding, as were the scallops bathed in meunière. With all of these superlatives, it's a shame that smoking is permitted in such tight quarters.

**THE BOATHOUSE**
401-846-7700.
636 Thames St., Newport,
RI 02840.
Open: Daily.
Price: Moderate.
Cuisine: American.
Serving: L, D.
Credit Cards: AE, D, MC, V.
Reservations: Accepted.
Smoking: Small smoking
section.
Handicap Access: Yes.

The thoroughly nautical atmosphere includes America's Cup memorabilia, yachting flags, fishing nets, buoys, even a neon sailboat advertising beer up at the bar. Besides specializing in large-scale lobster bakes, the Boathouse offers classic seafood dishes, such as baked-stuffed shrimp and bay scallops, but don't pass up the barbecued ribs — they're terrific. There are Cajun specials as well, plus lighter fare and children's menu. The clam chowder may not be the best, but there's Bass ale on tap. Reputed to be Ted Turner's favorite hangout in Newport.

Craig Hammell

*The Boathouse restaurant is awash in nautical memorabilia, both inside and out.*

**CAFÉ ZELDA**
401-849-4002.
528 Thames St., Newport,
   RI 02840.
Open: Daily.
Price: Moderate to
   Expensive.
Cuisine: Eclectic/Italian.
Serving: L, D, SB.
Credit Cards: AE, MC. V.
Reservations:
   Recommended.
Smoking: Bar only.
Handicap Access: One step.

Zelda's is something of a year-round, upscale hangout for Newport's nautical crowd. In fact, its bistro atmosphere makes it the locals' bar of choice in the winter. Word on the street is that Zelda's is a fun, friendly place, but the meals are so-so; I found the food better than expected. The menu offers soups, salads, and sandwiches, plus entrées, including pan-seared duck breast, shellfish bouillabaisse (a house specialty), and pan-seared black and blue tuna with key lime. Sunday brunch is reckoned to be a standout. Self-described as the "best little café between Bar Harbor and Key West."

**CANFIELD HOUSE**
401-847-0416.
5 Memorial Blvd.,
   Newport, RI 02840.
Open: Daily.
Price: Expensive to Very
   Expensive.
Cuisine: Continental.
Serving: D.
Credit Cards: AE, CB, D,
   DC, MC, V.
Reservations:
   Recommended.
Smoking: Bar only.
Handicap Access: No.

The Canfield House was built as a casino in 1897 by the creator of the card game solitaire and still has an old roulette wheel to prove it. Depending on how you feel (and are dressed), you can go upstairs to a vast, formal dining room with Gilded Age atmosphere (recently renovated) or downstairs to Patrick's Pub, a cozy spot with a nice fireplace that serves lighter fare; you can also order an entrée and eat at the bar. The large menu offers a full page of fish dishes — a friend had the best tuna steak of his life here — but rounds out the options with continentally prepared meat and fowl selections. Menus change every three to four months. Live jazz on Fri. and Sat. evenings (Wed.–Sun. in-season).

**CASTLE HILL INN AND RESORT**
401-849-3800.
Ocean Dr., Newport, RI 02840.
Open: Daily.
Price: Very Expensive.
Cuisine: Creative Continental.
Serving: L, D, SB (no dinner on Sun.).
Credit Cards: AE, D, MC, V.
Reservations: Recommended (jackets requested).
Smoking: Lounge only.
Handicap Access: Yes.
Special Features: Sun. from 1:00 p.m.–5:00 p.m. in-season seaside barbecue and live music on the lawn.

If you can afford it, Castle Hill will afford you a truly memorable dining experience. Located in an 1874 shingle-style mansion off Ocean Dr., the recently renovated dining rooms are subtly appointed and offer magnificent sea views. Service is professional, martinis are expertly prepared, and the wine list is extensive and tended to by a helpful steward. Meals are treated with an imaginative but light touch (the new chef uses no flour or butter sauces); appetizers include honey-roasted quail, clam chowder, and marinated venison; entrées range from seared tuna to lobster Thermidor to smoked barbecued duck. Well-traveled friends declared their dinner here to be the best that they've had in years and raved about the Stilton dessert plate, served with fresh blackberries and a blackberry-peach-ginger reduction sauce.

**CHEEKY MONKEY CAFE**
401-845-9494.
14 Perry Mill Wharf, Newport, RI 02840.
Open: Daily.
Price: Expensive.
Cuisine: British Colonial.
Serving: D.
Credit Cards: AE, DC, MC, V.
Reservations: Recommended.
Smoking: Bar only; smoking lounge upstairs.
Handicap Access: Yes.

Finally, there is a restaurant for people with a sense of humor who happen to crave well-prepared, creative food. The concept in this yellow, black, and leopard-spotted cafe is a takeoff on the British raj in India. Paintings of colonial types hang throughout; the catch is that they're colonial-type *chimps*. Despite the real glamour of the place, all this would seem silly if the food didn't follow suit — hearty fare with whimsical, Indian-inspired pairings — and weren't utterly top-notch. The menu is heavy on fish, but a couple of white-meat meals proved superb: grilled chicken rubbed with garlic and chili, served with corn bread pudding and black beans, and pork chops with banana-plantain chutney, smothered collard greens, black-eyed peas, and rice. Starters and salads are equally inventive, as is the homemade Indian nan bread. Live blues in the bar Thurs. night.

**CHRISTIE'S**
401-847-5400.
Christie's Landing, Newport, RI 02840 (off 351 Thames St.).
Open: Daily.

This biggest, oldest waterfront restaurant in Newport offers *superb* views and factory food. It's right on the harbor, which is visible in all its glory from either the outdoor patio or huge, rustic dining rooms. The place is always packed, with

Price: Moderate to
  Expensive.
Cuisine: Seafood.
Serving: L, D.
Credit Cards: AE, CB, D,
  DC, MC, V.
Reservations: Recommended
  on weekdays; not accepted
  weekends.
Smoking: Yes.
Handicap Access: Yes.

tourists drawn in by the location or to the live —
and extremely loud — weekend music. No one
comes for the food, which arrives in generous proportions but is standard at best. Expect seafood,
meat, and poultry dishes, and, unusual for such a
big spot, a cheerful waitstaff.

Craig Hammell

*The Clarke Cooke House —
home to a gourmet restau-
rant, an open-air porch where
casual fare is served, and a
nightclub called the Boom
Boom Room — is a venerable
presence on Bannister's
Wharf.*

**CLARKE COOKE HOUSE**
401-849-2900.
Bannister's Wharf,
  Newport, RI 02840.
Open: Daily.
Price: Bistro, Moderate to
  Expensive; Dining room,
  Very Expensive.
Cuisine: Bistro, Continental/
  Creative American;
  Dining room, French.
Serving: Bistro, L, D.;
  dining room, D.
Credit Cards: AE, CB, D,
  DC, MC, V.
Reservations:
  Recommended.
Smoking: Smoking section.
Handicap Access: No.
Special Features: The Candy
  Store becomes a disco
  called The Boom-Boom
  Room from 9:00 p.m.–1:00
  a.m.

The easy elegance of the Clarke Cooke House
belies its location in the thick of the harborside
throng. The formal French dining room (jackets
required) is upstairs and features a small, ever-
changing menu heavy on native fish, such as pan-
seared Atlantic salmon with saffron risotto, fresh
morels, and artichoke and fava bean puree, with
elegant meat and fowl entrées as well. The downstairs bistro, called the Candy Store, is extraordinarily attractive: open-air and breezy, its rattan
chairs and large, wainscoted bar, dominated by a
huge old model ship, hark back to the refined non-
chalance of the last century. Here you can get
lighter fare like soups, salads, and hand-tossed pizzas, as well as pastas, wood-grilled fish and meats,
even Mediterranean fish stew or twin lobsters. This
is a stalwart contender for the best restaurant in
Newport, whatever you're looking for.

**DRY DOCK SEAFOOD**
401-847-3974.
448 Thames St., Newport,
    RI 02840.
Open: Daily.
Price: Moderate.
Cuisine: Seafood.
Serving: L, D.
Credit Cards: No.
Reservations: No.
Smoking: Smoking section.
Handicap Access: One step.

*R*hode Island Monthly always includes this place in its "Cheap Eats" roundup (a best-for-less guide). The atmosphere is relaxed, and the straight-forward seafood is simply and perfectly cooked, with plenty of options that let you eat with your fingers, such as peel-and-eat shrimp, clam boils, and lobsters. The fried shrimp is some of the best on the planet. BYOB.

**ELIZABETH'S**
401-846-6862.
404 Thames St., Newport,
    RI 02840.
Open: Tues.-Sun.
Price: Expensive.
Cuisine: Continental/
    Seafood.
Serving: D.
Credit Cards: MC, V.
Reservations:
    Recommended.
Smoking: No.
Handicap Access: One step
    (rest rooms inaccessible).
Special Features: High Tea,
    2:30 p.m.–4:30 p.m.

*L*ove it or loathe it, Elizabeth's is different. In a new location on Thames St., the atmosphere is distinctly English country house: dark walls, William Morris prints, overstuffed chairs (nice to look at but difficult to dine in). The dinner menu features large platters to be shared by two; half-platters are available for odd-numbered parties, but ordering individual half-servings is discouraged. The cooking is healthy (some say that the side dishes are a bit bland), scarce on meats and fried foods, with stuffed sourdough bouillabaisse a favorite. Other entrées include scallop and shrimp Parmesan pie and stuffed chicken breast Marsala. The vegetable-cheese garlic bread is a winner. While many find Elizabeth's delightful, others think that the tandem-serving is an overpriced gimmick. BYOB.

**FRIEND'S PUB & EATERY**
401-846-3659.
32 Broadway, Newport, RI
    02840.
Open: Daily.
Price: Inexpensive.
Cuisine: American.
Serving: D (and snacks).
Credit Cards: No.
Reservations: No.
Smoking: Yes.
Handicap Access: Yes.

*T*his hole-in-the-wall on Broadway was voted "Best Place to be on a Tuesday Night" by *Rhode Island Monthly*. Better yet, insiders say it's where restaurant staff go after their shift to relax and get a burger — now that's high praise indeed. The atmosphere is friendly, the food tasty and unchallenging, and you can watch a model train run on suspended tracks above the bar. Go between 5:00 p.m.–7:00 p.m. and get a burger with fries, salad, and beverage for $5. Most tourists overlook it, which is their loss.

**LA FORGE CASINO
    RESTAURANT**
401-847-0418.
186 Bellevue Ave.,
    Newport, RI 02840.

*L*a Forge is all about atmosphere, and it is exceptional here even by Newport standards. The restaurant is part of the sprawling, shingle-style casino complex designed by McKim, Mead, and White in 1880; it also houses the International

Open: Daily.
Price: Moderate to
   Expensive.
Cuisine: American.
Serving: B (Sat. only), L, D,
   SB.
Credit Cards: AE, MC, T, V.
Reservations:
   Recommended.
Smoking: Smoking section.
Handicap Access: Yes.
Special Features: Sing-along
   piano music in the lounge.

**LA PETITE AUBERGE**
401-849-6669.
19 Charles St., Newport, RI
   02840.
Open: Daily.
Price: Very Expensive.
Cuisine: French.
Serving: D.
Credit Cards: AE, MC, V.
Reservations: Necessary.
Smoking: Bar only.

**LE BISTRO**
401-849-7778.
Bowen's Wharf, Newport,
   RI 02840.
Open: Daily.
Price: Very Expensive.
Cuisine: French.
Serving: L, D.
Credit Cards: AE, CB, D,
   DC, MC, T, V.
Reservations:
   Recommended.
Smoking: Smoking section.
Handicap Access: No.
Special Features: Live
   acoustic guitar at the
   second-floor bar every
   weekend.

Tennis Hall of Fame. La Forge's front rooms and porch offer a fairly standard light menu. For an authentic aristocratic experience, however, go farther back inside to a graceful, semicircular dining room that overlooks pristine grass tennis courts. (The bar alone, a classic example of warm, gleaming wood and 1890s' panache, rekindles the Gilded Age.) Meals are not haute or trendy but straightforward and dependable: seafood, steaks, veal, and chicken. The chateaubriand for two is a good choice. Go simply to go back in time.

La Petite Auberge, with its many fireplaces and Provençal appointments (lace tablecloths and curtains), is a visual and gastronomic delight and one of Newport's best. Several small dining rooms nestle in this 1714 colonial home. The menu is classic French with local and continental influences. Memorable appetizers feature escargot, goose liver pâté, and lobster bisque. Seafood entrées include trout with hazelnuts and lobster tail with truffles; fowl concentrates on chicken and duck; meats include a variety of beef preparations and saddle of lamb for two. Desserts are simple and tantalizing, and the wine list is extensive. Service can be slow, but the cooking is worth the wait. Casual courtyard dining in-season offers less expensive, simpler fare, such as burgers and roast chicken with creamed leeks.

Le Bistro specializes in French "low cuisine" — good, hearty fare with a few flights of fancy: bouillabaisse, steak au poivre with *real* "frites," sea scallops meunière, seven-hour lamb, cassoulet. The Savoyard — Gruyère, ham, and bèarnaise on French bread — is a favorite lunchtime option, as is The Great Bistro French Paradox: sausages, pâté, and prosciutto with crusty bread. Warm duck salad is also tasty, as is the restrained but delicious wild mushroom omelette. Desserts on the order of French bread pudding with bourbon sauce and bananas Foster are created in-house. Service can be excruciatingly slow, but the upstairs loft is a nice spot to wait.

**LONG WHARF STEAKHOUSE**
401-847-7800.
142 Long Wharf, Newport, RI 02840.
Open: Daily.
Price: Moderate.
Cuisine: American.
Serving: D.
Credit Cards: AE, MC, V.
Reservations: No.
Smoking: Yes.
Handicap Access: Yes.

The hike down to the end of Long Wharf may be off-putting, but once settled, the view may be the best in town; you're literally sitting above Newport Harbor. This restaurant in the Inn on Long Wharf is casual, offers generous portions cooked to preference, fast, professional service, and wisely sticks to what it does best: simple meat and seafood entrées. The wine list is pedestrian, but that's a small quibble; for a hearty, meaty meal at a budget price and a spectacular sunset, this is the place. Live, late entertainment on weekends.

**MAMMA LUISA ITALIAN RESTAURANT**
401-848-5257.
673 Thames St., Newport, RI 02840.
Open: Tues.–Sun.
Price: Moderate to Expensive.
Cuisine: Italian.
Serving: D.
Credit Cards: MC, V.
Reservations: Yes.
Smoking: No.
Handicap Access: One step (rest rooms inaccessible).

Down at the end of Lower Thames St., where old Newport lives on unhampered by T-shirt shops and traffic jams, is Mamma Luisa's, a quiet haven of understated calm and delicious food. Marco Trazzi, the host, has learned well from his mamma (a chef in Bologna), offering superior food in a delightful setting — two intimate dining rooms on either side of a center-hall colonial. Pastas are delicately cooked and flavored, and the homemade spinach gnocchi, a family specialty, is superb. Also memorable are the specials, including pork tenderloin and salmon steak. Homemade desserts are worth saving space for, and the wine list, though small, is well selected. A low-profile gem.

**THE MOORING**
401-846-2260.
Sayer's Wharf, Newport, RI 02840 (at the Newport Yachting Center).
Open: Daily.
Price: Moderate to Expensive.
Cuisine: American/New England.
Serving: L, D.
Credit Cards: AE, MC, V.
Reservations: Large parties only.
Smoking: In bar only.
Handicap Access: Yes.

Accessible, trendy, and recently renovated to add a new bar, outdoor patio, and lots of windows to highlight its harborside vista, The Mooring comes through in the food department as well. You can get a full range of appetizers, sandwiches, soups, salads, and entrées all day long; the Portuguese-style mussel appetizer (served with chouriço) is a standout. The menu isn't extensive — six fish, poultry, and meat items each — but the entrées are always reliable and well prepared. The Mooring's version of baked-stuffed shrimp is filled with huge pieces of scallops and crabmeat, and the tuna steak is top quality. The wine list, however, is a bit pricey. Mostly casual, but grows more formal as the evening progresses.

## MUDVILLE PUB

401-849-1408.
8 W. Marlborough St.,
  Newport, RI 02840.
Open: Daily.
Price: Inexpensive to
  Moderate.
Cuisine: American.
Serving: L, D.
Credit Cards: AE, MC, V.
Reservations: No.
Smoking: Yes.
Handicap Access: One step.

The Mudville Pub, beloved by the Newport police force, has a venerable reputation as the only place in town that serves *real* fresh-roasted and carved turkey sandwiches. A sports pub extraordinaire, it's a great place for lunch or a drink and snack with the game. Tiffany-style lamps hang above wooden booths; George, the longtime bartender, presides over a big bar; and the drone of ESPN, combined with warm, wood-paneled surroundings, invariably induces contentment. Sandwiches, clubs, and burgers are the way to go, though there are entrée specials that include steaks, chicken, plus a pasta and catch of the day. In-season, you can sit outside on the patio and watch *live* ball games at Cardines Field next door.

## MURIEL'S

401-849-7780.
58 Spring St., Newport, RI
  02840.
Open: Daily.
Price: Moderate.
Cuisine: Eclectic.
Serving: B, L, D, SB.
Credit Cards: AE, D, MC,
  V.
Reservations: Accepted for
  dinner, not for Sun.
  brunch.
Smoking: Discouraged.
Handicap Access: One step.

Muriel's looks like an attractive, hip French bistro. Tablecloths are overlaid with embroidery and glitter (all under glass), and funky antiques and lace lend atmosphere. In the first edition of this book, I judged Muriel's on the dinner offerings, which were uneven. Since then locals have confided that Muriel's is best for breakfast, and I wholeheartedly agree. Deliciously inventive options include chocolate pancakes; courthouse waffles, cooked with bacon inside and an egg and melted cheese on top; French toast "Grand Marnier," stuffed with cream cheese and dipped in liqueur batter; and crab cakes Benedict. The Jane Pickens Theater Special on Fri. and Sat. nights includes dinner and a movie for $12.95. A great bargain.

## MUSIC HALL CAFÉ

401-848-2330.
250 Thames St., Newport,
  RI 02840.
Open: Daily in-season,
  Thurs.–Sun. in winter.
Price: Moderate.
Cuisine: Southwestern.
Serving: L, D, SB.
Credit Cards: AE, D, MC, V.
Reservations: Accepted.
Smoking: Smoking section.
Handicap Access: Possible
  (rest rooms inaccessible).

There is only so much chowder a person can eat — for a change, try the Music Hall Café and its somewhat eclectic but mostly Southwestern fare. The building really was a music hall once, but now it's nicely outfitted in pale desert shades and a trompe l'oeil painting of an adobe village. The menu offers hip dishes like marinated grilled pork chops with black beans, fried bananas, polenta, and chicken breaded in blue corn flour. Everything is imaginatively concocted and nicely cooked; the ribs and chili nachos are all-time favorites of Newport-based friends. (By the way, you can get chowder, too.)

**NEWPORT BLUES CAFE**
401-841-5510.
286 Thames St., Newport,
    RI 02840.
Open: Daily in summer,
    Thurs.–Sat. off-season.
Price: Moderate to
    Expensive.
Cuisine: American/Creole.
Serving: D.
Credit Cards: AE, D, DC,
    MC, V.
Reservations: Parties of 8 or
    more.
Smoking: Bar only.
Handicap Access: Yes.

The food doesn't have to be top-notch in Newport's only blues dinner club, and it isn't. But it is better than average, and that's saying a lot for a spot that's got other things on its mind, principally different live music every night after 10:00 p.m. Look for an emphasis on grilled entrées, including pork, lamb, and chicken, and a slight touch of Louisiana, which shows up in dishes like shellfish Savannah, concocted of shrimp, scallops, littlenecks, mussels, and lobster over squid ink swirled in saffron tomato broth. The exterior is eye-catching — an old brownstone bank outfitted with blue neon signs, with an interior that is warmly welcoming. A unique newcomer that deserves to make it.

**PEZZULLI'S**
401-846-5830.
136 Thames St., Newport,
    RI 02840.
Open: Wed.–Sun.
Price: Expensive to Very
    Expensive.
Cuisine: Italian.
Serving: D.
Credit Cards: AE.
Reservations: No.
Smoking: No.
Handicap Access: No.

Pezzulli's is a haven of excellence. Relaxed, casual, and small (twelve tables), this family-run spot overlooking Brick Market Place offers slow, steady service in the European manner and some of the best food that you'll eat in a long time. The entrées all involve pasta, but the variety is great, ranging from crab and lobster over black fettuccine to shrimp tossed in ginger cream sauce to outstanding, homemade marinara dishes. The calamari is exquisitely seasoned, the hot Italian baguettes are homemade, and the desserts, including cappuccino bread pudding, tiramisu, and fresh fruit sorbets, are divine. Even the espresso is perfect. This is a place to savor superior food and conversation in a leisurely manner. Don't go if you're in a hurry, or dislike opera or Dean Martin music.

**PRONTO**
401-847-5251.
464 Thames St., Newport,
    RI 02840.
Open: Daily.
Price: Moderate.
Cuisine: Italian.
Serving: B Sat., Sun.; L, D.
Credit Cards: AE, MC, T, V.
Reservations:
    Recommended.
Smoking: Yes.
Handicap Access: Yes.

In the summer, the door stays open and bustling Thames St. is right outside, but the interior — chic in a elegantly funky way — can transport you to the European location of your choice. There's only one room (in which smoking is discouraged, but permitted), so reserve ahead. Creative pasta dishes, tossed with a cornucopia of nouvelle ingredients and seafoods, dominate the regular menu, which is supplemented by a generous choice of specials. Recent hits included grilled lobster and rib eye steak. The food is tasty and almost transporting. Serves beer and wine.

**PUERINI'S**
401-847-5506.
24 Memorial Blvd. West,
    Newport, RI 02840.
Open: Daily.
Price: Moderate.
Cuisine: Italian.
Serving: D.
Credit Cards: MC, V.
Reservations: No.
Smoking: No.
Handicap Access: Yes.

Simplicity, charm, and reasonable prices add up to an unpretentious winner. Three small dining rooms are cozy and casual, appointed with 1950s-style vases and original artwork. The menu is divided into chicken, beef, and vegetable selections, each offered in a variety of preparations over, or stuffed into, homemade pastas. The linguine with carciòfo (artichokes) is artistically presented and delicious; the veal baccèllo di vanìglia, with butter, prosciutto, and fresh vanilla bean, is a superb combination, packed with interesting flavors. Desserts range from sorbets and gelatos to flan and sinful chocolate things. Presentation has improved over the years while quality hasn't slackened.

**THE RED PARROT**
401-847-3140.
348 Thames St., Newport,
    RI 02840.
Open: Daily.
Price: Moderate.
Cuisine:
    Eclectic/American.
Serving: L, D.
Credit Cards: AE, D, MC,
    V.
Reservations: No.
Smoking: Smoking section.
Handicap Access: No.
Special Features: Live jazz
    sessions every weekend.

In an unmistakable black building — an 1898 meat-packing house on the National Register — at the heart of Newport's busiest, noisiest intersection, The Red Parrot is highly recommended for lunch and for late-night jazz; it's a bit too slick and frenetic for dinner. The menu is immense and offers silly drinks with names like Chocolate Monkey (chocolate liqueur, crème de banana, fresh banana, chocolate syrup, and ice cream), salads, burgers, pastas, quesadillas, a whole page devoted to lobsters, and desserts with descriptions like "it's a sexy, scary, chocolate thing." Getting beyond the hype, the food isn't bad; the barbecued pork sandwich is one of the best I've had.

**RESTAURANT
    BOUCHARD**
401-846-0123.
505 Thames St., Newport,
    RI 02840.
Open: Wed.–Mon.
Price: Very Expensive.
Cuisine: French.
Serving: D.
Credit Cards: AE, MC, V.
Reservations:
    Recommended.
Smoking: No.
Handicap Access: No.

Although it hasn't been around as long as other candidates for "best restaurant in town," Bouchard is often mentioned in their company. It's very expensive, very elegant, very romantic, and even quiet, despite it's location on Lower Thames St. Better yet, cooking and presentation are both magnificent, and the service is impeccable. Starters include lobster and asparagus tips in puff pastry and oyster ravioli in champagne sauce; entrées vary from rack of lamb in red wine and curry reduction to scallops flambé; and desserts — heavenly inventions, all — include individual soufflés with Grand Marnier sauce and profiteroles with vanilla ice cream. Attention to details, such as the selection of a fine house wine, a very able Merlot, takes Bouchard out of the ordinary (as do the steep, a la carte prices).

**THE RHUMB LINE**
401-849-6950.
62 Bridge St., Newport, RI
  02840.
Open: Daily.
Price: Expensive.
Cuisine: Seafood / Creative
  American.
Serving: L, D, SB.
Credit Cards: AE, MC, V.
Reservations:
  Recommended.
Smoking: Smoking section.
Handicap Access: One step.

The Rhumb Line has a reputation in Newport for being mismatched. Does it want to be a pub, a bistro, or a romantic little restaurant hidden in a colonial home in the Point Section of town? To some the culinary clash is too much; others are charmed by the red-and-white tablecloths, the chocolate bread pudding, the signature smoked bluefish pâté appetizer, and the first-rate wine list, complete with a selection of ports and cognacs. The menu is comprehensive, including beef, pork, veal, seafood, and pasta dishes, with such entrées as Thai pork and linguine and mesquite-spiced catfish.

**SALAS'**
401-846-8772.
345 Thames St., Newport,
  RI 02840.
Open: Daily.
Price: Inexpensive to
  Moderate.
Cuisine: Seafood / Italian.
Serving: D.
Credit Cards: AE, D, DC,
  MC, V.
Reservations: No; often a
  wait.
Smoking: Smoking section.
Handicap Access: No.

Salas' is a Newport fixture. It may be crowded and noisy and right in the heart of Thames St., but meals are cheap and tasty and everyone eats like crazy. Specialties include two market-priced versions of the individual clambake, and pasta or Oriental spaghetti by the pound (at $5, a quarter-pound with shrimp is too much for one person). There are plenty of additional seafood and Italian dishes, plus sandwiches and one steak entrée. Wine is not a highlight here; stick to the excellent draft beer or specialty drinks. Salas' is popular with Newport regulars, the sailing crowd (chic because it's unchic), and visitors who recognize a great deal.

**SALVATION CAFE**
401-847-2620.
140 Broadway, Newport, RI
  02840.
Open: Daily.
Price: Moderate.
Cuisine: Eclectic.
Serving: D.
Credit Cards: AE, MC, V.
Reservations: Large parties
  only.
Smoking: Smoking section.
Handicap Access: One step.

The Broadway area has become the East Village of Newport: funky, artsy, and a little seedy, but the place where restaurants and galleries pivot on the cutting edge. Salvation Cafe is as hip, in a bright, retro kind of way, as Newport gets. Inside are tables and a counter (don't kick the painted mural with your feet); out back is a a little patio (charming if you don't mind the messy, art school atmosphere) that overlooks the Newport Farmers' Market on Sun. Fresh, seasonal ingredients are the emphasis in the kitchen, with menus changing weekly. A recent selection included Pad Thai, chicken pesto, NY sirloin, and quesadillas. BYOB.

**SARDELLA'S**
401-849-6312.
30 Memorial Blvd. W,
   Newport, RI 02840.
Open: Daily.
Price: Moderate.
Cuisine: Italian.
Serving: D.
Credit Cards: AE, D, MC,
   V.
Reservations: Suggested.
Smoking: Smoking section.
Handicap Access: Yes.

Sardella's dishes are inspired by both northern and southern Italian traditions and are seasoned with the freshest ingredients. The petti di pollo Romano (chicken stuffed with mozzarella, garlic, fresh parsley, and wine) is excellent; the ravioli alla Parma and prosciutto, flavored with basil in a cream sauce is superb as is the vichyssoise starter. I'm glad to report that the wine list has grown over the years. Warm, dark tones in the casual dining room perfectly suit the heady Italian aromas and flavors. End with a great espresso and a truly mouthwatering napoleon. There's a wood-burning fireplace in the winter and outdoor patio dining in the summer.

**SCALES AND SHELLS**
401-846-3474.
527 Thames St., Newport,
   RI 02840.
Open: Daily.
Price: Expensive.
Cuisine: Seafood.
Serving: D.
Credit Cards: No.
Reservations: No.
Smoking: No.
Handicap Access: Yes.

Often mentioned as a personal favorite, Scales and Shells bills itself as the only restaurant in Newport to serve seafood exclusively. A blackboard notes what's fresh from the sea: tuna, bluefish, swordfish, scallops, red snapper — if it swims in local waters, it's been served here. House specialties include grilled lobster, calamari, and wood-grilled fish of all description. The raw bar merits high praise. The dining room is very informal and spills over into the open kitchen. Go early — there's often a wait. Beer and wine only. Note that in-season the owners operate a small spot upstairs called Upscales (no handicap access). It's quieter, more formal, accepts reservations, and features a full bar; meals are more intricate than the robust concoctions downstairs, and while fish is still featured, it often swims in southern Italian sauces.

**TUCKER'S BISTRO**
401-846-1811.
150 Broadway, Newport, RI
   02840.
Open: Daily.
Price: Expensive.
Cuisine: "Fusion."
Serving: D.
Credit Cards: D, MC, V.
Reservations: Yes.

From its cuisine, shaped by the flavors of Asia, Europe, and North America, to its eclectic decor, Tucker's has a very real touch of exoticism about it, harking back to Parisian bistros of the 1920s. Unique table settings, bookshelves, and original art and antiques all glow beneath home-made "chandeliers," concocted from Christmas lights and wire. The escargot appetizer, sautéed in

Smoking: Yes.
Handicap Access: Limited.

sun-dried tomato pesto, is flawless, while the jumbo shrimp smothered in curry-and-coconut baste lacks the appropriate zing. Entrées range from grilled pork chops in citrus-bourbon sauce to a Broadway burger to blackened mahimahi. Pasta specials are exceptionally good, as is the homemade banana bread pudding. The smallish wine list is well selected, and the service is pleasant if a little slow.

**VIA VIA CAFE**
401-848-0880.
372 Thames St., Newport,
 RI 02840.
Open: Daily.
Price: Inexpensive.
Cuisine: Italian.
Serving: L, D.
Credit Cards: MC, V.
Reservations: No.
Smoking: No.
Handicap Access: Yes.

"The best pizza in town." "Truly great pizza, you've got to try it." I listened, and did, and everything I heard is true. Via Via's pizza is some of the best that I've ever eaten (of the thin crust, trendy variety). Sample toppings include artichoke and feta, chicken and goat cheese, and shrimp and pesto — the biggest seller. The café also serves sandwiches, pastas, and chicken and veal dishes, which are tasty, a good deal for the money, and also available for takeout. BYOB. The delivery number is 401-846-4074. There's another location at 112 William St., Newport, RI 02840 (401-846-4070.

**THE WEST DECK**
401-847-3610.
1 Waites Wharf, Newport,
 RI 02840.
Open: D, Wed.–Sun., SB in
 winter, outdoor bar daily
 in-season.
Price: Expensive.
Cuisine:
 International/French.
Serving: D.
Credit Cards: AE, MC, V.
Reservations:
 Recommended.
Smoking: Yes.
Handicap Access: Yes.

The West Deck has a casual outdoor bar (sometimes with live music) that hits Newport's hedonistic, seaside mood right on its head; the small, indoor dining room is breezy but hip. All meals, which encompass a large variety of meats, fowl, and seafood, are prepared to customer's preferences; in general, simpler, classic dishes work better than more creative options. Recent appetizers (menus change weekly) have included house pâté of duck, rabbit, quail, foie gras, and escargots on a portabello mushroom. Entrées range from grilled swordfish with Jamaican jerk sauce to Oriental half-duckling, and desserts — exceptionally good — include frozen mango and cassis soufflé harlequin and strawberry-rhubarb cobbler. Despite the questionable policy of a blaring TV in the dining room, this is currently *the* hot spot in Newport.

**WHITE HORSE TAVERN**
401-849-3600.
Marlborough St., Newport,
 RI 02840.
Open: Daily.
Price: Very Expensive.

The building that houses the White Horse Tavern was constructed in 1673; in 1730, tavern keeper Jonathan Nichols named it the White Horse. It's been serving food and drink ever since, but make no mistake, this is no tourist attraction get-

Craig Hammell

*Generation upon generation have carried on the tradition of fine food and drink at the White Horse Tavern.*

Cuisine: Continental/
    Creative American.
Serving: L Wed.–Mon., D
    daily, SB.
Credit Cards: AE, CB, D,
    DC, MC, V.
Reservations:
    Recommended (as are
    jackets).
Smoking: Bar only.
Handicap Access: Limited.

ting by on its age and beamed ceilings. By all standards, the White Horse Tavern offers superb gourmet food and gracious professional service. A variety of seafood, meats, and poultry are on hand, all expertly prepared and presented. The mingled flavors of chicken stuffed with foie gras over wild rice takes poultry dishes to a new height; the wine and dessert selections are also superb. Fine colonial atmosphere and exceptional food offer a rare opportunity to hold the ordinary at bay — note, though, that escape doesn't come cheap.

**WINDWARD GRILLE**
401-849-2600.
Doubletree Newport
    Islander Hotel, Goat Is.,
    Newport, RI 02840.
Open: Daily.
Price: Expensive.
Cuisine: American.
Serving: B, L, D, SB.
Credit Cards: AE, MC, V.
Reservations:
    Recommended.
Smoking: Smoking section.
Handicap Access: Yes.

Truisms about hotel restaurants aside, the Windward Grille is a very fine spot. The atmosphere is restful, with an idyllic, seascape view of the Point Section and an air of spartan elegance. The service is top-notch, and the food — solid American fare, with just a few nouvelle touches here and there — is always fresh and well prepared. There's a great pea soup, plus raw bar selections amid a host of other interesting appetizers. The menu lists sirloin, salmon, chicken, and duckling entrées, plus lobster pot for two, and boasts fabulous desserts. One, fresh berries over a sweet cream sauce with a chocolate almond bar, approaches the divine. The wine list is moderate in scale and price. The Calypso Brunch on Sun. is famous throughout RI.

**YESTERDAY'S ALE
   HOUSE & WINE BAR
   AND GRILL**
401-847-0116.
28 Washington Sq.,
   Newport, RI 02840.
Open: Tues.–Sun.
Price: Expensive to Very
   Expensive.
Cuisine: Contemporary.
Serving: D.
Credit Cards: AE, MC, V.
Reservations: Yes (days in
   advance).
Smoking: Bar only.
Handicap Access: Yes.

Approach Yesterday's: the Ale House is to the left, the Wine Bar and Grill (aka The Place) is to the right. It's worth mastering this confusion, because both are utterly fabulous. The Place puts a unique spin on everything, then cooks it perfectly, with an inspired use of seasonings. Its Art Nouveau decor is enchanting, the service friendly and helpful, the dress casual, and the wine sampler (a tray of five small glasses) is an innovative introduction to the excellent wine list. The menu includes stuffed loin of pork with honey-almond crust, red snapper with lobster and guava, and a delicious crab ravioli with chèvre and ginger appetizer. A typically luscious dessert is key lime soufflé with fresh fruit. The Ale House menu is much lighter, simpler, and less expensive, with fresh salads, stellar clam chowder, and entrées like barbecue ribs and tuna with red chili crust; it also has a fine selection of beers.

**ZIA LIONELLA**
401-846-4477.
186-190B Thames St.,
   Newport, RI 02840.
Open: Tues.–Sun.
Price: Moderate.
Cuisine: Italian.
Serving: L, D.
Credit Cards: MC, V.
Reservations: Yes.
Smoking: No.
Handicap Access: No.

This Northern Italian restaurant is for folks who, after a long day at the beach, don't want to be challenged by epicurean sauces over anything made with squid ink. Traditional pasta and meat dishes are well prepared with a light touch; examples include cheese-filled spinach ravioli in meat sauce and veal scaloppine. A more up-dated special of wild mushroom ravioli with arugula proved excellent. The mascarpone dessert is a special of the house. Despite the almost kitschy Italian atmosphere, service by the Italian chef-owner is warm and personal. BYOB makes this spot a bargain.

# FOOD & BEVERAGE PURVEYORS

Note that starred listings (*) indicate a purveyor of local fame or of unusual or special merit.

## BAKERIES & COFFEEHOUSES

Thames Street is positively awash in coffee joints; the names are often transitory, but whatever the incarnation, they're always there. Current entries include **Best Dressed Bagel** (401-848-2245; 198 Thames); **Espresso Yourself** (401-847-1125; 337 Thames); **Starbucks** (401-841-5899; 212 Thames); **Steaming**

**Bean Espresso Cafe** (401-849-5255; 515 Thames); and **Uncle Josh's** (401-847-8030; 406 Thames). Street numbers increase from north to south. Off-Thames establishments include the following:

**Cappuccino's** (401-846-7145; 92 William St.) Trendy coffees, sandwiches, and salads to go or to eat in, plus fresh-baked goods. Just off Bellevue Ave.

**Coffee Corner** (401-849-2902; 283 Broadway) A down-to-earth spot noted as having one of the best breakfasts in town by readers of *Newport Life Magazine*.

**Coffee Grinder** (401-849-4325; 33 Bannister's Wharf) *The* ideal (and hard-to-find) place to have coffee, frozen cappuccino, sandwiches, or muffins, while sitting in a couple of Adirondack chairs at the very end of Bannister's Wharf.

\* **Ocean Coffee Roasters** (401-846-6060; 22 Washington Sq.) One of the most recommended places in town to get good biscotti, a cup of coffee, and a sandwich.

## BARS

A few bars are covered in the Restaurant section, including Friend's Pub & Eatery, Mudville Pub, Patrick's Pub in the Canfield House, and the outdoor bar at The West Deck. The following are primarily bars for eating and drinking; for bars that focus on entertainment and liquor, see the section Culture, under the heading Nightlife.

\* **Brick Alley Pub** (401-849-6334; 140 Thames St.) A *hugely* popular spot in the thick of the harborside din. It keeps winning local awards for best burgers, appetizers, etc., and has a gargantuan food and drinks menu. Always crowded — too crowded, perhaps. Stephen Spielberg and his crew came here when they shot the film *Amistad* in Newport in 1997.

**Craig's Place** (401-849-3203; 162 Broadway) A large sports bar with a pool table that attracts a young crowd for live music on weekends; voted best entertainment in *Newport Life Magazine* readers' poll.

\* **Marina Grille** (401-841-0999; Goat Island South) Although it offers a full dinner menu (London broil, lobster, etc.) in a city of superb restaurants, you'll probably want to give this one a miss. The outdoor patio, however, clings to the tip of Goat Is., directly opposite the harbor from the Trinity Church spire. There's absolutely no place better in Newport to sit outside, have appetizers and a drink, and watch the sun set into the sea.

**O'Brien's Pub** (401-849-6623; 501 Thames St.) A darn good Irish pub. In-season, drink alfresco on the patio and return to pub atmosphere when it gets cold. Breakfast, sandwiches, and full dinners.

**Sabina Doyle's** (401-849-4466; 359 Thames St.) Another darn good Irish pub, of which almost exactly the same can be said as that above.

**The Wharf Pub & Restaurant** (401-846-9233; 37 Bowen's Wharf) With thirty-six beers and cask-conditioned ale (whatever that means). Really terrific nachos, chowder, and black-and-tans, without having to leave the tourist throng. Live music on weekends.

## CONVENIENCE STORES

**Downtown Convenience** (401-842-0545; 202 Thames St.) Everything you need from newspapers to toothpaste to lottery tickets and an ATM; opposite Newport Harbor on Upper Thames.

**The Rum Runner** (401-847-7600; Goat Island South) A lifesaver for sailors tied up at Goat Island Marina. You can get beer, wine, liquor, breakfast, ice cream, sundries, and sandwiches to eat in, on the patio, or take away. Also a FedEx drop-off.

## FARM MARKETS

**Newport Farmers' Market** Held Thurs. 3:00 p.m.–7:00 p.m. at Easton Beach; Sun. 9:00 a.m.–1:00 p.m. at 77 Dr. Marcus Wheatland Blvd., behind the Salvation Cafe.

## FISH & MEAT MARKETS

**Aquidneck Lobster Company** (401-846-0106; Bowen's Wharf, off Thames St.) You know it's fresh when they give it to you whole or fillet it in front of you.

**Long Wharf Seafood** (401-846-6320; 17 Connell Hwy.) Recommended by some of Newport's best chefs for fresh fish and shellfish.

## GOURMET, DELI, GROCERY

* **Kathleen's Fantastic Food** (401-849-9034; 212 Broadway) This place is a smorgasbord of great smells and sights, including four potato salads and five chicken salads. The blueberry muffin here was voted best in the state. Also a location at 34 Narragansett Ave. in Jamestown, RI (401-423-0414).

* **The Market on the Boulevard** (401-848-2600; 43 Memorial Blvd.) The most-recommended grocery, deli, gourmet shop in town — one of Newport's finest chefs was recently spotted coming out the door with a big bag, surely a good sign. They put apricots in the chicken salad.

* **Sig's Market** (401-847-9668; 7 Carroll Ave.) Ask where to get a decent sandwich and this is where locals send you. It's really an overgrown grocery with a deli counter and soft ice cream. A selection of catered meals is also available (the whole caboodle from hors d'oeuvres, entrée, salad, dessert, to even the plastic cutlery). Great prices.

## ICE CREAM & SWEETS

**Bob and Gerry's Ices and Slices** (401-849-6904; 436-438 Thames St.) A big, clean shop with Hershey's ice cream, plus soft serve, frozen yogurt, and Italian ices. The "slices" refers to pies, not pizzas.

**Scoops** (401-848-0897; 359 Thames St.) An enduring ice-cream spot with lots of flavors; they do this one thing, and they do it right. Best-selling flavor: chocolate peanut butter cup.

**Treats** (401-847-8381; 458 Thames St.) Some call it a bakery, others say it's a sandwich shop. Most like the ice cream.

## SEASONAL FOOD FESTIVALS & SPECIAL DINING OPPORTUNITIES

*Clam and seafood lovers have a ball at the Great Chowder Cook-off, held annually at the Newport Yachting Center.*

Craig Hammell

**Great Chowder Cook-Off** (401-846-1600) Sponsored yearly (mid-Jun.) by the Newport Yachting Center, this is a terrific chance to taste over twenty-eight samples of clam and seafood chowder in one day (served up in tiny paper cups). Vote for your favorite.

**Kempenaar's Clambake Club** (401-847-1441; 37 Malbone Rd.) Arrange a private clambake for two or for a crowd up to 125, Apr.–Oct. The secluded clambake grounds are on Valley Rd. in Middletown, RI — there's even a pool. Kempenaar's holds a Public Clambake every 4th of July (choose between steak and lobster, plus all the fixings).

**Native American Clambake** (401-847-4242; Rose Island Lighthouse) Held rain or shine, this massive feast supervised by the Pokanoket Tribe is baked the traditional way, in a big pit dug in the sand, supervised by a bake-master, and includes lobsters, mussels, fish, corn, and fixings. Reservations required; also expect to take a $5 launch out to Rose Island.

**Newport Dinner Train** (800-398-RIBS; 19 America's Cup Ave.) Under new management, the dinner train cruises the shore of Narragansett Bay for two and a half hours as you dine; luncheon and dinner departures, as well as special barbershop quartet and murder mystery rides, plus a Sun. afternoon clambake. Expensive to very expensive.

**Oktoberfest** (401-846-1600) The Newport Yachting Center's big beer and wurst fest, held annually the second weekend in Oct.

**Taste of Rhode Island** (401-846-1600) The biggest of Newport Yachting Center's food festivals (late Sept.). Appetizer samples from over forty restaurants, plus cooking demonstrations and a Parade of Chefs. A similar **Taste of Newport** is held in Nov.

## TAKEOUT & CHEAP EATS

**Boston Chicken** (401-849-8990; 258 Bellevue Ave.) Although it's a Massachusetts chain, this rotisserie chicken is superb: moist, tender, and cheap. A big selection of cold salads, mashed potatoes, corn bread, and more to go with it.

**Café at Sayer's Wharf** (401-846-9740; corner America's Cup Ave. and Sayer's Wharf) It's in the touristy part of town, yet locals come here for cold cuts, to get a drink at the open-air bar, and to have a sandwich.

**Charlie's Good Egg** (401-849-7818; 12 Broadway) This is a little dinerlike spot with Formica tables, full of locals ordering inexpensive omelettes the way they like 'em. Anything but fancy.

**Gary's Handy Lunch** (401-847-9480; 462 Thames St.) A 1950s retro look — black-and-white checked floor, red-and-white tiled counter, swivel stools — lures both yuppies and local workers, who all return for the food; breakfast from 5:00 a.m. on; dinner Fri. and Sat. nights.

**Ocean Breeze Café** (401-849-1750; 580 Thames St.) Some like this place (not to be confused with Ocean Coffee Roasters), though others think that it's a little sterile. Fresh muffins, homemade soups, and chowders. Serves breakfast, lunch, and dinner.

**Poor Richard's** (401-846-8768; 254 Thames St.) A decent, not-fancy breakfast and lunch spot near the harbor. Good sandwiches and burgers.

* **St. Elmo's Galley** (401-847-7337; 18 Market Sq., in the Seaman's Church Institute) A personal favorite. This old-fashioned, genteel, comfy spot is hidden in the Seaman's Church Institute, a total contrast to the bright, noisy, yuppie panorama that surrounds it outside. Breakfasts and lunchtime sandwiches are cheap and simple.

# CULTURE

From colonial times through the Gilded Age to the present day, Newport has been a leader in American architecture, decorative and fine arts, and more recently, music.

## CINEMA

Because there are so few cinemas in this part of the world, theaters that are just beyond Newport's borders are also included.

**Holiday 7** (401-847-3001, W. Main Rd., Rte. 114, Middletown, RI).

**Jane Pickens Theatre** (401-846-5252; 49 Touro St., Newport) Note the dinner theater deal offered by Muriel's in the section Dining.

**Opera House** (401-847-3456; 19 Touro St., Newport).

**Starcase Cinemas** (401-849-7777; 1346 W. Main Rd., Rte. 114, Middletown, RI).

## DANCE

**Island Moving Company** (401-847-4470) Newport's resident dance company, IMC puts on a short series of outdoor summer dance concerts, plus a holiday show in Newport in Dec. All performances feature new works accompanied by live music. The summer series is on the campus of St. George's School in Middletown, RI. Bring a picnic dinner (or buy one there), and take in not only great dancing but a panoramic view of Second Beach. Cutting-edge performing artists in an idyllic setting.

## FINE ART GALLERIES

The bay area is well served by both contemporary artists and a fine legacy of Gilded Age art collecting (look for "de-accessioned" private collections now hanging in local galleries). It's no surprise that **Christie's Fine Art Auctioneers** maintains an office in Newport. Following is a selection of both commercial and not-for-profit art galleries, featuring fine and folk arts — paintings, works on paper, sculpture, and the like. Remember, most galleries are closed on Monday. (For craft galleries, see the section Shopping, under the heading Craft Galleries & Studios.)

**Arnold Art Gallery** (401-847-2273; 210 Thames St.) Third-floor space for exhibits by contemporary artists. Also art supplies and framing.

**Candida Simons Gallery** (401-848-0339; 221-223 Spring St.) An inviting gallery that specializes in antique prints and papers and original artwork by the owners.

**DeBlois Gallery** (401-847-9977; 138 Bellevue Ave.) The spot to get a preview of local talent. Two artists show for two weeks, then another group takes over. All local, mostly contemporary work.

**Fisher Gallery** (401-849-7446; 136 Bellevue Ave.) Look for small works in neon, plus framing done on the premises.

**Hydrangea House Gallery** (401-846-4435; 16 Bellevue Ave.) Guests of the Hydrangea House Inn (see the section Lodging) get to eat breakfast in the gallery, but anyone can stop in. Small but select monthly shows focus on contemporary works, especially still lifes and seascapes.

**Kulchur Modern Art** (401-847-7034; 164 Broadway) In the funky part of town, a contemporary gallery showing the work of young, local artists.

**Liberty Tree** (401-846-8465; 104 Spring St.) A fabulously full contemporary folk art gallery of great variety and richness.

**Long Wharf Fine Arts Ltd.** (401-847-6661; 201 Goddard Row, Brick Market Place) Slick, commercial, contemporary work from pop art to neosurrealism. Showcases Leroy Nieman.

**Maggie Gillis Art Barn** (401-849-1543; 32 Prospect Hill St.) Unusual pieces in a variety of media by local artists, shown in a real barn. Very neat stuff.

**McKillop Gallery** (401-847-6313; Salve Regina University, Ochre Point Ave.) Works by faculty, students, and contemporary artists.

**Norton's Oriental Gallery** (401-849-4468; 415 Thames St.) Eighteenth- and nineteenth-century Chinese silk embroideries are the highlight of this two-story gallery in a ca. 1835 home.

**Roger King Fine Arts** (401-847-4359; 22-23 Bowen's Wharf) A fine collection of nineteenth-century realist and Impressionist landscapes (primarily) hang in this three-story wharf space.

**Sheldon Fine Art** (401-849-0030; 59 America's Cup Ave.) Work by local artists as well as oils, photographs, and maritime art.

**Spring Bull Studio** (401-849-9166; 55 Bellevue Ave.) Contemporary work by artists residing in New England.

**Theodore Tihansky Fine Art Gallery** (401-841-5285; 24 Franklin St.) Work by Tihansky and guest artists; check out monthly performance art events.

**William Vareika Fine Arts** (401-849-6149; 212 Bellevue Ave.) Established in 1985, the William Vareika gallery offers two floors of beautifully mounted eighteenth-, nineteenth-, and twentieth-century American art of the highest quality. Look for works by American romantic and realist artist John La Farge.

## GARDEN TOURS

**Secret Gardens Tour** (401-846-0514) This highly successful and well-attended tour offers an opportunity to tour the private, walled gardens of colonial and Victorian homes in Newport's Point Section, which is something of a secret itself (a residential treasure trove of old homes and narrow streets abutting Newport Harbor). The gardens are delightful; it's considered a great honor to be included on the tour. The tour raises money for programs for public school children. Mid-Jun. Advance tickets $15; tour day $18.

## HISTORIC BUILDINGS & SITES

In 1933, a survey of historic properties concluded that there were nine truly exceptional public buildings from the colonial period still standing in the United States. Boston and Philadelphia tied for second place with two each — Newport was the winning city with three (the **Redwood Library,** the **Brick Market,** and the **Old Colony House**). These are magnificent buildings, but the significance of Newport's historic architecture rests upon the preservation of whole neighborhoods rather than one or two individual structures. Newport has over 300 pre-Revolutionary buildings alone, most of which remain private residences. Stroll through the **Historic Hill District** between Thames Street

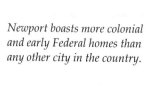

*Newport boasts more colonial and early Federal homes than any other city in the country.*

Craig Hammell

and Bellevue Avenue, roughly bordered by Touro Street on the north and Memorial Boulevard on the south. Here in the thick of things are calm side streets like Clarke and Division, where a sprinkling of seventeenth-, but mostly eighteenth- and early nineteenth-century homes nuzzle up against the sidewalks. (One of Newport's resident slave traders lived on Division, directly opposite the first free black church in Newport, which was also a stop on the Underground Railroad.) On the side streets off Lower Thames, in the district called the **Fifth Ward,** cluster many of the dwellings built by craftspeople who worked on the mansions, as homes of their own. Despite their modest size, many of these cottages, which now constitute their own historic district, display intricate tracery and fretwork, as befits the abodes of master craftsmen. For an uninterrupted taste of the past, cross Broadway at the other end of Thames and head to Newport's northwestern tip (right in the shadow of the Newport Bridge) to the **Point Section** of town.

The Point is a marvel. T-shirt shops and bars don't exist here; it's an exclusively residential area of quiet streets lined with well-kept homes that are one, two, and three centuries old; many of which were moved to the neighborhood by the Newport Restoration Foundation in the 1960s and 1970s. Only Williamsburg, Virginia, has a higher concentration of restored colonials. Helpful house plaques not only name original builders, but also often state what purpose the house served; for example, "John Pain House, ca. 1725. Pewter shop under a grant from King George III."

The waterfront is the busiest part of town, and in some ways, with four-lane America's Cup Avenue streaming through it, the most obviously adapted to the twentieth century, yet this is also the heart of colonial Newport. **Long Wharf** was already decades old when **Brick Market** (now home to the new **Museum of Newport History,** see below) was built in 1722 in a neoclassical design by famous local architect Peter Harrison. The graceful Palladian arches on the ground floor (now closed) were built wide enough to accommodate wagons laden with farm produce. (Don't confuse Brick Market with **Brick Market Place,** an outdoor mall adjacent to the building — see the section Shopping.)

Heading south down the harborfront, you'll come to **Bowen's Wharf** and **Bannister's Wharf.** The cobblestones belong to a recent restoration, but most of the buildings here, though they teem with chic shops, gourmet restaurants, and bars, date to the eighteenth and early nineteenth centuries. **Perry Mill,** at the convergence of America's Cup Avenue, Thames Street, and Memorial Boulevard, is a handsome granite structure built as a textile mill in 1835 by Alexander MacGregor, the stonemason who was also responsible for **Fort Adams.**

The "cottages" — mansions to those who don't live in them — are listed in their own section below. The following historical societies are wonderful sources of further information.

**Newport Historical Society** (401-846-0813; 82 Touro St., Newport, RI 02840).

**Preservation Society of Newport County** (401-847-1000; fax 401-847-1361; 424 Bellevue Ave., Newport, RI 02840) PSNC maintains many of the mansions.

**CHANNING MEMORIAL CHURCH**
401-846-0643.
135 Pelham St., Newport, RI 02840.
Services: Sun., 11:00 a.m.

This rough-cut granite church, built in 1880, was named for William Ellery Channing, founder of American Unitarianism. Take special note of the stained-glass windows by artist and sometime Newporter John La Farge (for more La Farge glass, see Newport Congregational Church). Julia Ward Howe was a member of the congregation.

**COMMON BURIAL GROUND**
Farewell St., Newport, RI 02840.

Where else would pragmatic colonists put the graveyard but on Farewell Street? It's a pity that this wonderful historic cemetery isn't in better repair, but beneath the overgrowth are more than 3,000 headstones and tombs, hundreds from the eighteenth century and many from the seventeeth. The eerie winged skull motif, a staple of colonial folk art, is here in force. Many of the early carvings are by local masters William Mumford and John Stevens and son. The southern part of the yard was reserved for "citizens" — northern slang for slaves. Also on Farewell St. check out the tiny and overgrown Historic Cemetery #9; these old graves also have heart-tugging decorative inscriptions.

**EDWARD KING HOUSE**
401-846-7426.
Aquidneck Park, 35 King St., Newport, RI 02840.

Envy the senior citizens of Newport: their community center is in the Edward King House, designed by Richard Upjohn ca. 1846 and considered one of the premier Italianate villas in the

Open: Year-round,
  Mon.–Fri., 9:00 a.m.–4:00
  p.m.
Admission: Free.

**FRIENDS MEETING
  HOUSE**
401-846-0813.
21 Farewell St., Newport,
  RI 02840 (Point Section).
Open: By appt.; call one
  week in advance.
Admission: Free.

**HUNTER HOUSE**
401-847-1000.
54 Washington St.,
  Newport, RI 02840 (Point
  Section).
Open: Daily May–Sept.;
  weekends Apr., Oct.;
  closed Nov.–Mar.
Admission: $6.50 adults;
  $3.50 children.

**JEWISH CEMETERY**
Bellevue Ave. and Kay St.,
  Newport, RI 02840.

**NEWPORT
  CONGREGATIONAL
  CHURCH**
401-849-2238.
Spring and Pelham Sts.,
  Newport, RI 02840.
Open: Mem. Day–Labor
  Day, Tues., Thurs., 10:00
  a.m.–12:00 noon.

**OLD COLONY HOUSE**
401-846-2980; 401-277-6790.

nation. The central hall is a majestic, riveting space. (Another Upjohn villa is Finnegan's Inn at Shadow Lawn in Middletown, RI.)

Constructed in 1699, expanded in 1729 and on several other occasions in the nineteenth century, this is the oldest religious structure in New England. In 1730, over half of the townspeople of Newport were Quakers and met here to worship. (During the Revolution, the Quakers' pacifism led many Newporters to consider them traitors to the cause; homes were burned and leading Quakers were jailed.)

Considered one of the ten best examples of colonial architecture in the country, this 1748 home is furnished with Newport's famous Townsend-Goddard furniture (see the section Shopping, under the heading Antiques for more information). The elaborate front door treatment, originally on the water side of the house, is complete with a carved pineapple on top. Take a look at the colonial garden, too.

If you feel as though you might overdose on Americana, take a stroll among these plots; the inscriptions, dating as far back as 1761, are in Hebrew, Latin, Portuguese, and Spanish, as well as English. Newport Jews purchased this land in 1677.

The congregation was founded in 1695, but the current structure dates to 1857. It's noteworthy for its massive Romanesque Revival design, but even more so as one of only two churches in the country with an interior decorative scheme by John La Farge still intact. La Farge (1835–1910) was an American romantic and realist who did his first notable painting in Newport in 1859. His trademark opalescent stained-glass windows and Byzantine-inspired wall murals are astounding.

This is another of Newport's early historical and architectural treasures, and where you can find

Craig Hammell

*Built in 1739, the Old Colony House is the second-oldest state capitol in the country.*

Washington Sq., Newport, RI 02840.
Open: Daily, mid-Jun.– Labor Day.
Admission: Free.

Gilbert Stuart's most famous portrait of George Washington. Built in 1739, the Old Colony House is the second-oldest capitol building in the country; until the State House was built in Providence in 1900, Rhode Island's assembly used to meet here for half the year, and in Providence the other half. Announcements made from the central balcony include King George III's coronation in 1760 and the Declaration of Independence in 1776.

**OLD STONE MILL/ VIKING TOWER**
Touro Park, Newport, RI 02840.

While Newport had taken to heart the notion that the stone tower was built by Vikings in the eleventh century (hence the city's original "847" telephone exchange, which spells out V-I-S), the theory was recently disproved by a team of scientists from Scandinavia. The latest word is that it was built by English colonists as recently as 1600. Oh well.

**REDWOOD LIBRARY & ATHENAEUM**
401-847-0292.
50 Bellevue Ave., Newport, RI 02840.
Open: Year-round, Mon.–Sat., 9:30 a.m.–5:30 p.m.
Admission: Free.

This architectural masterpiece is the oldest continuously used library in the country, with a collection of paintings nearly as fine as that of the Newport Art Museum next door. It was built in 1749-1750 in a neoclassical design by Peter Harrison, the same architect responsible for Brick Market and Touro Synagogue (of the three only the latter isn't included among the top ten public colonial structures in the country). Take a close look at the exterior — it's actually wood painted to look like stone. Henry James worked here.

Craig Hammell

*The Redwood Library, considered one of the most important colonial buildings in America, looks like stone but is actually built of wood.*

**SAMUEL WHITEHORNE HOUSE**
401-847-2448; 401-849-7300.
416 Thames St., Newport, RI 02840.
Open: May–Oct., Fri., 1:00 p.m.–4:00 p.m.; Sat.-Mon., 10:00 a.m.–4:00 p.m.
Admission: $5 adults; $1 students.

Captain Whitehorne, one of Newport's infamous triangle-traders, built this austere Federal-style home in 1811. Today it's filled with priceless Townsend-Goddard furniture and work by Newport silversmiths and pewterers, plus Far Eastern antiques and rugs. Don't miss the back garden. There's a great little cupola on the roof, caged in by matching chimneys.

**SEVENTH DAY BAPTIST MEETING HOUSE**
401-846-0813.
82 Touro St., Newport, RI 02840.
Open: Year-round, Tues.–Sat., 9:30 a.m.–4:30 p.m.
Admission: Free.

This meeting house is the oldest of its faith (also called Sabbatarian) in the country, built ca. 1729. Note the lovely pulpit and don't overlook the clock by famed Newport clock maker William Claggett — it's two centuries old and still ticking.

**ST. MARY'S CHURCH**
401-847-0475.
Spring St., Newport, RI 02840.
Open: Year-round, Mon.–Fri., 7:00 a.m.–11:30 a.m.
Admission: Free.

On September 12, 1953, Jacqueline Bouvier married John Kennedy in this lovely church, built in the English Gothic style in 1848–1852. Established in 1828, this is the oldest Catholic parish in RI.

**TOURO SYNAGOGUE**
401-847-4794.

Continuing Newport's litany of "oldests," this elegant Peter Harrison structure is the oldest

*Touro Synagogue, the oldest synagogue in North America, reputedly inspired Thomas Jefferson to design Monticello.*

Craig Hammell

85 Touro St., Newport, RI 02840.
Open: May–Oct., call for schedule; other times of year, by appt.
Services: Fri., 6:00 p.m.; summer, Fri. 7:00 p.m., Sat. 9:00 a.m.

synagogue in North America (the same may be said of its torah). It was constructed in 1763 to serve Newport's Jewish community, established by fifteen families from Holland in 1658 who were later joined by Sephardic Jews from Spain and Portugal. Despite the fact that Jews weren't allowed to vote until the Revolution, the synagogue preserves a letter from President Washington that states that the new country would give "bigotry no sanction and persecution no assistance." Harrison's design is said to have inspired Jefferson's plan for Monticello.

**TRINITY CHURCH**
401-846-0660.
Spring and Church Sts., Newport, RI 02840.
Open: Year-round.

A great landmark (look for the 150-foot clock tower) and rendezvous spot when touring Newport. Trinity was built in 1725–1726 from a design by Richard Munday, based on work by Christopher Wren. Inside is the only three-tiered

*The steeple of Trinity Church, inspired by the designs of Christopher Wren, has been a landmark to mariners since 1726.*

Craig Hammell

Services (Episcopalian):
    Sun., 8:00 a.m., 11:00
    a.m.; summer, 10:00 a.m.

wineglass pulpit in the country, plus Tiffany stained-glass windows, and a pipe organ donated by George Berkeley (see Whitehall Museum House in Chapter Four, *Narragansett Bay*) and tested by Handel himself before it was shipped from England. A $3-million restoration, funded by the congregation, was completed in 1987. Stand in the center aisle and let your eye run down the row of chandeliers — they don't line up because the main beam has gone askew with age.

**UNION CONGREGATIONAL CHURCH**
Division St., Newport, RI 02840.
Open: Year-round.
Admission: Free.

This fine Cottage Gothic structure, built in 1871, houses the first free black church in the United States. Twelve of Newport's leading African-Americans met in 1824 to form the Colored Union Church and Society; their first meeting house was built on the present site that same year.

**WANTON-LYMAN-HAZARD HOUSE**
401-846-0813.
17 Broadway, Newport, RI 02840.
Open: Tours by appt.
Admission: $4.

Built ca. 1675, this is the oldest house in Newport. In 1765, it was the home of Newport's stamp master, whose enforcement of the Stamp Act sparked a riot by Newporters during which the house was sacked. You'll see a wonderful winding staircase, medieval-looking beams and corner posts, and chimney details. The house is owned by the Newport Historical Society. It also features a colonial herb garden.

**WHITE HORSE TAVERN**
401-849-3600.
Marlborough and Farewell
   Sts., Newport, RI 02840.
Open: Year-round.

This is the oldest operating tavern in the country, built in the mid-1600s. In 1687, William Mayes, a local pirate, obtained a license to sell spirits. Today the White Horse is a superb restaurant (see the section Dining). Call ahead to arrange a private tour with the curator, or just stick your head inside for a quick visit to the seventeenth century; note the curved-wall fireplace, massive beams, and medieval stairway wrapped around the chimney.

## HISTORICAL TOURS

For annual house and garden tours, see the heading Garden Tours above.

**Newport Historical Society** (401-846-0813; 82 Touro St., Newport, RI 02840) Walking tours of the Historic Hill District leave from the Museum of Newport History (Brick Market, Thames St.) on Thurs., Fri., and Sat. mornings, and Sat. afternoon; price $5 (a combination museum admission and tour ticket is a substantial savings). Cliff Walk tours leave from Ochre Court (Salve Regina University, 100 Ochre Point Ave.) on Sat. mornings and afternoons; price $7. Both tours are held from May–Oct.

**Newport on Foot Guided Walking Tours** (401-846-5391; PO Box 1042, Newport, RI 02840) You might not get very far in an hour and a half (actually just over a mile on a ten-block loop), but you'll take in 150 years of history. Tour guide Anita Rafael leads you through graveyards and past colonial homes and landmarks (no mansions). By the end, you'll know a hipped roof from a gambrel at twenty paces. Groups are small and leave from the Newport Gateway Convention & Visitors' Bureau. Tours cost $7 per person and are offered year-round; children are free, and dogs are welcome. Bus escort guides are also available.

## LIBRARIES

**Newport Public Library** (401-847-8720; 300 Spring St.) The Newport Room has a wealth of local materials that are no longer available in bookshops. Open year-round; closed Sun.

## LIGHTHOUSES

The **Ida Lewis Rock Light** This lighthouse in Newport Harbor (inactive as of 1928, now the Ida Lewis Yacht Club) was named for the daughter of Captain Hosea Lewis, who had a stroke only six months after his appointment as the lighthouse keeper. Ida and her mother took over until Ida was named sole keeper in 1877. She went on to serve for fifty-nine years and became the most famous female lighthouse keeper in the country, frequently risking her life to save drowning swimmers and boaters. Before her death in 1911, Ida Lewis had received the Congressional Medal of Honor for bravery.

**Rose Island Lighthouse** The beacon was relit in August 1993. Accepts overnight guests. (See the section Lodging.)

## THE MANSIONS — "THE COTTAGES"

Contemporary architects have long glorified in "mansion bashing," considering these monuments to nouveau riche vanity to be just what Henry James called them — white elephants. But the tide is turning, and academic opinion is beginning to agree with the 800,000 visitors who each year troop through the "summer cottages" of the Astors, the Vanderbilts, and their friends. Some are magnificent buildings in their own right, created by designers of genius like Richard Morris Hunt, Henry Hobson Richardson, and Stanford White, the latter of the famous New York firm McKim, Mead, and White. (An aside: Sanford White was shot dead in 1906 by millionaire Harry Thaw, the spurned husband of actress Evelyn Nesbitt who Thaw believed was having an affair with White. Thaw chose a dramatic setting: the dining room of the old Madison Square Garden in New York City, which White had designed.)

The decade of the 1990s represents the centennial of many of the mansions, which were built throughout the "gay '90s," exactly one hundred years ago. One interesting feature of these Gilded Age icons that remains invisible to most visitors is their hardware. The reason that they've weathered the storm of the twentieth century so well is that beneath their alabaster walls and gilded ballrooms lies the same technology that built the great railroads and the *Titanic*. Of the nine Preservation Society mansions currently open to the public, almost all originally included central heating, indoor plumbing, and electrical wiring. The Breakers not only has two water systems — one fresh, one salty — but an underground coal tunnel the size of a New York City subway artery.

The best way to get a good look at some of the most famous mansions and to decide which ones you want to see on the inside — is to stroll the **Cliff Walk.** The Cliff Walk occupies the eastern coast of Newport's peninsula, running roughly parallel to lower Bellevue Avenue. It starts at Memorial Boulevard and continues south for three and a half miles to Bailey's Beach, *the* exclusive spot for Gilded Age bathers. To one side are crashing waves, to the other magnificent mansions. But be warned: it can be scary going in some spots and can be quite a drop to the rocks below. Where the path intersects Narragansett Avenue is a staircase called **Forty Steps,** which leads down to the water. In the summer, servants used to dance down there when The 400 were otherwise occupied.

The mansions tend to cluster along a number of famous thoroughfares: Bellevue Avenue, Ochre Point Avenue (thanks to an irregular coast, both parallel the Cliff Walk), and Ocean Drive, also known as "Ten Mile Drive." It follows the southernmost tip of the Newport peninsula and continues up the western side, past **Brenton Point State Park,** the **Castle Hill Inn and Resort,**

**Fort Adams State Park,** and **Hammersmith Farm.** Scenery here is windswept and rocky, with the romantic rooflines of great manor houses dominating the horizon.

Though many of these are still privately owned, the following are several of Newport's better-known mansions that are open to the public. Many are now maintained by the Preservation Society of Newport County (those mansions with the telephone number 401-847-1000). If you plan to visit more than one Preservation Society property, *be sure* to purchase a **combination ticket,** for any two properties to all nine, including the colonial Hunter House, Green Animals Topiary Gardens in Portsmouth, Rhode Island, and the soon to be opened Isaac Bell House. Combination tickets offer excellent savings. For further information, see Preservation Society of Newport County above.

**ASTORS' BEECHWOOD MANSION**
401-846-3772.
580 Bellevue Ave.,
Newport, RI 02840.
Open: Daily Jun.–
Thanksgiving; weekends
Feb.–mid-May; call in
Dec. for Christmas tour
reservations; closed Jan.
Admission: $8.50 adults;
$6.50 children.

This well-proportioned, stucco-over-brick mansion was built in 1852, well before size became the determining factor of success. Beechwood was home to "The Mrs. Astor," doyenne of Newport society throughout the Gilded Age, and who reigned over the "List of 400" like an American queen. You can experience something of what it was like to be a guest in her home, because unlike the other mansions, Beechwood employs costumed actors as guides, who pretend, with a great deal of good humor, that it's still the 1890s. See Seasonal Events below for special performances.

**BELCOURT CASTLE**
401-846-0669.
Bellevue Ave, Newport, RI
02840.
Open: Daily, Mem.
Day–Nov.; weekends,
Feb.–May; closed Jan.
Admission: $7.50 adults; $5
children.

This is Newport's only mansion with the owners still in residence. It was built by Richard Morris Hunt for Oliver Hazard Perry Belmont and the former Alva Vanderbilt (see Marble House below) in 1894 in the style of a Louis XIII hunting lodge at Versailles. This sixty-room castle boasts the largest collection of thirteenth-century stained glass in the country. The public rooms really constitute a museum of European treasures from armor to German throne chairs to a full-sized, gilded coronation coach. Ghost tours every Thurs. night in the summer; call for reservations.

**THE BREAKERS**
401-847-1000.
Ochre Point Ave., Newport,
RI 02840.

The mansion to end all mansions. Cornelius Vanderbilt — believe it or not, a man of simple tastes — had it built for his wife, Alice, in 1895 according to a design by Richard Morris Hunt.

Courtesy Preservation Society of Newport County

*Based on sixteenth-century Italian palazzos, the Great Hall of The Breakers rises a towering forty-five feet, its walls sheathed in marble and alabaster.*

Open: Daily, Apr.–Oct., Dec.; weekends, Nov.; closed Jan.–Mar. Admission: $10 adults; $4 children.

Hunt based the seventy-room seaside villa (it fronts on the Cliff Walk) on sixteenth-century northern Italian palaces. Massive and imposing, with a Great Hall that rises forty-five feet and walls sheathed in marble and alabaster, The Breakers may possibly be the most opulent private residence in the world — and decidedly the top single tourist attraction in RI. (The kitchen, in its simple immensity, is the most human room in the house.)

**CHATEAU-SUR-MER**
401-847-1000.
Bellevue Ave., Newport, RI 02840.
Open: Daily May–Sept., Dec.; weekends Jan.–Apr., Oct.–Nov.
Admission: $7.50 adults; $3.50 children.

One of the earliest Newport mansions, the Chateau is an extravaganza of American Victoriana, built for China trader William Wetmore in 1852, with extensive renovation by Richard Morris Hunt in the 1870s. The exterior is formidable, with a steep mansard roof and rough granite walls. Inside, the central hallway rises forty-five feet to a glass ceiling; open balconies of rich paneled wood wrap around each floor.

## THE ELMS
401-847-1000.
Bellevue Ave., Newport, RI
  02840.
Open: Daily May–Dec.;
  weekends Jan.–Apr.
Admission: $7.50 adults;
  $3.50 children.

Modeled by architect Horace Trumbauer on the eighteenth-century Château d'Asnieres near Paris, The Elms is an elegant, white marble summer residence, built in 1901 for Pennsylvania coal millionaire E.J. Berwind. The ball to celebrate the opening of The Elms was *the* event of the 1901 season; three orchestras and pet monkeys played as 125 couples danced under the stars. The formal sunken garden was designed by French landscape architect Jacques Greber.

## HAMMERSMITH FARM
401-846-7346.
Harrison Ave. and Ocean
  Dr., Newport, RI 02840.
Open: Call to check status
  (property for sale at time
  of publication).
Admission: $8 adults; $3
  children.

This twenty-eight-room, shingle-style cottage on the western bend of Ocean Dr., far from the one-upmanship games played on Bellevue Ave., was built for John Auchincloss in 1888. When Jacqueline Bouvier married John Kennedy in nearby St. Mary's Church, the reception was held here. The rooms are extraordinarily airy and bright, as befits a summer cottage overlooking Newport Harbor (note the majestic jade plants). The surrounding gardens are beautifully landscaped, and the farm, established in 1640, is still in operation — the last working farm in Newport.

## ISAAC BELL HOUSE
401-847-1000.
Bellevue Ave., Newport, RI
  02840.
Open: To be announced.
Admission: To be
  announced.

At the time of publication, the Isaac Bell House, purchased in 1994 and undergoing an extensive restoration by the Preservation Society of Newport County, is slated to open sometime in 1998. The house was designed by McKim, Mead, and White and completed in 1883. It's easily one of the finest examples of shingle-style architecture in the country, based on elements of the American colonial, English Queen Anne, and Japanese styles. The exterior is swathed in white cedar shingles cut to resemble waves and diamonds; the interior is dominated by a great hall with a monumental fireplace and wooden inglenook. A wonderful house, revolutionary and influential in its day.

## KINGSCOTE
401-847-1000.
Bellevue Ave., Newport, RI
  02840.
Open: Daily May–Sept.;
  weekends Apr., Oct.;
  closed Nov.–Mar.

Kingscote started the ball rolling: it's considered America's first "summer cottage," built in the Gothic Revival style in 1839 by Richard Upjohn for the Savannah millionaire George Noble Jones. The mahogany-paneled dining room with a cherry floor is Kingscote's tour de force, added by McKim,

Admission: $6.50 adults; $3.50 children.

Mead, and White in 1881 — note the wall of Tiffany glass tiles and cork ceiling.

**MARBLE HOUSE**
401-847-1000.
Bellevue Ave., Newport, RI 02840.
Open: Daily Apr.–Oct.; weekends Jan.-Mar.; closed Nov.–Dec.
Admission: $7.50 adults; $3.50 children.

Another of Richard Morris Hunt's sumptuous palaces, Marble House is based on elements of both the Grand and Petit Trianon at Versailles. It was completed in 1892 after four years of work at a cost of $11 million, ostensibly for William K. Vanderbilt though it was his wife Alva who truly reigned here. (Alva was one of Newport's "Great Triumvirate" of society dames — see Chapter One, *History* for more gossip.) Thanks to Alva's input, Marble House has a decorative harmony that many of the other showplaces lack: each room is decorated to reflect a different period of French history. Note the Chinese Tea House on the grounds, where Alva held suffragette meetings before divorcing Vanderbilt and moving across the street to Belcourt Castle.

**OCHRE COURT**
401-847-6650.
100 Ochre Point Ave., Newport, RI 02840.
Open: Year-round, Mon.–Fri., 9:00 a.m.–4:00 p.m.
Admission: Free.

Completed in 1892, Ochre Court was one of Newport's first truly palatial mansions. It was built (at a cost of $4.5 million) by Richard Morris Hunt for Ogden Goelet, who lived here a grand total of eight weeks a year. Hunt based the "cottage's" turrets, chimneys, and elaborate dormers on the late Gothic châteaux of the Loire Valley in France. Today Ochre Court houses the administrative offices of Salve Regina University, though the ground floor is open to visitors who wish to look around on their own. Don't miss this one: it summons up the age-old desire to inhabit a fairy tale.

**ROSECLIFF**
401-847-1000.
Bellevue Ave., Newport, RI 02840.
Open: Daily Apr.–Oct.; closed Nov.–Dec., Jan.–Mar.
Admission: $7.50 adults; $3.50 children.

Stanford White designed Rosecliff for Tessie Oelrichs in 1902 and based it on the Grand Trianon at Versailles. This exquisite, white terra-cotta mansion, overlooking the Cliff Walk is one of the most elegant in town. It's built in the shape of an H and features the largest private ballroom in Newport. The lovely marble staircase is curved in a heart-shaped design, and the garden terrace is based on one designed for Marie Antoinette. It's no surprise that Rosecliff was chosen as the set for the film *The Great Gatsby*.

*Built of glimmering white terra-cotta, Rosecliff is architect Stanford White's homage to the Grand Trianon at Versailles.*

## SEASONAL EVENTS

Note that many of the mansions are open in December and are elaborately decorated for Christmas. Call for more information.

**Black and White Ball** (401-351-5000, ext. 139; Rosecliff, Bellevue Ave.) An elegant annual affair held in early Oct. to benefit the Urban League of RI.

**Gatsby Ball** (401-423-1378; Rosecliff, Bellevue Ave.) This annual event brings twenties-worshipers out in droves. Arrive in your best flapper-era attire to dance the night away in Newport's biggest, most elegant ballroom. Early to mid-Jul.

**Governor's Ball** (401-847-6650, ext. 2381; Rosecliff, Bellevue Ave.) Another sparkling event held in the ballroom of Salve Regina University's Ochre Court.

**Newport Flower Show** (401-847-1000) A new, annual themed and competitive event held on the grounds of one of the Preservation Society of Newport County mansions (Marble House was the site for 1997). Artistic and horticultural classes as well. Tickets for general admission; reservations for seated luncheon. A very grand affair. Mid-Jul.

**Newport Symposium** (401-847-6543; Preservation Society of Newport County) This highly successful annual event, co-sponsored by Christie's auction house, has a different theme each year; in 1997, it was Art, Trade, and Empire. Architects, designers, and historians lecture on Newport houses, public buildings, and decorative arts. Reserve tickets *very early* because it's a sellout affair.

**Tea Dance Tours** (401-846-3772; Astors' Beechwood Mansion, 580 Bellevue Ave.) Victorian tea dances in the ballroom, featuring Mrs. Astor's famous chilled strawberry tea. Performed on Tues., Jun.–mid-Oct.; Murder Mystery evenings are held Jun.–Halloween. Call for a schedule.

## MILITARY MUSEUMS & SITES

**Artillery Company of Newport Military Museum** (401-846-8488; 23 Clarke St.) This is home to the oldest active military company in the U.S.; it received its charter in 1741 from King George III. The armory was built in 1836 and now houses perhaps the finest collection of foreign and domestic military memorabilia in the country, including four brass cannons — lent to the president for state occasions — cast by Paul Revere in 1797. Uniforms of Anwar Sadat, Prince Philip, and others. Open Jun.–Sept., Fri., Sat., 10:00 a.m.–4:00 p.m.; Sun., 12:00 noon–4:00 p.m. Adults $3; children $1.

**Fort Adams** (401-847-2800; Fort Adams State Park, off Harrison Ave. and Ocean Dr.) With an unparalleled strategic and scenic location, Ft. Adams is easily the most impressive military site in the state. It took twenty-three years to build the massive granite complex, but by the time it was finished in 1847, it was already obsolete (the huge walls, impenetrable to conventional muskets, would have been blown to bits by the powerful cannons invented during the Civil War). Ft. Adams was closed in 1945, but it now serves as a perfect acoustic soundstage for the Newport Jazz and Folk festivals. The same Scottish stonemason who built the fort, Alexander MacGregor, also built Perry Mill, the Newport Artillery Company, and many stone houses around town.

**Naval War College Museum** (401-841-4052; Coasters Harbor Island; public access through Gate 1 of the Naval Education & Training Center) The museum is housed in Founders Hall, a magnificent structure that served as Newport's poorhouse from 1820-1882, then as the first site of the Naval War College in 1884. The War College is the Navy's highest educational institution, considered one of the top military schools in the world. Exhibits highlight the history of naval warfare and the naval heritage of Narragansett Bay. Look for exhibits dedicated to Oliver and Matthew Perry, local boys who made good (Matthew was responsible for the opening of Japan in 1854). Open Oct.–May, Mon.–Fri., 10:00 a.m.–4:00 p.m.; Jun.–Sept., Sat.–Sun., 12:00 noon–4:00 p.m. Admission is free.

## MUSEUMS

The following represent most of the principal museums in Newport. Also take a look at the listings under the headings Historic Buildings & Sites and Military Museums & Sites.

**DOLL MUSEUM**
401-849-0405.
520 Thames St., Newport, RI 02840.
Open: Weekdays, 11:00 a.m.–5:00 p.m.; Sat., 10:00 a.m.–5:00 p.m.; closed Sun., Tues.
Admission: $2 adults; $1 children, under 5 free.

An interesting little collection of dolls from the eighteenth century to the present, as well as dollhouses, miniatures, and antique toys. Also offers antique dolls for sale.

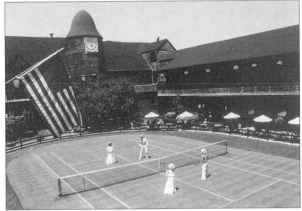

*The International Tennis Hall of Fame features thirteen historic grass tennis courts that are open to the public for play. Pictured here is a genteel doubles match on the famous Horseshoe Court.*

Michael Baz

**INTERNATIONAL TENNIS HALL OF FAME (NEWPORT CASINO)**
401-849-3990.
194 Bellevue Ave., Newport, RI 02840.
Open: Daily 10:00 a.m.–5:00 p.m.
Admission: $6 adults; $4 children.

This is a must-see for tennis, history, and architecture buffs alike. The Tennis Hall of Fame is housed in the old Newport Casino, a magnificent shingle-style complex designed by Stanford White in 1880. (The La Forge Restaurant is also in the casino complex; see the section Dining.) The casino was really a country club for Newport's Gilded Age vacationers, built by James Gordon Bennett, the New York publisher, after he was censured by the Newport Reading Room for challenging a friend to ride his horse across the front porch. Note the superb clock tower, Japanese detailing, horseshoe piazza, and latticed porches.

Above all, feast your eyes on thirteen beautifully tended grass tennis courts. The first national tennis championship was held here in 1881 (it became the U.S. Open at Flushing Meadows). The Hall of Fame galleries include photo exhibits and a host of tennis memorabilia. Don't miss the court tennis court, where the older version of the game is still played as it was in the thirteenth century. See the section Recreation for information on renting the courts and USTA tournaments.

**MUSEUM OF NEWPORT HISTORY**
401-841-8770.
Brick Market, Long Wharf and Thames St., Newport, RI 02840.
Open: Mon., Wed.–Sat., 10:00 a.m.–5:00 p.m.; Sun., 1:00 p.m.–5:00 p.m.; closed Tues.
Admission: $5 adults; $3 children.

This new museum curated by the Newport Historical Society just opened in December 1993. Don't miss it: interactive computers, photo installations, a children's discovery room, and exhibits ranging from local craftwork to Benjamin Franklin's brother's printing press, bring Newport's history to life. Look for interpretative exhibitions, focusing on the working waterfront, Newport in the Revolution, the Gilded Age, the city's multicultural communities past and present, and more.

**THE MUSEUM OF YACHTING**
401-847-1018.
Ft. Adams State Park, Newport, RI 02840.
Open: Daily 10:00 a.m.–5:00 p.m.
Admission: $3 adults; $6 family.

Did you know that the word "yacht" derives from the Dutch for "chasing?" A "jaght schip" means a fast, agile craft. Visitors here will sample such lore as well as gain a new appreciation for the beauty and grace of sailing vessels. The museum is dedicated to recording the history and development of yachting around the world. Featured is *Shamrock V*, the English challenger for the America's Cup in 1930; she's the only J class sloop in the world with a wooden hull that's still sailing, and her mast rises 155 feet. Call ahead to arrange a tour. The museum is next to Ft. Adams and overlooks Newport Harbor; also offers the Phil Weld Library, a school of yacht restoration, and regattas.

**NEWPORT ART MUSEUM**
401-848-8200.
76 Bellevue Ave., Newport, RI 02840.
Open: Daily, except Wed. year-round.
Admission: $4 adults; children under 5 free.

Here are works of art housed in a work of art — a rare combination of stick style with medieval-style half-timbering, designed in 1864 by Richard Morris Hunt (his first Newport commission); Hunt later designed many of the "proper" mansions as well. The collection includes both contemporary and historical works from Newport and New England. Look for works by Winslow Homer, George Inness, and others. The museum also fea-

Craig Hammell

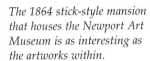

*The 1864 stick-style mansion that houses the Newport Art Museum is as interesting as the artworks within.*

tures classes in watercolors, pastels, and oils for all skill levels for both children and adults.

**NEWPORT HISTORICAL SOCIETY MUSEUM**
401-846-0813.
83 Touro St., Newport, RI 02840.
Open: Year-round, Mon., Wed.–Sat., 10:00 a.m.–5:00 p.m.; Sun., 1:00 p.m.–5:00 p.m.
Admission: $5 adults; $3 children.

In addition to rich research facilities, including early town records, merchant account books, and collections in architectural history and photography, the NPHS exhibits its generous holdings of silver, china, and Townsend-Goddard furniture. Also check out the Seventh Day Baptist Meeting House (built 1729) attached to the main building. For information on NPHS tours, see the heading Historical Tours above.

**RHODE ISLAND FISHERMEN & WHALE CENTER**
401-849-1340.
Seamen's Church Institute, 18 Market Sq., Newport, RI 02840.
Open: Year-round, Thurs.–Tues.
Admission: $2.50 adults; $1.50 children.

This marine discovery center is a great place for both children and adults. You can learn how to go quahogging, "pilot" a ship, and visit a unique kind of petting zoo that features sea urchins and horseshoe crabs. The museum is within the Seamen's Church Institute, a National Register building that's been "a haven for men and women of the sea" since 1919. Here you can find Newport's only public showers, plus rest rooms, washers, and dryers. See the section Food & Beverage Purveyors for St. Elmo's Galley, a great little breakfast and lunchroom in the Center.

**THAMES STREET SCIENCE CENTER**

A fun, informative, interactive, children-oriented spot with changing exhibitions and day

401-849-6966; 800-587-2872;
Web: www.thames
science.org.
77 Long Wharf, Newport,
RI 02840.
Open: Year-round, Mon.–
Wed., 10:00 a.m.–6:00
p.m.; Thurs.-Sat., 10:00
a.m.–7:00 p.m.; Sun. 12:00
noon–5:00 p.m.
Admission: $3 adults; $2
children.

camps. A recent show was called "Antarctica: Land of Extremes," which featured cool stuff like penguins (stuffed), meteorites, maps, and the gear of South Pole explorers. Note that the Center also offers adult courses in Celestial Navigation.

## MUSIC

*Thousands gather on land and sea to take in the tunes at the annual JVC Jazz Festival.*

Craig Hammell

Newport blows away the competition like a sou'east gale when it comes to music. This is the City by the Sea's specialty, and if classical, folk, jazz, R&B, or Irish music are your thing, make every effort to attend one of the festivals highlighted below. Don't be put off by crowds: Folk and Jazz Festival weekends are two of Newport's busiest, to be sure, but traffic control (of both vehicles and humans) is utterly superb.

**Ben & Jerry's Newport Folk Festival** (401-847-3700; PO Box 1221, Newport, RI 02840) This must be the most laid-back, politically correct, hip-and-cool, and all around good-time event in the world. People (around 7,500 to 9,000 each day) sit outside eating, talking, dancing, and listening to the country's best folk musicians. When it gets too hot, they just jump in the bay or get another

Cherry Garcia pop. Every year new artists make their debuts, but the famous are on hand as well. Return performers include the Indigo Girls, Gatemouth Brown, and Joan Baez. First weekend in Aug. One-day ticket costs: adults $36, children $15; both days, $60.

**British Cathedral Music Celebration** (401-848-2561; St. John's Church, Washington and Willow Sts., Newport, RI 02840) An annual visit by the choir of Magdalen College, Oxford. Services are free and open to the public. Mid-Jul.

**JVC Newport Jazz Festival** (401-847-3700; PO Box 1221, Newport, RI 02840) America's first jazz festival is now over forty years old. It's held the second weekend in Aug. after Ben & Jerry's Folk Festival in the same place (Ft. Adams). The same food sellers are on hand, too, and the harbor is filled with boats rocking to the beat. Only the audience and performers are different — the jazz crowd is older and more ethnically diverse, on hand to hear the jazz giants, such as Ray Charles, Grover Washington, Sonny Rollins, Tito Puente, Spyro Gyra, and Herbie Hancock, plus a host of up-and-comers. This is as good as it gets. One-day ticket costs: adults $36, children $15; both days, $60.

*During the acclaimed Newport Music Festival in July, concerts are held in the great halls and music rooms of the Newport mansions.*

Courtesy Newport Music Festival

**The Newport Irish Music Festival** (800-651-3990; Newport Yachting Center, America's Cup Ave., Newport, RI 02840) In addition to traditional and contemporary Irish music on the Yachting Center grounds, peripheral events include the Newport Celtic Games, Bagpipe Competition at Ft. Adams, and the Irish Mile Race, which features some of Ireland's best athletes. Third weekend in Sept. Tickets cost $10 per day, $15 for two days, $25 for three days.

**The Newport Music Festival** (401-846-1133, after Jun. 1 call 401-849-0700; PO Box 3300, Newport, RI 02840) This has been called "the most prestigious musical event in America." The schedule is ambitious: three concerts daily over a two-week period, performed by over 200 artists in spaces constructed for this purpose — the music rooms of Newport's mansions. As the Festival's longtime director, Mark Malkovich III, has said that music warms up the museumlike atmosphere of these grand, cold palaces and brings them alive. The Festival is respected for its musical daring and the coterie of international talent that it attracts, including past debuts by world-renowned pianists Jean-Phillipe Collard and Andrei Gavrilov. Mid-Jul.

**The Rockport Rhythm & Blues Festival** (401-847-3700; Web: www.rnb.rock-port.com; PO Box 128, Newport, RI 02840) This newest of the Ft. Adams State Park music festivals is already attracting the best talent there is — 1997 featured Patti LaBelle, Joan Osborne, Ben E. King, the Neville Brothers, and Aretha Franklin. Last weekend in Jul. One-day ticket costs: adults $36, children $15; both days, $60.

## NIGHTLIFE

"Zooport," as a recent *Providence Journal* article called it, has either a very good or very bad reputation as a party town, depending on your perspective (partyer or nonpartyer). One thing, however, is certain: walk down Thames Street (the major "party-artery") late on a summer night, and you'll get vibrant earfuls of different beats floating down from seaside patio bars. Like everything else in Newport, the atmosphere is casual, and the partying, especially by the twenty-something single crowd, is potent; the area more than earns its reputation as the "Riviera of Rhode Island."

The following list is hardly exhaustive; the best thing to do is to find a good little club for yourself. Many restaurants also have entertainment in-season, particularly on weekends. A few are noted below, but see the section Dining, as well as the section Food & Beverage Purveyors, under the heading Bars.

**Bad Bob's Boat** (401-849-2600; 4 Waite's Wharf) A slightly ramshackle, appropriately disreputable-looking old boat at the end of the wharf. Gets good and noisy.

**The Boom-Boom Room** (401-849-2900; The Candy Store at the Clarke Cooke House, Bannister's Wharf) By day a mild-mannered eatery — from 9:00 p.m.–1:00 a.m., a pretty wild disco and that's by Newport standards. Professional, twenty-something crowd reliving college days. Cover charge.

**Christie's** (401-847-5400; Christie's Landing, off 351 Thames St.) Forget the food; go to Christie's when you want to party. There's dancing to live music in the downstairs bar (a mixed-age crowd) and more live music on the outdoor deck overlooking Newport Harbor (a twenty-something pickup spot). Cover for outdoor patio.

**Club 3** (401-848-7851; 162 Broadway) Insiders call this the local musicians' favorite gig. It's small but packs a wallop; mostly local original rock bands, plus the odd acoustic booking.

**David's** (401-841-5431; 28 Prospect Hill St.) Newport's only enduring gay bar, it's popular with a straight crowd as well. DJ and disco dancing, with a fenced-in outdoor patio. Attracts a wide variety of ages.

**Newport Blues Cafe** (401-841-5510; 286 Thames St.) This place gets listed twice (it's also under the section Dining), because the food and music are both top-notch. Easily the best blues club covered in this book, with big names appearing nightly. Cover charge.

**One Pelham East** (401-847-9460; corner Thames and Pelham Sts.) Live and loud rock in an Irish pub setting, believe it or not; in the winter, the locals hang out here, in the summer, it attracts a nicely diverse crowd.

**Senor Froggs of Newport** (401-849-4747; 108 Williams St.) A second-floor disco that attracts the young singles crowd.

**Thames Street Station** (401-840-9480; Perry Mill Market, off Thames St.) A real dance club and Newport's biggest and most popular disco for the single, twenty-something set.

**Waverley's** (401-846-9233; 49 America's Cup Ave.) Real, live jazz in the Newport Harbor Hotel lounge.

## SEASONAL EVENTS & FESTIVALS

*Sumo wrestling is a highlight of the Black Ships Festival.*

Courtesy Japan-America Society

**Black Ships Festival** (401-846-2720; Headquarters, 28 Pelham St., Newport, RI 02840) Every year Newport celebrates the anniversary of hometown hero Commodore Matthew Perry's "opening of Japan" (the 1854 Treaty of Kanagawa), with Japanese art, origami, face-painting and flower-arranging demonstrations, plus a kite festival, sumo wrestling, formal tea ceremonies, Japanese beer tastings, fashion shows, and more. Events occur citywide. Sponsored by the Japan-America Society and Black Ships Festival of RI, Inc. Late Jul.

**Christmas in Newport** (401-849-6545; PO Box 716, Newport, RI 02840) Christmas in Newport, Inc. is a not-for-profit organization that for over twenty years has managed to orchestrate an event for nearly every day of Dec. and to turn the City by the Sea into a glittering fairyland of white lights (a Moravian custom). Some standouts include the following: the top-notch **Craft Show,** held the last weekend in Nov.; **Historic House Tours;** a production of Handel's *Messiah* at Trinity Church; **Kwanzaa,** the African-American celebration based on ancient African harvest rituals; and above all, the **Turtle Frolic.** Every year since 1752, when the first "frolic" was held — it featured a giant vat of turtle soup — subsequent frolics have commemorated the event in the same spot on the same evening, Dec. 23. It features eighteenth-century food, drink, and English country dancing. Come in your periwig and knee breeches if you have them. Many of the mansions also reopen on a daily basis throughout Dec. to show off their magnificent Christmas finery. For an advance peek at all of the festivities, order the *Christmas in Newport* video from Video Productions, PO Box 1024, Newport, RI 02840 (401-847-3229).

**Fort Adams Festival** (401-943-3308; Ft. Adams State Park, Newport, RI 02840) A low-key afternoon of arts and crafts, food, and a great view of Newport Harbor. Late Jul.

**Harvest Fair** (401-846-2577; Norman Bird Sanctuary, 583 Third Beach Rd., Middletown, RI 02842) Hay and pony rides, greased pole competitions, and even a Home & Garden Competition (enter your prized giant squash), plus scarecrow and apple pie contests. Tour the sanctuary, too.

**Maritime Arts Festival** (401-849-2243; Bowen's and Bannister's Wharves, Newport, RI 02840) Where else can you listen to live music and watch the nation's finest scrimshaw artists demonstrate their craft, while your kids attend a ship-in-a-bottle making workshop? Lots of local arts, crafts, and performers. Mid-May.

**Newport Outdoor Art Festival** (401-683-4009; 401-245-3793; Long Wharf Mall and Eisenhower Park, Washington Sq. area, Newport, RI 02840) This is a long-running, fine-arts-only show, with competitions and exhibits in oils, acrylics, pastels, watercolors, graphics, photography, and sculpture. Mid-to-late Jun.

**Newport Winter Festival** (401-847-7666; citywide) In case you thought Newport was dead in the winter, show up the last weekend in Jan. through the first week in Feb. for this annual festival, which includes horse-drawn hayrides, ice carving and snow-and-sand sculpting contests, a progressive dinner party, and — get ready for it — the polar bear plunge. Crazy people may also want to know that there's an annual New Year's Day Plunge as well (for Jamestown's famous Penguin Plunge, also held on New Year's, see the section Recreation, under the heading Beaches in Chapter Four, *Narragansett Bay.*

## THEATER

**Newport Playhouse & Cabaret Restaurant** (401-848-PLAY; 102 Connell Hwy., Newport, RI 02840) A year-round dinner theater, featuring local professionals. Call to find out what's playing; box office open daily, closed Tues.

# RECREATION

The word "yacht" comes from the Dutch for "sleek, agile craft." Yachts are to Narragansett Bay what coals are to Newcastle: this is their home, their breeding ground, and over the years racing yachts have brought fame and fortune back to the waters that spawned them. Between 1893 and 1934, the Herreshoff Boatyard in Bristol, Rhode Island, designed and built more America's Cup defenders than any other shipyard in the world. The New York Yacht Club, based in Newport, held the cup for thirty years; although it was stolen away by Australia in 1983, Newport's yachting tradition continues, and throughout the summer Narragansett Bay is alive with racing craft.

One reason Newport is a boater's paradise is the wind. Called the "billion dollar breeze" when the prevailing southwesterlies sweep through the Bellevue Avenue mansions (nineteenth-century air-conditioning), the wind off Narragansett Bay is a perpetual force that never stops blowing, or billowing sails. Like the "cottages" themselves, boating arrived in Newport with Gilded Age vacationers in the late nineteenth century. James Gordon Bennett, who built the Newport Casino, was one of the most notorious — his personal yacht had a full-sized Turkish bath and a miniature dairy. Back on land, "The 400" attacked wickets, shuttlecocks, and balls as earnestly as they did the waves. The first national tennis and golf tournaments were held in Gilded Age Newport, and sports, such as polo, croquet, and foxhunting, were all raised to new levels of achievement.

Today Newport is still the place for international polo matches and even professional-level croquet — the New England Regional Croquet Championships are held at the Tennis Hall of Fame — but it's also home to surfing and sumo wrestling championships. Like all kinds of diversity, sporting eclecticism thrives in the City by the Sea.

## BASEBALL

Watch local leagues do battle at **Cardines Field,** across the street from the Newport Gateway Convention & Visitors' Bureau, on the corner of America's Cup Avenue and West Marlborough Street. For a schedule, call 401-847-1398; sometimes celebrity softball teams like the New England Patriots play here as well. Games are free.

## BEACHES

Beaches listed below are for saltwater bathing; fees, except where noted, are per car rather than per person. (Beach attendants start taking your money in mid-June and stop after Labor Day). For beaches in towns surrounding Newport, see the section Recreation, under the heading Beaches in Chapter Four, *Narragansett Bay.*

**Bailey's Beach** This small, unspectacular beach at the southern end of the Cliff Walk was *the* most exclusive spot as far as Gilded Age bathers were concerned. Go figure. Most of it is private but for a small public portion.

**Easton Beach** Also known as First Beach, this is the gray strip of sand at the bottom of the Cliff Walk. It's three-quarters of a mile long and sometimes offers great surf (wet-suited surfers hang out here all year). A brand new cabana and pavilion complex was built in 1993 — Hurricane Bob did in the previous one — with a merry-go-round, miniature golf, a refreshment stand, and the Newport Aquarium. It gets crowded, but you can see the mansions and be seen. 3,960 feet long; 737 parking spaces; $8 weekdays, $10 weekends (for out-of-staters).

**Fort Adams State Park Beach** This calm, clean beach offers peace and quiet, park facilities, and a superb view of Newport Harbor. It's small but a nice spot. 225 feet long; 423 parking spaces; $2.

**Gooseberry Beach** This modest, privately owned beach out along Ocean Dr. is open to the public (it's next to Bailey's); it offers great swimming within a protected, sandy cove; good for young children. Parking and concessions available; $5–$15.

**King Park Beach** Near the Ida Lewis Yacht Club, off Wellington Ave., this little harbor beach is an ideal spot for a picnic; it's really more park than beach. Free.

## BICYCLING

The best place to bicycle in Newport is **Ocean Drive** (aka Ten Mile Drive), which begins on Bellevue Avenue at the International Tennis Hall of Fame and continues in a curvy, coast-hugging loop past Hammersmith Farm and the Castle Hill Inn and Resort before winding up back into town at the harbor. The scenery here is as romantically windswept and rock-strewn as it gets; but, everyone else is cycling here, too. Another option is to use a bicycle to tour the side streets of the Point Section. There's no better way to get a good look at the colonial homes.

### BICYCLE RENTALS & SHOPS

Make sure your bicycle rental includes a map, helmet, and lock, for no additional charge. (See the heading Sky & Water Sports below for large outfitters that rent all kinds of sports equipment, including bicycles.

**Instant Replay** (401-848-0133; 8-10 Marlborough St.) A consignment and retail sporting goods shop that rents mountain, racing, and vintage bicycles.

**Newport Bicycle** (401-846-0773; 162 Broadway) Runner-up for best bicycle shop in *Newport Life Magazine* readers' poll.

**Ten Speed Spokes, Ltd.** (401-847-5609; 18 Elm St.) Bicycle sales, service, and rentals. Winner of best bicycle shop in *Newport Life Magazine* readers' poll.

## CROQUET

**M**any inns have croquet sets for their guests to use. But if a friendly game of croquet turns your loved ones into cunning thrill-seekers who would rather send your ball flying into the bushes than win, take in a professional match instead. The **New England Regional Croquet Championships** are held at the International Tennis Hall of Fame (401-849-3990; 194 Bellevue Ave.) in early August. The best mallet swingers in the area compete for berths in the USCA National Open (U.S. Croquet Association).

## FISHING

**I**f it swims in Narragansett Bay, odds are it's been caught by Rhode Island fishermen. And quite a lot swims here. Inshore, try fly and bottom fishing by boat, or surf casting; look for striped bass, blues, cod, pollack, tautog, mackerel, fluke (summer flounder), and flounder. Offshore, in serious sportfishing on the open seas, look for tuna, shark, and white marlin. The surf casting is good almost anywhere; ask the people at the bait shop what's running, what's good for catching it, and where. Don't forget essential fishing items: standard bait and tackle, gaff, net, lots of rags, pail, knife, and a full hip flask.

*Surf casting is a favorite pastime on the shores of Narragansett Bay.*

Craig Hammell

Most of the boats listed under Charters in Sailing & Boating below offer deep-sea fishing trips to inshore and offshore locations; some will even take you on an overnighter out to Georges Bank and other open-ocean grounds. Note that the price of the charter includes bait and tackle; the crew will usually clean your catch for you, too. There are two kinds of fishing charters: 1) party ("head") boats take between forty to about 110 passengers for bottom-fishing excursions; you don't normally need a reservation, and boats leave on a set schedule, usually 6:00 a.m.–2:30 p.m.; sometimes you have to rent your tackle;

2) fishing charters require reservations and sail at your bidding; you get enough people (usually between four to six) and plan your own route.

Remember there's a general six-a-day state limit on any catch. There are special restrictions on stripers (at least twenty-eight inches, one per day); blues (ten per day); tautog, also called blackfish (must be twelve inches); and flounder — throw it back — there is a total ban on keeping flounders, and you can be charged up to $500 for each flounder in your possession. Know the difference between fluke and flounder: flounder have small, toothless mouths, while fluke have large mouths studded with sharp teeth. Contact the Rhode Island Tourism Division (401-277-2601; 800-556-2484; 7 Jackson Walkway, Providence, RI 02903) for their comprehensive pamphlet *Boating & Fishing in Rhode Island.*

## LESSONS

**The Saltwater Edge** (401-842-0062; 559 Thames St., Newport, RI 02840) Expert guides will take you saltwater light tackle and fly-fishing, or teach you how.

## GOLF

Newport was a pioneer in the realm of golf as well. In 1895, the city hosted the first national open golf tournament in the U.S. at the Newport Country Club (alas the club's course, wedged between Ocean Drive and the Atlantic, is reserved for members only). For public courses near Newport, see the section Recreation under the heading Golf in Chapter Four, *Narragansett Bay.*

## HIKING & WALKING

The most famous place to walk in Newport, of course, is the illustrious **Cliff Walk** (see the section Culture, under the heading The Mansions). This three-and-a-half-mile trail is the Cadillac of walking paths, snaking around Newport's rocky coast with the ocean on one side and the mansions on the other. But there are many other locations as well; an excellent idea source is Ken Weber's *Walks & Rambles in Rhode Island* series (see the section Bibliography in Chapter Six, *Information).*

## HORSEBACK RIDING & POLO

The Gilded Age lingers around Newport, but not so much in the mansions as out on the fields. The City by the Sea is still the polo capital of the world, and the **Newport International Polo Series,** which began in 1886 and was resurrected in 1992, packs in the fans. Matches take place every Saturday afternoon (rain date, Sunday) from the first weekend in June through early September at Glen Farm, a restored farming estate on East Main Road, Route 138 in Portsmouth, Rhode Island, about a twenty-minute drive from Newport.

Banners mark the spot at the head of the long lane down to the playing fields: "Team U.S.A. vs Argentina" — or the U.K., Egypt, Italy, and India, among others. This is Olympic-level polo and is taken very seriously, though the crowd is more casual than dressed to kill. For more information, call 401-847-7090 (tickets: adults $8; children free). If you ride and are interested in learning to play polo, see the listing for **Glen Farm** below. They claim that after only a few lessons you'll be ready for the annual **Governor's Cup Match** (401-846-0200), which ends the series in mid-September.

The following stables offer a variety of trail rides, indoor ring riding, and lessons.

**Glen Farm** (401-847-7090; Glen Rd., Portsmouth, RI 02871) Polo and riding lessons, plus trails through miles of farmland, woods, and beaches. Polo scrimmages on Tues. and Thurs. evenings, 7:00 p.m. Also hosts a variety of polo league competitions, including a women's league.

**Newport Equestrian Academy** (401-847-7022; 800-8-HORSES; 287 Third Beach Rd., Middletown, RI 02842) Instruction at all levels, plus weekly summer riding camp (five to eighteen years old). In-season, trail rides on the beach ($65 for two hours). Also carriage rides by reservation.

**Surprise Valley Farm** (401-847-2660; 200 Harrison Ave., Newport, RI 02840) Located on forty acres just off Newport's Ocean Dr., this farm offers lessons, training, boarding, and guided trail rides on the estate. Also summer camp for children.

## SAILING & BOATING

Newport played host to America's Cup competition for fifty-three years until the Aussies won it away in 1983. So the Cup is gone, and with it the international yachting set — everyone from Ted Turner to the Aga Khan — who would arrive every four years to sail, spend, drink, and play.

But there's more to the legacy of cup competition than America's Cup Avenue; in fact, the sailing scene in Newport is livelier today than ever. Not-for-profit institutions, such as the **Sail Newport Sailing Center,** the **Newport Yachting Center,** and the **Museum of Yachting,** attract a steady stream of prestigious sailing events to Newport's waters; a better state of affairs, in the long run, than one big bash every four years. From the **Michelob Regatta** to Rolex's **International Women's Keelboat Championships,** there's still a lot of glamour out on the seas.

In recent years, Newport has become something of a yacht restoration center as well. The **International Yacht Restoration School** (401-849-3060; Thames St.) is a fascinating place to watch old racing craft coaxed back into life. Don't miss it.

For information on kayaking, see the heading Sky & Water Sports below.

### Charters, Rentals, Lessons

In Newport, you can hire a boat to go fishing, whale watching, or simply cruising around Narragansett Bay. Regularly scheduled sight-seeing cruises

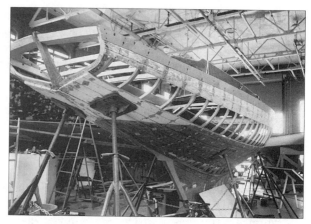

*The public is always welcome to take a peek as old ships are brought back to life at the International Yacht Restoration School.*

Craig Hammell

("sight sailing," as one promoter calls it) are noted under the heading Tours, though there's naturally some overlap. Chartering a boat usually refers to renting a crewed boat (the skipper remains onboard and in charge — these are often called "term charters") and to following an agenda of your own choosing or one recommended by the captain. It's your responsibility to get a group together (usually no more than eight) to share expenses. There are also "bareboat" charters — meaning that you hire just the boat and crew it yourself — available for both sail and powerboats. You can either call one of the outfits listed below directly, or contact the Newport Gateway Convention & Visitors' Bureau (401-849-8098; 800-326-6030); they'll give you the name of a yacht bro-

---

### The America's Cup

Captain Nat Herreshoff, Sir Thomas Lipton, Ted Hood, Harold Vanderbilt, and Dennis Connor: these are just some of the names associated with the America's Cup, the oldest international sporting competition in the world. It all began in 1851, when Britain invited other nations to race yachts around the Isle of Wight. That competition was won by *America* (hence the America's Cup), whereupon the U.S. achieved a stranglehold on the once-every-four-years competition. Thomas Lipton (of tea fame) had to grin and bear it as all five of his *Shamrocks* were beaten by American defenders (*Shamrock IV* came the closest in 1920, but *Resolute*, skippered by Charles Francis Adams, came from behind to win). From 1893, when the daring design of *Vigilant* revolutionized yacht racing, through *Resolute* in 1920, all of the America's Cup defenders were designed and built by Captain Nat Herreshoff at the Herreshoff Boatyard in Bristol, Rhode Island (see the section Culture in Chapter Four, *Narragansett Bay* for more on the Herreshoff Marine Museum and the America's Cup Hall of Fame). Cup racing first came to Rhode Island waters in 1930 when the New York Yacht Club moved to Newport; it left with the Australians in 1983. The rest, as they say, is history.

ker (brokers revolve daily) who will recommend a boat to fit your needs. Brokers and yachts are members of the Newport Yacht Charter Association.

The **Newport Recreation Department** (in conjunction with the Sail Newport Sailing Center, see below) offers children's sailing lessons throughout the summer. Call 401-846-1398.

**America's Cup Charters** (401-849-5868) A full day's cruising around Narragansett Bay for up to twelve people aboard one of five classic, twelve-meter wooden racing yachts (the only America's Cup winners available in the U.S.). You can pack a lunch, or they'll do it for you. Full-day rentals cost $1,700, half-day $1,200.

*Aurora* (401-849-6999; Goat Island Marina, Newport, RI 02840) Newport's largest schooner, a 101-foot wooden beauty, is available for charters, sunset sails, island clambakes, whatever you want.

**Fishin' Off, Inc.** (401-683-5557; 1 Washington St., Newport, RI 02840) Inshore and offshore fishing trips, full- or half-day or personalized charters aboard a thirty-six-foot trojan sportsfish sedan. Also overnight/weekend trips to Block Is. American shipyard at Goat Island Causeway.

**Flaherty Charters** (401-848-5554; Castle Hill Cove, Newport, RI 02840) Full- or half-day fishing trips or self-designed charters on a twenty-five-foot Boston whaler with a native Newport guide. Maximum six passengers.

**J. World Sailing School** (401-849-5492; 24 Mill St., Newport, RI 02840) All levels of instruction from beginning to championship racing. A weekend course costs $345.

**Long Wharf Yacht Charters** (401-849-2210; Long Wharf Marina, Newport, RI 02840) Bare-boat rentals, plus sportfishing and cruising charters; they also offer catering, and a B&B (see the section Lodging).

**The Museum of Yachting** (401-847-1018; Ft. Adams State Park) Educational programs include a school of yacht restoration and courses in offshore navigation, celestial navigation, yacht design for sailors, and yacht surveying (see the section Culture, under the heading Museums).

**Newport Sailing School and Tours** (401-246-1595; 401-848-2266; Goat Island Marina, Newport, RI 02840) Sailing instruction available daily, plus one- and two-hour tours of Newport Harbor and Narragansett Bay.

**Oldport Marine Services** (401-847-9019; Sayer's Wharf, Newport, RI 02840) Offers sail or powerboats from twenty-eight to fifty feet, bare-boat or crewed. Twenty-foot daysailer for rent. Also narrated cruises of Newport Harbor and lower Narragansett Bay.

**Sail Easterner** (401-847-5007; 800-420-7766; Web: www.amcup12.com; PO Box 1218, Newport, RI 02840) A gorgeous, wooden twelve-meter with a mahogany hull; accommodates up to twelve people; crewed private or corporate charters. Catering available.

**Sail Newport Sailing Center** (401-849-8385; 401-846-1983; Ft. Adams State Park, Newport, RI 02840) This nonprofit group formed to preserve Newport's sailing tradition after the loss of America's Cup in 1983 and to promote public recreational sailing. Offerings include sailboat rentals, tours, private and group instruction, and special events (see Seasonal Sailing & Boating Events below). Open May–Oct.

**Tiedmann Collection** (401-847-5007) Over 100 boats available for charter, including five restored, vintage yachts from a sixty-two-foot rumrummer (1918) to a seventy-foot America's Cup Class sloop (1938).

## MARINAS

These marinas offer public docking slips and/or moorings in Newport. Most have "full-service" facilities, which generally include electrical hookups, gas, diesel, and propane, bilge pumps, fresh water, ice, and telephone (those that are lacking are noted). Most have more, including a marine store, toilets, showers, and other amenities. *Call for specifics and to make a reservation in high-season.*

In **Newport Harbor** look for four state guest moorings on the south shore of Brenton Cove at the entrance to the smaller, inner cove; the quietest anchorage, though, is further out toward the head. Anchor south of the orange ball buoys between Fort Adams and the Newport Gas Company.

**Bannister's Wharf** (401-846-4500; Bannister's Wharf) Thirty-five guest slips.

**Bowen's Wharf** (401-849-2243; 13 Bowen's Wharf).

**Brown & Howard Marina** (401-846-5100 in-season; 401-274-6611 out-of-season; Brown & Howard Wharf) Transient and seasonal dockage for boats up to 250 foot, plus parking.

**Christie's Landing** (401-847-5400; Christie's Landing, 351 Thames St.) Thirty-five guest slips.

**Coddington Landing** (401-849-2419; 27 Coddington Wharf) A small wharf on Coaster's Is. in Newport Harbor.

**Goat Island Marina, Inc.** (401-849-5655; Goat Island) Guest slips and the usual. Voted best marina by *Newport Life Magazine* readers.

**Newport Harbor Hotel & Marina** (401-847-9000; 800-955-2558; 49 America's Cup Ave.) 100 guest slips with all the works; engine, electrical, and minor hull repairs. More kudos from *Newport Life Magazine* readers.

**Newport Onshore Ltd.** (401-849-0480; 405 Thames St.) Seventy-five guest slips.

**Newport Yachting Center** (401-847-9047; PO Box 549, America's Cup Ave.) 3,000 linear feet of guest slips. The NYC is a very active organization that sponsors many top-flight events (see the section Food & Beverage Purveyors, under the heading Seasonal Food Festivals & Special Dining Opportunities).

## SEASONAL SAILING & BOATING EVENTS

The following is a representative sampling of Newport sailing events; any copy of the free publication *Newport Summer Guide* will give you more.

Craig Hammell

*Boats find shelter at the Ida Lewis Yacht Club in Newport Harbor.*

**Annapolis to Newport Race** (401-846-1000; New York Yacht Club, Halidon Ave.) Early to mid-Jun.

**The Bermuda One-Two** (401-846-9410; Newport Yacht Club) A curious race: lone skippers sail from Newport to Bermuda where their partners, who flew down to the island, join them in sailing home to Newport. Early Jun.

**Classic Yacht Regatta** (401-847-1018; Museum of Yachting, Ft. Adams State Park) A great chance to see the old beauties afloat. Early Sept.

**Frostbite Regatta** (401-847-1613) Two annual events that traditionally mark the beginning (Apr.) and the ending (Nov.) of the sailing season.

**Nantucket Gold Regatta** (401-253-1264; Doubletree Newport Islander Hotel, Goat Is.) This new regatta benefits the Hasbro Children's Hospital of RI; at latest count over sixty boats took part. Early Jun.

**Newport International Boat Show** (401-846-1600; Newport Yachting Center, America's Cup Ave.) With over 300 boats and 400 accessory displays, this is the largest sail and powerboat show in the Northeast. Catch the special promos, including free harbor cruises. Mid-Sept.

**Newport Regatta** (401-846-1983; Sail Newport Sailing Center, Ft. Adams State Park) This is an immensely popular, Michelob-sponsored event. Racing for 300 boats and 1,500 people, plus socializing in the park afterwards. Mid-Jul.

**New York Yacht Club's Annual Regatta** (401-846-1000; New York Yacht Club, Halidon Ave.) Open to IMS yachts; 1998 is their 144th year. Mid-Jun.

**Rolex International Women's Keelboat Championship** (401-846-1969; Sail

Newport Sailing Center, Ft. Adams State Park) Biennial event hosted by the Ida Lewis Yacht Club. Women-only teams from all over the world race in forty to fifty J/24-class sailboats. Mid-Sept.

**Sail Newport National Regatta for the Blind** (401-846-1983; Sail Newport Sailing Center, Ft. Adams State Park) Six teams compete; the skipper of each boat must be blind or visually impaired. Mid-May.

**Sail Newport Sailing Festival** (401-846-1983; Sail Newport Sailing Center, Ft. Adams State Park) This free sailing event — harbor cruises offered on the rental fleet of J/22s and Rhodes 19s — has kicked off each summer sailing season for over ten years. The Museum of Yachting (next door) is free to anyone with a Sail Newport pass. The annual Barbecue Bash rounds out the day. The **Bank of Newport Memorial Day Regatta** (401-846-1983) is also held at the Ida Lewis Yacht Club. Mem. Day weekend.

**Wall Street Challenge Cup** (401-846-2316; Newport Harbor) Wall Street brokerage firms race one another on vintage America's Cup yachts to raise money for others for a change.

**Wooden Boat Show** (401-846-1600; Newport Yachting Center, 4 Commercial Wharf) The largest wooden boat show in the U.S. On land and in the water, 200 featured craft, plus demonstrations, races, regatta, and children's boat-building lessons. Late Jun.

## USEFUL TELEPHONE NUMBERS

**Newport Marine Electric** (401-847-8870).
**Newport Mooring Service** (401-846-7535).
**Newport Nautical Supply** (401-847-3933).
**Trident Rigging** (401-849-9466).
**Yacht Service & Resources** (401-849-8470).

## SKY & WATER SPORTS

This section highlights sports in the air and in the water rather than on the water. Fans of **Kayaking, Parasailing, Scuba Diving, Surfbiking** (surf-bikes, or seacycles, are surfboards fitted with seats, pedals, and steering rudders) **Surfing,** and **Windsurfing** will find what they're looking for. Lessons, sales, and rentals are readily available.

**Surfers,** WBRU (95.5 FM) broadcasts daily surf reports at 8:35 a.m. The best surfing beach in Newport is **Easton** (aka First) **Beach** at the foot of the Cliff Walk. Minutes away, however, is **Second Beach** in Middletown, RI, which has even bigger breakers.

**Adventure Sports** (401-849-4820; 142 Long Wharf, Newport, RI 02840) They rent it all: bicycles, surfbikes, powerboats, sailboats, kayaks, canoes, and fishing rods; they also offer charters, lessons, guided tours, and diving trips.

**Alpine Ski & Sports** (401-849-3330; Bellevue Plaza, Newport, RI 02840) Diving sales, rentals, lessons, and repair of equipment; also in-line skates, plus tennis rackets, water skis, and regular old beach gear.

**Atlantic Outfitters** (401-848-2920; 152 Bellevue Ave., Newport, RI 02840) This is the place to go for sea and surf kayaking: sales, rentals, demonstrations (surf kayaking refers to the sit-on-top style), and tours (see the heading Tours, "On the Water" below).

**Freeman Thomas Diving Service** (401-847-4985; 55 Chaple St., Newport, RI 02840).

**Newport Diving Center** (401-847-9293; 800-DIVING-0; 550 Thames St., Newport, RI 02840) A true diver's haven, with gear, lessons, charters, and repairs.

**Skydive Newport** (401-841-9545; 800-656-3663; Newport State Airport, Middletown, RI 02842) How to kill either half a day or yourself: jump out of a plane (a skydiving photographer will even jump with you if you like and take photos to prove to others that you really are crazy). Reservations necessary. You must be over 18 and under 230 lbs.

**Water Brothers Surf & Sport** (401-849-4990; 39 Memorial Blvd., Newport, RI 02840) Surfboard and skateboard sales and rentals; also clothing and accessories.

SEASONAL EVENTS

**Swim the Bay** (401-272-3540) Swimmers have been breaststroking their way from Newport to Jamestown for almost twenty years now. Check-in is 9:00 a.m. and starting time is 11:00 a.m. for this two-mile swim across the bay — you get lunch on the beach when you finish. Preregistration is mandatory. Mid-Aug.

## STATE PARKS

State parks are open from sunrise to sunset; naturalists are on duty only during the summer months. Pets must be on leashes; rest rooms are usually available. For more on state parks, contact the **Department of Environmental Management, Division of Parks and Recreation** (401-277-2632; 2321 Hartford Avenue, Johnston, Rhode Island 02919).

**Brenton Point State Park** (401-846-8240; Ocean Dr., Newport) Superb ocean views, plus picnic tables, fishing, and a visitor center with a full schedule of nature programs. The sculptures are a monument to Portuguese navigators.

**Fort Adams State Park** (401-847-2400; off Harrison Ave. and Ocean Dr., Newport) On the tip of the peninsula that shelters Newport Harbor, Ft. Adams not only boasts the old fort (see the section Culture, under the heading Military Museums & Sites), but the best views in the state — to one side is the harbor, the other Jamestown and the bay. Offers swimming, fishing, boating, and picnicking; Sail Newport Sailing Center and the Museum of Yachting are also here. $4 entrance fee for nonresidents, $50 for a three-month season pass.

## TENNIS

As a pastime, tennis is centuries old, the original "Sport of Kings" played indoors on court tennis courts. As an American institution, however, outdoor lawn tennis began in Newport. The first National Tennis Championship was held in 1881 at the Newport Casino, now the **International Tennis Hall of Fame,** where it remained until 1915 when the tournament moved to Forest Hills, New York. (Now it's ensconced in Flushing Meadows as that great Labor Day event, the U.S. Open.)

This doesn't mean that the Hall of Fame's thirteen immaculate grass courts (the only competition grass courts available for play in the country) lie languishing. Tournaments are still held here each summer (see "Seasonal Events" below). If you feel your tennis togs (and your pocketbook) are up to it, book one of the grass beauties as a holiday treat, or call town halls for the location of municipal courts. Also see the section Lodging for inns, hotels, and B&Bs with tennis courts; these are often available to the public for a fee.

**International Tennis Hall of Fame** (401-849-3990; Newport Casino, 194 Bellevue Ave.) For information on the Hall of Fame and Newport Casino, see the section Culture, under the heading Museums. Rent one of thirteen historic grass courts from mid-May–early Oct. at $35 per person per ninety minutes; have your serve speed clocked by radar. Hard courts are a bargain at $20 per court per ninety minutes. Lessons are also available at $50 per hour. Pro shop. Wear white.

### Seasonal Events

While it's tempting to sit courtside at tournaments at the Newport Casino/Int'l Tennis Hall of Fame, go for the cheaper bleacher seats. The view is just as good, and if it's a hot July day in Newport, the bleachers are the only place where you can catch a breeze. Bring a cooler, plus seat pads, hats, sunscreen, and spray bottles filled with water to spritz yourself and others. All of the events below take place at the **International Tennis Hall of Fame** (see information above).

**Miller Lite Hall of Fame Tennis Championships** (401-849-6053) The only professional men's tournament played on grass in the U.S. As part of the IBM/ATP tour, it's an important stop, but doesn't draw top names — players are afraid of grass these days. Nonetheless, the quality of play is high. Early to mid-Jul. $13-$35.

**Tennis Hall of Fame Enshrinement Ceremony** (401-849-6053) Held on semifinals day (Sat.) of the Virginia Slims and Miller Lite tourneys, this hour-long event (speeches and exhibition matches) honors recent inductees. It's worth going just to see what Bud Collins will wear. Mid-Jul.

**Tennis Hall of Fame Expo & Fair** (401-849-3990) Exhibits from the makers of top tennis accoutrements. Mid-late Jun.

**U.S. Ladies Court Tennis Championships** (401-849-6772) Watch court tennis as it was originally played centuries ago. Mid-May.

**Virginia Slims Hall of Fame Invitational** (401-849-6053) Not the big Newport Virginia Slims tournament of yore, which featured the likes of Martina and Chris; it's now a four-day special event that attracts mid-ranking players. Early to mid-Jul. $17-$35.

## TOURS

A diverse range of tours by air, sea, land, and on foot are noted below. The boats listed here offer sight-seeing cruises, with regularly scheduled departures (see the heading Sailing & Boating for other sailing options). For historic walking tours, see the section Culture, under the heading Historical Tours.

### BY AIR

**Aquidneck Aviation** (401-848-7080; Newport State Airport, Middletown, RI 02842) Sight-seeing, aerial photography, and flying instruction; if you're qualified, they'll rent you a plane of your own.

**Newport Air Services** (401-846-8877; Newport State Airport, Middletown, RI 02842) Avoid the traffic with twenty to twenty-five-minute helicopter tours of the city.

### ON THE WATER

*Adirondack* (401-846-3018; Newport Yachting Center, Newport, RI 02840) Two-hour cruises through Newport Harbor aboard a seventy-eight-foot schooner. Call for private charters.

*Flyer* (401-848-2100; 800-TO-FLYER; 142 Long Wharf, Newport, RI 02840) Sail aboard a custom, fifty-seven-foot catamaran. Takes up to sixty-five passengers; full bar. Sails from May-Oct., two-hour guided cruises of Newport Harbor. Leaves from the Inn on Long Wharf (see the section Lodging).

*Spirit of Newport* (401-849-3575; Newport Navigation, PO Box 331, Newport, RI 02840) Departs every ninety minutes for a one-hour cruise of the bay and harbor. Biggest boat in town — seats 200, with full bar. Leaves from the Newport Harbor Hotel & Marina (see the section Lodging) off America's Cup Ave.

*Viking Queen* (401-847-6921; Viking Tours, PO Box 330, Newport, RI 02840) Sail aboard the 140-passenger *Viking Queen* for a one-hour cruise of Newport Harbor, or a two-and-a-half-hour cruise with a stop to tour Hammersmith Farm (see the section Culture, under the heading The Mansions). Tickets at Viking Boat Dock, Goat Is., or the Newport Gateway Convention & Visitors' Bureau. Mid-May–mid-Oct.

**The Kayak Center at Atlantic Outfitters** (401-848-2920; 152 Bellevue Ave., Newport, RI 02840) Choose from a range of guided kayak tours; no previous experience or equipment necessary. Explore Ocean Dr. and Newport Harbor, paddle out to Rose Is. for a picnic, or plan your own itinerary. From $45–$85.

**Sight Sailing of Newport** (401-849-3333; Bowen's Wharf, Newport, RI 02840) One-hour sailing tours of the harbor and the bay.

**Yankee Boat Peddlers** (401-849-3033; Bannister's Wharf, Newport, RI 02840) Both the seventy-two-foot schooner *Madeleine* and the sixty-foot motor yacht *Rum Runner II* sail daily for harbor cruises from Bannister's Wharf. Both available for private charters.

### BY CAR OR BUS

**Driving Cassette Tape Tour of Newport** (401-849-8048; Newport Gateway Convention & Visitors' Bureau, 23 America's Cup Ave., Newport, RI 02840) Pickup one of these at the Visitors' Bureau and pop it in: a narrated tour of the mansions and Ocean Dr., complete with sound effects. (Good luck sticking to the right speed.)

**The Paper Lion** (401-846-5777; 24 Long Wharf Mall, off America's Cup Ave., Newport, RI 02840) Another auto tape tour of the City by the Sea. You can rent a tape player and cassette for the day, or order ahead by mail and get the tape (and map) for about $12.

**Viking Bus Tours of Newport** (401-847-6921; Newport Gateway Convention & Visitors' Bureau, 23 America's Cup Ave., Newport, RI 02840) Four different narrated motor coach tours (air-conditioned!) of colonial Newport, the Bellevue Ave. mansions, and Ocean Dr. Tours depart daily from Apr.–Oct.; from Nov.–Mar. on Sat. mornings only. Adult tickets range from $13 for one and a half hours to $27 for four and a half hours.

### ON FOOT

**Jane S. Jacques** (401-884-8805; 30 Longfellow Dr., N. Kingstown, RI 02852) Custom-prepared tour guide service to Newport or elsewhere.

### BY HORSE

**Surprise Valley Carriage Company** (401-847-2660) Horse-drawn carriage rides around the city; pick one up either at the Newport Blues Cafe on Thames St. or the Newport Marriott on America's Cup Ave. $35 per carriage-full.

### BY RAIL

**Old Colony and Newport Railroad** (401-624-6951; PO Box 343, America's Cup Ave., Newport, RI 02840) The station is directly across from the Newport Gateway Convention & Visitors' Bureau; this is the same line that serves the

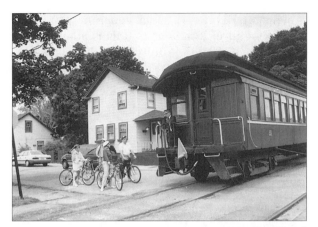

Cyclists approach the Newport Dinner Train in Newport's quiet Point Section.

Craig Hammell

**Newport Dinner Train** (see the section Dining). Gaze at the bay from an 1884 parlor car or a 1904 open platform touring car during the nine- or eighteen-mile round-trip. Weekends from May–Jun., Sept.–mid-Oct.; Tues., Wed., Thurs., Sat., Sun. from Jul.–Sept.; Sun. only from mid-Oct.–mid-Nov. Adult fares from $5.50–$10.

## VOLLEYBALL

Throughout the summer the "Bud Light" beach volleyball tour makes repeated visits to Easton's (First) Beach on Memorial Boulevard. Both Shot Block Amateur Volleyball matches are held, as well as Men's and Women's Pro tournaments. Also look for the Jose Cuervo Pro-Am Beach Volleyball tour. Check local "What's Doing" newspaper listings for dates and times.

## GRAB BAG

A miscellany of fun things to do, many ideal for children.

**Children's Night** (401-846-1398; Newport Recreation Department, 280 Spring St., Newport, RI 02840) Every Thurs. evening in-season at 6:30 p.m. — free entertainment with music, magic, puppets, and stories.

**Butterfly Zoo at Newport Butterfly Farm** (401-846-3148; Aquidneck Ave., Middletown, RI 02842) Two twelve-foot flight areas house over twenty-five species of native butterflies bred by Marc Schenck, who also sells monarch, swallowtail, and caterpillar garden kits. Avoid wearing strong perfume (attracts bees) or the color red (the butterflies love it and will roost on you). Open daily mid-May-Sept.; closed rainy days. Adults $5; children $3.

**Newport Aquarium** (401-849-8430; Easton's (First) Beach, Memorial Blvd.,

Newport, RI 02840) A small aquarium with hands-on exhibits, featuring animals found in local waters (this is your chance to pet a live shark!). Daily 10:00 a.m.–5:00 p.m. Adults $3.50; children $2.50.

*The perpetual wind at Brenton Point State Park makes for ideal kite-flying conditions.*

Craig Hammell

**Newport Kite Festival** (401-846-3262); Brenton Point State Park, Ocean Dr.) A major event that brings together kite makers and kite flyers from up and down the eastern seaboard. Also kite-flying lessons and demonstrations.

## SHOPPING

Newport dominates Narragansett Bay in the shopping department. The town is brimming with stores of all description, but be warned that the turnover rate is ferocious. Rents are high, and many little boutiques can't sustain the swings of a seasonal economy. The shops listed below are examples of the kinds of stores typical of the area; it's inevitable that some of them will be history by the time that you visit. On the other hand, there are some constants, including the gift shops at historic houses and museums, a selection of which are noted below. Museum shops often have unusual items of excellent quality unavailable anywhere else.

It's convenient to organize Newport into distinct shopping areas. **Bellevue Avenue** shops are fairly swanky; clothing tends toward the preppy, expensive, and traditional (Talbots is here). Note the superb commercial architecture along the Casino block (this said, there's an Almacs supermarket directly across from the International Tennis Hall of Fame). The arty, on-the-cusp **Broadway area** is the place to go for funky galleries and secondhand clothing and gift stores. **Thames Street** has a dual personality: Upper Thames from

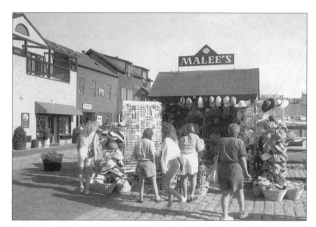

*Sunglasses are never in short supply on Bowen's Wharf.*

Craig Hammell

Washington Park to Memorial Boulevard can give the impression that Newport has cornered the market on souvenir and beachy clothing shops, while Lower Thames is an eclectic universe unto itself, with boutiques both bizarre and glamorous selling everything from lawn ornaments to low-fat dog bones. Shop here for more hip, cool clothes. **Brick Market Place,** off Upper Thames, has plenty of benches for the tired of foot, with midrange clothing and souvenir shops. **Bowen's and Bannister's Wharves** are more upscale, with designer footwear and sportswear, fine art galleries, and the wonderful Museum Shop of the Preservation Society of Newport County. Finally there's **Spring Street,** the commercial stretch that runs from Memorial Boulevard to Washington Square. This is my favorite area: not too fancy, not too trendy, with one-of-a-kind shops and antique galleries.

## ANTIQUES

Newport has a longstanding reputation as an antiques center, with both a regional and international legacy on which to draw. First came the China trading days of the eighteenth and nineteenth centuries and then the Gilded Age, when expensive baubles of every description filled the mansions. Many items from both periods are now for sale in shops and galleries throughout town, and they set an impressive standard; quality can be dizzyingly high, with prices to match. Much here is of Asian or European origin, rather than colonial or Early American. Shops in Newport are concentrated on **Franklin Street** (only one block long and packed with shops — a great option for the footsore), **Spring Street,** and **Lower Thames Street,** as well as **Bellevue Avenue.** Look for a pamphlet available at the Newport Gateway Convention & Visitors' Bureau called *Antique Shops in Newport, Rhode Island,* which includes a map.

**A & A Gaines** (401-849-6844; 401-846-0538; 40 Franklin St.) A superb shop: Chinese porcelains, nauticals, clocks, and top-quality, nineteenth-century furniture. Prices to match.

**Alice Simpson Antiques** (401-849-4252; 40 1/2 Franklin St.) Specializes in Victorian silver plate, textiles, and jewelry. Reasonable prices.

**The Armory Antiques & Fine Art** (401-848-2398; 365 Thames St.) A conglomerate of shops in the former Armory building, featuring china, glass, paintings, estate jewelry, and some furniture. 125 dealers represented. Public rest rooms, too.

**The Ball & Claw** (401-848-5600; Bowen's Wharf) See the heading Craft Galleries & Studios below.

**The Burbank Rose** (401-849-9457; 111 Memorial Blvd.) See the section Lodging for the B&B of the same name; the shop offers small antiques, collectibles, and sports memorabilia.

**Courtyard Antiques** (401-849-4554; 142 Bellevue Ave.) Packed to the gills with an eclectic mix, some good, some not.

**Drawing Room Antiques** (401-841-5060; 152-154 Spring St.) Merchandise as highfalutin as the name: Baccarat chandeliers, Hungarian pottery, all manner of museum-quality, nineteenth-century furnishings.

**Eclectics** (401-849-8786; 5 Lee's Wharf) Antiques, crafts, books, maps, and prints. This shop down at the end of the wharf has a nice feel to it.

**Exotic Treasures** (401-842-0040; 622 Lower Thames St.) A sometimes-campy trove of Victorian, Edwardian, and Asian pieces.

**Fine Arts and Antiques** (401-846-2105; 35 Franklin St.) High-quality, nineteenth- and twentieth-century paintings and accompanying antiques.

**Forever Yours** (401-841-5290; 220 Spring St.) Voted best antiques shop by *Newport Life Magazine* readers' poll, it features Victorian and French antiques gussied up with silk and dried flower arrangements.

**The Griffon Shop** (401-848-8200; 76 Bellevue Ave.; inside the Newport Art Museum) Don't miss it: a fine selection of antiques from Newport estates.

**Harbor Antiques** (401-848-9711; 134 Spring St.) A fun collection of funky old things; for instance, an antique barber's chair reupholstered in floral print fabric.

**JB Antiques** (401-849-0450; 33 Franklin St.) Furniture, paintings, and accessories, all top quality, such as an eye-catching Arts and Crafts pottery piece painted with scenes from the Bayeux Tapestry.

**John Gidley House** (401-846-8303; 22 Franklin St.) A small space with high prices and excellent items, ranging from marble fireplace mantels to oil lamps and lighting fixtures.

**Mainly Oak, Ltd.** (401-846-4439; 489 Thames St.) Good quality oak furniture, restored on the premises.

**New England Antiques** (401-849-6646; 60 Spring St.) A personal favorite, with fairly priced American art (paintings and works on paper), nauticals, glass, oil lamps, even a collection of daguerreotypes. Excellent in an unstuffy sort of way.

**Newport Antiques** (401-849-2105; 471 Thames St.) A cluttered haven of estate jewelry, coins, and a variety of china and collectibles.

**Newport China Trade Co.** (401-841-5267; 8 Franklin St.) Porcelains, silver, mirrors, and furniture from the eighteenth- and nineteenth-century China trade.

**Patina** (401-846-4666; 26 Franklin St.) Decorative arts, Americana, silver, copper, and furniture.

**Petteruti Antiques** (401-849-5117; 105 Memorial Blvd. W) Antique wicker, nineteenth-century bronzes, and generally fine, interesting stuff.

**Renaissance Antiques** (401-849-8515; 42 Spring St.) Clocks, antique lighting fixtures and lighting restoration services, glass shades, and more.

**Smith Marble Ltd.** (401-846-7689; 44 Franklin St.) English and European antiques; specializes in china and silver, with some large pieces of furniture.

SEASONAL EVENTS

**Newport Antiques & Collectibles Festival** (617-863-1516; Glen Farm, E. Main Rd., Rte. 138, Portsmouth, RI 02871) 400 dealers at a gala outdoor antiques event. First weekend in Jun.

**Newport County Antiques Week** (401-846-7010; The Newport County Antique Dealers Assoc., PO Box 222, Newport, RI 02840) Features shows, tours, lectures, and shop events. Last week in Apr.

---

### *Of Furniture & Clocks*

Before the Revolutionary War, Newport craftsmen achieved a standard of excellence unequaled anywhere else in the colonies. The Townsend and Goddard families, in particular, led the way with exquisite furniture that today commands towering prices. The Nicholas Brown desk, a Townsend-Goddard piece that belonged to the Brown family of Providence, was auctioned by Christie's in 1989 for $11 million: the highest price ever fetched by an artwork other than a painting. If that leaves you out of the bidding, stop by the **Newport Historical Society,** the **Hunter House,** and especially the **Samuel Whitehorne House** (see the section Culture) to view examples of Townsend-Goddard furniture. You can also stroll by the houses that these master cabinetmakers erected for themselves, all in the **Point Section** of town. Christopher Townsend's home and workshop complex was built at 74-76 Bridge Street in 1725, with another for Job Townsend at 68-72 Bridge, sometime before 1758. John Goddard was originally apprenticed to Job, but he went on to cabinetmaking fame and glory himself and built 81 Second Street. More of the families' homes are throughout the area.

Nearby, at 16 Bridge Street, is the 1725 home of William Claggett, Newport's equally famous master clock maker. Claggett was a mechanical genius of the first order, and many of the clocks and organs that he built are still working. You can see for yourself at the **Seventh Day Baptist Meeting House** (see the section Culture).

## BOOKS, CARDS, MUSIC

For more on books about Newport or by Rhode Island authors, see the Bibliography section in Chapter Six, *Information.*

**Anchor and Dolphin Books** (401-846-6890; 30 Franklin St.) A rare and used book shop that specializes in architecture, applied arts, and gardening. Try in the afternoon, or by appt.

**The Armchair Sailor** (401-847-4252; 543 Thames St.) A well-stocked shop specializing in marine and travel books. Also seafood cookbooks, children's books, magazines, and much more. Complimentary coffee and tea.

**The Bookmark** (401-847-4544; 152 Broadway) A trove of fine and used books in hardcover and paperback, including military, nautical, children's, culinary, and history books and other nonfiction.

**The Corner Bookstore** (401-846-8406; 46 Marlborough St.) A large selection of used books for browsers and collectors.

**The Newport Book Store** (401-847-3400; 116 Bellevue Ave.) Excellent old and rare material; specialties include Americana, military, and RI.

**Papers** (401-847-1777; 178 Bellevue Ave.) Cards, loose writing paper, Crane's stationery, and gifts.

**The Third & Elm Press** (401-846-0228; 29 Elm St.) A unique find in a unique part of town (the otherwise residental Point Section), selling original woodblock prints, private-press books, and notepaper. Commissions for calligraphy and letterpress printing.

## CHILDREN

**Gentle Jungle** (401-849-8210; 57 America's Cup Ave.) Stuffed animals galore, plus toys and books.

**The Zoo** (401-849-9466; Bannister's Wharf) An all-animal theme shop of toys, plush creatures, dog dishes, and much more.

### SEASONAL EVENTS

**Newport Maritime Teddy Bear Show & Sale** (860-628-8582; Doubletree Newport Islander Hotel, Goat Is.) An annual event that features teddy bear designers throughout the U.S. Look for one-of-a-kind and famous bears, plus free bear-making demonstrations. Late Aug.

## CLOTHING & ACCESSORIES

**Brahmin Leather Factory Outlet** (401-849-5990; 22 Bannister's Wharf) Discounted leather handbags, briefcases, etc.

**Cabbage Rose** (401-846-7006; 493 Thames St.) Funky new and used women's clothing and hats.

**Chico's** (401-849-8286; 130 Thames St.) Really wearable women's clothes; unusual prints in 100 percent cotton. Expensive, but worth it.

**Cole-Haan Co. Store** (401-846-4906; 206 Bellevue Ave.) Men and women's leather footwear and accessories. Very upscale.

**Diva** (401-846-7788; 489 Thames St.) More hip and cool women's clothing.

**Edna Mae's Millinery** (401-847-8665; 424 Thames St.) Great hats made by hand from vintage and new materials.

**The Last Mango** (401-848-2842; 6 Franklin St.) Casual, artsy, comfortable women's clothing.

**Lily's of the Alley** (401-846-7545; 64 Spring St.) A friendly shop with comfortable, earthy, contemporary women's clothes. Good prices, lots of cotton prints.

**Michael Hayes/Michael Hayes for Kids** (401-846-5440; 202 and 204 Bellevue Ave.) Serious, classic, expensive wear for men (suits in particular), women, and children by a famous Newport clothier. Also a location at 19 Bowen's Wharf.

**The Shoe Cellar** (401-846-0052; 6 Bowen's Wharf) Pricey women's shoes from over fifty labels; weekly shipments of new footwear.

**Suit-Systems** (401-847-7848; 359 Thames St.) Computer-measured swimwear for men and women (do you really want a computer to know your measurements?).

**Team One Newport** (401-848-0884; 800-847-4327; 547 Thames St.) Very serious sailing gear, plus swimwear and sports clothes. Call ahead for their catalogue.

**Timberland** (401-846-4410; 16 Bannister's Wharf) Sturdy leather hiking boots and accessories.

**Tropical Gangsters** (401-847-9113; 375 Thames St.) Way cool clothing and accessories for men and women.

**Tropique** (401-848-5570; 470 Thames St.) Very "village" stuff. Cool, trendy clothing for thin women; lots of strokable, unusual fabrics.

**The Weathervane** (401-849-6219; Long Wharf Mall) Good, middle-of-the-road women's clothing at reasonable prices. If the temperature drops, pick up a cotton sweater here.

## CRAFT GALLERIES & STUDIOS

**The Accidental Artist** (401-841-8809; 516 Thames St.) Paint it yourself pottery — a great idea for kids.

**The Ball & Claw** (401-848-5600; Bowen's Wharf) An exceptional shop, showcasing the exquisite craftsmanship that furniture maker Jeffrey Greene lavishes upon pieces designed for, as he puts it, "the eighteenth-century home." Highly recommended.

**Collage** (401-849-4949; 25 Bowen's Wharf) Hand-designed jewelry, furniture, clocks, frames, etc. by RISD graduates and other artists.

Craig Hammell

*Master furniture maker Jeffrey Greene crafts pieces "fit for the eighteenth-century home," which he displays at his shop The Ball & Claw.*

**The Erica Zap Collection** (401-849-4117; 477 Thames St.) Top-quality international crafts.

**MacDowell Pottery** (401-846-6313; 140 Spring St.) A small place with a good selection of serviceable pottery, plus cards and gifts. Watch the potter at work.

**Newport Scrimshanders** (401-849-5680; 800-635-5234; 14 Bowen's Wharf) Scrimshaw (the art of engraving on ivory) has fallen into disfavor, though no elephants died for the scrimshaw exhibited here. The owner works mostly with prehistoric mammoth and walrus ivory. Nantucket lightship baskets, too.

**Thames Glass** (401-846-0576; fax 401-846-0579; 688 Thames St.) At the end of Lower Thames is a fabulous glassblowing studio and shop. These beautifully fashioned vases, paperweights, perfume bottles, goblets, candlesticks, etc. make everything else look cheap. There's also a shop at 8 Bowen's Wharf, 401-842-0597. Note the annual Second's Sale, beginning on Thanksgiving and running for ten days.

**Thames Street Pottery** (401-847-2437; 433 Thames St.) Pottery thrown on the spot, plus work in wood, clay, and glass from artisans around the country. Native American pottery, too.

**Tropea-Puerini** (401-846-3344; 391 Thames St.) A fine craft gallery with cutting-edge wares.

**Wave** (401-847-6303; 424 Thames St.) Good quality (occasionally slick and/or cutesy) handmade stuff in a small, crowded shop: jewelry, lamps, teapots, vases, etc.

## GIFTS

**Cabbages & Kings** (401-847-4650; 214 Bellevue Ave.) "Gifts and decor designed for gracious living" — an upscale gift shop.

**Cadeaux du Monde** (401-848-0550; 140 Bellevue Ave.) Unusual art and artifacts from South America, Asia, and Africa.

**A Myriad of Things** (401-847-5520; 6 Broadway) A unique collection of decorative accessories.

**The Newport Preservation Society Museum Store** (401-849-9900; 1 Bannister's Wharf) A fine selection of museum reproductions from Newport and around the world.

## HOUSE & GARDEN

*Statuary from The Aardvark might be the perfect, if heavy, souvenir.*

Craig Hammell

**The Aardvark** (401-849-7232; 475 Thames St.) The address refers to a jumbled antique shop, but four doors down is a yard full of great statuary from imposing to campy and downright silly.

**Bellevue Florist** (401-847-0145; 159 Prospect Hill St.) This elegant little shop tucked down a tiny side street off Bellevue Ave. looks like it belongs in London. They carry only a small selection of wicker and home accessories, but it's worth a peek.

**The Gilded Age** (401-847-1272; 146 Bellevue Ave.) Original, handmade pillows, throws, and table runners inspired by the glory days of the last century.

**The Linen Shop** (401-846-0225; 196 Bellevue Ave.) Imported linens for bed, bath, and table; a former branch of E. Braun & Co., Vienna.

**Rue de France** (401-846-3636; 78 Thames St.) This little gem would be at home on the Ile St. Louis in Paris — it's a revelation in Newport. Reams of French lace, fabrics, bed linens, and country home furnishings. Write for their catalogue.

## JEWELRY

**David R. Rough Jewelers** (401-846-0598; 120 Bellevue Ave.) The oldest jewelry store in Newport (opened in 1913); new and estate jewelry, plus baby gifts, jewelry and watch repair, and bead restringing.

**Down Under Jewelry** (401-849-1078; 479 Thames St.) Contemporary and traditional jewelry, with and without gemstones. More fun than haughty.

**Firenze Jewelers** (401-849-7070; 301 Swan's Wharf Row, Brick Market Place) Estate, antique, and modern jewelry.

**Geoclassics** (401-849-5587; 61 America's Cup Ave.) Jewelry and other pretty things at this gem and mineral shop.

**The Golden Dog** (401-849-1444; 888-GOLD-DOG; 1 Bannister's Wharf) Sleek, modern jewelry in gold, silver, platinum, and mixed metals, and a real Golden Retriever named Sailor.

**J.H. Breakell & Co.** (401-849-3522; 800-767-6411; E-mail: jafl95a@prodigy.com; 132 Spring St.) A very fine silversmith's shop. All the exquisite pieces that you see are designed and forged on the premises. Don't miss this one — send ahead for the catalogue.

**Platinum House** (401-848-7528; 209 Goddard Row, Brick Market Place) Hand-crafted jewelry in gold, silver, and platinum. Takes on custom work.

## KITCHEN

**The Runcible Spoon** (401-849-3737; 180 Bellevue Ave.) Elegant, and expensive, kitchen and tableware and gifts. A runcible spoon is "a fork with three broad prongs, one of which is sharp-edged and curved like a spoon," according to Webster.

## MARINE SUPPLY

**J.T.'s Ship Chandlery** (401-846-7256; Web: www.jtschanglery.com; 364 Thames St.) Nautical heaven. This shop has it all, from serious marine hardware to clothing, charts, books, hermit crab hand puppets, even cool plastic champagne glasses for your yacht (or your home). Check out the bulletin board advertising sail makers, riggers, craft for sail, engine repair, boatbuilders, etc.

**Nautor's Swan** (401-846-8404; Bowen's Wharf) Yacht sales and brokerage; parts distribution center.

*J.T.'s Ship Chandlery has everything from sound charts to rope cables, and much more.*

Craig Hammell

**Northrop & Johnson** (401-848-5500; Brown and Howard Wharf) Yachts sales and brokerage, charters, and new construction.

## PHARMACIES & NEWSSTANDS

**Bellevue News** (401-847-0669; 111 Bellevue Ave.) A great little newsstand with magazines, candy, the works.

**Carroll Michael & Co. Pharmacy** (401-849-4488; 115 Bellevue Ave.) Make a point of stopping here — it's more like a gallery than a shop, with exquisite displays of perfumes, soaps, gifts, and other elegant, luxurious items (prescriptions, too). They decorate with flair at Christmas.

## SOUVENIRS & NOVELTIES

**The Souvenir Stop** (401-849-6717; 115 Swinburne Row, Brick Market Place) No-nonsense Newport bric-a-brac and clothing. The place to come when you need to stock up on souvenirs in a hurry.

**Scrimshaw Market Place** (401-849-4430; 170 Thames St.) Lots of Newportized stuff in addition to custom scrimshaw engraving; a lot more browseable than the bigger, slicker shops.

## SPECIALTY

**Buddy's Tattoo Shop** (401-245-5645; 4 Marlborough St.) A master of the tattoo trade, Buddy's been at it for almost half a century. Skin sketches average about $40.

**Ebenezer Flagg Co.** (401-846-1891; 65 Touro St.) Their logo says "We Make or Procure Any Flag." A great flag maker's shop with a colorful, international collection. Bring a design, and they'll make one for you.

**The Gourmet Dog** (401-841-9301; 476B Thames St.) A self-described doggie bakery, featuring six flavors of all natural, low-fat dog biscuits and other items. Don't forget to pet Milton, the in-shop taster.

**High Flyers Flight Co., Inc.** (401-846-3262; 492 Thames St.) A colorful kite shop with an extraordinary range of wares.

**Miniature Motors of Newport** (401-847-0857; 318 Broadway) Die-cast collectibles by Matchbox and other manufacturers; cars, trucks, banks, even NASCAR models.

**Miniature Occasions** (401-849-5440; 800-358-4285; 57 Bellevue Ave.) Purveyors of fine miniatures for dollhouses, plus the miniature abodes themselves. Also carries Julie-Bond Kruger dolls.

**Nautical Nook** (800-841-6810; 86 Spring St.) Nautical antiques, ship models, boats-in-bottles, that kind of thing. Also does restoration.

**Newport Hobby House, Ltd.** (401-847-1515; 235 Spring St.) From car and plane models to masterful, miniature wooden ships and toy train sets, this is the place. Their specialty is a host of sailboat models in wood, plastic, and fiberglass; kits range from eighteen to fifty-five inches (for display or for sailing with radio control). If you can't find your own sailboat model on the shelves, have blueprints made, and they'll build it for you.

**The Painted Canvas** (401-841-5685; 22 Bellevue Ave.) Another needlepoint shop, specializing in hand-painted designs.

**Ransom House** (401-847-0555; 36 Franklin St.) *The* place for lamps, lamp shades, candle shades, sconces, and more.

## VINTAGE CLOTHING SHOPS

**Insanity** (401-848-5379; 154 Broadway) A hip and kooky spot, selling hip and kooky used clothing. If you wore it already in the 1970s, give it a miss; if not, this place is for you.

**Newport Consignment** (401-849-9488; W. Marlborough St., next to Mudville Pub) A very large, no-nonsense used clothing store; received high marks from readers of *Newport Life Magazine.*

**True Colors** (no telephone; 30 Broadway) Eccentric used clothes and old stuff. Very retro.

# CHAPTER FOUR
# *Rocky Shores & Rolling Fields*
## NARRAGANSETT BAY

Narragansett Bay carves a great hole in Rhode Island's landmass, making for a state that's really more sea than shore. On either side of this big marine playground are coasts that shelter historic settlements well over 300 years old, rural areas of pastureland and tilled fields, horse farms and nurseries, shingle-style beach cottages, seaside restaurants, and communities where blue-blooded Yankees and descendants of Portuguese and Italian immigrants have mingled together for over a hundred years.

Craig Hammell

*The Jamestown Windmill, built in 1787, occupies a high, windy hill above Narragansett Bay.*

Because the bay is horseshoe-shaped, the state of Rhode Island borders it on either side. This chapter is accordingly grouped into two designations, East and West, in hopes that geographical order makes more sense for drivers than alphabetical order. The communities on Aquidneck Island, excepting Newport, which has its own chapter, are included under the East Bay heading; Jamestown Island is grouped under the West Bay.

On the West Bay are the towns East Greenwich, North Kingstown, and Narragansett. Of these East Greenwich is the least tourist oriented, though over the past few years its Main Street has shaken off a decades-old sleepiness, thanks to an influx of young restaurateurs, artists, and shopkeepers. The gem of sprawling North Kingstown is Wickford, an idyllic little village on a harbor with a host of interesting shops and galleries; a new kayaking center and change in the liquor code (Wickford used to be dry) have turned it into a hopping spot. Narragansett, an old rival of Newport, maintains some of the best

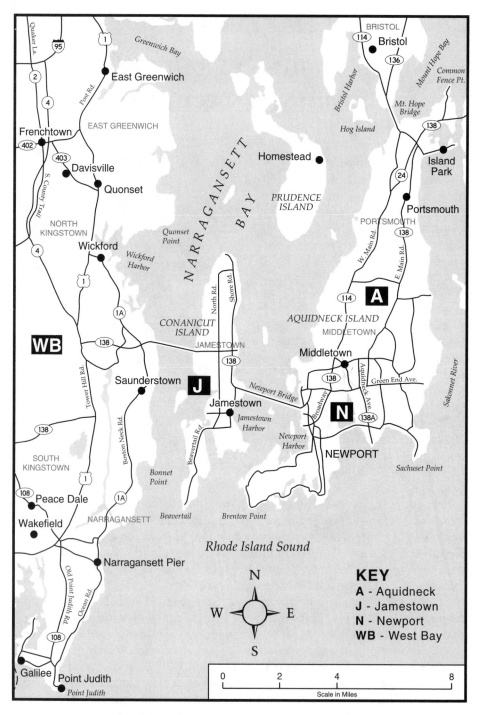

**West Narragansett Bay: West Bay and Jamestown**

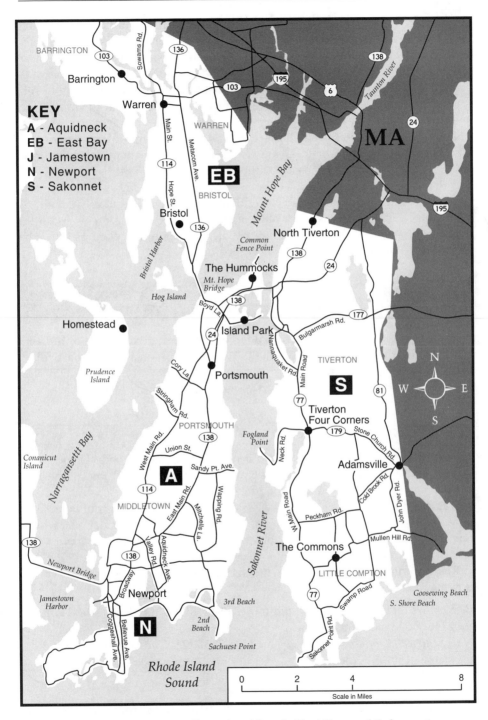

**East Narragansett Bay: Aquidneck, East Bay and Sakonnet**

turn-of-the-century beach cottages in the state and boasts a fine town beach and boardwalk, while Jamestown, also known as Conanicut Island, has succeeded in keeping a low, earthy profile despite its proximity to Newport.

On the East Bay are the northern towns of Bristol and Warren — two historic, waterfront communities with exceptional architecture from the late eighteenth and early nineteenth centuries. Bristol is the more restored and upscale of the two, with a growing art and antique profile, though Warren's sleepy, waterfront character has a rough appeal. The sprawling, farming towns of Portsmouth and Middletown share Aquidneck Island with Newport; Portsmouth also administers Hog and Prudence Islands, two little droplets of land in the bay that are ideally discovered by bicycle. In the extreme southeast of Rhode Island lie Tiverton and Little Compton, which occupy a hidden, little-known, and utterly delightful world of fields and farm stands, old homes and older cemeteries — and little else — all framed by the Narragansett Bay as a reminder that here, as throughout the state, the sea is land's constant companion.

# LODGING

While lodging is scarce in the Sakonnet region, there are more options in the East Bay and even more in the West Bay. Narragansett, in particular, used to be an upscale resort to rival Newport late last century, and it still claims a sizeable share of breezy old beach cottages, many of which are now open to guests.

## LODGING NOTES

**Tax.** Most prices are quoted without the seven percent Rhode Island sales tax; to that add another five percent room (also called bed) tax. If the full twelve percent tax is included in the price, this is noted.

**Handicap access.** This chapter's assessment of what is and is not accessible at each lodging is more casual than established government regulations, which few inns, especially those in old houses, can meet. Be sure to ask about your specific requirements.

**Reservation services.** The following services are free to folks trying to hunt down a room.

*Bed & Breakfast of Rhode Island* (401-849-1298; PO Box 3291, Newport, RI 02840) Covers the entire state.

*Narragansett Chamber of Commerce* (401-783-7121; The Towers, Ocean Rd., Narragansett, RI 02882).

## *Rates*

Rates are based on one night, double occupancy (most rooms are doubles) and reflect high-season prices (generally from Memorial Day to Labor Day).

Off-season prices are often substantially lower. I've noted the few cases in which breakfast is not included or rooms do *not* have private baths.

### *Lodging Price Code*

| | |
|---|---|
| Inexpensive | Under $60 |
| Moderate | $60 to $120 |
| Expensive | $120 to $200 |
| Very Expensive | Over $200 |

### *Credit Cards*

| | |
|---|---|
| AE — American Express | DC — Diners Club |
| CB — Carte Blanche | MC — MasterCard |
| D — Discover | V — Visa |

## *WEST*

## WEST BAY

### *Jamestown*

*The Bay Voyage Inn on Jamestown was originally built in Middleton and barged across the bay — hence the name.*

Craig Hammell

**BAY VOYAGE INN**
Manager: John Ludwick.
401-423-2100; 800-225-3522.
150 Conanicus Ave.,
    Jamestown, RI 02835.
Open: Year-round.
Price: Moderate to Very
    Expensive.
Credit Cards: AE, D, DC,
    MC, V.

The name "Bay Voyage" literally describes the history of this shingle-style beach cottage, which was hauled across the bay by steamer from Middletown in 1889 (the owner considered Jamestown more exclusive). Today its one-bedroom suites are appointed with colonial-style furniture, TVs, and telephones; kitchenettes have microwaves and coffeemakers. The atmosphere is one

Smoking: Yes.
Handicap Access: Yes.
Restrictions: No pets.
Special Features: Outdoor
 pool, exercise room,
 Jacuzzi.

step above chain hotels — it's the magnificent view that makes all the difference. Continental breakfast is served in the dining room, which is open to the public for dinner and a sumptuous Sunday brunch (see the section Dining). Ask about the "buy-back" token policy for the otherwise expensive ($2 each way) Newport Bridge.

**JAMESTOWN B&B**
Owner: Mary Murphy.
401-423-1338.
59 Walcott Ave., James-
 town, RI 02835 (no sign).
Open: Year-round.
Price: Moderate.
Credit Cards: No.
Smoking: Not encouraged.
Handicap Access: No.
Restrictions: No pets.

**M**ary's home near Jamestown village is comfortable and spacious, with three second-floor guest rooms (there's a choice of queen, full, or twin beds) that share two baths between them. The rooms aren't fancy, but attractive, airy, and spotlessly clean. Guests are welcome to use a first-floor TV room and the deck out back. Best of all, Mary cooks up a full breakfast, including those famous Rhode Island jonnycakes. A quiet, friendly, economical base for touring Newport.

## *Narragansett*

**HISTORIC HOME B&B**
Owners: Nancy & Steven
 Richards.
401-789-7746.
144 Gibson Ave.,
 Narragansett Pier, RI
 02882 (no sign).
Open: Year-round.
Price: Moderate to
 Expensive.
Credit Cards: No.
Smoking: No.
Handicap Access: No.
Restrictions: No pets, or
 children under 12.

**L**ined up as if for roll call along Gibson Ave. are some of Narragansett's loveliest old beach cottages. Just before the street dead-ends, at the left through a gap in high hedges is the loveliest house of all: a gabled stone cottage built in 1884. Secluded and veiled in ivy, it looks like a modest English manor. The interior retains an atmosphere of gracious calm. On hot afternoons, the rooms are coolly shaded by old trees and show their age honestly and charmingly by way of freestanding radiators, worn Oriental rugs, immense closets, and bathrooms with claw-foot tubs (baths are both private and shared). All four guest rooms have working fireplaces and complimentary decanters of sherry. Furnishings reflect the casual, seaside air — old and charming but not imposing. There's also a two-room suite with connecting sitting room. Work off the full breakfast by strolling through formal gardens, over the immense lawn, and along a wooded path down to the beach. Nancy's planning a new water garden for the spring of 1998.

**MON REVE**
Owners: Eva & Jim Doran.
401-783-2846.

**M**on Reve is the epitome of a Victorian beach cottage (built ca. 1890). High Victoriana reigns in the living room, with a wonderfully

41 Gibson Ave., Narragan-
sett Pier, RI 02882.
Open: Year-round.
Price: Moderate.
Credit Cards: No.
Smoking: In living room
only.
Handicap Access: No.
Restrictions: No pets.

**MURPHY'S B&B**
Owners: Martha & Kevin
Murphy.
401-789-1824.
43 South Pier Rd.,
Narragansett Pier, RI
02882.
Open: May–Oct., weekends
off-season.
Price: Moderate.
Credit Cards: No.
Smoking: Porch only.
Handicap Access: No.
Restrictions: No pets, or
children under 8.

crowded selection of paintings. Usually only four guests are accepted at a time (though the house will take more) and are given their pick of second- and third-floor rooms decorated in "country Victorian" style. Limiting the number of guests means that Eva can fuss over them and serve them a delicious full breakfast.

**M**artha Murphy is the author of *The Bed and Breakfast Cookbook*, and her full breakfasts show her expertise. She's also a seasoned traveler, and her B&B is well appointed to suit visitors' needs. Guests have the first-floor living room to themselves, including use of the big fieldstone fireplace. The second floor is reserved for the family, with guest rooms on either side of the spacious third-floor landing, insuring privacy for all. One room has a queen-sized bed, and the other has twin beds that convert to a king; both have lots of sunlight, walk-in closets, and cupboard TVs. The larger room has a view of the ocean, just a block away. This 1894 "cottage" is simply but elegantly appointed throughout, with a mix of comfy furniture, antiques, and marine art. From the hanging baskets on the front porch to Martha's map with pins marking guests' hometowns, it's a special place. See the section Bibliography in Chapter Six, *Information* for more on Martha's latest cookbook, *A New England Fish Tale*.

**THE 1900 HOUSE B&B**
Owners: Bill & Sandra
Panzeri.
401-789-7971.
59 Kingstown Rd.,
Narragansett Pier, RI
02882.
Open: Year-round.
Price: Moderate.
Credit Cards: No.
Smoking: On porch only.
Handicap Access: No.
Restrictions: No pets,
children not encouraged.

**W**hen a guest book indicates lots of return business, the owners are obviously doing something right. In this case, Bill and Sandy are being themselves: kind, friendly, fun. Their wonderful home, with a lavender front door, first- and second-floor window boxes, and pretty garden, is on a quiet side street. Of the three guest rooms, one has a private bath, the others share. Each room is unique, but all include country antiques, wooden bed frames, thick Oriental rugs, and best of all, small special touches like the marriage certificate of the original owners. The Panzeris keep updating and adding new antiques all the time. A full breakfast is served in the dining room.

**THE OLD CLERK HOUSE**
Owner: Patricia Watkins.
401-783-8008.
49 Narragansett Ave.,
  Narragansett Pier, RI
  02882.
Open: Year-round.
Price: Moderate.
Credit Cards: No.
Smoking: No.
Handicap Access: No.
Restrictions: No pets, or
  children.

Patricia is from Wales but now runs a graceful, British-style B&B in the heart of Narragansett Pier. The front walkway of this century-old home is draped with roses. Inside, the charming front parlor (reserved for guests) is filled with family heirlooms and antiques, including a splendid grandfather clock made in 1775. One guest room offers a queen-sized bed; the other, with king-sized bed and private sitting room, has two walls of nearly all windows that overlook Patricia's new backyard fishpond. Both rooms include color/cable TV with VCR; a guest refrigerator is also available. French doors open off the parlor onto a bright, plant-filled sunroom, where a three-course breakfast is served on crystal and china. All in all a warm, welcoming, gracious spot.

**STONE LEA B&B**
Owners: The Lancellotti
  family.
401-783-9546.
40 Newton Ave.,
  Narragansett Pier, RI
  02882.
Open: Year-round.
Price: Moderate.
Credit Cards: No.
Smoking: No.
Handicap Access: No.
Restrictions: No pets, or
  children under 10.

McKim, Mead, and White, who designed the Newport Casino and Rosecliff, among other landmarks, built this magisterial shingle-style cottage around 1884. It sits just south of Narragansett Pier village, alone on a bluff overlooking the ocean. Recently the Lancellotti family purchased the house and are restoring it to its former, high Victorian splendor (even to putting the kaiser peaks back on the windows). Views here are stupendous; the back porch looks across an expansive lawn to the sea and the horizon beyond. Common areas are paneled and stately, and the four spacious guest rooms are handsomely outfitted with antique Victorian furnishings; two have nonworking fireplaces. A full, hearty breakfast is served in the morning.

**TOTUS TUUS**
Owners: Chris & Diane
  Wilkens.
401-789-4785.
67 Narragansett Ave.,
  Narragansett Pier, RI
  02882 (no sign).
Open: Apr.–Oct.
Price: Moderate.
Credit Cards: No.
Smoking: Not encouraged.
Handicap Access: No.
Restrictions: No pets.

Totus Tuus is Latin for "totally yours," and that's just what this over-the-garage apartment is. With a queen-sized bedroom, living-cum-dining room that can sleep two, a small kitchen (with stove, refrigerator, and microwave), TV, and full bath, plus private deck and entrance, this is the place of choice for young families. Chris and Diane have lots of kids of their own and welcome playmates of all ages; Diane has a full supply of toys and kid gear that she's happy to loan. The apartment is light and airy, decorated in child-proof contemporary. The kitchen is stocked with fixings for a make-your-own continental breakfast.

**THE VILLAGE INN**
Manager: Pi Patel.
401-783-6767.
1 Beach St., Narragansett
Pier, RI 02882.
Open: Year-round.
Price: Expensive.
Credit Cards: AE, CB, D,
DC, MC, V.
Smoking: Nonsmoking
rooms available.
Handicap Access: Several
rooms.
Restrictions: No pets.
Special Features: Children
under 12 free.

You can't miss this one — it's the big weathered-shingle complex in Pier Marketplace, a sprawling shopping center across from Narragansett Town Beach. If you value convenience over charm, stay here. There are two restaurants on the premises (breakfast isn't included), plus an indoor pool and Jacuzzi. Each of the sixty rooms has air-conditioning, TV, and telephone and is decorated in "American motel" style. For a water view, request the third floor; first-floor verandas feature the parking lot more than the ocean.

**WHITE ROSE B&B**
Owners: Pat & Sylvan
Vaicaitis.
401-789-0181.
22 Cedar St., Narragansett
Pier, RI 02882.
Open: Year-round.
Price: Moderate.
Credit Cards: No.
Smoking: No.
Handicap Access: No.
Restrictions: No pets, or
children under 6.
Special Features: Private
charters available on the
sloop *White Rose.*

"Casual but elegant" fits the White Rose perfectly. Just a block from the beach, this big, airy Victorian has taken on the sporty and relaxed attitude of its owners. Big shade trees keep it cool; white roses twine around the back porch. Two shared-bath guest rooms are decorated in a simple, unfussy style: brass beds, hardwood floors, lace curtains, floral wallpaper. There's an upstairs sitting room with a TV and a refrigerator stocked with complimentary beer and wine. A baby grand is in the front hallway. Croquet, horseshoes, darts, bicycles, bocci, and gear for diving and fishing are also available.

### North Kingstown

**JOHN UPDIKE HOUSE**
Owners: Mary Anne & Bill
Sabo.
401-294-4905.
19 Pleasant St., Wickford,
RI 02852 (no sign).
Open: Year-round.
Price: Moderate.
Credit Cards: No.
Smoking: On deck only.
Handicap Access: No.
Restrictions: No pets.
Special Features: Private
sandy beach.

Built in 1745, the Updike House is the second oldest in Wickford. On a quiet side street, this sturdy old Georgian backs up to the waterfront, with a private beach at the end of a manicured lawn. The arrangements are conveniently flexible: rent the second floor as an apartment, or each of the two bedrooms individually (shared bath; both have fireplaces). The comfortable common room (with TV) in between the bedrooms is dominated by a huge fireplace. For an additional $15, you can have full use of the adjoining kitchen, with a washer and dryer and separate telephone. Best of all is the second-floor deck that runs the full length of the house and overlooks Wickford Harbor. A "continental-plus" breakfast is served (even if you've rented the kitchen).

### MONTE VISTA MOTOR INN
Manager: William Alamonte.
401-884-8000; 800-524-8001.
7075 Post Rd., N. Kingstown, RI 02852.
Open: Year-round.
Price: Moderate.
Credit Cards: AE, D, DC, MC, V.
Smoking: Nonsmoking rooms available.
Handicap Access: One room.
Restrictions: No pets.

If you're looking for a motel, this Best Western-run motor inn is the pick of a group of motels that cluster on Rte. 1 near Wickford. Benefits include a pool screened from the road by flowering hedges, complimentary breakfast, forty-nine clean units with cable TV, and Pastrami's Restaurant, open for breakfast and lunch.

# EAST

## AQUIDNECK

### Middletown

### ATLANTIC HOUSE B&B
Owner: John E. Flanagan.
401-847-7259.
37 Shore Dr., Middletown, RI 02842.
Open: Daylight-saving months.
Price: Moderate to Expensive.
Credit Cards: No.
Smoking: No.
Handicap Access: No.
Restrictions: No pets, or children.

The Atlantic House is built smack on the sea at Easton Point. Just to the north, the coast curls around to form First (Easton) Beach; directly opposite, the mansions line up along Newport's famous Cliff Walk. The three guest rooms aren't fancy, but they're crystal clean and filled with the smells and sounds of the sea — not to mention the jaw-dropping views. One room has a private bath, all have TVs. John, a retired lawyer, serves a full breakfast and may even show you around his law library if you ask nicely. There's also a separate apartment for rent.

### HEDGEGATE B&B
Owners: Anna & Francis Parente.
401-846-3906; 401-849-4109.
65 Aquidneck Ave., Middletown, RI 02842.
Open: Mid-May–Columbus Day.
Price: Moderate.

"Like staying at your Aunt Mary's" is how Anna describes this turn-of-the-century Dutch colonial that has been in her family for years. It has a wraparound veranda, complete with rockers, and a terrific view of Easton Pond and First (Easton) Beach. The snack bars and surfing shops of Aquidneck Ave. are nearby, but behind the Hedgegate's high namesake privets you don't notice. There are

Credit Cards: No.
Smoking: On veranda only.
Handicap Access: No.
Restrictions: No pets.

six guest rooms, basic but clean, furnished with hand-me-downs just the way beach houses used to be. The shared bath space can be tight, but there are additional facilities in a bathhouse out back. Since the owners live in an adjacent home on the property, guests have full run of the house and receive a full complimentary breakfast at a coffee shop down the street. There's a TV in the living room, but head to the gazebo-style "teahouse" in the lovely back garden instead. (All available for rent by the week.)

*Shadows really do fall across the sweeping lawns at the Inn at Shadow Lawn in Middletown.*

Craig Hammell

**INN AT SHADOW LAWN**
Managers: Selma & Randy Fabricant.
401-847-0902; 800-352-3750; Web: www.shadowlawn. com.
120 Miantonomi Ave., Middletown, RI 02842.
Open: Year-round.
Price: Expensive.
Credit Cards: AE, D, DC, MC, V.
Smoking: No.
Handicap Access: No.
Restrictions: No pets, but children welcome.

Take the "lawn" in the name seriously — an immense expanse of grass sets off this magnificent Italianate home, built by Richard Upjohn in 1853 and now on the National Register. New owners have done a superb job restoring the dining room and upstairs and downstairs hallways. Basket weave floors gleam, hand-painted friezes run brightly around the ceilings, and the original door knockers have been found and returned to place; also note the elephant skin on the library walls. Eight guest rooms (all named after Victorian writers) are bright and spacious, with working fireplaces, refrigerators, telephones, and cable TV. Furnishings don't share the grandiosity of the common rooms, which isn't a drawback; they're comfortable and familiar, like in real bedrooms. Breakfast is continental style. Despite the inn's proximity to Newport, peace reigns here. Ask the owner to tell you about the Underground Railroad connection.

**LITTLE SUMIYA B&B**
Owner: Mary Ellen Fatulli.
401-847-7859.
48 Kane Ave., Middletown,
    RI 02842.
Open: Year-round.
Price: Expensive.
Credit Cards: AE, MC, V.
Smoking: Discreet smoking
    permitted.
Handicap Access: No.
Special Features: Pool, pets
    and children welcome.

Little Sumiya means "Little House on the Corner" in Japanese. This contemporary residence in a quiet neighborhood offers two second-floor guest rooms that share a separate entrance and sitting area, with refrigerator and microwave; each has a private bath, air-conditioning, fluffy robes, and cable TV. Best of all, the rooms overlook Mary Ellen's pride and joy, a heated pool set in landscaped gardens. A gazebolike shelter at one end is laden with flowers — often frequented by hummingbirds — where full breakfast is served in the summer, including homemade Danish and other goodies. The outdoor wet bar provides drinks after your swim. Ask Mary Ellen about picnic basket lunches and have a talk with Alex, the family parrot.

**POLLY'S PLACE B&B**
Owner: Polly Canning.
401-847-2160; Web:
    www.bbonline.com/ri/p
    ollysplace/.
349 Valley Rd., Rte. 214,
    Middletown, RI 02842.
Open: Year-round.
Price: Moderate.
Credit Cards: No.
Smoking: No.
Handicap Access: No.
Restrictions: No pets, or
    children under 12.

Out on the trellis-covered back deck gazing over a meadow of wildflowers, in the new garden gazebo, or in the midst of a cookout with Polly and your friends, you'll feel miles from busy Newport, just over the town line. Polly has a true B&B — a home shared with guests. There are four bedrooms; the two upstairs have private baths, the two downstairs share. All are bright and very attractively furnished, with ceiling fans and a variety of bed sizes. Polly invites you to watch TV in her living room — take a look at the Newport Mansions video before going into town. The full breakfast usually involves fresh garden vegetables and entrées like raspberry-baked pancakes. There's also a fully-equipped basement apartment that rents weekly.

**SEA BREEZE INN**
Owners: Telly & Leeza
    Amarant.
401-849-1211; 401-846-8335.
147 Aquidneck Ave.,
    Middletown, RI 02842.
Open: Year-round.
Price: Expensive.
Credit Cards: AE, MC, V.
Smoking: Nonsmoking
    rooms available.
Handicap Access: One
    room.
Restrictions: No pets.

If you prefer to stay between First (Easton) Beach and Second Beach rather than in Newport proper, this is the motel of choice. Eight rooms are bright and comfortable, with cable TV, telephone, and air-conditioning; all but the handicap accessible room have private decks that look across busy Aquidneck Ave. to Easton Pond. Guests eat breakfast at Telly's, the Amarant's ice-cream parlor/restaurant. This spot may remind you of modern guest houses on the Mediterranean.

$109/nt.

**SEAVIEW INN**
Owners: David & Marina
Stanfield.
401-846-5000.
240 Aquidneck Ave.,
Middletown, RI 02842.
Open: Year-round.
Price: Moderate.
Credit Cards: AE, D, MC,
V.
Smoking: Nonsmoking
rooms available.
Handicap Access: Yes.
Special Features: One pet
room.

**D**on't be fooled by the Industrial Park sign — the road to the industrial complex also serves as the Seaview driveway. There's a spectacular view of Easton Pond and the ocean from Seaview's perch; you can even see Newport's famous Cliff Walk across the way. This white clapboard motel has been recently revamped, top to bottom. All forty rooms have a panoramic view, two double beds, TV, and telephone. Complimentary continental breakfast and bicycles come with an evening's stay, as well as access to a neighboring sport and fitness facility, with indoor pool.

**STONEYARD B&B**
Owner: Anne Cooper.
401-847-0494.
13 Fairview Ave.,
Middletown, RI 02842.
Open: May-mid-Nov.
Price: Moderate to
Expensive.
Credit Cards: No.
Smoking: No.
Handicap Access: No.
Restrictions: No pets, or
children.

**A**nne Cooper lovingly renovated her 1921 bungalow on a quiet, residential street in Middletown and lavished the same care on the separate-entrance apartment at the rear. This is a find for two people: attractive, private, with full bath and small kitchen (including microwave), TV, air-conditioning, and private patio. Anne equips the kitchen daily for a full, gourmet breakfast, including fresh home-baked goods and coffee beans. You can take your meal outside to the patio or to the gazebo in the garden; it's so inviting that it's easy to forget that Newport is around the corner.

## *Portsmouth*

**BEST WESTERN
BAYPOINT INN AND
CONFERENCE
CENTER**
Manager: Sarah Malik.
401-683-3600; 800-289-0404.
144 Anthony Rd.,
Portsmouth, RI 02871.
Open: Year-round.
Price: Moderate to
Expensive.
Credit Cards: AE, CB, D,
DC, MC, V.
Smoking: Nonsmoking
rooms available.
Handicap Access: Yes.
Restrictions: No pets.

**I**n addition to the eighty-five guest rooms, the Baypoint has an indoor pool, sauna, and exercise room, free movie-channel TV, and two adjacent golf courses. Bridge's Restaurant serves breakfast and dinner. Note that the motel is adjacent to the excellent golf course at Montaup Country Club (see the section Recreation, under the heading Golf).

## BROWN'S BED & BREAKFAST

Owners: Roger & Dot Brown.
401-683-0155.
502 Bristol Ferry Rd., Portsmouth, RI 02871.
Open: Year-round.
Price: Moderate.
Credit Cards: No.
Smoking: On deck only.
Handicap Access: No.
Restrictions: No pets.

Owner Dot Brown says that she "puts her heart and soul" into her guest house, and it's obvious. This weathered-shingle cottage was built at the turn of the century on three acres, with a spectacular view of Narragansett Bay. The five guest rooms, two with private bath, all with color TV, are spotlessly clean and decorated in gracious, grandmotherly style — stately but comfortable. Guests are welcome to use a lovely old-fashioned parlor but most prefer the back porch, flanked by open decks overlooking the bay. This is where the delicious full breakfast is served, which may include Dot's homemade muffins and local Portuguese specialties; try the wickedly delicious malassadas, a fried sweetbread dough. Guests return here year after year.

## WHITE CAP CABINS

Owner: Joan DeMello.
401-683-0476.
Vanderbilt Ln., Portsmouth, RI 02871.
Open: May–Oct.
Price: Inexpensive to Moderate.
Credit Cards: No.
Smoking: Yes.
Handicap Access: No.

Never was there a better place to get away from it all: a dirt and gravel lane leads through arching farmland to a copse of woods, then continues to the Sakonnet River. Three tiny, beautifully kept cabins cluster in utter privacy at the shoreline. One has just two twin beds; another is the bathroom; the third has a kitchenette, wood-burning stove, and double bed. There's no phone and no electricity; the cabins are lit with kerosene and gaslight (with rechargeable lamps for kids if they're occupying one of the sleeping cabins). Joan has also installed a new device called a Power-It that provides electricity for small appliances, including a new TV. This is the place to bring kids and pets, or go by yourself and write the great American novel. There's also a pebble beach, swing, and stone grill. Linens and towels are provided.

## EAST BAY

### *Bristol*

## BRADFORD-DIMOND-NORRIS HOUSE

Owner: Suzanne Adams.
401-253-6338.
474 Hope St., Bristol, RI 02809.
Open: Year-round.
Price: Moderate.
Credit Cards: MC, V.
Smoking: No.

Located in one of Bristol's most magnificent homes (built in 1792), the house was so artfully enlarged in the 1840s by architect Russell Warren that it became known as "The Wedding Cake House" — this B&B gets everything right. Three of the four guest rooms are ultraspacious (the fourth is cozy) and decorated with antiques to create a formal colonial atmosphere that's never stuffy nor intimi-

Handicap Access: Yes.
Restrictions: No pets, or children under 12.

dating. Just as bedrooms speak of age (despite discreet, cable TVs), brand new bathrooms speak to modern comforts. Magnificent common rooms are appointed with fireplaces, Oriental rugs, even a grand piano. A creatively prepared, full breakfast is served in the dining room. Architecture buffs should note that the new owners have undertaken a rigorous restoration campaign: the house is full of delights like intricate moldings, sidelights with etched red glass, and a Victorian wrought-iron "screen" door.

**JOSEPH REYNOLDS HOUSE B&B**
Owners: Wendy & Richard Anderson.
401-254-0230.
956 Hope St., Bristol, RI 02809.
Open: Year-round.
Price: Moderate.
Credit Cards: No.
Smoking: No.
Handicap Access: No.
Restrictions: Pets welcome, not suitable for children under 12.

The Joseph Reynolds House is the oldest three-story home in New England, as the superb hearth paneling in the parlor suggests: the lines run charmingly askew in all directions. As the National Register plaque indicates, the house was built in 1698, and plans are underway for a gala 300th anniversary celebration. Lafayette slept here (he was only twenty-one years old at the time and was mistaken for a servant), and so can you, in one of five comfortable guest rooms, only one of which doesn't have a private bath; a suite with private bath is also available. Sturdy, easy-to-live-with antiques create a warm, relaxed atmosphere. Full breakfast (as featured in *Yankee Magazine*) is a triumph of home cooking. A friendly Lab-mix pup is on hand as well.

Craig Hammell

*Rockwell House Inn is one of several elegant inns in the historic town of Bristol.*

**ROCKWELL HOUSE INN**
Owners: Debra & Steve Krohn.

The four guest rooms at the Rockwell are decorated in colonial high style with antiques that are rich and dignified yet still comfortable. Two

401-253-0040.
610 Hope St., Bristol, RI
   02809.
Open: Year-round.
Price: Moderate.
Credit Cards: AE, D, MC,
   V.
Smoking: No.
Handicap Access: Yes.
Restrictions: No pets, or
   children under 12.

rooms have gas-log fireplaces; all include hair dryers and fluffy, terrycloth bathrobes. Nightly turn-down service is optional. The full breakfast features Debra's "famous homemade granola" and a hot entrée, such as cheese-stuffed French toast. In the winter, breakfast is served by candlelight in the dining room; in the summer, it is served on the rear porch or courtyard. Afternoon tea is served between 4:00 p.m.–5:00 p.m. Guests are welcome to watch TV in the magnificent front parlor where Debra also offers sherry in the evening.

**WILLIAM'S GRANT INN**
Owners: Mike & Mary
   Rose.
401-253-4222.
154 High St., Bristol, RI
   02809.
Open: Year-round.
Price: Moderate.
Credit Cards: AE, CB, D,
   DC, MC, V.
Smoking: On back porch.
Handicap Access: No.
Restrictions: No pets, or
   children under 12.

Family heirlooms and creative touches, such as a panoramic mural of Bristol Harbor in the entrance hall, create a warm and original atmosphere at the William's Grant Inn that's both memorable and distinctive. The three bedrooms on the first floor have private baths, the two on the second-floor share; all have fireplaces and a journal in which to share thoughts with other guests. The "Middleburg Virginia Room" has walls hand-rubbed with rich, golden paint and a trim of deep plum. The common room has a piano, games, and sherry. Mike serves a full breakfast; a specialty is his famous Huevos Rancheros, made from homegrown vegetables. This is a friendly, whimsical, historic gem of an inn on a quiet stately street. The owners are delightful, as are their pets: two Terrier-mix dogs and a cat.

## Warren

**NATHANIEL PORTER
   INN**
Owners: Viola & Robert
   Lynch.
401-245-6622.
125 Water St., Warren, RI
   02885.
Open: Year-round.
Price: Moderate.
Credit Cards: AE, D, DC,
   MC, V.
Smoking: Not in bedrooms.
Handicap Access: No.
Restrictions: No pets,
   children welcome.

Built in the eighteenth century by a local sea captain, the inn is deservedly on the National Register. Its three guest rooms, two with canopied double beds and one with twin beds, slope whichever way their wide, listing floorboards lead them. The furnishings are in a straightforward Early American style. All rooms have air-conditioning, nonworking fireplaces, and share a common sitting room. Continental breakfast is included. The downstairs dining room (actually a number of small rooms) is one of the best restaurants around (see the section Dining).

## SAKONNET

### *Little Compton*

**THE ROOST**
Innkeepers: Jen & Larry.
401-635-8486, reservations;
   401-635-8407, innkeepers.
170 W. Main Rd., Little
   Compton, RI 02837 (no
   sign).
Open: Year-round.
Price: Moderate.
Credit Cards: MC, V.
Smoking: Downstairs only,
   not in rooms.
Handicap Access: No.
Restrictions: No pets, or
   children under 12.

**S**atisfying is the word to describe this 1920s cottage on the edge of Sakonnet Vineyards (bookings are made through the winery). It's simple and casual, full of sunlight and strong colors, just as a beach cottage should be. A fairly steep staircase leads to the three second-floor bedrooms, each with a queen, full, or set of twin beds. Continental breakfast is at a communal table in the sunny kitchen or on the deck out back. It's an idyllic walk to the winery or a short drive to the beach.

**THE STONE HOUSE
   CLUB**
Owners: Virginia & Tod
   Moore.
401-635-2222.
120 Sakonnet Point Rd.,
   Little Compton, RI 02837.
Open: Year-round.
Price: Moderate to
   Expensive.
Credit Cards: MC, V.
Smoking: Not in public
   rooms, discouraged in
   guest rooms.
Handicap Access: One
   room.
Restrictions: No pets.

**B**uilt in 1836 out near Sakonnet Point, this imposing granite mansion has high ceilings and walls two feet thick. There are eleven guest rooms in the main house (nine with private baths) and two more in the renovated barn, which also accommodates conferences and group events. The furnishings look seasoned rather than antique and complement the secluded, they-can't-find-me-here feel of the place. Note that this is a club: nonmembers are welcome but must add $20 to lodging and $5 to meal costs, bringing the prices up no higher than average. Continental breakfast is included with lodging. There's also a dining room in the main house (see the section Dining), a lovely pond, ocean views, and a beach within walking distance.

### *Tiverton*

**BONNIEBIELD
   COTTAGE**
Owners: Nancy &
   Raymond Lundgren.
401-624-6364.
Neck Rd., Tiverton, RI
   02878 (no sign).
Open: Year-round.
Price: Moderate.
Credit Cards: No.
Smoking: Outside only.
Handicap Access: No.

**T**his cottage behind the Lundgren's home is surrounded by flowers and shade trees, has a lawn with a fieldstone grill and a picnic table, a coop with seven purebred Rhode Island Red chickens, and a clay tennis court (bring flat tennis shoes if you want to play). The cottage is modest, pleasant, very clean, and offers a small living room with kitchenette, dining area, and full bath; a second-floor room with twin beds is bright with white wainscoting (for a little bit extra, there's a cot for a

Restrictions: No pets, or children.
Special Features: Clay tennis court.

third person). Nancy doesn't serve breakfast but often leaves fresh eggs and vegetables from the garden so guests can make their own. A short walk leads to a private beach on the Sakonnet River.

## DINING

Rhode Island is a food state. From the haute cuisine of Providence and Newport (often conjured up by graduates of the famed culinary school at Johnson and Wales University in Providence) to local favorites like coffee "cabinets" and "stuffies," people take food here very seriously. Eating well is simply a matter of mastering the local lingo: cabinets are milk shakes (frappés to some); a grinder is a submarine sandwich; jonnycakes (white cornmeal pancakes) are an old Yankee treat.

Most important of all, however, is the mighty quahog (pronounced "co-hog"). Quahogs are big, hard-shell clams, not to be confused with littlenecks (small hard-shell clams) or soft-shell clams. The quahog is frequently used to make "chowdah," of which several kinds abound. There's the classic white variety, known as New England style; the local favorite, Rhode Island Red, in a tomato-based broth; the so-called Block Island style, which comes as a clear broth; and finally seafood chowder, packed with all sorts of cooked crustaceans.

But that's not all. Get ready for fried clams (the whole plump creature), clam strips, clam cakes (these are actually fritters, about the size of a golf ball — nothing like crab cakes), and the local favorite, stuffed quahogs, universally known as stuffies (chopped clams in a bread-based stuffing, put back into the shell). The shores of Narragansett Bay are brimming over with purveyors of these delicacies from formal restaurants to seafood shacks. Note that the two poles of haute cuisine in the state, at the head and mouth of the bay, are Providence and Newport; in fact, Providence has so many innovative restaurants that I've included a list of eleven favorites at the end of this section. In between, with some exceptions, menus tend to be far more conservative and traditional. The standard by which restaurants are judged in Chapter Three, *Newport* is therefore different from that applied in this chapter.

Ethnic cooking in the bay area — generally Portuguese or Italian — features native catches, including swordfish, bluefish, lobsters, mussels, and, of course, quahogs. Throughout the nineteenth and twentieth centuries, Portuguese speakers have come to work in Rhode Island's maritime industries, and the culinary traditions that they've brought from places like the Azores, Cape Verde, and Madeira, as well as Portugal itself, still flavor local menus. Look for linguiça and chouriço (spicy garlic sausages — chouriço is hotter), malassadas (fried sweetbread dough), caldo verde (kale soup), and "blade meat" (marinated pork).

## The Quahog Stops Here

*Cartoonist Don Bosquet is a native Rhode Islander who lives in Narragansett. He claims that he once held a regular job, but one day snapped and decided to become a cartoonist. Bosquet has penned many books of cartoons lampooning life in the Ocean State, mostly starring that cute, hard-shelled crustacean, the quahog. The Quahog Stops Here (Douglas Charles Press, $8.95 pb) was Rhode Island's best-seller for 1993. More recently he's issued The Illustrated Rhode Island Dictionary, a collaboration with Providence columnist Mark Patinkin (Covered Bridge Press, $8.95 pb), The Rhode Island Album: 10 Years of Don Bosquet (Douglas Charles Press, $10.95 hc), and his latest, Don Bosquet's Next Book (Douglas Charles Press, $9.95 pb). Not surprisingly, Don Bosquet's favorite meal involves pasta and — get ready for it — seafood.*

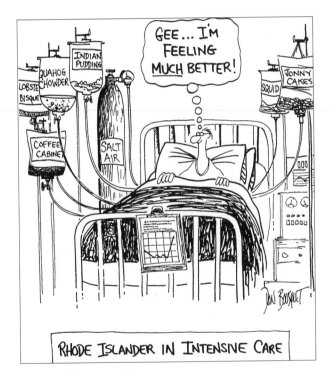

*The following restaurant listing offers a cross section of the area's many and varied eateries. The section Food & Beverage Purveyors lists the best spots for provisions for everything from gourmet picnics to essential ice-cream stops.*

*The price range reflects the cost of a single dinner meal, including appetizer, entrée, dessert, and coffee or tea. Alcoholic beverages, tax, and tip are not included in the price scale.*

## Dining Price Code

| | |
|---|---|
| Inexpensive | Up to $15 |
| Moderate | $15 to $25 |
| Expensive | $25 to $35 |
| Very Expensive | Over $35 |

## Credit Cards

| | |
|---|---|
| AE — American Express | MC — MasterCard |
| CB — Carte Blanche | T  — TransMedia |
| D  — Discover | V  — Visa |
| DC — Diner's Club | |

# WEST

## WEST BAY

### East Greenwich

**CATHAY GARDEN**
401-884-7776.
363 Main St., E. Greenwich, RI 02818.
Open: Tues.–Sun.
Price: Inexpensive.
Cuisine: Chinese.
Serving: L, D.
Credit Cards: AE, D, MC, V.
Reservations: No.
Smoking: Smoking section.
Handicap Access: Possible.

The dinner buffet is popular with locals, who arrive in surprising numbers to eat in rather than to take out; the decor is smart, and there's a full bar. A mandarin special, Moo Shi Pork (shredded meat with dried lily flowers, mushrooms, cabbage, and bamboo shoots with tortillalike pancakes) is hot, spicy, and delicious. Local business people make for a brisk lunch trade.

**THE GRILLE ON MAIN**
401-885-2200.
50 Main St., E. Greenwich, RI 02818.
Open: Daily.
Price: Moderate.
Cuisine: American.
Serving: L, D.
Credit Cards: AE, D, DC, MC, T, V.
Reservations: No.
Smoking: Smoking section.
Handicap Access: Yes.

With more eateries than you could shake a snake at, Main St. in E. Greenwich nonetheless lacked an upscale bar until The Grille on Main opened (one of four locations in RI). It's sleek and attractive, putting postmodern touches on the standard bar-and-grill theme. There's a sidewalk bistro atmosphere in-season (front windows pop out for an alfresco feeling), plus a backup bar that only opens on Fri. and Sat. nights to take up the overflow. The ubiquitous portabello mushroom makes an appearance on the menu, but nicely placed on a Caesar salad; also serves chowder, pizzas, sandwiches, and minor entrées.

## HARBORSIDE LOBSTERMANIA

401-884-6363.
33 Water St., E. Greenwich, RI 02818.
Open: Daily.
Price: Moderate.
Cuisine: Seafood/ American.
Serving: L, D.
Credit Cards: AE, D, DC, MC, V.
Reservations: Accepted.
Smoking: Smoking section.
Handicap Access: Yes.
Special Features: Early-Bird specials, 4:00 p.m.–6:00 p.m.

It's great fun to sit outside at this glorified clam shack on the East Greenwich Harbor and watch big boats get in each others' way (in fact, much of the clientele arrives by water). Choose to dine upstairs, downstairs, or al fresco. The sizeable menu has four appetizer categories: cold, hot, soups and stews, and salads — diverse options range from snail salad to scallops wrapped in bacon to excellent quahog chowder. The main menu offers sandwiches from the simple (grilled cheese) to the elaborate (lobster club), plus dinners from fish and chips to baked scrod. Summer-help service could be better, but all in all a fun spot with better-than-average seaside food.

## JIGGER'S DINER

401-884-5388.
145 Main St., E. Greenwich, RI 02818.
Open: Daily.
Price: Inexpensive.
Cuisine: American.
Serving: B, L.
Credit Cards: No.
Reservations: No.
Smoking: Yes.
Handicap Access: No.

This 1950 Worcester diner car, perpendicular to Main St., is reminiscent of an old ship's cabin inside, full of warm, mellowed wood and — a nice contrast — stainless steel counter stools (it was restored in 1992). Not a tourist hangout but a local favorite, it claims "Best East Bay Jonnycakes," and "Best Diner Breakfast" awards. Sandwiches and Blue Plate Specials are first-rate; pies, cakes, and ice cream are all homemade. In fact, the "coffee bean," full of flecks of ground-up beans, is *the* best coffee ice cream that I've ever eaten. Open from 6:00 a.m.–2:00 p.m. Mon.–Thurs.; 6:00 a.m.–8:00 p.m. Fri.; and 6:00 a.m.–1:00 p.m. Sun. Make this be the reason that you visit E. Greenwich.

## THE KENT

401-884-9855.
223 Main St., E. Greenwich, RI 02818.
Open: Daily.
Price: Inexpensive to Moderate.
Cuisine: American.
Serving: B, L, D.
Credit Cards: MC, V.
Reservations: No.
Smoking: Smoking section.
Handicap Access: Potential.

The Kent has a niche: it offers midday dinners from 3:00 p.m.–6:00 p.m., bland atmosphere, and its luncheon specials sound like they were made by Beaver's mom: meat loaf, turkey croquettes, meatballs, and liver and onions. In a word, it's an old people's restaurant. But let's not be age-discriminatory here, you can also get almost anything that you've ever desired for breakfast, one of the most inexpensive lobster rolls in RI, sandwiches from pizza to clubs, and more contemporary dinner specials on Fri. and Sat. nights. Where else have you been lately that serves homemade pudding and fruit cup for dessert?

## Jonnycakes

It's no typo: real, honest-to-goodness Rhode Island jonnycakes have no H; the spelling is actually protected by Rhode Island state law. If white cornmeal is made exclusively from White Cap Flint corn (an ancient, persnickety strain native to this area) and stone-ground in Rhode Island, it may be called "jonnycake meal" — anything else is merely the stuff that makes johnnycakes.

The name jonnycake probably derives from the colonial term "journey cakes," so named because the flat cornmeal pancakes were ideal for packing to take on the road. Typically, Rhode Islanders can't agree on how to cook their most famous homegrown product. There's the East Bay method, which produces large, thin, lacy jonnycakes that look like crêpes, and the West Bay style, which calls for smaller, thicker cakes the size of half-dollars. Every year jonnycakes are the staple of Rhode Island's traditional **"May Breakfasts."** There are thirty-five or so "breakfasts" held throughout the state on or near the first weekend of the month, sponsored by groups ranging from churches to yacht clubs. Call the Rhode Island Department of Economic Development (401-277-2601; 800-556-2484) for a list.

Believe it or not, there is a Society for the Propagation of the Jonnycake Tradition in Rhode Island (PO Box 4733, Rumford, RI 02916). You can watch jonnycake meal being ground at the following gristmills, which also offer mail-order service.

**Carpenter's Gristmill** (401-783-5483; Moonstone Beach Rd., Perryville, RI 02879) Carpenter's (ca. 1703) is the only mill that still runs on water power. The meal is available at Wickford Gourmet in Wickford, RI.

**Gray's Grist Mill** (508-636-6075; PO Box 422, Adamsville, RI 02801) Operating continuously since 1670; buy the product (as well as other flours and meals) in Gray's own shop.

**Kenyon's Gristmill** (401-783-4054; Glen Rock Rd. Usquepaug, RI 02892) The mill was built ca. 1711, but they use *alien* white corn and must call their product johnnycake meal.

*Tim McTague keeps local food traditions alive at Gray's Grist Mill, built ca. 1670, in Adamsville.*

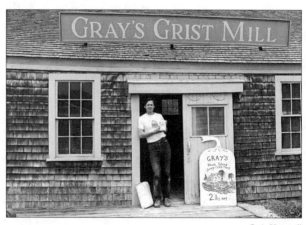

Craig Hammell

**OUTBACK
　STEAKHOUSE**
401-886-4543.
1000 Division St., E.
　Greenwich, RI 02818.
Open: Daily.
Price: Moderate.
Cuisine: Australian.
Serving: D.
Credit Cards: AE, D, MC,
　V.
Reservations: No.
Smoking: Yes.
Handicap Access: Yes.

Although part of an international conglomerate (this is one of 425 Outback Steakhouses worldwide), it's worth a mention for two reasons: one, it's a family spot located in the East Greenwich Shopping Center, opposite the big West Bay movie theater complex (good for a rainy day); and two, for rib and steak lovers, the food is an excellent value. Prime ribs, "ribs on the barbie," and a variety of steaks are all choice cuts and cooked to order, accompanied by well-prepared vegetables and Aussie chips. Kids should enjoy the Down Under theme.

**POST OFFICE CAFE**
401-885-4444.
11 Main St., E. Greenwich,
　RI 02818.
Open: Tues.–Sun.
Price: Moderate to Very
　Expensive.
Cuisine: Italian.
Serving: D.
Credit Cards: AE, D, MC, T,
　V.
Reservations: Yes.
Smoking: Smoking section.
Handicap Access: Yes.

That the cafe was once really a post office is clear from the outside and from the decor, which cleverly retains features of the building's former incarnation. The menu leans to creative Italian, reveling in exceptionally tasty pastas (note that most specials are priced higher than the regular menu). The calamari appetizer is a fine achievement, both flavorful and tender. In addition to a nicely balanced, if not extensive, wine list, desserts are worth saving room for; homemade banana-pecan ice cream served with raspberry bread pudding is to most desserts what next-day air is to snail mail. Service is prompt and efficient; unobtrusive live music on Fri. nights. A very fine restaurant.

**RAPHAEL'S BAR-RISTO**
401-884-4424.
5600 Post Rd., E.
　Greenwich, RI 02818.
Open: Tues.–Sun.
Price: Very Expensive.
Cuisine: Northern Italian.
Serving: D.
Credit Cards: AE, MC, V.
Reservations: Yes.
Smoking: Lounge only.
Handicap Access: Yes.

Raphael's began life as a *way* hip bistro in Providence; this is the suburbia version, a little less funky, a little more tasteful, quiet, bourgeois (and in a strip mall). But it's the food that counts, and that remains superb. Salads are original and fresh; appetizers range from antipasto to smoked salmon and grilled squid; entrées include pizzas, pastas, and more substantial seafood and meat dishes from roasted cod with lobster to pork chops and grilled ham. Hazelnut-crusted salmon is tasty and perfectly cooked; veal Parmigiana is served over homemade ravioli stuffed with spinach, unsmothered by sauce. Wines range in price from $16–$40, and the service is top-notch. Desserts are elegant and intense, and the atmosphere is delightful, with postmodern colors and interesting fabrics.

**TWENTY WATER STREET**
401-885-3700.
20 Water St., E. Greenwich, RI 02818.
Open: Daily.
Price: Expensive.
Cuisine: Seafood / American.
Serving: L, Mon.–Fri.; D, Mon.–Sat. (tavern daily).
Credit Cards: AE, D, DC, MC, V.
Reservations: Recommended.
Smoking: Smoking section in-season; tavern only off-season.
Handicap Access: Yes.

On historic Water St. next to a small harbor of pleasure yachts, this nineteenth-century stone building really began life as a warehouse. Now it's a sleek restaurant popular with well-to-do suburbanites (the valet-only parking lot is full of expensive sport utility vehicles). The menu leans to seafood with a few beef and chicken dishes; traditional preparations like baked-stuffed shrimp are more successful than those with innovative pretensions (chicken breast with dried cherry and hazelnut crust was a good idea poorly executed). Waitstaff on a busy summer night tends to get frazzled. Tip: ask to sit in the Sky Room, a spectacular balcony dropped from the second floor with water views on all sides. The Warehouse Tavern offers lighter fare downstairs and wharfside in-season.

## *Narragansett*

**ANGEL'S**
401-782-2300.
140 Pt. Judith Rd., Narragansett, RI 02882.
Open: Wed.-Sun.
Price: Moderate to Expensive.
Cuisine: Italian.
Serving: D.
Credit Cards: AE, MC, V.
Reservations: Yes, for 5 or more.
Smoking: Smoking section.
Handicap Access: One step.

Cherubim and seraphim are here in force: on the wallpaper, hanging from the ceiling. Perhaps they're guardians of good pasta, on which Angel's has built its reputation. Standard *cucina nuòva* dishes dominate the menu from puttanesca to four-cheese; a nice touch is paella made with orzo instead of rice. Appetizers include polenta e Gorgonzola, cozze fritte (fried squid with hot peppers), and Roman egg drop soup. Don't eat too much of the herbed bread, temptingly served with rosemary-infused olive oil; save room for homemade Italian desserts. This is a winner in a strip mall, Mariner's Square Mall.

**AUNT CARRIE'S**
401-783-7930.
1240 Ocean Rd., Pt. Judith, RI 02882.
Open: Mon.–Sun., Jun.–Labor Day.
Price: Inexpensive.
Cuisine: Seafood.
Serving: L, D.
Credit Cards: No.
Reservations: No.
Smoking: Yes.
Handicap Access: Yes.

A debate rages in Rhode Island as to who has the best clams — cakes, stuffies, fried, in chowder, you name it. Evelyn's and Flo's are the other contenders (see below). Each lady has her own adherents, but they'll all treat you well. Aunt Carrie's, which has been around for over seventy years, is in a big, old, handsome beach house, which is open, airy, and casual, with a great view of the sea from the large dining room. The bluefish special is a bargain, as are the clam cakes and chowder. Nice fresh fruit pies, too. Also has takeout and a kid's menu.

## BASIL'S

401-789-3743.
22 Kingstown Rd.,
　Narragansett Pier, RI
　02882.
Open: Wed.–Sun.
Price: Very Expensive.
Cuisine: French/
　Continental.
Serving: D.
Credit Cards: AE, MC, V.
Reservations:
　Recommended.
Smoking: No.
Handicap Access: No.

You can't miss Basil's: it's a townhouse (painted bright yellow) in a small shopping plaza, just across from Pier Marketplace. Inside, elegant French provincial decor takes over, as does a team of professional waiters who perform their tasks with alacrity and good cheer. The place is small (only ten tables), and the menu is ambitious and unashamedly unnouvelle, beginning with frogs legs and fettuccine Alfredo and moving on to duck à l'orange, steak Diane, and the house specialty, veal à la Basil's (medallions in a light cream and mushroom sauce). Béarnaise and cream sauces abound. Appropriately, the wine list features whites, and the desserts are wildly rich. Old-style, indulgent food at Newport prices.

## CASA ROSSI

401-789-6385.
90 Pt. Judith Rd.,
　Narragansett, RI 02882.
Open: Daily.
Price: Moderate.
Cuisine: Italian.
Serving: D.
Credit Cards: AE, CB, D,
　DC, MC, V.
Reservations: Yes, for 6 or
　more.
Smoking: Smoking section.
Handicap Access: Yes.

This is a find: a clapboard house marooned in a sea of miniature golf courses and fast-food joints, with authentic Italian cooking. All of the pastas are homemade, as is the excellent bread. Hard-to-find dishes turn up here like bracciola, which is rolled beef stuffed with eggs and spices. Appetizers begin with snails, squid, and antipasto. The huge menu is divided into beef, veal, chicken, and fish selections, plus lots of seafood combos over pasta. Portions are large, but leave room for the homemade cannoli, which is first-rate. Fresh gnocchi, pastas, and sauces to go.

## CHAMPLIN'S SEAFOOD

401-783-3152.
256 Great Island Rd., PO
　Box 426, Galilee, RI 02882.
Open: Daily.
Price: Inexpensive.
Cuisine: Seafood.
Serving: B, L, D.
Credit Cards: MC, V.
Reservations: No.
Smoking: Smoking section.
Handicap Access: Limited.

Galilee is the home of Rhode Island's fishing fleet, so you know that the seafood is fresh here. But where to get it can be confusing; George's (401-783-2306), right next door, is equally good, but Champlin's occupies the optimum spot at the mouth of Pt. Judith Pond. Eat inside or out on the deck, or get some fried clams or a lobster roll to eat on the way to Block Is. Order at the window and they'll call your number. Every permutation of RI seafood is here, including baked-stuffed shrimp, fried squid, stuffies, fish and chips, and chowder. The prices are right, the fish is fresh, there's a full liquor license, and you can even get breakfast or ice cream downstairs. Highly recommended retail fish market, too.

**CHEZ PASCAL**
401-782-6020.
944 Boston Neck Rd., Rte.
 1A, Narragansett, RI
 02882.
Open: Tues.-Sat.
Price: Moderate to
 Expensive.
Cuisine: French.
Serving: D.
Credit Cards: MC, V.
Reservations: Suggested.
Smoking: No.
Handicap Access: No.

If a restaurant is to be judged by the authenticity and freshness of its cuisine, the lack of pretension of its setting, and the value it offers for the money, Chez Pascal must be the finest restaurant in RI. Both the chef (Pascal) and his creations are scrupulously, indisputably *French*. Salads are simple and fresh; appetizers include Pascal's pâté of the day, plus exquisite specials like white boudin. Entrées, a classic parade of beef, fowl, fish, and poultry, are prepared with flair and humility. Confit of duck with garlic potatoes sings with flavor without being ostentatious or heavy. Pascal makes all of the desserts himself, including picture-perfect fruit tarts. The setting is simple (from the outside it looks like a trailor) but crisply and elegantly appointed. A new wine list is small but well selected.

**COAST GUARD HOUSE**
401-789-0700.
40 Ocean Rd., Narragansett
 Pier, RI 02882.
Open: Daily.
Price: Expensive.
Cuisine: Seafood /
 Continental.
Serving: L, D, SB.
Credit Cards: AE, CB, D,
 DC, MC, V.
Reservations: Yes, for 8 or
 more.
Smoking: Nonsmoking
 section with limited
 water view.
Handicap Access: Yes.

You can't get much closer to the water than this. The Coast Guard House was built in 1888 as a lifesaving station just feet from Narragansett Bay — the main dining room offers one of the best water views in the state. With this location, the food doesn't have to be good, but it is. Sole Véronique in a delicate white sauce with green grapes and grilled swordfish with honey-mustard glaze are both delicious. For nonfish lovers, there are plenty of other options. The decor is surprisingly elegant for a waterfront place, but beware: it can get noisy. The outdoor rooftop bar has lighter fare and was named by *Rhode Island Monthly* as the best waterfront bar in RI.

**OCEAN VIEW CHINESE**
401-783-9070.
140 Pt. Judith Rd.,
 Narragansett, RI 02882.
Open: Wed.–Mon.
Price: Inexpensive.
Cuisine: Chinese.
Serving: L, D.
Credit Cards: No.
Reservations: No.
Smoking: Smoking section.
Handicap Access: No.

In Mariner's Square Mall, this is *the* Chinese place in the West Bay — people even come from Newport for the authentic mandarin and Szechuan specials. The menu is enormous and virtually every choice is a good one, with great service, fair prices, and takeout. (Tip: pick up a couple of pint containers on the way to Block Is., where there is no Chinese food.)

## PANCHO O'MALLEY'S

401-782-2299.
140 Pt. Judith Rd.,
   Narragansett, RI 02882.
Open: Daily.
Price: Inexpensive.
Cuisine: Mexican/
   American.
Serving: L, D.
Credit Cards: AE, D, DC,
   MC, V.
Reservations: No.
Smoking: Nonsmoking
   room.
Handicap Access: Yes.

How postmodern: Pancho O'Malley's calls itself "an Irish pub with Mexican grub," which is exactly right. Located in Mariner's Square Mall, the bar has two TVs, and the decor is unassuming, but once the drinks arrive you'll know that you're in a spot that cares about quality. The margaritas are full-flavored and generous, and the sangria is homemade; a creative palate lies behind on-tap beers. The Mexican menu doesn't wander out of the ordinary, but nothing is skimped. The chicken quesadilla oozes with cheese and tender pieces of fajita-grilled chicken; cheese enchiladas sizzle as they should. If the taste isn't scruptiously *authentic*, no matter, this is New England, which means that the chowder and fish and chips are good, too. Live Irish entertainment on Sun. afternoons.

## SPAIN

401-783-9770.
1144 Ocean Rd.,
   Narragansett Pier, RI
   02882.
Open: Daily.
Price: Expensive to Very
   Expensive.
Cuisine: Spanish.
Serving: D.
Credit Cards: AE, D, DC,
   MC, V.
Reservations: Yes, for 6 or
   more.
Smoking: Smoking section.
Handicap Access: Yes.

Although Spain has moved down the street from its former location — it's now one block from the sea, without a view — the kitchen still offers that rare treat: authentic Spanish cuisine on the RI coast. Paella for two is available only on Fri. and Sat. nights; be prepared to wait. The dish brims full of blue mussels, shrimp, scallops, chicken, clams, chouriço (spicy sausage), and a whole lobster — it makes a second meal the next day. Also on hand is chicken breast stuffed with artichokes in tequila sauce, monkfish with shrimp and clams in marinara, and salmon fillets with crab, shrimp, and scallops. End the meal with a perfect cup of espresso and a slice of flan. Service is stately (slow), but always utterly professional. A new Spanish restaurant has filled Spain's former quarters. Don't confuse the two.

## THE STEAK LODGE

401-789-1135.
945 Boston Neck Rd., Rte.
   1A, Narragansett, RI
   02882.
Open: Daily, D; Wed.–Sun.,
   L.
Price: Moderate to
   Expensive.
Cuisine: American.

This log cabinlike "lodge" has a wonderful ocean view and a pretty, linen-tablecloth look that belies the rustic exterior. The beef dishes are available with a variety of house sauces. Prices are low, and quality is high — carnivores will have a field day here. Other red meats, chicken, and seafood are also on the menu, as is a very reasonable children's selection. This is a family restaurant

Serving: L, D.
Credit Cards: MC, V.
Reservations: Accepted.
Smoking: Smoking section.
Handicap Access: No.

## WOODY'S
401-789-9500.
Pier Marketplace,
    Narragansett Pier, RI
    02882.
Open: Wed.–Sun., D.
Price: Expensive to Very
    Expensive.
Cuisine: Creative
    American.
Serving: D.
Credit Cards: MC, V.
Reservations: Yes.
Smoking: No.
Handicap Access: Yes.

### North Kingstown

## GREGG'S
401-294-5700.
4120 Quaker Ln., Rte. 2., N.
    Kingstown, RI 02852.
Open: Daily.
Price: Inexpensive.
Cuisine: American.
Serving: L, D.
Credit Cards: AE, D, MC, V.
Reservations: No.
Smoking: Smoking section.
Handicap Access: Yes.

## RED ROOSTER TAVERN
401-884-1987; 401-295-8804.
7385 Post Rd., Rte. 1., N.
    Kingstown, RI 02852.
Open: Tues.–Sun.
Price: Moderate to
    Expensive.
Cuisine: Continental/
    American.
Serving: D.
Credit Cards: AE, D, DC,
    MC, V.
Reservations:
    Recommended.
Smoking: Smoking section.
Handicap Access: Yes.

with sophistication and a view: a rare thing in a fast-food world.

What Woody's lacks in space (there are only twelve tables), it makes up for in supremely imaginative cuisine. For starters, the tapas menu includes masterpieces like the Mezza Platter, with spicy white beans, olives, roasted reds, tomato relish, and goat cheese, served with flat bread, or, if that's not enough, grilled scallops in crispy tortillas with smooth avocado-corn relish. The main menu — fetchingly called "Birds, Grains, Animals, and Swimmer" — cooks up pistachio-crusted lamb, yellowfin tuna, grilled and smoked pork chop in black currant sauce, and vegetarian options. Happily, this is a restaurant that's all about food.

It's too resolutely cheerful, and the big, laminated menu is overwhelming, with its vast selection of sandwiches (from clubs to grilled cheese to New York combos like corned beef and chopped liver), salads, burgers, daily specials, pastas, and dinners, most for under $10. But desserts are the real reason to go to Gregg's. The cakes and pies are the most gloriously, wantonly luscious that you've ever seen. Get a slice or buy a whole one to go (see the display case). Better yet, skip lunch entirely and just indulge.

A RI tradition, the Red Rooster Tavern is a throwback in both menu and decor to a time before the 1980s, when words like "trendy" and "nouvelle" didn't refer to restaurants. Prices are far lower than those at fashionable Newport eateries. With some exceptions, like sole baked with bananas, grapefruit juice, and curry, the menu is traditional; the baked seafood platter still comes with Ritz cracker topping. The grilled chicken with roasted red peppers and sausage is very good — not outstanding, but good enough to make the Red Rooster a terrific deal. The award-winning wine list was named one of the best in the country by *Wine Spectator* magazine. Don't miss the Grape-Nut pudding, chosen "best traditional dessert" in the state. Early-Bird specials.

**SEAPORT TAVERN**
401-294-5771.
16 W. Main St., Wickford, RI 02852.
Open: Daily, L; Wed.–Sat., D.
Price: Moderate to Expensive.
Cuisine: International.
Serving: L, D.
Credit Cards: AE, D, MC, V.
Reservations: Yes.
Smoking: Outside only.
Handicap Access: Yes.

Now that it's no longer dry, Wickford should become a mecca for good restaurants. It's picturesque, upscale, and locals and tourists alike possess sophisticated palates. The Seaport Tavern, nestled onto a dock overlooking the tidal inlet opposite Wickford Harbor, is the first to fill the void. Word on the food is uneven; reports so far claim that the pasta with pink Alfredo sauce is utterly delightful, the Caesar salads are not-so-great, and a chicken dish was dry. This said, it's the tavern's first season in a glorious location: give it a chance. Also pastas, sandwiches, and, a nice plus, a fine selection of ports.

Craig Hammell

*Not the cartoon character but Pauline Bacon, pictured here with her husband Raymond, is in charge of Snoopy's Diner in North Kingstown.*

**SNOOPY'S DINER**
401-295-1533.
4015 Quaker Ln., Rte. 2, N. Kingstown, RI 02852.
Open: Daily.
Price: Inexpensive.
Serving: B, L.
Credit Cards: MC, V.
Smoking: Yes.
Handicap Access: No.

This classic Art Deco diner is done up inside and out in gleaming stainless steel and lustrous, mint green tiles. Owner Snoopy serves up wonderful diner fare in the form of meat loaf sandwiches and hearty plates of steak and eggs for breakfast (not to mention all kinds of pancakes and waffles, available all day). The diner is open from 4:00 a.m.–3:00 p.m., except Fri. and Sat., when it's open from 11:00 p.m. the previous evening until 3:00 p.m. the next day. Eat in a booth or on one of the spin-around counter stools.

**WICKFORD GOURMET**
401-295-8190.
21 W. Main St., Wickford,
  RI 02852.
Open: Daily.
Price: Inexpensive.
Cuisine: Café.
Serving: B, L.
Credit Cards: AE, MC, V.
Reservations: No.
Smoking: No.
Handicap Access: No.

The sights and aromas at this gourmet shop and café — chocolate truffles, more kinds of olives than you can pronounce, rich, dark bins of coffee beans, cheeses with rinds like topographical maps — create a sensory overload of the best kind. The tiny but tasty eat-in/take-out café has the most upscale, imaginative fare in Wickford. Don't overlook the catalogue of made-up gift baskets. Also has terrific kitchen and tableware, including work by acclaimed local potter Thomas Ladd.

## Jamestown

**BAY VOYAGE INN**
401-423-2100.
150 Conanicus Ave.,
  Jamestown, RI 02835.
Open: Mon.–Sat., D; SB
  only.
Price: Very Expensive.
Cuisine: Classic
  Continental.
Serving: D, SB.
Credit Cards: AE, D, DC,
  MC, V.
Reservations:
  Recommended.
Smoking: No.
Handicap Access: Yes.

Known for its mammoth brunch, the Bay Voyage Inn is a treat restaurant, good for anniversaries and parental birthdays. Believe it or not, this shingle-style cottage was barged across the bay from Middletown in 1889 (see the section Lodging); the dining room offers compelling sea views from all angles. The all-buffet brunch, with a prix fixe of $15.95, includes both breakfast and lunch offerings, plus made-to-order omelettes and waffles, also trifles and elegant cakes. Vegetarians beware. Dinner options are grand in the traditional style: Caesar salad for two (tossed tableside), lobster Thermidor, rack of lamb, grilled Angus sirloin, stuffed jumbo shrimp, roast duck framboise, veal piccata. The oysters on the half-shell appetizer is a standout. A tavern menu offers lighter fare, plus modest dinners.

**CHOPMIST CHARLIE'S**
401-423-1020.
40 Narragansett Ave.,
  Jamestown, RI 02835.
Open: Daily.
Price: Mostly moderate.
Cuisine: Seafood.
Serving: L, D.
Credit Cards: AE, MC, V.
Reservations: No.
Smoking: Smoking section.
Handicap Access: Yes.

Here's the new kid on the seafood block, come to give the Oyster Bar (see below) a run for its money. Traditional favorites are well represented: all manner of broiled and fried seafood; a veal, chicken, and steak option for landlubbers; and barbecue pork and cheese steak sandwiches for lunch, plus some nice twists. Adventurers look for marinated conch salad, Zeek's lobster bisque (Zeek's is a local fish/bait market), and Block Is. swordfish nuggets in a special sauce, as the standout appetizer. The atmosphere is low-key and informal, as befits the island.

**JAMESTOWN OYSTER BAR**
401-423-3380.
22 Narragansett Ave.,
Jamestown, RI 02835.
Open: Daily, D; Sat.-Sun.,
L.
Price: Moderate to
Expensive.
Cuisine: Seafood.
Serving: L, D.
Credit Cards: AE, MC, V.
Reservations: No.
Smoking: Smoking section.
Handicap Access: Yes.

Some locals won't go anywhere else to celebrate an occasion. This, they say, is an unsung wonder, far from the crowds, formality, and high prices of Newport. Appetizers include RI "stuffies" (stuffed quahogs), lobster ravioli, fried calamari, and, of course, oysters. Best of all is the grilled, broiled, and blackened seafood, though you can also get inexpensive items like fish and chips, burgers, and sandwiches. The "raspberry bash," a concoction of chocolate cake, white chocolate, and raspberries, is out of this world. Both the staff and clientele are friendly and informal. This is the island's time-honored seafood spot.

*The Schoolhouse Cafe is one of several restaurants clustered together on Narragansett Avenue in Jamestown village.*

Craig Hammell

**SCHOOLHOUSE CAFE**
401-423-1490.
14 Narragansett Ave.,
Jamestown, RI 02835.
Open: Daily.
Price: Moderate to
Expensive.
Cuisine: American.
Serving: B, L (Sat.), D, SB.
Credit Cards: AE, MC, V.
Reservations: Suggested.
Smoking: Bar only.
Handicap Access: No.

Even though it's one of the few "upscale" places in town, the Schoolhouse Cafe is right at home on Jamestown, which is a decidedly laidback place. The dining room is airy and casual (it really was a one-room schoolhouse and general store, built in 1829), and the food and prices are both middle-of-the-road. The evening menu rounds up usual suspects from sirloin and chicken to seafood and pasta, all well prepared with French and Italian influences. Sunday brunch serves up creative options, including French toast made from Portuguese sweetbread. Two tries found the service friendly but incompetent.

**TRATTORIA
  SIMPATICO**
401-423-3731.
13 Narragansett Ave.,
  Jamestown, RI 02835.
Open: Daily, D; Wed.–Sun.,
  L.
Price: Very Expensive.
Cuisine: Northern Italian.
Serving: L, D.
Credit Cards: AE, MC, V.
Reservations:
  Recommended.
Smoking: Smoking section.
Handicap Access: Yes.
Special Features: Jazz
  in-season on the terrace.

Other than pizza places, Trattoria Simpatico is the only "ethnic" restaurant on Jamestown; yet despite the lack of competition, it offers the best Italian fare around. Two beige-toned dining rooms, a screened-in porch, and a shady terrace, with outdoor bar and grilling area, set a relaxing tone. The kitchen specializes in wrapping local fish and produce in earthy-but-elegant Mediterranean presentations: delicate calamari, sweet littlenecks with zesty relish, poached pear and prosciutto salad, with Gorgonzola, walnuts, and champagne vinaigrette. Main dishes concentrate on pasta (fresh tagliatelle with shrimp and scallops) and fish, but include hearty meat fare as well. Portions are large, and desserts are picturesque. This is an ideal choice for a *leisurely* meal.

## EAST

## AQUIDNECK

### *Middletown*

**ANDREW'S**
401-848-5153.
909 E. Main Rd., Rte. 138.,
  Middletown, RI 02842.
Open: Daily.
Price: Expensive.
Cuisine: Eclectic American.
Serving: L, D, SB.
Credit Cards: AE, MC, V.
Reservations:
  Recommended.
Smoking: Smoking section.
Handicap Access: Yes (not
  facilities).
Special Features: Early-
  Dinner Club, Mon.–
  Thurs., 4:30 p.m.–6:30
  p.m., $9.95; Sizzling
  Steaks, Sun., 3:00 p.m.–
  9:00 p.m.; Reservations
  advised for both.

Not enough can be said in praise of Andrew's. Despite its unlikely location — on Middletown's nursery flats, in a former car showroom — the food, served ultrafresh in enormous portions, is utterly delicious. Innovative twists are given to familiar fare: starters include fried calamari with Dijon pecans and balsamic vinegar sauce, and seafood nachos; salads are crisp and served with homemade dressing; meat, poultry, and seafood entrées are simply and perfectly prepared; and pastas are hearty and original. Wines include neighboring Newport Vineyards offerings, and desserts are not to be overlooked — the raspberry chocolate ice-cream pie is pure heaven. Recommendation: portions are so generous that it's wise to order a selection of appetizers.

**CODDINGTON
  BREWING COMPANY**
401-847-6690.

It looks like a chain restaurant (a Chili's or an Applebee's), and it's in an awkward location for the Newport tourist trade. But the great copper

210 Coddington Hwy.,
   Middletown, RI 02842.
Open: Daily.
Price: Inexpensive to
   Moderate.
Cuisine: American.
Serving: L, D.
Credit Cards: AE, MC, V.
Reservations: No.
Smoking: Smoking section.
Handicap Access: Yes.

vats visible behind glass remind you that Coddington's is a unique enterprise. Accordingly, the beer at this microbrewery is excellent; try the five-glass sampler or the mellow pale ale. The immense menu serves up everything from pizzas to pastas to ribs, plus dinners, including sirloin in a whisky cream sauce, and a few atypical items like souvlaki and German sausage platter. Fish and chips are fresh and lightly battered; the chicken barbecue sandwich falls flat. Two pool tables are in the smoking area.

Craig Hammell

*Old-fashioned seafood with a smile at Johnny's Atlantic Beach Club in Middletown.*

## JOHNNY'S ATLANTIC BEACH CLUB
401-847-3059.
53 Purgatory Rd.,
   Middletown, RI 02842.
Open: Daily.
Price: Moderate.
Cuisine: Seafood.
Serving: L, D.
Credit Cards: AE, D, DC,
   MC, V.
Reservations: Yes.
Smoking: Section available.
Handicap Access: One step.

The high tide hurricanes of 1938 and 1954 swept Johnny's away; the current incarnation is built on a sturdy concrete foundation, which is a good thing, since Johnny's deserves to be around a while. It's a seafood restaurant of the old school: red vinyl-covered captain's chairs, mounted game fish on the walls, a superb location on the beach, and classic seafood dishes from fried scallops to broiled lobster served with a big scoop of coleslaw. The seafood kabob (swordfish, shrimp, and scallops) is modest in size but tasty.

## SEA SHAI
401-849-5180.
747 Aquidneck Ave.,
   Aquidneck Green 1B,
   Middletown, RI 02842.

Japanese food-loving friends tried this restaurant and pronounced it the very best that they've been to on the East Coast. Describing the decor as "Laura Ashley goes Japanese," they nonetheless claimed the flowered tablecloths, pastels, and sushi

Open: Daily.
Price: Expensive.
Cuisine: Japanese / Korean.
Serving: L, D.
Credit Cards: AE, MC, V.
Reservations: Accepted.
Smoking: Patio only.
Handicap Access: Yes.

bar made for a lovely, tranquil atmosphere. They began with eel sushi and sunomono (raw fish with vinegared seaweed) and miso soup — all perfectly prepared — then moved to Korea, so to speak, for main courses. Cod stew arrived in a spicy fish broth, with tofu chunks and kinchee, a pickled cabbage, on the side; chicken in Korean ginger sauce was expertly flavored, delicate yet potent. Maintaining Asian tradition, desserts are minimal: ginger, green tea, and fried ice cream, all excellent. Full-bar service includes Sapporo and other Japanese beers.

**TITO'S CANTINA**
401-849-4222.
651 W. Main Rd., Rte. 114,
  Middletown, RI 02842.
Open: Daily.
Price: Inexpensive.
Cuisine: Mexican.
Serving: L, D.
Credit Cards: AE, D, MC,
  V.
Reservations: No.
Smoking: No.
Handicap Access: Yes.

How can you beat good, cheap Mexican food in a setting that's a cross between burger chain and Mexican kitsch? Tito's bills itself as a "Mexican Quick-Service Cantina" — a good description. The Bandito Burrito, a sixteen-ounce monster with the works, is a real crowd pleaser; Tito's quesadilla is also very tasty. In addition to a wide variety of tacos, fajitas, burritos, and the like, there's also a "Little Amigos" menu and a selection of desserts from flan to chimi-chiquita (deep-fried banana in a flour tortilla with chocolate sauce). Wine and Mexican beer and Tito's own brand of tortilla chips and salsa are on hand, plus there's takeout.

## Portsmouth

**15 POINT ROAD**
401-683-3138.
15 Point Rd., Portsmouth,
  RI 02871.
Open: Wed.–Sun.
Price: Moderate.
Cuisine: American
  Bistro / Continental.
Serving: D.
Credit Cards: D, MC, V.
Reservations: No.
Smoking: No (flexible).
Handicap Access: Yes.

The big picture windows in 15 Point Road command a fabulous view of the Sakonnet River, with little Stone Bridge Marina in the foreground; the interior is decorated in fresh, contemporary colors and light woods. Seafood predominates among the signature specials, which include cod Mediterranean sautéed with peppercorns, capers, black olives, green onions, garlic, and white wine. Pasta concoctions are certainly passable, but not memorable. Char-grilled specials and traditional New England favorites are also on hand. If you have to wait for a table at the bar, try the fabulous deluxe margarita.

**THE MELVILLE GRILLE**
401-683-2380.
East Passage Yachting
  Center, Portsmouth, RI
  02871.

In the 1940s, the Mosquito Fleet, the Navy's elite team of PT boat crews, trained here. Before that the East Passage Yachting Center was a resort called Portsmouth Grove, though now only the

Open: Daily.
Price: Moderate.
Cuisine: American.
Serving: L, D.
Credit Cards: D, MC, V.
Reservations: Accepted.
Smoking: Smoking section.
Handicap Access: Patio
  only.
Special Features: Free
  dockage while you eat.

**SEA FARE INN**
401-683-0577.
3352 E. Main Rd., Rte. 138,
  Portsmouth, RI 02871.
Open: Tues.–Sun.; closed
  Sun. off-season.
Price: Very Expensive.
Cuisine: Creative
  Continental/American/
  Greek.
Serving: D.
Credit Cards: AE, MC, V.
Reservations:
  Recommended.
Smoking: One smoking
  room.
Handicap Access: Yes.

**EAST BAY**

*Bristol*

**AIDAN'S PUB**
401-254-1940.
5 John St., Bristol, RI 02809.
Open: Daily.
Price: Inexpensive to
  Moderate.
Cuisine: Irish/American.
Serving: L, D, Sat.–Sun.
  Brunch.
Credit Cards: AE, MC, V.
Smoking: Yes.
Handicap Access: Yes.

naval heritage remains. But for the pleasure yachts, it still looks like a base; the grille even occupies a Quonset hut and is decorated in World War II memorabilia. While the lunch menu is served all day, don't miss dinner, which includes chicken, seafood, and pasta offerings. Lemon goat cheese ravioli served with grilled vegetables is a gourmet bargain. The same goes for the Seafood Sauté, but save room for the Depth Charge: a chocolate macaroon cookie with vanilla ice cream and chocolate chips. The waitstaff serves with pride and courtesy.

Master Chef George Karousos is a recipient of the prestigious Ambassador Award from the International Institute for Dining Excellence. One visit and you'll want to give him a medal, too. Karousos calls himself a "culinary archaeologist" and is fond of reinterpreting standard recipes, using only fresh seasonal ingredients and light sauces. A starter of baked mushrooms stuffed with lobster and the entrée of poached salmon in lemon wine sauce with scallops and clams are heavenly. Homemade Greek yogurt with raspberries is a perfect ending. Try the house dressing with feta for the salad and the house potatoes, mashed with bacon, asparagus, and other wonderful tidbits. Choose between seven elegant, antique-filled dining rooms, all in a richly renovated Victorian mansion in a parklike setting. Despite the grandeur, this family-run restaurant is warm and friendly.

Aidan's is an ideal hybrid: an Irish pub with American spit and polish. The smoke is authentic, but the lace curtains and light woods are very New World. The food follows suit. You can get chowder, clam cakes, and burgers, but also a host of Irish specialties like shepherd's pie, a corn beef dinner (Thurs.), banger's and mash, Irish mixed grill, etc. This is *real* pub food: tinned peas, wonderous, creamy mashed potatoes, Irish link sausages. And, of course, there's a sea of beers on tap, served in imperial pints. A lovely Irish brunch on weekends features rashers and bangers, black-and-white pudding, Irish brown bread, and a pot of tea.

**THE LOBSTER POT**
401-253-9100.
121 Hope St., Bristol, RI
  02809.
Open: Tues.-Sun.
Price: Expensive.
Cuisine: Seafood.
Serving: L, D.
Credit Cards: AE, CB, D,
  DC, MC, V.
Reservations: Suggested.
Smoking: Smoking section.
Handicap Access: Yes.

Again and again The Lobster Pot is rated best seafood restaurant in RI. The terrific bay views remind you why: everything from bouillabaisse (the house specialty — there's also a vegetarian variety) to scallops Nantucket (baked with cheddar cheese and sherry) is straight-off-the-boat fresh. You could make a meal of escargot, smoked salmon, crab cakes, or calamari, and these are only the appetizers. Entrée options include baked-stuffed lobster, surf-and-turf dishes, and a personal clambake ($25). Featured on the extensive wine list are half a dozen RI selections. It's no criticism that this isn't a trendy place — the slightly old-fashioned atmosphere is just right.

**QUITO'S**
401-253-9040.
411 Thames St., Bristol, RI
  02809.
Open: Wed.–Sun.
Price: Inexpensive.
Cuisine: Seafood.
Serving: L, D.
Credit Cards: MC, V.
Reservations: No.
Smoking: Yes.
Handicap Access: Yes.

Quito's used to be a wee shack of a fish market clinging to Bristol Harbor, where you could also get good fried seafood; the booths were lumpy, and the ceiling leaked when it rained. Now it's gussied up a bit: new shingles, new roof, outdoor seating under a canopied deck. The fish market's still in the back. But the fresh seafood is the same as ever — flaky, fresh, perfectly cooked to eat in or to take out. Also offers red-and-white chowder, ice cream, and wine and beer — an endearing spot with a good kitchen.

**REDLEFSEN'S
  ROTISSERIE AND
  GRILL**
401-254-1188.
425 Hope St., Rte. 114,
  Bristol, RI 02809.
Open: Tues.–Sat., L;
  Tues.–Sun., D.
Price: Moderate to
  Expensive.
Cuisine: Grill/Continental.
Serving: L, D.
Credit Cards: AE, CB, D,
  MC, V.
Reservations: Accepted.
Smoking: Smoking section.
Handicap Access: Yes.

Originally a German restaurant, Redlefsen's has branched out into pastas and grilled fare; in fact, sadly, Wiener schnitzel is the only German entrée left on the menu. Most preparations are straightforward and well prepared: chicken, veal, fish, and steak, plus a house specialty, delicate pasta puttanesca (also served with chicken breast). The bistro and lunch menus offer lighter versions of similar fare. The European bistro atmosphere is charming: strings of white lights and a forest green tin ceiling, with lace curtains on large, storefront windows. This is a restaurant with a conscience; it's too bad that the trade couldn't support a more unique, ethnic menu.

**THE SANDBAR**
401-253-5485.
775 Hope St., Rte. 114,
  Bristol, RI 02809.
Open: Daily.
Price: Inexpensive.
Cuisine: Seafood / Italian /
  Portuguese.
Serving: L, D.
Credit Cards: No.
Reservations: No.
Smoking: Yes.
Handicap Access: One step.

The Sandbar is small, busy, unpretentious (Formica tables, vinyl chairs, cigarette smoke), and cheap. The food isn't subtle, but it's tasty. Though seafood lovers could do better elsewhere — fried clams are a little like rawhide, scallops are overcooked, shrimp are lost in a sea of heavy batter — the fare is perfect for squeamish fish eaters like me. In addition to fried seafood, The Sandbar offers two kinds of clam chowder, sandwiches, and entrées, ranging from pastas and lasagna to baked fish Portuguese style (the latter is tender and fresh if lacking zip). A local favorite.

**S.S. DION**
401-253-2884.
520 Thames St., Bristol, RI
  02809.
Open: Mon.-Sat.
Price: Moderate.
Cuisine: Seafood /
  American.
Serving: D.
Credit Cards: AE, CB, DC,
  MC, V.
Reservations: Suggested.
Smoking: Bar only.
Handicap Access: Yes.

The S.S. Dion isn't a former steamship, though the bay views from its front windows are almost as good as if you were standing on deck. "S.S." refers to owners Sue and Steve Dion, who keep their regulars happy with unchallenging, well-prepared seafood served in a modern dining room with nautical accents, including a tank of gargantuan carp. A selection of fresh grilled fish is the house specialty, which comes with a choice of homemade sauces. More elaborate concoctions include scrod stuffed with fresh crabmeat in a creamy Romano sauce; nonseafood dishes receive equal attention. There's also lighter fare to offset the rich desserts. Dinner-for-two bargains Wed. and Thurs.

**"TWEET'S" (aka
  BALZANO'S)**
401-253-9811.
180 Mt. Hope Ave., Bristol,
  RI 02809.
Open: Daily in-season; in
  winter Fri.–Sun. only, L.

Tweet's is greatly beloved as *the* RI family restaurant. Everyone comes here — kids, moms, dads, grandparents, politicians — to down heaping plates of spaghetti ordered by the pound. All the traditional dishes are on hand from lasagna to manicotti, plus a host of seafood choices. It's noisy and

---

### Dinner Cruise

**Bay Queen Dinner Cruises** (401-245-1350; 800-439-1350 in Rhode Island; 461 Water Street, Warren, Rhode Island 02885) Have lunch, brunch, or dinner buffet aboard the sleek dining ship *Vista Jubilee*. The brunch cruise puts you ashore for two hours in Newport; the lunch trip offers a narrated tour of Newport Harbor; and the dinner cruise has dancing. Charters available for private parties. May through December.

Price: Inexpensive.
Cuisine: Italian.
Serving: L, D.
Credit Cards: AE, MC, V.
Reservations: Yes, for 8 or
  more.
Smoking: Lounge only.
Handicap Access: Yes.

## _Warren_

**BULLOCKS**
401-245-6502.
50 Miller St., Warren, RI
  02885.
Open: Daily.
Price: Mostly Inexpensive.
Cuisine: American.
Serving: D.
Credit Cards: MC, V.
Reservations: Yes, for 6 or
  more.
Smoking: Yes.
Handicap Access: Yes.

**NATHANIEL PORTER
  INN**
401-245-6622.
125 Water St., Warren, RI
  02885.
Open: Daily, D; Mon.–Fri.,
  L.
Price: Expensive.
Cuisine: Gourmet
  American.
Serving: L, D, SB.
Credit Cards: AE, CB, D,
  DC, MC, V.
Reservations: Strongly
  recommended.
Smoking: Accommodated
  when possible.
Handicap Access: Yes (not
  facilities).

absolutely packed with people, and there's not a porcini mushroom or sun-dried tomato in sight.

**B**ullocks is highly recommended as the best place in Warren to get a sandwich or light meal. Easy to miss, it _is_ the charming, European-looking spot half-covered in ivy, with awning-shaded outdoor tables bordered by lovely flower boxes (it's hard to see the sign). There's a handsome bar and more tables inside in the small, warmly lit dining room. Soups, salads, and sandwiches are offered, plus a short and simple dinner menu, augmented by nightly specials. The lobster roll, studded with huge chunks of fresh lobster, is one of the best bargains anywhere; the Marsala burger, served with mushrooms on a locally baked Portuguese muffin, was deservingly voted best in the state by _Rhode Island Monthly_.

**W**ith all of the magnificent eighteenth-century homes in RI, you'd think more would be occupied by restaurants, but the Nathaniel Porter Inn is one of only a few. The current owner, a descendant of the sea captain who built the house in 1795, has restored it to the highest standards. Several small dining rooms are decorated with antiques and glow with candlelight; in the winter, blazing fireplaces add to the atmosphere. A well-rounded menu offers starters, including seafood chowder (a house specialty), smoked mussels, and grilled shrimp Caesar salad; entrées range from smoked filet mignon with hazelnut sauce to nut-crusted trout. For dessert, the Bartlett pear baked in puff pastry is elegant and tasty. The creativity and quality of the offerings equal that of far more expensive restaurants in Providence or Newport. Inquire about the Yule Log Ceremony — six special dinners held during the holiday season.

**THE RESTAURANT &
  CAFE**
401-245-4770.
437 Main St., Warren, RI
  02885.
Open: Daily.
Price: Inexpensive to
  Moderate.
Cuisine: American/Greek.
Serving: B, L, D.
Credit Cards: MC, V.
Reservations: No.
Smoking: Smoking section.
Handicap Access: Yes.

This little spot on Main St. is a good choice anytime of day for an inexpensive meal. In addition to a long list of sandwiches, salads, clubs, and traditional American dinner entrées are the dishes closest to the chef's heart: souvalki, hearty Greek salads, baked eggplant Mediterranean, and his pork, beef, and lamb gyros. The latter, served on a grilled pita, feature carved, marinated slices of cooked meat rather than the ground, preprocessed stuff that so many places buy from food service companies. A good bet.

**TAV-VINO**
401-245-0231.
267 Water St., Warren, RI
  02885.
Open: Tues.–Sun.; closed
  Tues. off-season.
Price: Moderate.
Cuisine: Seafood.
Serving: D.
Credit Cards: AE, MC, V.
Reservations: Accepted.
Smoking: Smoking section.
Handicap Access: Yes.

Stroll past old houses and antique shops to a white, crushed-shell drive, and Tav-Vino is at the end, right on the bay. The dining room is attractive (lots of glass and wood), and there's deck dining in-season. The emphasis is on fresh fin fish (as opposed to shellfish) from sole to tautog, salmon to trout. The mud pie has been ranked "Best Decadent Dessert" in the state. Great fish; lots of noise.

**WHARF TAVERN**
401-245-5043.
215 Water St., PO Box 69,
  Warren, RI 02885.
Open; Daily.
Price: Moderate.
Cuisine: Seafood.
Serving: L, D.
Credit Cards: AE, D, MC,
  V.
Reservations:
  Recommended.
Smoking: Smoking section.
Handicap Access: Yes.

Both the enclosed deck and the more rustic dining room are right on the Warren River — the views are exceptional. The Wharf Tavern caters to seafood lovers, but the charbroiled menu gets equal time, making surf-and-turf options a good choice. Lobster is a specialty and is prepared in a variety of styles from Thermidor and Newburg to pot boiled, all offered at reasonable prices. Poultry and pastas are on hand as well; the luncheon menu offers low-calorie plates and sandwiches in addition to entrées. A very reasonable set-price dinner is offered Mon.–Wed. and includes a bottle of wine. Take-out menu and docking are available, too.

# SAKONNET

## *Little Compton*

**ABRAHAM
  MANCHESTER
  RESTAURANT &
  TAVERN**

This former 1820s general store is a gathering place for the community. Little League photos and work by local artists hang on the walls, wines

401-635-2700.
Adamsville Rd., Little
　Compton, RI 02837.
Open: Daily.
Price: Inexpensive to
　Moderate.
Cuisine: American/
　Seafood/Italian.
Serving: L, D.
Credit Cards: MC, T, V.
Reservations: No.
Smoking: Smoking section.
Handicap Access: Yes.

from nearby Sakonnet Vineyards are on offer, and in addition to predictable American and Italian standards, specials like conch salad and fresh fish dishes reflect the Portuguese heritage of many locals. The combination of relatively sophisticated offerings and basic fare (in large or small portions), plus a relaxed atmosphere (kids are even given crayons) make this a great place for families. Mud pie is a house specialty.

*George Crowther knows how to make East Bay jonnycakes at the Commons Lunch in Little Compton — his are the best.*

Craig Hammell

**COMMONS LUNCH**
401-635-4388.
The Commons, Little
　Compton, RI 02837.
Open: Daily.
Price: Inexpensive.
Cuisine: New England.
Serving: B, L, D.
Credit Cards: No.
Reservations: No.
Smoking: Yes.
Handicap Access: Yes.

The Commons Lunch is *the* quintessential RI restaurant — a little place with tables, booths, and counter service, just across from Little Compton's ancient churchyard. The cuisine, served in immense portions, is pure New England. Not only can you get East Bay jonnycakes made with cornmeal ground at Gray's Grist Mill just down the road, but also you can indulge in a tasty, generous helping of fish and chips, quahog chowder *and* quahog pie, a variety of grinders, fried seafood, and kale soup (a Portuguese influence), plus "American" meals like liver and bacon and baked ham. Save room for Indian, Grape-Nuts, or bread puddings, or choose a slice of homemade pie for dessert. A real local gem.

**COUNTRY HARVEST**
401-635-4579.

The Country Harvest is a blessing in Little Compton, where eateries are few and far

67 W. Main Rd., Rte. 77,
   Little Compton, RI 02837.
Open: Wed.–Mon.; closed
   Mon. off-season.
Price: Expensive.
Cuisine: American.
Serving; D, SB.
Credit Cards: AE, D, MC,
   V.
Reservations: Suggested.
Smoking: Smoking section.
Handicap Access: Yes.

between. It occupies a choice spot looking west over a meadow and the Sakonnet River — sunsets can be breathtaking. The menu isn't adventurous, but every meal is cooked absolutely to order. The chef is wonderfully accommodating and will gracefully make substitutions upon request. Poultry, beef, veal, seafood, and pastas are all here, along with truly fresh vegetables; the fresh fruit sherbet is good, too. A nice touch is the inclusion of many local selections on the wine list. The dining room is rustic and attractive, and there's a pub room and patio bar, too.

## THE STONE HOUSE CLUB

401-635-2222.
122 Sakonnet Point. Rd.,
   Little Compton, RI 02837.
Open: Daily in-season;
   Fri.–Sun., mid-
   Sept.–mid-Jun.
Price: Moderate to
   Expensive; Tap Room,
   Inexpensive.
Cuisine: American.
Serving: D.
Credit Cards: MC, V.
Reservations: Yes.
Smoking: No.
Handicap Access: No.

The Stone House Club (see the section Lodging) is an atmospheric old place near the end of Sakonnet Point. It's restaurant, the Tap Room, is warm and welcoming with low ceilings, pine paneling, and stone hearths (a real winter environment). The menu, like the crowd, tends to be a bit elderly, featuring options like veal Marsala and shrimp scampi, run-of-the-mill pastas, duck, chicken, and steak dishes, as well as a number of more contemporary seafood specials. The mesclun salad with goat cheese was heavy-handed, and my chicken arrived woefully undercooked, for which (to his credit) the chef didn't charge me the standard $5 table fee for nonclub members. Desserts are old-fashioned, and the wine list is ordinary, except for some local Sakonnet vintages. Best recommendation: go off-season for Soup and Sandwich on Sat. night — the "ends of the earth" atmosphere is worth it.

## *Tiverton*

## BARCELLOS FAMILY RESTAURANT

401-624-6649.
1214 Stafford Rd., Rte. 81,
   Tiverton, RI 02878.
Open: Daily.
Price: Inexpensive to
   Moderate.
Cuisine: Portuguese/
   American/Spanish.
Serving: L, D.
Credit Cards: AE, CB, D,
   DC, MC, V.

This is a real New England-Portuguese restaurant. It smells of smoke and has tacky decor but has good, supremely inexpensive Portuguese wines (opt for a red Garrafeira or white vinho verde), superb local bread, and marvelously strong- flavored, hearty cuisine. The shrimp Mozambique appetizer, flavored with orange, is an exotic dream and a bargain; entrées include codfish gomes sa (shredded, sun-dried cod with onions, potatoes, and egg), paella Valenciana, which features all manner of crustaceans with chicken and chouriço, and a per-

Reservations: Yes.
Smoking: Smoking section
(ineffectual).
Handicap Access: Yes.

**EVELYN'S DRIVE-IN**
401-624-3100.
2335 Main Rd., Rte. 77,
Tiverton, RI 02878.
Open: Wed.–Mon.
Price: Inexpensive.
Cuisine: Seafood/
American.
Serving: B, L, D (closed by
8:00 p.m.).
Credit Cards: No.
Reservations: No.
Smoking: Yes.
Handicap Access: Outdoor
tables.

**FOUR CORNERS GRILL**
401-624-1510.
3841 Main St., Rte.77,
Tiverton-Four-Corners,
RI 02878.
Open: Daily.
Price: Inexpensive to
Moderate.
Cuisine: Creative
American.
Serving: B, L, D.
Credit Cards: AE, D, MC,
V.
Reservations: No.
Smoking: No.
Handicap Access: Yes.

**THE HERE & NOW
RESTAURANT AND
TEA ROOM**
401-624-2890.
2753 Main Rd., Rte. 77,
Tiverton, RI 02878.
Open: Tues.–Sun.
Price: Inexpensive to
Moderate.
Cuisine: English/
American.
Serving: L, D (on weekends
only), Afternoon Tea.

sonal favorite, pork with potatoes and littlenecks (only $8.95 and enough for two). Be assured that there is plenty for the timid palate as well. One caution: avoid the crabmeat, it's imitation.

Evelyn's is a 1950s-style roadside dream. The outdoor picnic tables overlook lovely Nannaquaket Pond; the indoor "dining room" looks like it belongs in a seaside beach cottage. Order at the take-out window, while crunching crushed white shells underfoot. In addition to the usual array of local fresh seafood, you can also get sandwiches and full dinners that range from chow mein to grilled lemon pepper chicken, meat loaf, ham, and veal cutlet. The huge stuffie is great, seasoned with an Italian flair. Orders of clam cakes and fried shrimp are generous and tasty.

This is *the* restaurant of choice for Tiverton residents. Everyone seems to know each other, the kitchen is frenetic, the food is surprisingly inexpensive, and for a little dinerlike spot in the country, the Four Corners is unusually creative. Burgers are built with exotic toppings, and the standard BLT comes with avocado. In addition to light fare, you can also get entrées like grilled salmon steak, plus a very decent range of beers and wines, including local Sakonnet Vineyards options. Eating here is a terrific bargain and a good way to meet the natives.

Taking over the reins of a former lackluster restaurant is a very pleasant English tearoom, sharing the space with a frilly gift shop/patisserie called **Past & Presents.** You can get afternoon tea anytime, which consists of scones, clotted cream and jam, finger sandwiches, desserts, and, naturally, a pot of tea, all for $10; for high tea on Sun. at 4:00 p.m., add cold and hot items as well, including meat pies, fish cakes, and quiche. There's also a somewhat come hither lunch and dinner menu that offers soup, seafood, chicken, and even the trifle

Credit Cards: AE, MC, V.
Reservations: Yes, D only.
Smoking: No.
Handicap Access: No.

**MOULIN ROUGE**
401-624-4320.
1403 Main Rd., Rte. 138,
   Tiverton, RI 02878.
Open: Wed.–Mon.
Price: Moderate.
Cuisine: French.
Serving: D.
Credit Cards: AE, CB, DC,
   MC, V.
Reservations: Accepted.
Smoking: Smoking section.
Handicap Access: Two
   steps.

"of the moment" (i.e. whatever's fresh and strikes the chef's fancy).

There's a mini Eiffel Tower out front with Christmas lights (the moulin is around to the side) and a menu with listings like escargot, chicken cordon bleu, and crêpes Suzette — traditional French food à l'Amerique. Nonetheless, the crab entrée is equal to the best, and the sole bonne femme is perfectly cooked and delicious in a white wine cream sauce with mushrooms and shrimp. The wine list includes a fine selection of cognacs and liqueur-laced coffees.

---

### Providence Restaurants

Only a forty-five-minute drive from Newport, Providence now harbors some of the best restaurants in the country. Here's a selection of eleven personal favorites for a very special evening out.

**Al Forno** (401-273-9760; 577 South Main Street) One of the spots that put Providence on the culinary map. The *International Herald Tribune* named it "Best Casual Restaurant in the World." Wood-grilled pizzas, fabulous Italian fare.

**Cafe Nuovo** (401-421-2525; 1 Citizens Plaza) Beautifully crafted meals (especially the "architectural" desserts) in a contemporary Art Deco setting overlooking the Providence River. Lemon risotto with seared sea scallops is a knockout.

**Down City Diner** (401-331-9217; Eddy and Weybosset Streets) "Diner" comes from the great Art Deco surroundings, not the avant-garde food. Less expensive than the others, meals are just as imaginative, if a little rougher around the edges. Terrific Cajun crab cakes.

**The Gatehouse** (401-521-9229; 4 Richmond Square) A real nineteenth-century gatehouse on the Seeknok River that serves up local fare with New Orleans and Mediterranean overtones. The food more than lives up to the view.

**Grappa** (401-454-1611; 525 South Water Street) Entrées like wood-grilled shrimp risotto in a very contemporary setting, smack at the mouth of the Providence River. Lots of trendy grappas.

**Grill 262** (401-751-3700; 262 South Water Street) A very hip and cool spot overlooking the waterfront, with choice grilled fare and superb mashed potatoes.

**L'Epicurio** (401-454-8430; 238 Atwells Avenue) In the heart of Providence's Little Italy — a bastion of Old World cooking — is L'Epicurio, an ultrachic spot with outstanding wood-grilled fare and pastas.

*(continued)*

**New Rivers** (401-751-0350; 7 Steeple Street) Great American bistro food in a warm, intimate setting, between RISD (Rhode Island School of Design) and the new Providence riverfront. Try the spring roll to start and the praline ice cream to finish.

**Pizzico** (401-421-4114; 762 Hope Street) One of the best Italian restaurants in town isn't on Federal Hill but in a residential neighborhood about five minutes from Brown University. "Glowing" is the word to describe both the food and the earth-toned atmosphere. The creative pastas are divine, as is the wine list.

**Pot au Feu** (401-273-8953; 44 Custom House Street) Truly classic French food is served upstairs, and bistro food is offered in the brick-walled basement. A rare five-star rating from *Rhode Island Monthly*.

**XO** (401-273-9090; 125 North Main Street) Highly creative cuisine in a casual setting; the ubiquitous portabello mushroom makes an appearance here *not* on a bun but as a tall stack of mushroom "french fries." The crème brûlée tray, with chocolate, white chocolate, and anise custards, is literally a work of art

# FOOD & BEVERAGE PURVEYORS

*Famous for their ice cream, Newport Creamery is a Rhode Island institution.*

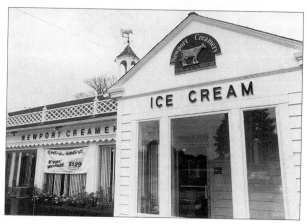

Craig Hammell

The food and beverage purveyors listed here are, for the most part, one-of-a-kind establishments that offer a variety of alternatives to restaurant dining. For picnic or party provisions, backpackable eats, or just a coffee or ice cream stop, see below.

Some local chains are also well worth a visit. "Local" here means only or mostly in Rhode Island, and "chain" refers to any place with over three locations. A sampling follows:

**Bess Eaton Donuts** (twenty-eight locations in RI) Local doughnut chain with a great name.

**Newport Creamery** (twenty-three locations in RI) A cross between Friendly's and an old-fashioned ice-cream parlor (with old-fashioned prices), it offers great ice cream, plus burgers and sandwiches.

**Ocean Coffee Roasters** (three locations in RI) This new gourmet coffee/bakery chain is turning up everywhere. The quality is right up there with your local coffeehouse. A good bet for breakfast.

Note that starred listings (*) indicate a purveyor of local fame or of unusual or special merit.

## BAKERIES & COFFEEHOUSES

## WEST

### *West Bay*

* **Allie's Donuts** (401-295-8036; 3361 Quaker Ln., Rte. 2, N. Kingstown) It's a RI tradition to get Allie's doughnuts on the way to the beach; the whole state is *crazy* about them. The chocolate-frosted doughnuts are to die for, but there are lots of other treats, too.

**Felicia's** (401-885-5444; 333 Main St., E. Greenwich) In addition to coffees and teas, choose from twenty kinds of bagels, including coffee and jalapeño salsa, twelve kinds of muffins, whole cakes (like angel rum), nine kinds of NY-style cheese cakes, pies, biscotti, and more. Another location at 5757 Post Rd., Rt. 1.

---

### *Del's Lemonade vs Coffee Milk*

It comes as no surprise that a state with a jonnycake law would want to put something on the books about Rhode Island's favorite beverage. It sounds benign, but a small war broke out in 1992 between Del's Lemonade diehards and the Coffee Milk crowd when the Rhode Island Legislature tried to name the state's official beverage. When the smoke cleared, Coffee Milk had won the day, though this is still a touchy issue. Decide for yourself.

**Del's Lemonade.** Established in 1948, Del's has spread recently beyond Rhode Island. There's a story of a potential but hesitant franchiser in California who got a Providence telephone book and called people out of the blue to see what they thought of Del's. He opened his franchise right away. There are Del's shops, trucks, and streetcarts all over the state. There's at least one real lemon peel in each cup of this sweet, slurpy stuff, guaranteed by the owner.

**Coffee Milk.** Invented by the Autocrat Company in 1895 and again by Eclipse Foods in 1914, coffee syrup is like sweet liquid gold. Both brands are still available, but are now manufactured by the same people (Autocrat). Mix your own syrup into a glass of cold milk, or buy ready-mixed cartons (coffee milk outsells chocolate four-to-one in Rhode Island convenience stores). The good news is that one ounce of coffee syrup has less caffeine than eight ounces of a cola drink.

**The Gathering Ground** (401-886-5282; 250 Main St., E. Greenwich) *The* local coffeehouse; sandwiches are served on home-baked bread, and locals claim that the soup is the best on the West Bay. The coffee is ground by Ocean Coffee Roasters (see above).

**Real Muffins** (401-783-8380; 1014 Boston Neck Rd., Rte. 1A, Narragansett) The apple muffins have been voted best in the state.

**Wild Flour** (401-295-1944; 45 Brown St., Wickford) A new, upscale venture with the latest baked goods and coffee. Great name.

## *Jamestown*

**Slice of Heaven Bakery & Cafe** (401-423-3970; 32 Narragansett Ave., Jamestown) This year-round breakfast and lunch spot makes terrific desserts; try the chocolate wish cake or the apple pie.

# EAST

## *East Bay*

Bristol is a town of bakers: cruise the streets east of Hope St. and you'll find a wealth of Portuguese and Italian spots baking fresh breads, pies, pizzas, and the like.

**Bristol Bagel Works** (401-254-1390; 420 Hope St., Bristol) A locally owned shop that bakes fresh bagels daily.

**Oliver Street Bakery** (401-253-1660; 60 ½ Oliver St., Bristol) It's worth a turn off the main drag to this side street spot. The pizzas, breads, and spinach pies taste truly homemade. Go Sunday mornings for fresh malassadas (fried sweetbread dough). Closed Mon.

**Sip & Dip Donuts** (401-247-1060; 487 Metacom Ave., Rte. 136, Warren) Get a dozen homemade doughnuts, a breakfast sandwich, or an inexpensive grinder for lunch. Malassadas on Sun. morning.

**Sunset Bakery** (401-253-6607; 499 Hope St., Rte. 114, Bristol) Since 1929 this traditional bakery, with fresh French, Portuguese, and Italian breads and a host of sweet treats, has made artwork of birthday cakes. More hometown than trendy.

## *Sakonnet*

* **The Barn** (401-635-2985; Adamsville Rd., Little Compton/Adamsville) Voted "best breakfast in a country setting," The Barn earns its kudos with authentic atmosphere (it really was a barn) and excellent food from corned beef hash to French toast.

* **Olga's Cup and Saucer** (401-635-8650; at Walker's Roadside Stand, 261 W. Main Rd., Rte. 77, Little Compton) Olga's is Little Compton in a nutshell: swanky stuff in a modest setting. Elegant offerings like iced cappuccino, fresh ginger lemonade, squash-and-onion pizza, and fabulous baked goods,

including fresh-baked pies, explain why it's been featured in *Metropolitan Home*. There's a new Cup and Saucer in Providence.

## BARS

### WEST

#### *West Bay*

**The Irish Pub** (401-294-9761; 8220 Post Rd., Rte. 1, N. Kingstown/Wickford) Looks like a dive, but *the* place to go for fish and chips; they use flounder, not white fish.

**Twin Willows** (401-789-8153; 865 Boston Neck Rd., Rte. 1A, Narragansett) A big Irish bar with a great view; the homemade chowder is some of the best around; also fine stuffies, ESPN on TV, and a good roster of draught beers.

#### *Jamestown*

**Narragansett Café** (401-423-2150; 25 Narragansett Ave., Jamestown) Voted "Best Dive Bar in Rhode Island." Tavern fare available, plus live entertainment on weekends.

### EAST

#### *East Bay*

**Gillary's** (401-253-2012; 198 Thames St., Bristol) A real waterfront bar with entertainment on weekends.

**The Topsider Bar & Grill** (401-253-9110; 805 Hope St., Bristol) Also on the harbor, but totally different than Gillary's: more Beach Boys than the blues.

#### *Sakonnet*

**Li'l Bear Lounge & Restaurant** (401-624-9164; 983 Main Rd., Rte. 138, Tiverton) Not quite a dive, not quite a family restaurant. Drink with the local fishermen (ask about the silly wagon train lamp as an icebreaker), or get tasty regional food like jonnycakes, chouriço, and the fried local catch at rock bottom prices.

## FARM STANDS & MARKETS

### WEST

#### *West Bay*

**Cranston Farm** (401-295-1985; 7490 Post Rd., Rte. 1, N. Kingstown) Pick up fresh vegetables, condiments, and fruit pies.

**EAST**

*Aquidneck*

* **Aquidneck Growers' Market** (401-848-0099; PO Box 1481, Newport; 909 E. Main Rd., Rte. 138, Middletown) Held on the grounds of Newport Vineyards & Winery. Around twenty growers from RI and MA meet twice-weekly from mid-Jun.-late Oct. to sell their wares. Sat. 9:00 a.m.–1:00 p.m.; Wed. 2:00 p.m.–6:00 p.m.

**De Castro Farm** (401-683-4688; 1780 E. Main Rd., Rte. 138, Portsmouth) Extensive selection of locally grown fruits and vegetables, plus flowers and dairy products.

* **Farmlands** (401-847-1233; 474 Wapping Rd., Portsmouth) A beautiful, quiet spot to pick up peaches, and in the fall, apples and cider. The shingled barn is a New England treasure.

*East Bay*

**D. Alves Pure Honey** (Long Rd., E. Warren, opposite the Rod & Gun Club) A charming roadside stand that sells fresh honey and homegrown vegetables. Drive down to Touisset Point to find lots more fresh produce for sale, usually stacked on a cart at the end of someone's drive and sold on the honor system.

*Sakonnet*

* **Walker's Roadside Stand** (401-635-4719; 261 W. Main Rd., Rte. 77, Little Compton) Rhode Islanders call this the best in the state — it's certainly the most attractive. You'll find the freshest of everything, including the sweetest corn and plums on earth. If it's crowded, several smaller stands cluster nearby on W. Main Rd.

**FISH & MEAT MARKETS**

**WEST**

*West Bay*

**Butcher Block Gourmet Deli** (401-885-0530; 5647 Post Rd., Rte. 1, E. Greenwich) Self-described as "the only old-fashioned meat market" in town. It's really three shops in a row: gourmet and deli, butcher shop, and pizza place. The pizza is great.

* **Handrigan Seafood** (401-789-6201; Great Island Rd., Narragansett/Galilee) Near the Block Is. ferry, it sells everything that you can name and some things that you can't straight-off-the-(nearby)-dock fresh. Several other fish markets cluster nearby, including **Brownie's** (401-792-9346) and **ABC Lobster** (401-782-8088). The above star means that these spots are the closest outlet for the RI fishing fleet.

**Seafood Marketplace** (401-885-8100; 6995 Post Rd., Rte. 1, N. Kingstown) Have them ship your clambakes anywhere in the world, or just get fresh lobsters, clams, or fish to go. There's also a eat-in/take-out menu with lots of fried seafood, plus red, white, broth, or seafood chowder. In the winter, try the quahog chili.

### Jamestown

* **Watson Farm** (401-423-0005; 455 North Rd., Jamestown) A rare find: stop at this old island farm to select fresh cuts of lamb or Black Angus beef for your freezer. Also wool yarns are for sale.
**Zeek's Creek** (401-423-1170; N. Main Rd., Jamestown) A little shack in the marshes; get your bait and tackle here, as well as fresh seafood.

## EAST

### Aquidneck

**Portsmouth Meat Market** (401-683-1484; 108 Chase Rd., Portsmouth) Choice cuts of meat, plus fish and Portuguese sausage. Boxed specials to go.

### East Bay

**Andrade's Catch** (401-253-4529; 186 Wood St., Bristol) Here the seafood comes both fresh and fried, straight from the owner's boat. They "dig and deliver" their own shellfish. Open to the public, Fri. and Sat. only.
**Azorian Butcher Shop** (401-253-7724; Wood and Franklin Sts., Bristol) Want authentic chouriço and linguiça? The locals get it here.
**Hall's Seafood** (401-245-0225; 8 Turner St., Warren) When in Warren, this is where to pick up fresh fish, lobster, scallops, crabs, etc.

### Sakonnet

*Lobster boats haul in the catch at Sakonnet Harbor in Little Compton.*

Craig Hammell

**Manchester Seafoods** (401-624-8000; 2139 Main Rd., Rte. 77, Tiverton) Look for the neon lobster; fresh and smoked fish, plus live lobsters and shellfish, wholesale and retail. If they're out of something, try **Bridgeport Sea Food Market** next door.

**Sakonnet Lobster Company** (401-635-4371; Sakonnet Point Rd., Rte. 77, Little Compton) Pick up some dripping wet lobsters and seafood. (Locals' advice is to skip the markets and buy straight off returning boats early in the morning, down at Sakonnet Point.)

## GOURMET, DELI, GROCERY

## WEST

### *West Bay*

**Back to Basics Grocery** (401-885-2679; 500 Main St., E. Greenwich) Natural foods and homeopathic body care.

\* **Chef-a-Roni Fancy Foods** (401-884-8798; 2832 S. County Trail, Rte. 2, E. Greenwich) This place is so good that it has out-of-state regulars. It's a large gourmet market with a deli counter, prepared foods, a bakery, and its own brand of spices. Closed Tues.

**The Coffee Bean and Deli** (401-782-6226; 20 Woodruff Ave., Narragansett) The deli counter smells like the Lower East Side; fresh-baked goods and over thirty kinds of coffee. Middle Eastern appetizers, too. Highly recommended.

**Galilee Grocery** (401-783-5164; Great Island Rd., Narragansett/Galilee) Last mainland outlet for provisions before heading out to higher prices on Block Is.

\* **MarketPlace Gourmet** (401-782-3663; 15 Pier Marketplace, Narragansett Pier) An exceptional new spot — get coffee, breakfast fare, sandwiches, pastries, you name it — with a funky, mix-and-match atmosphere of wall murals, sofas and stuffed chairs, original artwork (for sale), and bookshelves. BYOB dinners on Fri. nights (accompanied by live entertainment) feature items like ripe pears stuffed with Brie, Asian black duck, and roasted curried vegetables. Customized catering includes five- or nine-course European dinners brought to your home, hotel room, or boat. A find.

**Papa's Country Grocery** (401-783-1230; 123A Boon St., Narragansett Pier) A fun country store with everything from Duke's Texas-sized muffins to Mrs. Papa's coffee cake, penny candy, and hand-quilted pillows.

**Pick Pockets Deli** (401-884-0488; 431 Main St., E. Greenwich) Here's something refreshing in the land of fried seafood and portabello mushroom burgers: soups, salads, sandwiches, and falafels with a Middle Eastern flavor (hummus, tabouli, kabobs, and the like). Frequented by the alternative set.

**The Picnic Basket** (401-782-2284; 20 Kingstown Rd., Narragansett Pier) A gourmet deli with sandwiches, soups, salads, plus fresh-baked breads and bagels. Also frozen yogurt and Ben & Jerry's ice cream. Get a picnic basket for the beach.

**Ryan's Market** (401-294-9571; 70 Brown St., N. Kingstown/Wickford) An old-fashioned market with groceries, plus prepared foods to go; the macaroni and cheese is a bargain.

## EAST

### *Aquidneck*

**Foodworks** (401-683-4664; 3030 E. Main Rd., Rte. 138, Portsmouth) Smell the aroma of fresh-baked breads, pastries, and work-of-art gourmet pizzas. Also has deli sandwiches and salads.

**Marcie's General Store** (401-683-9200; 401-683-9811; ferry landing, Homestead Village) The only store on the island, with maps, gear, some groceries, and soft drinks. Check in before you go wandering.

**Nature's Goodness** (401-847-7480; 510 E. Main Rd., Rte. 138, Middletown) Natural foods grocery store; it gets points for opening right next to a Tastee Freeze.

\* **Pastabilities** (401-847-7894; 124 Aquidneck Ave., Middletown) Over twenty flavors of fresh pasta from sweet curry to saffron to chocolate. A myriad of shapes are available, plus ravioli, tortellini, gnocchi, stuffed shells, and more. Sauces too, plus European breads. Call in your order or to find out what's being made fresh that day.

### *East Bay*

**Aguiar's Market** (401-253-1775; 585 Metacom Ave., Rte. 136, Bristol) This place is so authentic that even the signs are in Portuguese. Come here for linguiça, chouriço, and other Portuguese specialties.

**Basically British** (401-253-5722; 219 High St., Bristol) British and Irish food-stuffs, plus frozen and canned imports and chocolates.

**Cafe la France** (401-253-0360; 483 Hope St., Rte. 114, Bristol) Originally called Peaberry's, la France is still the same trendy, 1990s-style bakery serving gourmet coffees; pick up epicurean foodstuffs and sandwiches, too.

**Golden Goose Deli** (401-253-1414; 365 Hope St., Rte. 114, Bristol) An attractive café right on the main street. Bring soups and salads home from the deli counter, or have a sandwich made up on the spot. Good desserts, ice cream, and espresso.

### *Sakonnet*

\* **The Provender** (401-624-8084; 3883 Main Rd., Rte. 77, Tiverton Four Corners) Located in a majestic Victorian house, this is the only upscale gourmet deli in the region. Splurge and buy a whole Austrian plum torte, or pick up a deli sandwich or croissant. They do superb picnic lunches and take MC, V.

**Wilbur's Store** (401-635-2356; 50 Commons, Little Compton) Get everything here from baked goods to a pound of hamburger to hardware. Where all of Little Compton comes to shop.

## ICE CREAM & SWEETS

### WEST

#### *West Bay*

* **Brickley's Ice Cream** (401-294-7970; 30 Ten Rod Rd., N. Kingston) A small, family-run spot with rich, homemade ice cream. Enormously popular.

**The Chocolate Delicacy** (401-884-4949; 800-MR-WONKA; 149 Main St., E. Greenwich) Handmade truffles and much more. A rare find.

**Nana's Ice Cream & Pastry** (401-782-2705; 6A Pier Marketplace, Narragansett Pier) The usual fattening treats, plus Dolewhip: a low-fat, lactose-free "ice cream" that actually tastes good.

**Scrumptious** (401-884-0844; Marketplace Plaza, E. Greenwich) The super-rich desserts here live up to their billing.

**Treats of Wickford** (401-295-1140; 83-D Brown St., Wickford) A sweetshop with the best location in town. Eat your ice cream, cookies, and candy at the end of the pier, overlooking the Wickford Harbor.

### EAST

#### *Aquidneck*

**Telly's Ice Cream** (401-849-1211; 401-846-8335; 147 Aquidneck Ave., Middletown) Ice cream and frozen yogurt, plus breakfast and sandwiches until 9:00 p.m.

#### *East Bay*

* **Delekta Pharmacy** (401-245-6767; 496 Main St., Rte. 114, Warren) Don't miss this 1858 apothecary with full, old-fashioned fountain service. The coffee cabinets are the best in the state. It has lovely wood trim and tiled floor, and the shelves are full of attractively packaged soaps and bottles.

**Sam I Am** (401-245-1177; 10 State St., Bristol) This breakfast-and-lunch-all-day spot is straight out of Dr. Seuss's *Green Eggs and Ham*. A little girl swore to me that their homemade ice cream is "the best." How can you not like a place with a peanut butter-and-banana triple-decker on the menu?

#### *Sakonnet*

**Corner Cones** (Willow Ave., Little Compton) Just down from The Commons, don't miss this small summer-only spot, featuring local Bliss ice cream.

\* **Gray's Ice Cream** (401-624-4500; 16 East Rd., Rte. 77, Tiverton Four Corners) The quintessential Sunday-drive-in-the-country ice-cream barn. The home-made product is as rich and creamy as it gets (try the Grape-Nuts flavor). Also frozen yogurt and sherbet for the calorie-shy. A much-loved landmark.

**Helger's Ice Cream** (401-624-4560; 2474 Main Rd., Rte. 77, Tiverton) Soft ice cream and take-out items where Helger's Produce Market used to be.

## SEASONAL FOOD FESTIVALS

The Newport and Narragansett Bay area is rich with food festivals of every kind. Below are some of the major events. You can also find small local fairs, fondly referred to as "clamslurpers," almost every summer weekend.

**Harvest Festival and Apple Pie Contest** (401-783-5400) A big annual tradition at the South County Museum in Narragansett, featuring jonnycakes, clam cakes, chowder, cider, and, of course, apple pie. Early to mid-Oct.

**International Quahog Festival** (401-294-9606) This decade-old Wickford event features a pro/am baked-stuffed quahog (stuffies) cook-off, plus clam-shucking contests. Held at the Wickford Festival Grounds, Tower Hill Rd., Wickford. Late Aug.

**Lobstermen's Festival** (401-783-1543) Yawgoo Bakes provides clam chowder, fresh fish, corn, burgers, and, of course, lobster at this annual Narragansett event in Galilee. Late Jun.

**Pick-Your-Own** Look for strawberries in Jul., blueberries in Aug., and apples in Sept. and Oct. Locations include the following:

> *The Berry Farm* (401-847-3912; 19 Third Beach Rd., Middletown) Straw-berries.
>
> *Devecchio's Farm* (401-884-9598; 302 Potter Rd., N. Kingstown) Blueberries.
>
> *Quonset View Farm* (401-683-1254; 895 Middle Rd., Portsmouth) Straw-berries and blueberries.

**Traditional Rhode Island Public Clambake** (401-245-1977; E. Warren Rod and Gun Club, Long Ln., Rte. 103, Warren) An excellent chance to scarf down steamers, scrod, hot dogs, potatoes, yams, quahogs, sweet corn, and water-melon. Mid-Jul.

## TAKEOUT & CHEAP EATS

## WEST

### *West Bay*

**Adriana's** (401-783-3550; 1157 Pt. Judith Rd., Narragansett/Pt. Judith) Get fresh fried seafood at the take-out window or eat in the miniscule-but-charming dining room.

**Brown's Cafe & Deli** (401-294-1150; 85 Brown St., Wickford) A real local spot with breakfast, sandwiches, calzones, coffee, beer, and wine. Open daily 6:00 a.m. until early evening. No smoking.

\* **Crazy Burger** (401-783-1810; 144 Boon St., Narragansett Pier) A newspaper review called this spot, opened recently by the former chef of Rue de l'Espoir in Providence, the hottest and hippest place in Narragansett. It's seaside-funky, with all kinds of nouvelle burgers (how does freshly ground salmon mixed with pistachio pesto, topped with orange-chili mayo grab you?), including vegan adaptations, plus smoothies and way cool milk-shakes.

**Ed's Roost** (401-885-3358; 357 Main St., E. Greenwich) A veteran breakfast and lunch spot with patina and charm; of the "Customer Favorites," Rick's Delight, broiled turkey and ham on a bulkie roll with melted cheese, is aptly named. (Just up the street at 315 Main St., **Audra's Cafe** has similar offerings in a slicker space.)

**Fillipou's Pizza** (401-294-4467; 670 Ten Rod Rd., N. Kingstown/Wickford) Try "George's Special" — pizza with the works minus anchovies. Highly endorsed by many Wickfordites.

**Frank & Johnny's Restaurant & Pizzeria** (401-884-9751; 401-884-1221; 186 Main St., E. Greenwich) The thin-crust pizza was voted one of the ten best in the state; entrées, however, are uneven. Some say the veal stuffed with eggplant and the pasta dishes are excellent, others remain skeptical. No deliveries.

**Harborside Grill** (401-295-0444; 68 Brown St., Wickford) One of three little breakfast and lunch eateries in the middle of Wickford; choose from a huge menu and eat at the counter or take out. Just down the street is the sweetly unassuming **Wickford Diner.**

**J.L.'s Take Out** (401-789-2020; State Pier off Great Island Rd., Narragansett/Galilee) Great Island Rd. is packed with seafood restaurants and takeouts, but this is the most convenient to the Block Is. ferry. Decent fried everything.

**Mandarin** (401-294-6776; 7769 Post Rd., Rte. 1, N. Kingstown) Of several Chinese restaurants on Rte.1 between E. Greenwich and N. Kingstown, this is the best. Try the orange-flavored beef or the Seafood Treasure. The menu is extensive and a little pricey.

**Peppers** (401-783-2550; 83 Narragansett Ave., Narragansett Pier) The hands-down choice for an inexpensive breakfast in Narragansett Pier. It occupies the front room of a somewhat seedy boardinghouse, but don't let that stop you. The lunch menu has a Mexican flair, but goes as far as burgers and falafel pockets. Takeout, too. Closed Tues.

**PJ's Pizza & Family Restaurant** (401-789-4950; 909 Boston Neck Rd., Rte. 1A, Narragansett) An essential pizza place with Greek overtones. Try the spinach and broccoli pies or the Greek cheese pizza. Cheap pasta dinners, too. Delivery.

\* **Wiley's at Middlebridge** (401-782-3830; 90 Middlebridge Rd., Narragansett)

Breakfast and lunch daily, plus Fri. and Sat. dinners in this tiny, off-the-beaten-track spot overlooking the Narrow River. Good fish and chips. Star is for location.

## *Jamestown*

**East Ferry Deli** (401-423-1592; 47 Conanicus Ave., Jamestown) An indoor/outdoor café overlooking Jamestown Harbor, serving coffees, pastries, sandwiches, quiches, and salads. The view is better than the pasta salad, however.

**Spinnakers Cafe** (401-423-3077; 3 Ferry Wharf, Jamestown) Bakery and deli items, plus soups, salads, ice cream, and frozen yogurt — the closest place to the harbor.

## EAST

## *Aquidneck*

**Atlantic Grill** (401-849-4440; 91 Aquidneck Ave., Middletown) This is where guests at the Hedgegate B&B get the breakfast part of their stay, so you know that it's good. A big breakfast and lunch menu, with take-out service.

*Flo knows her clams — get 'em here in Middletown or at the original Flo's Clam Shack on Island Park in Portsmouth.*

Craig Hammell

* **Flo's Clam Shack** (Park Ave., Portsmouth) Flo's is a RI fixture. A previous incarnation of the shack was swept out to sea in the 1938 hurricane, so you know that Flo's has been around awhile. Terrific, plump fried clams, plus stuffies, chowder, and burgers. You can tell this is vintage RI, because they offer vinegar for the fries. There's another, more elaborate Flo's opposite First (Easton) Beach in Middletown (401-847-8141), with a larger menu. You can't get fried shrimp at the Portsmouth spot, only clams and fish, but it's a RI landmark.

**No. 1 Buffet Chinese Food** (401-847-8588; 665 W. Main Rd., Rte. 114, Middletown) The TV add shows happy folk chowing down on a gargantuan, all-you-can-eat buffet dinner for $8.95. Despite the hype, the food is actually good. Also Japanese and American a la carte options.

**Tommy's Delux Diner** (401-847-9834; 159 E. Main Rd., Middletown) A *real* diner marooned amidst the mall sprawl of Middletown. Be different: eat here, skip McDonald's this once.

## East Bay

* **Amaral's Fish & Chips** (401-247-0675; 4 Redmond St., Warren) Eat in (at Formica booths) or take home superb fresh seafood fried in the lightest of batters. Wildly popular with the locals. Closed Sun.

**Barnacle B's Beef on the Reef** (401-253-9010; 448 Thames St., Bristol) A cheap, smoky breakfast and lunch joint.

* **Cabral's Gourmet Chicken** (401-253-3913; 585 Metacom Ave., Rte. 136, Bristol) Experts in rotisserie chicken way before it became trendy and expensive. Lots of other choices, including chouriço pies, stuffed peppers, and stuffies.

**Castigliego's** (401-245-4640; 485 Metacom Ave., Rte. 136, Warren) A slick seafood palace in a strip mall, with stuffies, chowder, clam cakes, smelt, fried squid, and lobster. Take it home or eat there in a small, pretty dining room.

**The Hope Diner** (401-253-1759; 742 Hope St., Rte. 114, Bristol) Nothing fancy, just the most recommended breakfast place in town. Lunch, too.

**The Riptide** (401-253-2122; 271 Wood St., Bristol) A small sweet spot two streets removed from the posh part of town, with sandwiches, breakfasts, and fried seafood. Open for breakfast and lunch, plus dinner on weekends. Comes well recommended.

* **Sam's Restaurant & Pizzeria** (401-253-7949; 149 Bradford St., Bristol) Don't miss this one. Their oblong pizzas (homemade sauce and crust worth saving for the last bite) were voted best in the state by *Providence Journal* readers. Friendly, fifties atmosphere, plus other entrées from scungilli salad to grinders to entrées like linguine and roast veal, make this the best Italian take-out option on the East Bay.

## Sakonnet

**Mykonos Restaurant** (401-625-5780; Main Rd., Rte. 77, Tiverton) A pleasant spot, a tremendous view, and a menu with enough flair to satisfy the adventurous, plus plenty of burgers and fried seafood to make traditionalists happy. Italian, Greek, and seafood specialties (shrimp in wine sauce with feta is a winner), plus chicken and chops — even baklava for dessert. Beer and wine, plus takeout.

**Phoenix Pizza** (401-624-8400; 750 East Rd., Tiverton) Choose from twelve kinds of pizza, or make up your own. Also burgers, salads, and sandwiches. Free delivery.

## WINERIES

In addition to visiting bay area wineries, visitors can contact The Wine Experience (401-782-1478; PO Box 472, N. Kingstown, RI 02852). It's a wine education organization that offers tastings, a wine-finding service, wine adventure packages, and more. Ask for Lynette Brodeur.

**Greenvale Vineyards** (401-847-377; 582 Wapping Rd., Portsmouth) Tours, tastings, and purchases are by appointment only. The opportunity to tour this historic farm and vineyard along the banks of the Sakonnet River (complete with gorgeous shingle-style house and outbuildings) is more than worth the trip.

**Newport Vineyards & Winery** (401-848-5161; fax 401-848-5162; 909 E. Main Rd., Rte. 138, Middletown) The winery is in a strip mall (albeit surrounded by tree nurseries rather than mall sprawl), but reward yourself with a short drive to Indian Ave. along the Sakonnet River, where the vineyards grow in majestic surroundings. Back at the winery, tours are held daily 1:00 p.m. and 3:00 p.m., May–Oct. and on weekends, Nov.–Apr. All wines, including a promising port, are available for tastings.

*Keeping tabs on the vintage at Sakonnet Vineyards in Little Compton.*

Craig Hammell

**Sakonnet Vineyards** (401-635-8486; 162 W. Main Rd., Rte. 77, Little Compton) Burrow deep down a dirt lane into beautiful countryside to reach the winery. Sakonnet is the biggest — and given its medals, the best — winery in New England. Stroll the grounds, take a tour of the caves, and stay for a free tasting. White wines are best suited to Narragansett Bay soil and climate, though the Cabernet Franc is very nice indeed.

# CULTURE

The shores of Narragansett Bay have much to recommend themselves both historically and artistically. When you're in the mood for a short day-trip north, however, don your cushion-soled museum shoes and head to Providence. **The Rhode Island School of Design Museum** — aka **The RISD Museum,** pronounced Riz-dee (401-454-6100; Benefit Street) — is easily one of the best small art museums in the country. Its European and American painting galleries have just been refurbished and are looking resplendent.

When in Providence don't overlook the eighteenth-century **John Brown House** (401-331-8575; 52 Power Street), which John Quincy Adams called "the most magnificent private mansion" that he'd seen in America, nor the **Governor Henry Lippitt House Museum** (401-453-0688; 199 Hope Street), a veritable temple to high Victorian design. Or, if you're staying on the West Bay, call the **University of Rhode Island** (401-792-2200) in nearby Kingston for a schedule of events.

Finally, for one of the most unique evenings that you can spend in an American city, head up to Providence for **Water/Fire,** an art installation that's become an institution on the Providence River. Artist Barnaby Evans and a team of volunteers stoke logs onto forty wrought-iron braziers built directly atop the water, then ignite "singing bonfires," which burn from sunset to midnight, while low, chanted music plays in the background. It's an intoxicating and nearly medieval experience to smell wood smoke in the skyscrapered downtown of a modern city. Restaurants set up outdoor tables, and thousands stroll the streets on foot. For lighting dates, call the **Rhode Island Convention and Visitors Bureau** (401-274-1636).

## ARCHITECTURE

When it comes to architecture, Rhode Island's size is ideal. You can travel centuries within miles here. Individual streets and even some towns seemingly were built for no other purpose than to serve as pattern books of American architecture.

One type of colonial building was actually named for the state: the seventeenth-century Rhode Island stone-ender. These farmhouses were built on medieval lines and featured a massive fieldstone hearth along one wall. While there are none in the Narragansett Bay area (the nearest is the **Clemence-Irons House** in the village of Manton, in Johnston), the largest seventeenth-century home in New England can be found in Bristol: the three-story **Joseph Reynolds House** (1694), which is also a B&B (see the section Lodging). Bristol is well known for its Federal and especially for its Greek Revival homes. The former represents a restrained, slightly more severe version of the Georgian style practiced during the colonial period (see the **William's Grant Inn** in the section Lodging for a typical five-bay Federal clapboard structure); the little village of Wickford, on the western side of the bay in North Kingstown, also boasts a fine collection of colonial and Federal homes, particularly on Main Street.

The Greek Revival came into vogue in the early to mid-nineteenth century as an architectural corollary to the principles of the representative democracy. Its templelike roofs, gable end to the street, and massive Doric, Ionic, and Corinthian columns were meant to summon associations with the Athenian democracy of ancient Greece. Bristol's Hope Street (the main thoroughfare) has some wonderfully massive examples of this style; peek down side streets for smaller, cottage-sized versions.

Not surprisingly for "America's First Resort," Rhode Island is also rich with Victorian resort architecture. While the Newport mansions represent the most lavish flowering of this phase, don't miss their less ostentatious, and in many ways more picturesque, Queen Anne and shingle-style neighbors in Narragansett Pier's historic district and on Beaver Tail peninsula on Jamestown.

## CINEMA

**B**ecause there are so few cinemas in this part of the world, theaters just beyond the region's borders are also included.

### WEST

#### *West Bay*

**Narragansett Theater** (401-782-2077; Pier Marketplace, Narragansett Pier).
**Showcase Cinemas 1-12** (401-885-1621; 1200 Quaker Ln., Rte. 2, Warwick; Exit 8A southbound, 9A northbound off Rte. I-95).

### EAST

#### *Aquidneck*

**Jane Pickens Theatre** (401-846-5252; 49 Touro St., Newport).
**Opera House** (401-847-3456; 19 Touro St., Newport).
**Starcase Cinemas** (401-849-7777; 1346 W. Main Rd., Rte. 114, Middletown).

#### *East Bay*

**Bristol Cinema** (401-253-4312; 91 Bradford St., Bristol).
**Showcase Cinemas 1–8** (508-336-6020; 800 Fall River Ave., Rte. 114, Seekonk, MA); **9 & 10** (508-336-3420; 775 Fall River Ave., Rte. 114, Seekonk, MA).

## DANCE

### EAST

#### *Aquidneck*

**Island Moving Company** (401-847-4470) Newport's resident dance company is actually in Middletown. The IMC puts on a short series of outdoor summer dance concerts, plus a holiday show in Newport in Dec. All performances feature new works accompanied by live music — cutting-edge performing artists in an idyllic setting. The summer series is on the campus of St. George's School in Middletown. Bring a picnic dinner (or buy one there), and take in not only great dancing but also a panoramic view of Second Beach. Their annual Blues Ball is held at the International School of Yacht Restoration in Newport in mid-Sept. (401-847-4470).

### *East Bay*

**Roger Williams University Dance Theatre** (401-254-3624; Old Ferry Rd., Bristol) Call for a schedule of dance concerts performed by faculty, students, and guest artists.

## FINE ART GALLERIES

The following is a selection of both commercial and not-for-profit art galleries, featuring fine and folk art: paintings, works on paper, sculpture, and the like. Note that most galleries are closed on Monday. (For craft galleries, see the section Shopping, under the heading Craft Galleries & Studios.)

## WEST

### *West Bay*

**The Artist's Gallery of Wickford** (401-294-6280; 5 Main St., Wickford) A co-op of fine artwork by RI artists.
**Gallery at Updike Square** (401-294-7773; 16 W. Main St., Wickford) Fine art, plus a gaggle of gargoyles.
**Studio Zwei** (401-295-5907; 800-760-5907; 2 Main St., Wickford) Paintings in watercolor and oil by Elsie Kilguss (her studio is in the back), plus botanical illustrations.
**Wickford Art Association Gallery** (401-294-6840; 36 Beach St., N. Kingstown/ Wickford) An active local arts organization that sponsors shows year-round; tends to focus on juried competitions and work by local artists. All media.

## EAST

### *East Bay*

**Main Street Studio Gallery** (401-245-4583; 543 Main St., Rte. 114, Warren) A rotating selection of oil and watercolor works, photography, and graphics.
**Roger Williams University School of Architecture Gallery** (401-254-3605; 1 Old Ferry Rd., Bristol) Works by faculty, students, and guest artists.

## Sakonnet

**Donavan Gallery** (401-624-4000; 3879 Main Rd., Rte. 77, Tiverton Four Corners) Works by an ever-changing roster of contemporary New England artists.

**Sakonnet Painters Cooperative Gallery** (401-635-8958; 3946 Main Rd., Mill Pond Shops, Tiverton Four Corners) Paintings of the Sakonnet region by members of the co-op.

**Virginia Lynch Gallery** (401-624-3392 Main Rd., Rte. 77, Tiverton) One of the best galleries in the state. Look for work by internationally known artists in everything from glass to photography. It could be in Soho, but it's in Tiverton.

## GARDENS & GARDEN TOURS

### WEST

#### West Bay

**A Celebration of Gardens** (401-884-1776; Gen. James Mitchell Varnum House, 57 Pierce St., E. Greenwich) House and garden tours in E. Greenwich's historic district, plus plant sale and displays by local florists.

**Histwick Garden Tour** (401-295-8813; Wickford Village Association, Wickford) An annual tour of gardens throughout historic Wickford Village. Late Jul.

### EAST

#### Aquidneck

**Green Animals Topiary Gardens** (401-847-1000; Cory's Ln., off Rte. 114, Portsmouth) Down a long lane near the bay is a modest nineteenth-century estate. Behind the house eighty sculpted trees and shrubs are considered to be the best topiary garden in the country. Bring the kids to marvel over sixteen animals and birds, including a bear, unicorn, giraffe, dinosaur, even a peacock, all growing (some to twenty-six feet) from the green leaves of privet hedges and yews. Open daily Jun.-Sept.; $6.50 adults, $3.50 children.

#### East Bay

**Blithewold Gardens & Arboretum** (401-253-2707; 101 Ferry Rd., Rte. 114, Bristol) These grounds — thirty-three acres overlooking Narragansett Bay — harbor one of the first and most innovative arboretums in America, with exotic trees, shrubs, and flowers not grown anywhere else in New England, including the largest giant redwood east of the Rockies. In April, Blithewold hosts **Daffodil Week** — one of the largest daffodil displays in the country, featuring over 30,000 blooming bulbs. Open year-round for self-guided tours; $5 adults, $.75 children. See below for information on Blithewold Mansion.

*From tail to snout, the beasts at Green Animals Topiary Gardens in Portsmouth are all sculpted of privet and yew leaves; together they make up the finest topiary garden in the country.*

**Bristol Historical House & Garden Annual Tour** (401-253-7223; 48 Court St., Bristol) Sponsored by the Bristol Historical & Preservation Society, this annual tour offers an unparalleled chance to see Bristol's exceptional homes and well-tended gardens. Usually scheduled toward the end of Sept.

## HISTORIC BUILDINGS & SITES

The Narragansett Bay region is as rich in historic places as it is in quahogs, maybe more so. The real significance of this wealth lies not in the magnificence of one or two houses, but of the preservation of whole neighborhoods. Towns like Wickford, East Greenwich, Bristol, Warren, and Little Compton boast splendid nests of historic houses, most of which are still occupied and functioning as *homes* rather than museums. For more on historic architectural styles, see the heading Architecture above.

Local historical societies are a terrific source of information and often may be able to arrange private tours to homes not usually open to visitors. The following list will get you started.

**Bristol Historical & Preservation Society** (401-253-7223; 48 Court St., Bristol, RI 02809).

**East Greenwich Preservation Society** (401-884-4988; 110 King St., E. Greenwich, RI 02818).

**Jamestown Historical Society** (401-423-0784; 92 Narragansett Ave., Jamestown, RI 02835).

**Little Compton Historical Society** (401-635-4559; 635 W. Main Rd., Rte. 77, Little Compton 02837).

**Middletown Historical Society** (401-849-1870; Green End Ave. and Valley Rd., Middletown, RI 02842).

**Narragansett Historical Society** (401-783-4695; The Towers, Narragansett Pier, RI 02882).

**Portsmouth Historical Society** (401-683-9178; 870 E. Main Rd., Rte. 138, Portsmouth, RI 02871).

**Rhode Island Historical Society** (401-331-8575; Providence, RI 02903).

**Tiverton Historical Society** (401-624-8881; Tiverton, RI 02878).

## WEST

### *Jamestown*

**JAMESTOWN WINDMILL**
401-423-1798.
North Rd., Jamestown, RI 02835.
Open: Mid-Jun.–mid-Sept., Sat.–Sun.
Admission: Free.

Erected in 1787 on a high, windy hill above the bay, this weathered-shingle monument to colonial know-how was restored by the Jamestown Historical Society. It was a tradition here that whenever the mill stones were regrooved (an event that caused some grit to get mixed in with the grain), the miller, were he a Democrat, would select a Republican's grist to grind and vice versa.

**WATSON FARM**
401-423-0005.
North Rd., Jamestown, RI 02835.
Open: Jun.–Oct. 15, Tues., Thurs., Sun., 1:00 p.m.–5:00 p.m.
Admission: $3 adults; $1.50 children.

A mid-nineteenth-century farmhouse (moved to this spot) and 280 acres open for self-guided touring (enjoy the great bay vistas) are the attractions. Still a working farm, it's operated by the estimable Society for the Preservation of New England Antiquities.

### *West Bay*

**CANONCHET FARM**
401-783-5400.
Strathmore St., Narragansett Pier, RI 02882.

A cloudy day treat: a small nineteenth-century working farm set within a 174-acre park. Poke around the cemetery (graves date back to 1700), hike the fitness and nature trails, picnic, or visit

Open: Daily, daylight hours.
Admission: Free.

South County Museum (see the heading Museums below) which is also here.

*The Casey Farm in North Kingstown is an elegant reminder of plantation-style estates that once swept across western Rhode Island.*

Craig Hammell

**CASEY FARM**
401-295-1030.
Boston Neck Rd., Rte. 1A, N. Kingstown, RI 02852.
Open: Jun.–mid-Oct., Tues., Thurs., Sun., 1:00 p.m.–5:00 p.m.
Admission: $4 adults; $2 children.

This large, white clapboard structure looks almost too elegant to be an eighteenth-century farmstead. Built ca. 1750, it overlooks Narragansett Bay and is encompassed by fields, woodlands, outbuildings, freestanding stone walls, and a family cemetery. This is a rare example of a Yankee plantation, inherited by a succession of gentlemen farmers. The property is maintained by the Society for the Preservation of New England Antiquities. (Don't miss the bullet hole in the parlor door — a memento from the Revolutionary War.)

**GENERAL JAMES MITCHELL VARNUM HOUSE**
401-884-1776.
57 Pierce St., E. Greenwich, RI 02818.
Open: Mem. Day–Labor Day, Tues.–Sat., 1:00 p.m.–4:00 p.m.
Admission: Nominal.

Built ca. 1773, this is a mansion-sized house filled with excellent examples of colonial furniture and fabrics. Note especially the magnificent paneling, and don't forget to see the eighteenth-century garden.

**GILBERT STUART BIRTHPLACE**
401-294-3001.
815 Gilbert Stuart Rd., N. Kingstown, RI 02852.

Not just anybody's ca. 1751 home, but that of Gilbert Stuart, the man responsible for all of those portraits of George Washington. This deep colonial red homestead is tucked in the woods between Rtes. 1 and 1A. A real treat is the operating

Open: Apr.–mid-Nov.,
Thurs.–Mon., 11:00
a.m.–3:45 p.m.
Admission: $3 adults; $1
children.

**OLD NARRAGANSETT
CHURCH**
401-294-4357.
Church Ln., N. Kingstown,
RI 02852.
Open: Jul.–Labor Day, Fri.-
–Mon., 11:00 a.m.–4:00
p.m. and by appt.
Admission: Free.

**SMITH'S CASTLE**
401-294-3521.
55 Richard Smith Dr., N.
Kingstown, RI 02852.
Open: May–Sept., Fri.–Sun.;
Jun.–Aug., Thurs.–Mon.;
12:00 noon–4:00 p.m.
Admission: $3 adults; $1
children.

**THE TOWERS**
401-83-7121.
Ocean Rd., Narragansett
Pier, RI 02882.
Open: Jul. 4–Labor Day,
Sat.–Sun., 12:00
noon–4:00 p.m.
Admission: Free.

**EAST**

*Aquidneck*

**OLD SCHOOL HOUSE**
401-683-9178.
E. Main Rd., Portsmouth,
RI 02871.
Open: Mem. Day–Labor
Day, Sat.–Sun., 1:00
p.m.–4:00 p.m.
Admission: Free.

eighteenth-century snuff mill (the first in America), complete with waterwheel. Stuart was born here but lived much of his adult life in Europe.

Take the "old" in the name seriously. Built in 1707, this is one of the oldest Episcopal churches in the country; it possesses the oldest church organ (1680) in North America. Of note are the Queen Anne communion silver, old-fashioned box pews, elegant wineglass pulpit, and slave gallery. Gilbert Stuart (see above) was baptized here.

In 1678, Roger Smith rebuilt a "blockhouse," or fortified trading post, which had been destroyed in King Philip's War. (Roger Williams had originally established the fort forty-two years earlier.) Smith called the wood-frame structure "Cocumscussoc" for the Native American name for the area; others simply called it Smith's Castle. Now considered one of the oldest plantation houses in America, it's set on twenty-seven square miles of coastal lands and gardens. Have fun imagining it full of English-style squires and their families. There's also an archaeological dig on the premises.

You can't miss these massive stone landmarks on Ocean Rd., right next to the Coast Guard House restaurant. The 1885 towers and the arch that they bear are all that's left of Stanford White's magnificent 1883 Narragansett Pier Casino (it burned to the ground in 1900). Today The Towers still summon up a powerful, romantic image of seaside days past.

Built in 1716, this is the oldest schoolhouse in America. It features a collection of antique desks, school bells, and textbooks.

**PRESCOTT FARM**
401-847-6230; 401-849-7300;
401-849-7301.
2009 W. Main Rd., Rte. 114,
Middletown, RI 02842.
Open: Apr.–Oct., Mon.–Fri.,
10:00 a.m.–4:00 p.m.
Admission: $2 adults; $1
children (for tour of
guardhouse & windmill;
grounds are free)

A forty-seven-acre reconstructed colonial farm, Prescott is named not for its Yankee owner but for the British commander who was captured here in 1777. The main house is closed to the public, but you can visit the little 1730 gambrel-roofed guardhouse where Prescott was captured. Wander around with goats, lambs, and geese, and watch the grinding of cornmeal in a ca. 1812 English windmill; you can buy the meal at a country store on the property, built in 1715 as the Portsmouth ferry master's home and moved to this site.

**WHITEHALL MUSEUM HOUSE**
401-846-3116; 401-847-7951,
off-season.
311 Berkeley Ave.,
Middletown, RI 02842.
Open: Jul.–Aug., Tues.–
Sun., off-season by appt.
Admission: $3 adults; $1
children.

Whitehall came into this world in the seventeenth century as a farmhouse, but upon the arrival of Irish clergyman and philosopher George Berkeley in Newport in 1729, it was enlarged to become an elegant manor home. Berkeley introduced elements unusual in New England at the time: a formal façade, hipped roof, and false double-front doors. He lived here just three years before returning to England, whereupon he deeded the house to Yale University, which lent it out as a tavern. Today the stately red home is in prime repair, but its former view of open fields has been replaced by rows of condos.

**WITHERBY SCHOOL HOUSE**
401-849-1870.
Green End Ave.,
Middletown, RI 02842.
Open: Aug. weekends or by
appt.
Admission: Free.

The Witherby schoolhouse is a patterned-shingle gem from the last quarter of the nineteenth century. It now houses the Middletown Historical Society, which mounts exhibitions in Aug.

*East Bay*

**BLITHEWOLD MANSION**
401-253-2707.
101 Ferry Rd., Rte. 114,
Bristol, RI 02809.
Open: Mid-Apr.–Oct.,
Tues.–Sun.; grounds
open year-round.
Admission: $7.50 adults
(mansion and gardens);
$5 adults (gardens only).

If any forty-five-room, turn-of-the-century mansion can be called charming and unpretentious, it's Blithewold. While a bit overshadowed by the spectacular gardens and arboretum (see Gardens & Garden Tours above), the mansion has its attractions, too. It was built by coal magnate Augustus Van Wickle in 1908 to resemble a seventeenth-century, stone-and-stucco English manor house, and indeed it does. A great place to watch the bay and

*Blithewold Mansion in Bristol is the centerpiece of one of the largest and most exotic arboretums in New England.*

Craig Hammell

daydream about being rich. The mansion reopens in late Nov. for a special Christmas exhibition.

**COGGESHALL FARM MUSEUM**
401-253-9062.
Colt State Park, Bristol, RI 02809.
Open: Year-round.
Admission: Nominal.

The fields, woods, and rocky shores of Colt State Park (see the section Recreation, under the heading State Parks & Wildlife Refuges) settle comfortably into Poppasquash peninsula. Nestled within the park is Coggeshall Farm, an eighteenth-century farmstead, featuring a team of oxen, colonial crafts and games, and historical herb and vegetable gardens. Write for a calendar of events, which includes the blessing of the animals (Aug.), sheepshearing (May), maple sugaring (Mar.), and other traditional events. Look for now-rare breeds of animals once common to eighteenth-century farms.

**LINDEN PLACE**
401-253-0390.
500 Hope St., Bristol, RI 02809.
Open: May–Columbus Day, Thurs.–Sat., 10:00 a.m.–4:00 p.m.; Sun., 12:00 noon–4:00 p.m.; late Nov.–Dec., 12:00 noon–8:00 p.m.
Admission: $4.

An architectural confection more than a Federal mansion, this 1810 home, designed by Russell Warren, represents the pinnacle of Bristol's "fair houses." It's every inch the impressive showplace owner George De Wolf intended (although he decamped in 1825 after he overspeculated and brought the town to financial ruin). The delicately curved, snail shell of a staircase is magnificent. The outbuildings include a carriage barn and a 1906 ballroom, which houses exhibitions by local and regional artists.

---

### A Word About Warren

Sandwiched between the upscale, bay-oriented, and far more tourist-friendly town of Bristol and the upscale, Providence-oriented suburb of Barrington, Warren is often overlooked by visitors. But make an effort to take a stroll in the old neighborhood between Main Street (Route 114) and Water Street, which borders the Warren River. Utterly out of the loop of tourist Rhode Island, the quiet side streets will nonetheless reward you with both grand and modest examples of late eighteenth- and early nineteenth-century homes: five-bay Federals, tiny pre-Revolutionary farmhouses (a plaque on one of these notes that its builder participated in the Boston Tea Party), early, cottage-sized Greek Revivals, mid-nineteenth-century villas. Some have been restored, others haven't. It's a real neighborhood of living homes, with each cross street offering a view of the working waterfront and river beyond.

---

**MASONIC TEMPLE**
401-245-7652.
Baker St., Warren, RI 02885.
Open: By appt.

This nineteenth-century temple is the oldest in New England. Make an appointment, if only to see twin Federal-style doorways — masterpieces of elaborate carpentry — built from timbers of British frigates sunk in Newport Harbor during the Revolution.

**MAXWELL HOUSE**
401-245-0392.
59 Church St., Warren, RI 02885.
Open: Year-round, Sat., 10:00 a.m.–2:00 p.m.
Admission: Free.

Prepare to be awed by the massive central chimney (complete with two beehive baking ovens) that dominates this gambrel-roofed colonial home built ca. 1750. This National Register property was recently refurbished to exacting eighteenth-century standards by the Massasoit Historical Society. Fireplace cooking, candle-dipping, and other eighteenth-century skills are frequently demonstrated. Annual events include a Fall Fair on the last Sat. in Sept. and a Christmas Open House the first weekend in Dec.

## Sakonnet

**ALPACAS OF HENSEFORTH FARM**
401-624-4184.
460 East Rd., Tiverton, RI 02878.
Open: Year-round.
Admission: Free.

This farmstead, built in 1740, was moved to this site all the way from Woonsocket in northern RI. Visitors are welcome to tour the house even though it's a family home. The main attractions however, are the twelve alpacas, plus guinea hens, ducks, chickens, and fish. In-season, visitors can purchase eggs, flowers, and yarn (call before visiting to find out when they're carding wool). Mind the "Alpaca Crossing" sign at the head of the driveway.

## CHASE-COREY HOUSE
401-624-8881.
3908 Main Rd., Rte. 77,
  Tiverton Four Corners,
  RI 02878.
Open: By appt.
Admission: Free.

**B**uilt in 1730, this gambrel-roofed colonial home is now maintained by the Tiverton Historical Society, which mounts special exhibitions in-season.

*"Here lyeth ye bode of Elisabeth ye second wife of William Pabodie who dyed Decem ye 14th 1717 aged about 45 years." This ancient inscription is one of many still legible in the Commons Burial Ground in Little Compton.*

Craig Hammell

## COMMONS BURIAL GROUND
The Commons, Little
  Compton, RI 02837.

**T**he triangular Burial Ground is at the heart of Little Compton's Commons, the most picturesque village center in RI. You can get shivers in this graveyard just from reading the dates. Betty Pabodie lies here, the first white woman born in New England, daughter of pilgrims Priscilla and John Alden. Also look for Elizabeth Mortimer (1712-76), whose inscription reads "In memory of Elizabeth, who should have been the wife of Mr. Simeon Palmer . . ." (they were married but lived apart at her request; Simeon didn't consider her conduct becoming of a real wife).

## GRAY'S STORE
401-635-4566.
4 Main St., Little Compton,
  RI 02837.
Open: Year-round.

**I**f this isn't *the* oldest operating general store in the country, it's right up there. Built in 1788, it contains Little Compton's first post office, plus the original soda fountain, candy and tobacco cases, and ice chest. You can buy Gray's jonnycake meal and even vintage clothing here.

## WILBOR HOUSE, BARN & QUAKER MEETING HOUSE
401-635-4559.

**T**his is one of those New England jigsaw puzzle houses: bits were fitted together in each ensuing century from the seventeenth through the nineteenth. Now restored and filled with colonial

W. Main Rd., Rte. 77, Little Compton, RI 02837. Open: Mid-Jun.–mid-Sept., Thurs.–Mon., 2:00 p.m.–5:00 p.m. Admission: $4 adults; $.75 children.

appointments, it's operated by the Little Compton Historical Society. The barn has a display of old farm tools, utensils, and vehicles.

## LIBRARIES

Whether you stop in to peruse a mystery or plan to spend hours doing genealogical research, local libraries are a great, often overlooked, resource. Those listed below contain rich materials on local history, including out-of-print books and collections donated by townspeople (everything from menus and scrapbooks to Peruvian artifacts). Note that all libraries are open year-round and closed on Sunday, except where noted.

## WEST

### *Jamestown*

**Jamestown Philomenian Library** (401-423-7280; 26 North Rd., Jamestown) Includes the **Sydney L. Wright Museum** of colonial and Native American artifacts; recently, as stipulated under the Native American Grave Protection and Reparation Act, most of the latter, including a stone bowl buried 3,400 years ago, are being returned to the Narragansett Tribe.

### *West Bay*

**Davisville Free Library** (401-884-5524; Davisville Rd., N. Kingstown) Open Mon., Wed., Fri. in summer; Tues., Thurs., Sat. in winter.

**East Greenwich Free Library** (401-884-9511; 82 Pierce St., E. Greenwich).

**Narragansett Public Library** (401-789-9507; Kingstown Rd., Narragansett) Closed Sat.–Sun. in summer.

**North Kingstown Free Library** (401-294-3306; 100 Boone St., N. Kingstown).

**Willet Free Library** (401-294-2081; Ferry Rd., N. Kingstown).

## EAST

### *Aquidneck*

**Middletown Public Library** (401-846-1573; 700 W. Main Rd., Rte. 114, Middletown).

**Portsmouth Free Public Library** (401-683-9457; 2658 E. Main Rd., Rte. 138, Portsmouth).

### *East Bay*

**George Hail Free Library** (401-245-7686; 530 Main St., Rte. 114, Warren)

Closed Sat.–Sun., Jul.–Aug. Includes the Charles R. Carr Collection of Pre-Columbian, Peruvian, and Native North American artifacts.

**Rogers Free Library** (401-253-6948; 525 Hope St., Rte. 114, Bristol) Closed Sat.–Sun., Jul.–Aug.

### Sakonnet

**Brownell Library** (401-635-8562; The Commons, Little Compton).

**Essex Public Library** (401-625-6799; 238 Highland Rd., Tiverton).

## LIGHTHOUSES

There are currently twenty-four working lighthouses in Rhode Island. Here are two landmarks, one on each side of the bay.

## WEST

### Jamestown

**Beaver Tail Lighthouse** (401-423-9941; Beaver Tail Point, Beaver Tail State Park, Jamestown) Strategically located at the tip of Conanicut Is., Beaver Tail was the first lighthouse in RI, originally built in 1749. The current granite tower was erected in 1856.

### West Bay

**Point Judith Lighthouse** (401-789-0444; 1460 Ocean Rd., Narragansett/Pt. Judith) This substantial, red-and-white tower was built in 1810. It has a white light that flashes three times every fifteen seconds. Access to the lighthouse and Coast Guard Station is restricted.

## MILITARY SITES & MUSEUMS

## WEST

### West Bay

**Quonset Aviation Museum** (401-294-9540; 488 Eccleston Ave., N. Kingstown/ Quonset-Davisville Air Base) This new museum is housed in the only brick hanger on the East Coast and features a glamorous collection of twenty-five aircraft (the oldest is from 1931), including a Russian MIG-17, World War II fighters, and an A-6 Intruder. Also New England aircraft memorabilia. Open year-round, Fri.–Sun., 1:00 p.m.–3:00 p.m.; $4 adults; children free.

**Varnum Military Museum** (401-884-4110; 6 Main St., E. Greenwich) A collection of artifacts from U.S. wars through World War I is displayed in a wonderful old armory that looks like a miniature, brick castle. Open by appt.

## EAST

### *Aquidneck*

**Butts Hill Fort** (off Sprague St., Portsmouth) These ruined redoubts mark where the Battle of Rhode Island took place on August 29, 1778 (see Chapter One, *History*). Drive down to Middletown and look for **Green End Fort** off Vernon Ave.; the redoubts there mark British defense lines for Newport.

### *Sakonnet*

**Fort Barton** (Highland Rd., Tiverton) This Revolutionary War redoubt was originally named Tiverton Heights Fort for its strategic location; it was feared that the British in Newport would cross to the mainland at Tiverton and attack Boston. One night in 1777, a certain Col. Barton stealthily sailed from the fort to capture the British general Prescott in Middletown (see **Prescott Farm**) — hence the name change. A nature walk leads from the fort over the wonderfully named Sin and Flesh Brook. Open year-round, sunrise to sunset.

## MONUMENTS & MEMORIALS

Craig Hammell

*Today a monument marks the spot where the chief of the Narragansetts met with Roger Williams on Conanicut Island (Jamestown).*

Not only monuments or memorials, but also just indications of good-spirit-edness, fun, and civic pride. For example, when in Warren check out the **fire hydrants;** they're all individually painted to look like people: soldiers, fire fighters, police officers, and the like. Very clever.

## WEST

### *West Bay*

**Canonchet Memorial** (on the Green at Exchange Place, Narragansett) This

6,000-pound limestone memorial to Narragansett chief Canonchet was sculpted in 1977 by artist Robert Carsten.

**Narragansett Indian Monument** (Kingstown Rd. and Strathmore St., Narragansett Pier) A twenty-three-foot sculpture carved from a single Douglas fir by artist Peter Toth, this is one of a series of forty-one monuments throughout the country honoring Native Americans.

## EAST

### *Aquidneck*

**Black Soldier's Memorial** (W. Main Rd., Rte. 114, Portsmouth) At the spot marked by the flagpole, the first company of African-Americans to fight for the country encountered the British on August 29, 1778, at the Battle of Rhode Island.

**Founder's Brook** (signposted off Boyd's Ln., Portsmouth) A bronze marker shows the spot where Anne Hutchinson and her fellow settlers landed in 1638 and subsequently made history. (See Chapter One, *History* for more information on Hutchinson and the Portsmouth Compact.)

### *Sakonnet*

**Rhode Island Red Monument** (Main St., Adamsville) One of only two monuments to chickens in the world (the other is in Georgia), this 1924 plaque honors the famed Rhode Island Red, first bred here in 1854.

## MUSEUMS

The following represent most of the principal museums in the Narragansett Bay area. Also take a look at the listings in **Historic Buildings & Sites, Libraries,** and **Military Sites & Museums.**

## WEST

### *Jamestown*

**JAMESTOWN MUSEUM**
401-423-0784.
92 Narragansett Ave.,
  Jamestown, RI 02835.
Open: Mid-Jun.–Aug.,
  Tues.–Sun.
Admission: Free.

This nineteenth-century schoolhouse makes an ideal seaside museum. It's a little musty, but the material is fascinating, featuring a permanent exhibit on the Jamestown ferries. The Jamestown-to-Newport route was established in 1675 and ran until 1969: the oldest transportation line in America served by the longest-operating ferry service. Special exhibits each season. Home of the Jamestown Historical Society.

## *West Bay*

**NEW ENGLAND
    WIRELESS & STEAM
    MUSEUM**
401-885-0545;
    fax 401-884-0683.
Frenchtown and Tillinghast
    Rds., E. Greenwich, RI
    02818.
Open: By appt. (very
    accommodating).
Admission: Nominal.

A small but very entertaining engineering museum with exhibits of early radio, telephone, and telegraph equipment, plus engines of all description. There's also a reference library of early scientific texts for researchers and students. Yankee Tune Up Day, featuring the radios, is held in the summer (call for date); Yankee Steam Up is held annually in mid-Sept.

**SOUTH COUNTY
    MUSEUM**
401-783-5400.
Canonchet Farm,
    Narragansett, RI 02882.
Open: May–Oct.,
    Wed.–Sun., 11:00
    a.m.–4:00 p.m.
Admission: $3.50 adults;
    $1.75 children.

Exhibits on rural life in eighteenth- and nineteenth-century RI, including a country kitchen, general store, cobbler shop, antique carriage collection, and a featured show of early American crafts. There's an operating printing shop in a separate building. Annual quilt show in late Aug.

## EAST

## *Aquidneck*

**PORTSMOUTH
    HISTORICAL SOCIETY**
401-683-9178.
E. Main Rd. and Union St.,
    Portsmouth, RI 02871.
Open: Mem. Day–Labor
    Day, Sat.–Sun. afternoons.
Admission: Free.

The PHS has a small but fascinating collection, including early household conveniences and farm implements. This was the former Christian Sabbath Society Meeting House; Julia Ward Howe preached here.

## *East Bay*

**BRISTOL HISTORICAL
    & PRESERVATION
    SOCIETY MUSEUM &
    LIBRARY**
401-253-7223; 401-253-5705.
48 Court St., Bristol, RI
    02890.
Museum: Jun.–Sept., Sun.,
    1:00 p.m.–4:00 p.m.; or
    call for appt.
Library: Wed., 2:00
    p.m.–5:00 p.m.
Admission: Free; $3.50 for
    use of library.

This county jail was constructed in 1828 from stone ballast used in Bristol sailing ships. Today it houses a library with very good genealogical materials and a collection of 300 years of Bristolian artifacts.

**FIREMAN'S MUSEUM**
401-245-7600.
42 Barker St., Warren, RI
02885.
Admission: By appt.

A restored fire barn that once housed Narragan-sett Steam Fire Co. #3, this is a great place for kids to look at old fire-fighting equipment and climb aboard Little Hero, Warren's first fire engine purchased in 1802.

*A Western Apache storage basket, ca. 1900, is among the highlights at the Haffenreffer Museum of Anthropology in Bristol.*

Craig Hammell

**HAFFENREFFER MUSEUM OF ANTHROPOLOGY**
401-253-8388.
Mt. Hope Grant, Tower St.,
Bristol, RI 02809.
Open: Jun.–Aug.,
Tues.–Sun.; weekends
off-season; closed Jan.
Admission: $2 adults; $1
children.

It seems as if you're penetrating primeval wood-land to reach the place, but once here, a magnifi-cent view of the Sakonnet River opens before you. Temporary shows and permanent exhibits trace various cultures of the Americas, including the Canadian and Alaskan North, the Southeast, the Great Plains, Mesoamerica, and more. A network of nature trails (be careful of the poison ivy) comb the 500-acre grant, which was once the ancestral homeland of the Wampanoag Tribe. The museum is administered by Brown University and plans to move to Providence in the near future.

**HERRESHOFF MARINE MUSEUM**
401-253-5000.
7 Burnside St., Bristol, RI
02809.
Open: May–Oct.,
Tues.–Sun., 1:00
p.m.–5:00 p.m.
Admission: $3 adults; $5
family.

The Herreshoff Shipyard built eight consecu-tively successful America's Cup Defenders between 1893 and 1954 (see Chapter One, *History*). This is their collection of thirty-five sleek and graceful sailing and power yachts, plus photos and memorabilia from the Golden Age of Yachting, including hand-carved models of Herreshoff-designed boats. The Herreshoff Manufacturing Co. was founded in 1863 by John Brown Herreshoff and his brother Capt. Nat (Nathaniel Green), who

*America's Cup winners and other sleek racing yachts make up the collection of the Herreshoff Marine Museum in Bristol.*

Craig Hammell

was known as the "Wizard of Bristol." Check out the **America's Cup Hall of Fame** for racing memorabilia in the new wing.

## MUSIC

### WEST

#### *West Bay*

**Lafayette Band Summer Concerts** (401-885-1125; N. Kingstown Town Beach, Band Shell, N. Kingstown) The Lafayette Band is one of the oldest community bands in the country (established 1882). Have a beach picnic and hear them play for free. Call for dates.

**North Kingstown Arts Council Summer Concert Series** These free concerts are held at the harbor's edge behind 55 Brown St. in Wickford Village on Tues. nights at 7:00 p.m. Bring blankets or lawn chairs. Everything from Dixieland to Irish, horns and pop.

### EAST

#### *East Bay*

**Summer Concerts By-the-Bay** (401-253-2707; Blithewold Mansion, 101 Ferry Rd., Rte. 114, Bristol) Concerts on Blithewold's beautiful grounds are held all summer; call for a schedule. Season pass costs $40.

---

### *Providence Nightclubs*

Here are several Providence-area clubs that are too good to miss.

**AS220** (401-831-9327; 115 Empire Street) A very casual, funky, spontaneous alternative art and performance space, incorporating a gallery and café with a stage and soundsystem. Live performances, readings, and concerts are held nightly, as befits a city with more working artists than anywhere else in the country. Cover charge $3 to $5.

**CAV** (401-751-9164; 14 Imperial Place) CAV stands for "Coffee Antiques Venture." It's a one-of-a-kind coffeehouse, with interesting food (including brunch) and even more interesting antiques. Best of all is the amazingly diverse live music, ranging from African to contemporary folk.

**Lupo's Heartbreak Hotel** (401-272-5876; 239 Westminster Street) Lupo's is a famous Providence rock-and-roll landmark and intimate venue for local and international bands, cutting-edge and big names alike. Cover charge $5 to $15.

---

## NIGHTLIFE

The following list is selective; the best thing to do is to find a good little club for yourself. Many restaurants also have entertainment in-season, particularly on weekends. Some standouts are noted below, but see the section Dining as well, plus the section Food & Beverage Purveyors, under the heading Bars.

## WEST

### *West Bay*

**Blue Parrot** (401-884-2002; 28 Water St., E. Greenwich) Live waterside jazz.

**Bon Vue Inn** (401-789-0696; 1238 Ocean Rd., Narragansett) Live rock and roll down by the sea.

## EAST

### *East Bay*

**The Clubhouse** (401-253-9844; 95 Tupelo St., Bristol) A popular spot to catch local rock bands.

## SEASONAL EVENTS & FESTIVALS

From the largest outdoor art show on the East Coast to the annual Blessing of the Fleet, Narragansett Bay has a festival for everyone.

## WEST

### *West Bay*

**Blessing of the Fleet** (401-783-7121; Great Island Rd., Narragansett/Galilee) A bishop blesses the fishing fleet, which is suitably decorated for the occasion, plus any pleasure craft on hand, then they all join in a floating parade.

**Blessing of the Fleet** (401-884-6363; E. Greenwich Cove, Water St., E. Greenwich) Same as the above, but for private boats; dock party follows at three waterfront restaurants.

**Jamestown Annual Art Show** (401-423-2436; Jamestown Community Center, Conanicus Ave. and Union St., Jamestown) There are paintings, photos, works on paper, sculpture, and more. This will be a twenty-five-year event in 1999. First weekend in Aug. The **Conanicut Island Craft Show** is the second weekend in Aug.

**Model Train Show** (401-783-5400; South County Museum, Canonchet Farm, Boston Neck Rd., Rte. 1A, Narraganasett) An annual event hosted by the Mohegan-Pequot Railroad Club, with miles and miles of track and many rare "choo-choos."

**Narragansett Heritage Days** (401-783-7121; Veteran's Memorial Park, off Ocean Rd., Narragansett Pier) Crafts, food, and nightly entertainment. Late Jul./early Aug.

**Waterfront Fest & Feast** (401-885-0020; Main St., E. Greenwich) A good time: 125 arts and crafts exhibitors, a 5-K road race, live music, and best of all, food sampling at Norton's Marina. Old-fashioned trolley cars cruise along Main St. and the waterfront. Late Aug.

**Wickford Art Festival** (401-294-6840; sidewalks of Wickford, Brown and Main Sts., N. Kingstown/Wickford) This is one of the oldest and largest annual art

*Onlookers peruse works at the Wickford Art Festival, one of the oldest and largest art shows on the East Coast*

shows on the East Coast. With exhibits by over 250 artists, it literally takes over the whole town. Good quality work but on the safe side; go to galleries for the avant-garde. Early to mid-Jul.

## EAST

### *Aquidneck*

**Annual Lawn Party** (401-846-9700; St. Mary's Episcopal Church, 324 E. Main St., Rte. 138, Portsmouth) They've been doing this in Portsmouth for over 120 years. Don't miss the baby parade, dunk tank, bakery and white elephant tables, local crafts, plus great food from clam cakes to chowder.

**Harvest Fair** (401-846-2577; Norman Bird Sanctuary, 583 Third Beach Rd., Middletown) Hay and pony rides, greased pole competitions, and even a Home & Garden Competition (enter your giant squash), plus scarecrow and apple pie contests. Tour the sanctuary, too. Early Oct.

### *East Bay*

**Bristol Civic, Military & Fireman's Parade** (401-253-7215; Hope and Chestnut Sts., Bristol) First held in 1785, this is the oldest Fourth of July Parade in the country. You know that when the center lines along the parade route are painted red, white, and blue — year-round — that this is no ordinary event. Crowds line up twelve-deep (those in front have probably been there since 5:00 a.m.) to watch over 3,000 marchers, floats, teams of Clydesdale horses, clowns, even a guy with a brass drum strapped to his lawn mower. The marching bands represent the pick of the national crop; don't miss yearly appearances by the famous Philadelphia Mummers, Tom McGrath's

*Bristol's venerable Civic, Military & Fireman's Parade, first held in 1785, is the oldest in the country.*

Craig Hammell

Marching Clambake Band from Newport, and especially the Centennial Legion Division — fife and drum corps in full eighteenth-century regalia. The parade is heralded by Bristol's town crier and lasts about three hours. If you want to join the 200,000 other folks who attend this annual extravaganza, heed some warnings: the parade starts at 10:30 a.m. but roads are blocked off by 8:30 a.m., so arrive early — you can begin setting up blankets and chairs along the sidewalks any time after 5:00 a.m. Plan to park at a distance; police recommend side streets, Colt State Park, and the Newport Creamery lot on Rte. 114 north of the town center. Either walk or bicycle in on the East Bay Bike Path, though it too gets crowded. Don't forget to bring cold drinks (no alcohol), sunscreen, and a hat. Or, if crowds give you the heebie-jeebies, watch full coverage on TV (it's carried by Channel 6, Providence's ABC affiliate).

**Civil War Reenactment** (401-783-5400; South County Museum, Canochet Farm, Boston Neck Rd., Rte. 1A, Narragansett) Watch as the Artillery Company of Newport reenacts drills, skirmishes, battles, etc. of the Civil War. Also demonstrations and a parade. Mid-May.

**Warren Art Festival** (401-245-4583; Burr's Hill Park, Water St., Warren) Artists from all over New England sell their work.

## *Sakonnet*

**Tiverton Four Corners Center for Arts & Education** (401-624-2600; 3852 Main Rd., Tiverton Four Corners) sponsors a wealth of cultural events from Jun.-Aug.: flower, antique, craft, and children's shows, plus storytellings and readings, in addition to rotating exhibitions by local artists. Call for a schedule.

## THEATER

R hode Island is home to one of the very best small repertory companies in the world: Trinity Repertory Company in Providence (401-351-4242; 201 Washington Street). A Trinity production is well worth a drive to Rhode Island's "Big City." Call ahead for a list of the season's performances. In the bay area, you'll also find the following excellent choices.

## WEST

## *West Bay*

**Greenwich Odeum Theatre** (401-885-9119; 59 Main St., E. Greenwich) This former movie house has reopened and not as a cineplex, but as a venue for nationally known singers, musicians, and comedians, as well as dramatic productions. In 1997, the National Shakespeare Co. presented *Much Ado About Nothing* and *Richard III*.

# EAST

## *Aquidneck*

**Rhode Island Shakespeare Theatre** (401-849-7892; St. George School, Purgatory Rd., Middletown) A superb, small theater company in summer residence on the beautiful campus of St. George's prep school (take a peek into nearby Purgatory Chasm before the show). Play selections are ambitious, and the acting is consistently good. It's a tiny space, so call for tickets ahead of time.

## *East Bay*

**Roger Williams University Performing Arts Center** (401-254-3626; box office, 401-254-3666; Roger Williams University, 1 Old Ferry Rd., Bristol) This shared space is busy year-round. During the academic year, plays are performed by Roger Williams students and faculty. In July, the college community teams up with professionals to perform as the **Barn Summer Theatre,** and in August, the **Bristol Theatre Company** of community performers takes the stage, literally. Call the box office for a performance roster.

# RECREATION

Probably the best recreational activity on Narragansett Bay is simply gazing at the natural magnificence of land and sea. The coast is often spectacularly rocky, as along the romantic shoreline of Beaver Tail State Park on Jamestown. But great swatches of sand poke through to offer some of the best beaches in New England, including the crashing surf at Second Beach in Middletown and the peace and quiet of Goosewing Beach in Little Compton.

Don't miss out on the time-honored pleasure of driving around and taking in the scenery. Many of the bicycle rides outlined under the heading Bicycling below are also suitable for car touring; cruise around with the windows down and enjoy a bay breeze.

## BASEBALL

From April through August, Rhode Island's own minor league team, the **Pawtucket Red Sox** (known simply as "The Pawsox") play at McCoy Stadium, just north of Providence (401-724-7300; 1 Columbus Avenue, Pawtucket). Tickets are just a couple of bucks, and they sell ice cream in upside-down, miniature batting hats (reason enough for going). Several times a summer Pawsox players hold free clinics to teach kids how to bat, field, and throw. Who knows? Next year these guys might be in the big leagues.

## BEACHES

Go on, get wet in the Ocean State. Beaches are the cushiony highlight of Narragansett Bay's 400 miles of coastline. Those listed below are all saltwater, and the fees, except where noted, are per car rather than per person. (Beach attendants start taking your money in mid-June and stop after Labor Day).

For **beachcombing** or shell hunting, first visit the **Sachuest Point National Wildlife Refuge** visitor center in Middletown and study their display of local shells to know what to look for (see State Parks & Wildlife Refuges below). The inside word is that **Brenton Point State Park** in Newport (see the section Recreation, under the heading State Parks in Chapter Three, *Newport*) is good for oyster drills, periwinkles, and surf clams; **Roger Wheeler State Beach** in Narragansett has dog whelks, blue mussels, and moon snails; **Fort Getty** on Jamestown is often less picked over than other spots and is good for slipper shells, mermaid's purses, and clam, quahog, and conch shells; and **Purgatory Chasm** and **Sachuest Point,** both in Middletown, offer up sea urchins and conch and clam shells. Happy hunting.

## WEST

### *Jamestown*

**Mackerel Cove** (Jamestown) Along the causeway leading to the Beaver Tail peninsula, this isn't the place for people who like sheltered, hidden spots, but the water is shallow and warm, so it's good for kids. Not the most beautiful spot in RI. 2,640 feet long; lifeguard, rest rooms; 150 parking spaces; $10.

### *West Bay*

**Narragansett Town Beach** (off Rte. 1A, Boston Neck Rd.) A long, flat beach in the middle of Narragansett Pier. There's usually a crowd here, good waves,

*Making their own fun on Narragansett Town Beach.*

Craig Hammell

and boardwalk-style fun. 2,640 feet long; full cabana service; car park; $5 walk-on fee.

**Roger Wheeler State Beach** (Narragansett) off Sand Hill Cove Rd. in Galilee, this is a family-style place with good playground facilities. 1,650 feet long; full cabana service; 2,000 parking spaces; $4 weekdays, $5 weekends.

**Salty Brine State Beach** (Narragansett) Formerly Galilee State Beach, this is just west of Roger Wheeler State Beach. It's small, but a major teen-spot-to-be-seen. 150 feet long; rest rooms; 100 parking spaces; $4 weekdays, $5 weekends.

**Scarborough State Beach** (Narragansett) It runs alongside Ocean Rd. on the way down to Pt. Judith. With your windows down, you can smell the Coppertone. *Rhode Island Monthly* says "Big hair, hard muscles, more mousse and mascara than SPF 15." 2,000 feet long; all facilities; 2,900 parking spaces; $4 weekdays, $5 weekends.

## EAST

### *Aquidneck*

**Sandy Beach** (Prudence Is.) Aptly named, as it's the only one on the island. This lovely rim of sand is on the northwestern arm of Prudence (about a fifteen-minute bicycle ride from the ferry landing at Homestead). It's absolutely undeveloped here — trees grow thick right up to the sand. The state has more or less abandoned this beach, but there's no reason not to use it — great views of the Newport and Jamestown bridges. 6,600 feet long.

**Sandy Point Beach** (Portsmouth) At the end of Sandy Point Ave., off E. Main Rd., Rte. 138, this Sakonnet River beach is a sheltered, calm spot, good for young paddlers. (The water is harmlessly murky due to the lack of surf.) 2,640 feet long; full cabana service; 150 parking spaces; $5.

**Second Beach** (Middletown) Take Aquidneck Ave. to the end and head left, pass the Purgatory Chasm sign, and wind up at Second Beach. Wide open sand and sea, with a land's end feeling. 7,920 feet long; full cabana service; 1,600 parking spaces; $10 weekdays, $15 weekends.

**Teddy's Beach** (Portsmouth) On Park Ave. in Island Park (very near the ruins of Stone Bridge), this is a small, quiet spot. 575 feet long; no lifeguards, but the surf isn't rough; 12 parking spaces; free.

**Third Beach** (Middletown) Head east from Second Beach and take a left to Third Beach (a right leads to Sachuest Point; see State Parks & Wildlife Refuges below). It's secluded here and popular with families and windsurfers. 2,640 feet long; rest rooms; 200 parking spaces; $10 weekdays, $15 weekends.

### *East Bay*

**Bristol Town Beach** (Colt State Park) So the bay up here has ripples instead of waves, and the shore has pebbles instead of sand — the water still feels good. 300 feet long; full cabana service; 400 parking spaces; $3 weekdays, $5 weekends.

## Sakonnet

**Fogland Beach** (Tiverton) Take Neck Rd. off Main Rd., Rte. 77 and turn right on Fogland Rd.(a beautiful drive). It's a pebbly bay beach, but it's nicely marooned on a tiny peninsula. 2,640 feet long; lifeguard, rest rooms; 250 parking spaces; $5.

**Goosewing Beach** (Little Compton) An idyllic spot, but beware, there's no longer direct access to Goosewing. Park at the town beach lot and walk eastward, crossing a little rivulet. Behind you are fields, cows, and an eighteenth-century stone barn; ahead is the Atlantic Ocean. 1,300 feet long.

**Grinnell's Beach** (Tiverton) Near the old Stone Bridge, facing Island Park in Portsmouth just across the water, this is a teenager-hangout beach. 1,320 feet long; lifeguard, rest rooms; 150 parking spaces; $5.

**South Shore Beach** (Little Compton) Also known as Little Compton Town Beach, it's a little tricky to find. Head south on W. Main Rd., Rte. 77 almost to the end, turn left on Swamp Rd.; at the point Swamp Rd. makes a ninety-degree bend to the left, take the road to the right (there's a small sign) to the beach, which is clean but somewhat stony. 1,300 feet long; lifeguard; 300 parking spaces; $9 weekdays, $13 weekends.

## BICYCLING

This is ideal cycling territory. Not only is the whole region fairly flat, the scenery is never redundant. Southern Rhode Island can seem like an abridged version of the whole of New England — seascapes, farm scenes, and wooded areas all mingled together.

Rules for safe cycling are the same here as everywhere: use a headlight and/or wear reflector clothing at night, and wear a helmet. A tip: never trust Rhode Island drivers. They are especially infamous for failing to use turn signals. (There's a Don Bosquet cartoon of a used car salesman delivering the pitch: "And the turn signals are like new!") Finally, bring a decent lock, and always use it.

The following are some recommended rides for each region, though for a thorough guide see *Short Bike Rides in Rhode Island* by Howard Stone (see the section Bibliography in Chapter Six, *Information*). Most routes make good motor tours as well.

## WEST

### Jamestown

The best choice for West Bay cycling is Conanicut Island (Jamestown's other name), which is a cyclist's paradise. On the southern end, head down Beaver

Tail Road to the lighthouse of the same name or out to Fort Wetherill State Park on the eastern promontory. Or head up East Shore Road to the northern tip, then come down North Road on the western side; there's not much here but farms and a scattering of old houses.

Another, somewhat busier, choice is to cycle around the Historic District in Narragansett Pier. It's flat and a fine way for architecture enthusiasts to get a good look at a number of handsome, shingle-style beach cottages. Although it comes to a dead end, don't miss Gibson Avenue; the houses are knockouts.

## EAST

### *Aquidneck*

A route through eastern Middletown and Portsmouth, from Third Beach Road to Wapping Road, finishing at Sandy Point Avenue, offers great views of the Sakonnet River. Cut onto Indian Avenue via Howland Avenue off Third Beach Road for a look at the vineyards that supply the Newport Winery; it's Bordeaux-beautiful out here. The Island Park and Hummocks area of northeastern Portsmouth is also fun to explore by bicycle; it's a classic New England marshscape of water, boats, and seagulls. The best time is late September when the marsh reeds turn burnt umber.

On Prudence Island, the ferry schedule leaves you nearly a full day to explore, and there's hardly any traffic (though some roads are of tightly packed gravel, so bring a cushion). Get a map from Marcie's General Store, then take off. The island is a tangle of woods and vines grown over abandoned fields; look for the old stone walls and for deer — Prudence has the densest deer population in New England. Don't miss a tour of South Prudence Bay Island Park, a former military installation that now makes a perfect bike path.

### *East Bay*

The **East Bay Bike Path** is the crowning glory of Rhode Island's bicycle routes. It runs fourteen and a half miles from Providence to Bristol, offering access to several parks and the bay en route; it also intersects a total of forty-nine streets, so obey the miniature stop signs, they're for real. The path is ten feet wide, paved with a centerline for two-way traffic, and equipped with four-foot shoulders (the rule is bikers to the right, walkers to the left, and dogs on leashes). Best of all, you don't even have to be in shape to go the distance — it's entirely flat. Stop at **Quito's Seafood** near the southern terminus (see the section Dining). They serve great fried clams.

Better yet (in my opinion), take a right on Child Street, Route 103 off Metacom Avenue, Route 136 in Warren and follow it to Long Lane; turn right and follow it to the end, then turn left on Barton Avenue; follow it to a right on Touisset Road, and then on to the bay. This is East Warren, also known as the Touisset Section of Warren; realtors bill it as "Rhode Island's forgotten hamlet." It's true: there's little here but farms, stables, and, at the very tip of the

*The East Bay Bike Path runs from Providence to Bristol — a great way to see the bay.*

Craig Hammell

Touisset peninsula, an old community of beach houses (modest by Newport standards). The bay opens before you, and the cycling is perfectly flat.

### *Sakonnet*

A suggested starting place is Tiverton Four Corners; take East Road into Adamsville, follow signs for **Sneekers** (a convenient restaurant and bar) into the Little Compton Commons, and head north on West Main Road to a left on Fogland Road (a brief detour to the beach here), then continue north on Neck Road, which leads back into Tiverton Four Corners and, happily, **Gray's Ice Cream.** This is pristine countryside; you'll see horses, cows, gulls, farm stands, fields, and the sea, but only one traffic light.

### EVENTS & ORGANIZATIONS

### WEST

### *West Bay*

**Tour de Cure — Bike to the Bay through South County** (401-789-4422; 800-548-4662) Experts and novices cycle twenty-, fifty-, or 100-K to raise money for diabetes research. The start/finish is at Narragansett Town Beach. Late May.

### EAST

### *East Bay*

**East Bay Bike-a-Thon** (401-253-7482) An annual event that begins at Independence Park in Bristol and finishes up at India Point Park in Providence.

*Sakonnet*

**Narragansett Bay Wheelmen** (401-831-1494) The Wheelmen are one of the biggest and oldest cycling clubs in the country; they hold organized rides every Sun. (and some Sats.), plus what's billed as **The Flattest Century in the East** on the Sun. after Labor Day (traditionally 100 miles, though you can do fifty or twenty-five; it starts in Tiverton). Their newsletter, *The Spoken Word*, lists all events. Send SASE to PO Box 428, Tiverton, RI 02878.

BICYCLE RENTALS & SHOPS

**WEST**

*West Bay*

**Narragansett Bikes** (401-782-4444; 1153 Boston Neck Rd., Rte. 1A, Narragansett) A complete bicycle shop.

**EAST**

*East Bay*

**Bay Path Cycles** (401-254-1277; 25 Homestead Ave., Barrington) The only bicycle shop in the East Bay vicinity that rents bicycles for the East Bay Bike Path (see above). Over 150 bicycles on display. Repairs and sales, too.

**BIRD-WATCHING**

Narragansett Bay is on the Atlantic Flyway, so during the spring and fall, the area plays host to diverse species of songbirds, shorebirds, and waterfowl — even the endangered peregrine falcon. Refuges (see State Parks & Wildlife Refuges below) attract over sixty species of nesting birds, including the woodcock, osprey, great blue (and little green) heron, snowy egrets, cormorants, and the endangered piping plover. Bird lovers have even seen pairs of bald eagles nesting on the southern shores of Narragansett Bay. **Ninigret National Wildlife Refuge Complex** (401-364-9124; Box 307, Charlestown, RI 02813) publishes a free wildlife calendar that notes the species to find during different seasons.

**BOWLING**

**WEST**

*West Bay*

**Kingstown Bowl** (401-884-4450; 6125 Post Rd., Rte. 1, N. Kingstown).
**Wickford Lanes** (401-294-9886; Post Rd., Rte. 1, N. Kingstown).

## EAST

### *Aquidneck*

**Aquidneck Lanes** (401-846-2729; 173 E. Main Rd., Rte. 138, Middletown) Tenpin and duckpin bowling, plus pro shop, snack bar, and drinks.

**Ryan Family Amusement Center** (401-849-9990; 105 Chases Ln., Middletown) Candlepin and tenpin bowling; also at 266 Thames St., Newport (401-846-5774). See Grab Bag below for other Ryan Center activities.

## CAMPING

**H**ard to believe that woodlands still cover sixty percent of the most densely populated state in the union. Burrowed into these enclaves are a host of state, municipal, and private campgrounds. Remember to get a permit for every fire that you build. Rates usually run from $15 to $25 per night, depending on your equipment (tent or trailer). Most trailer sites include electric, water, and sewer hookups; general facilities usually feature hot showers, rest rooms, dumping stations, and picnic tables. Extras are noted below.

## WEST

### *Jamestown*

**Fort Getty Recreation Area** (401-423-1363; Fort Getty Rd., PO Box 377, Jamestown, RI 02835) A recommended spot (by the photographer of this book) on the spectacular Beaver Tail peninsula. 100 trailer sites and twenty-five tent sites. Facilities include boat ramp and fishing dock. Season: Mem. Day weekend-Columbus Day.

### *West Bay*

**Fishermen's Memorial State Park** (401-789-8374; 1011 Pt. Judith Rd., Rte. 108, Narragansett, RI 02882) 147 trailer sites (forty include sewer hookups) and thirty-five tent sites. Tennis, basketball, horseshoe courts, and children's playground. Reservations required; write in advance to Division of Parks and Recreation, 2321 Hartford Ave., Johnston, RI 02919. Season: Mid-Apr.–Oct.

**Long Cove Marina Family Campsites** (401-783-4902; Long Cove Marina, off Pt. Judith Rd., Rte. 108, Narragansett, RI 02882) 155 trailer sites and twenty tent sites. Facilities include the usual, plus launching ramp, saltwater fishing, and dockage with twenty-four slips. Allow only one pet, must be leashed. Season: May-mid–Oct.

## EAST

### *Aquidneck*

**Meadowlark Recreational Vehicle Park** (401-846-9455; 132 Prospect Ave.,

Middletown, RI 02842) Forty trailer sites. No tent sites; leashed pets only. Season: Mid-Apr.-Oct.

**Melville Ponds Campground** (401-849-8212; 181 Bradford Ave., off W. Main Rd., Rte. 114, Portsmouth, RI 02871) Sixty-six trailer sites (thirty-three include sewer hookups) and fifty-seven tent sites. Features include 116 fire rings and on-site fishing. Playground and beach privileges, too. Season: Apr.-Oct.

**Middletown Campground** (401-846-6273; Second Beach, 350 E. Main Rd., Middletown, RI 02840) Thirty-six trailer sites, all with sewer hookups. No tent sites. Access to the beach (a favorite) comes with the deal. No pets. Season: Mid-May–late Sept.

**Paradise Mobile Home Park** (401-847-1500; 459 Aquidneck Ave., Middletown, RI 02842) Sixteen trailer sites. No tent sites; public telephone; no pets. Season: May–mid-Oct.

## FISHING

Most of the boats listed under Charters, under the heading Sailing & Boating below offer deep-sea fishing trips to inshore and offshore locations; some will even take you on an overnighter out to Georges Bank and other open-ocean grounds. Note that the price of the charter includes bait and tackle; the crew will usually clean your catch for you, too. There are two kinds of fishing charters: 1) party ("head") boats take between forty to about 110 passengers for bottom-fishing excursions. You don't normally need a reservation, and boats leave on a set schedule, usually 6:00 a.m. to 2:30 p.m.; sometimes you have to rent your tackle; 2) fishing charters require reservations and sail at your bidding — you get enough people (usually between four to six) and plan your own route. Some of the best local spots include **Nebraska Shoals** off Charlestown for bluefish; **Coxes Ledge** east of Block Island for cod; near **Point Judith Light** and **Matunuck Point** for bass.

Then there's always freshwater fishing for the compleat angler. A freshwater license is about $10 and is available at most bait and tackle shops. Trout season opens on the second Saturday in April at sunrise; look for stocked ponds of brown, rainbow, and brook trout. For further license information, call 401-277-3576 or 401-789-3094. Good bets are **St. Mary's** and **Melville Ponds** in Portsmouth and **Tiverton Trout Pond** in Tiverton.

For restrictions, see the section Recreation, under the heading Fishing, in Chapter Three, *Newport*.

### LESSONS

### WEST

### *West Bay*

**Fin & Feather Lodge** (401-885-8680; 95 Frenchtown Rd., E. Greenwich) Free fly-casting instruction on Sat. 9:00 a.m.–12:00 noon, weather permitting. Canoe rentals.

## RENTALS, BAIT, TACKLE

For more options on bait and tackle shops, see Marinas under the heading Sailing & Boating below and the section Shopping, under the heading Marine Supply.

## WEST

### *Jamestown*

**Zeek's Creek Bait & Tackle** (401-423-1170; 194 North Rd., Jamestown) Look for Zeek's "Hook, Line & Sinker" column in *The Jamestown Press.*

### *West Bay*

**John's Bait & Tackle** (401-885-3761; 135 Frenchtown Rd., N. Kingstown).
**Quaker Lane Bait & Tackle** (401-294-9642; 4019 Quaker Ln., Rte. 2, N. Kingstown) The obvious, plus canoe and kayak sales and rentals.

## EAST

### *Aquidneck*

**Edward's Fishing Tackle** (401-846-4521; 36 Aquidneck Ave., Middletown) A complete line of fresh- and saltwater tackle, plus live and frozen bait. Also try **Sam's Bait and Tackle** (401-848-5909; 936 Aquidneck Ave.).

### *East Bay*

**Neves Marine, Bait & Tackle** (401-253-5358; Metacom Ave., Bristol).

## SHELLFISHING

The commercial fishing fleet out of Galilee owes its livelihood to lobsters, but a host of other shelled and spiny creatures can be found in Rhode Island waters as well. Nonresidents of Rhode Island are required to apply for a license from the Division of Licensing (401-272-3576) before harvesting shell-fish (not required for Rhode Islanders). Nonresidents are allowed half a bushel of scallops and a quarter-bushel each of quahogs, soft-shell and surf clams, oysters, and mussels per day, except in shellfish management areas; Rhode Island residents are allowed twice the take on all shellfish. Ask the bait shops where to go, but good bets for clamming always include **Escape Road** in Galilee, **Fogland Point** on the Sakonnet River in Tiverton, and **Bissell Cove** in North Kingstown. All you need is a rake, a bucket, and a set of rules on sizes — you can get these at most of the bait shops listed above.

If it's lobsters or nothing, for $20 residents only can buy a noncommercial lobster license (five lobster pots a day) or a lobster driving license (five lobsters per day). Again, get a set of rules, which are available from the Division of Law Enforcement (401-277-2284). Or better yet, visitors and residents alike can build their own lobster trap at a class offered by URI on its East Farm location (401-792-6211; Rte. 108, Kingston, RI 02881), near the Narragansett Pier. If the trap doesn't work, use it as an end table.

## SEASONAL EVENTS

**Snug Harbor Shark Tournament** (401-783-7766; Snug Harbor Marina, Gooseberry Rd., S. Kingstown) A quest for prize-winning sharks of all breeds. Mid-Jun. Immediately followed by the **Snug Harbor June Moon Madness Striper Tournament;** this is the region's only striped bass tourney, with separate competitions for surf casters and boat anglers. For entry form, contact Tournament Enterprises, Dept. SH, PO Box 803, Greenville, RI 02828.

**Tuna Tournament** (401-737-8845; North Docks, Narragansett/Galilee) An over thirty-five-year old event that includes over 100 boats and 400 anglers. Early Sept.

## GOLF

The following golf courses, clubs, and driving ranges are open to the public. For custom club design, repairs, and used and new sales, try **Ocean State Golf** (401-295-5511; 7360 Post Road, Route 1, North Kingstown).

## WEST

### *Jamestown*

**Jamestown Golf Course** (401-423-9930; E. Shore Rd., Jamestown) 9 holes, 3,344 yards, par 72, carts available. Snack bar, lounge. It's said that this is the oldest nine-holer in the country.

### *West Bay*

**North Kingstown Municipal Golf Course** (401-294-4051; Quonset Access Rd., N. Kingstown/Quonset Point) 18 holes, 6,300 yards, par 70, carts available. Snack bar. On the list of RI's fifteen best courses.

**Rolling Greens** (401-294-9859; Ten Rod Rd., N. Kingstown) 9 holes, 3,059 yards, par 35, carts available. Snack bar.

**Woodland Golf & Country Club** (655 Old Baptist Rd., N. Kingstown) 9 holes, 3,180 yards, par 70, carts available. Lounge.

## EAST

### *Aquidneck*

**Green Valley Country Club** (401-847-9543; 371 Union St., Portsmouth) 18 holes, 6,500 yards, par 71, carts available. Restaurant, bar. Described as "a beast" in a *Rhode Island Monthly* roundup of the state's best courses; three par-five holes.

**Montaup Country Club** (401-683-9882; Anthony Rd., Portsmouth) 18 holes, 6,300 yards, par 71, carts available. Dining room, bar. The fifteenth hole is described as ". . . the Calvin Klein of golf holes . . . first-class, simple, under-stated, with just enough mystery to always make it worth your investment."

**Tee Time Golf Practicing Center** (401-841-8454; 1305 W. Main Rd., Rte. 114, Middletown) A fifty-station driving range with covered and grass tees. Pro shop, private lessons.

### *East Bay*

**Bristol Golf Club** (401-253-9844; 95 Tupelo St., Bristol) 9 holes, 6,060 yards, par 71, carts available.

**Pocasset Country Club** (401-683-2266; 807 Bristol Ferry Rd., Portsmouth) 9 holes, 2,770 yards, par 34, carts available. Restaurant, lounge.

### HIKING & WALKING

In addition to the suggestions in State Parks & Wildlife Refuges below, also see the section Culture, under the heading Museums for more sites with hiking trails. Another source is Ken Weber's excellent *Walks & Rambles in Rhode Island* series (see the section Bibliography in Chapter Six, *Information*). The seasonal listings below contain energetic events for runners, too.

### WEST

### *Jamestown*

**Beaver Tail State Park** (Jamestown) Meandering trails follow the coast from

*Park rangers lead guided tours along the rocky coast beneath Beaver Tail Lighthouse on Jamestown.*

Craig Hammell

one side of the headland to the other. The western route is probably too rigorous for children, but it's more private, and the views are superb; on the eastern shore, note the granite blocks chiseled in delicate floral patterns; they were destined for a building in Virginia but went down in an 1859 wreck, only to be tossed ashore in the 1938 hurricane. The whole hike (rock scrambling makes it a hike rather than walk) is three miles.

## EAST

### *Aquidneck*

**Norman Bird Sanctuary** (Middletown) Eight miles of well-marked trails lead through a variety of wildlife habitats and some spectacular sea view scenery.

### *East Bay*

**Haffenreffer Museum of Anthropology** (Bristol) A network of mapped nature trails runs like a maze through 500 acres of woodland, overlooking Mt. Hope Bay.

### *Sakonnet*

**Ruecker Wildlife Refuge** (Tiverton) A mild one-and-a-half-mile walk through saltwater marshes and wooded uplands; the way is well marked.

**Weetamoo Woods** (Tiverton) Pristine hiking trails lead through a forest, past ponds, brooks, and to an historic village site. For trailhead: drive south on Main Rd., Rte. 77, turn left onto Lafayette Rd. An entrance will be signposted.

### Seasonal Events

**Rhode Island Marathon** (401-861-RACE) In Providence, RI, in early Nov.

## HOCKEY

The Providence Bruins (known behind their backs as the Baby Bruins — Boston's Minor League team) skate at the Civic Center in Providence, Rhode Island, throughout hockey season. More people come to see them than any other professional hockey team in the country. Join the crowd. Call 401-273-5000 for tickets.

## HORSEBACK RIDING & POLO

The following stables offer trail rides, indoor ring riding, and lessons.

## EAST

### *Aquidneck*

**Glen Farm** (401-847-7090; Glen Rd., Portsmouth, RI 02871) Polo and riding lessons, plus trails through miles of farmland, woods, and beaches. For more on the polo opportunities at Glen Farm, see the section Recreation, under the heading Horseback Riding & Polo in Chapter Three, *Newport.*

**Newport Equestrian Center** (401-848-5440; 401-847-1774; 287 Third Beach Rd., Middletown, RI 02842) Instruction at all levels, plus trail rides on the beach ($65 for two hours) and more. See this listing in the section Recreation, under the heading Horseback Riding & Polo in Chapter Three, *Newport.*

**Sandy Point Stables** (401-849-3958; Sandy Point Ave., Portsmouth, RI 02871) Lessons, indoor/outdoor summer riding camp, and pony parties.

**Upson Downs Stables** (401-683-0453; 401-683-4838; White Horse Ter., Portsmouth, RI 02871) Riding lessons for $12 per hour; indoor ring riding.

### East Bay

**Arcadian Run Farm** (401-245-1994; Barton Ave., E. Warren, RI 02885) Lessons, training, and sales of sport horses in a lovely spot in rural E. Warren.

### Sakonnet

**Roseland Acres Equestrian Center, Inc.** (401-624-8866; 594 East Rd., Tiverton, RI 02878) Instruction for beginning, intermediate, and advanced riders; also one- and two-hour guided trail rides.

**Sakonnet Equestrian Center** (401-625-1458; 3650 Main Rd., Rte. 77, Tiverton, RI 02878) English riding lessons, boarding; six shows per year.

### SAILING & BOATING

Contact the Rhode Island Tourism Division (401-277-2601; 800-556-2484; 7 Jackson Walkway, Providence, Rhode Island 02903) for their comprehensive pamphlet *Boating & Fishing in Rhode Island.*

For information on kayaking, see the heading Water Sports below.

#### CHARTERS, LESSONS, RENTALS

Charter boats are available for fishing, whale watching, and simply cruising around Narragansett Bay. Regularly scheduled sight-seeing cruises ("sight sailing," as one promoter calls it) are noted under the heading Tours below. Chartering a boat refers to renting a crewed boat (the skipper remains onboard and in charge) and to following an agenda of your own choosing or one recommended by the captain. It's your responsibility to get a group together (usually no more than eight) to share expenses. Several of the listings below also include "bare-boat" charters — meaning that you hire just the boat and crew it yourself. Charter listings also include several party fishing boats that depart for scheduled trips and generally take upwards of twenty passengers.

## WEST

### *West Bay*

**Bob's Boat, Bait & Tackle** (401-295-8845; 23 Brown St., N. Kingstown, RI 02852) Sailing lessons.

**The Frances Fleet** (401-783-4988; 800-662-2824; PO Box 3724, Peace Dale, RI 02883) Deep-sea fishing (half- and three-quarter day trips, plus extended trips to Georges Banks; call for special cod and bluefish dates); moonlight cruises and whale watching. The whale watching lasts five hours and costs $30 adults, $20 children. Departs regularly from the Galilee docks in Narragansett.

**Greenwich Bay Sailing Association** (401-885-1231; 401-884-7700; East Greenwich Yacht Club, E. Greenwich, RI 02818) Offers a four-week beginner program for adults ($250), plus classes for children and private lessons.

**Mill Cove Yacht Sales and Charters** (401-295-0504; 1 Phillips St., N. Kingstown, RI 02852) All levels of instruction on your boat or theirs. Also rents Lasers, Sunfish, and sixteen-foot powerboats daily, plus twenty-two- and forty-two-foot sailboats either bare-boat or crewed. They'll sell you a boat, too.

*Persuader* (401-783-5644; 110 Avice St., Narragansett, RI 02882) Join Capt. Denny Dillon aboard the *Persuader* for half- and full-day and special evening trips. Will also do pickups on Block Is.

*Seven B's V* (401-789-9250; Galilee Docks, Dock RR, Narragansett, RI 02882) Custom eighty-foot yacht for special events, fishing, whale watching, and moonlight cruises. Maximum six passengers. Sails from Galilee Charter Boat Docks.

**West Bay Sailing** (401-885-4532; Box 757, E. Greenwich, RI 02818) Lessons.

## EAST

### *Aquidneck*

**Myles Standish Charters** (401-846-7225; 4 Smithfield Dr., Middletown, RI 02842) Offers both sport and bottom fishing, plus sight-seeing excursions aboard the *Mayflower*.

### *Sakonnet*

**Sportfisherman** (401-635-4292; Sakonnet Point., Little Compton, RI 02837) This party boat sails on a schedule from Sakonnet Point; call Capt. Bud Phillips.

### MARINAS

These marinas offer public docking slips and/or moorings on and around Narragansett Bay. Most have full-service facilities, which generally include electrical hookups, gas, diesel, propane, bilge pumps, fresh water, ice, and telephone (those that are lacking are noted). Most have more, including a marine store, rest rooms, showers, and other amenities. *Call for specifics and to see if you'll need a reservation in high-season.*

**WEST**

*All manner of pleasure craft moor in Jamestown Harbor, beneath the elegant backdrop of the Newport Bridge.*

Craig Hammell

## *Jamestown*

**Conanicut Marina** (401-423-1556; 1 Ferry Wharf, Jamestown Harbor, Jamestown) Fifteen guest slips, twenty guest moorings. Full repairs.
**Dutch Harbor Boat Yard** (401-423-0630; 252 Narragansett Ave., Jamestown).
**Jamestown Boatyard** (401-423-0600; Racquet Rd., Jamestown) Five guest slips. Full repairs (not many other amenities). Near Fort Wetherill State Park.

## *West Bay*

Anchorage is also available in Point Judith Pond (a quiet, well-dredged basin; the **Rhode Island State Pier** at Galilee is here, too), and there are three guest moorings behind the breakwaters in Wickford's outer harbor. Off Jamestown, the best anchorage is in Jamestown Harbor, south of the ferry landing.

**Long Cove Marina** (401-783-4902; Old Pt. Judith Rd., RR #9, Box 76, Narragansett) Forty-five guest slips.
**Pleasant Street Wharf** (401-294-2791; 160 Pleasant St., N. Kingstown/Wickford) One guest slip, two guest moorings. Minor repair work.
**Wickford Bait & Tackle** (401-295-8845; 1 Phillips St., N. Kingstown/Wickford) One guest slip. Repairs, bait and tackle.
**Wickford Cove Marina** (401-884-7014; Reynolds St., N. Kingstown/Wickford) Transient slips available. Engine, hull, and rigging repairs.
**Wickford Shipyard** (401-294-3361; 125 Steamboat Ave., N. Kingstown/Wickford) Twelve guest slips. Inner harbor.

**EAST**

## *Aquidneck*

**Brewer's Sakonnet Marina** (401-683-355; Narragansett Blvd., Portsmouth).
**East Passage Yachting Center/Coggeshall Marina** (401-683-4000; 800-922-2930; 1 Lagoon Rd., off W. Main Rd., Rte. 114, Portsmouth) On the grounds

of the Navy's old PT Boat training ground (The Melville Grille is also here; see the section Dining), this bills itself as the state's largest and most secure marina. Many guest slips; reservations accepted; all the usual amenities, plus shuttle van service to Newport.

**Little Harbor Marine** (401-683-7100; One Little Harbor Landing, Portsmouth).

**Pirate Cove Marina, Inc.** (401-683-3030; 109 Point Rd., Portsmouth) Five guest slips, five guest moorings. Full repairs.

**Point Boat Yard** (401-683-0433; 199 Narragansett Ave., Portsmouth).

**Potter's Cove** off **Prudence Island** offers three state guest moorings; it's one of the best undeveloped anchorage sites in Narragansett Bay. There are five more state guest moorings off Prudence Bay Island Park, but these tend to be crowded. For information, call the Rhode Island Tourism Division (401-277-2601; 800-556-2484).

**Stone Bridge Marina** (401-683-1011; 41 Point Rd., Portsmouth) Two guest slips. Nice view of the old Stone Bridge, at the foot of 15 Point Rd.; the restaurant 15 Point Road is here (see the section Dining).

### *East Bay*

There are three state guest moorings at the extreme head of **Bristol Harbor** and a state pier on the eastern shore; you can also anchor in the **Warren River** (middle of Smith Cove). For information, call the Rhode Island Tourism Division (401-277-2601; 800-556-2484).

### *Sakonnet*

In additon to the marinas below, there are several anchorage spots along the Sakonnet River. In Tiverton, try the east shore (watch the strong current between the bridges in Tiverton Harbor). Also try Fogland Harbor, though it's not particularly sheltered on the northern side, and Sachuest Cove in the lower river is good except in north or east winds.

**Riverside Marine, Inc.** (401-625-5181; 211 Riverside Dr., Tiverton).

**Sakonnet Point Marina** (401-635-4753; Sakonnet Point, Little Compton).

**Standish Boat Yard, Inc.** (401-624-4075; 1697 Main Rd., Rte. 77, Tiverton).

## SEASONAL SAILING & BOATING EVENTS

**Fool's Rules Regatta** (401-423-1492; Jamestown Yacht Club, East Ferry Beach, Jamestown) This is an annual silly sailing event. Construct your boat at 9:00 a.m. on the beach and use anything but standard marine materials. Then race it 500 yards beginning at 11:00 a.m. Late Aug.

## STATE PARKS & WILDLIFE REFUGES

Narragansett Bay is a naturalist's dream; its rocky shores, coastal wetlands, and rolling dunes shelter hosts of indigenous and migratory animals.

Environmental watchdog groups, especially **Save The Bay,** preserve its integrity and have helped restore it as well. For information on their programs, contact Save The Bay, 434 Smith St., Providence, Rhode Island 02908 (401-272-3540).

State parks are open from sunrise to sunset; naturalists are on duty only during the summer months. Pets must be on leashes; rest rooms are usually available. For more on state parks, contact the **Department of Environmental Management, Division of Parks and Recreation** (401-277-2632; 2321 Hartford Avenue, Johnston, Rhode Island 02919). At wildlife refuges, surf casting is allowed but no bicycles, motor vehicles, or kites. For more information, call the Refuge Manager (401-364-9124). A word of warning about **ticks:** wear protective clothing and *always* check for ticks afterward. Wood ticks are common, especially after paths have been mowed, but the tiny deer tick is the one to watch out for (the carrier of Lyme disease).

## WEST

### *Jamestown*

**Beaver Tail State Park** (401-423-9941; Jamestown) At the southern tip of Conanicut Is., Beaver Tail is one of the best places in the state to set a Gothic romance: rocky, windswept, beautiful. **Beaver Tail Lighthouse** (see the section Culture) guards the point.

**Fort Wetherill State Park** (401-243-1771; Jamestown) From here, look across the bay to Ft. Adams; both former military installations are still standing guard at the entrance to RI waters. Wetherill is on a small peninsula at the southeastern end of Jamestown; it offers a rocky shoreline, paths, and terrific views.

### *West Bay*

**Goddard State Park** (401-884-2010; Ives Rd., E. Greenwich) Right on Greenwich Bay, the park offers swimming, bathhouses, fishing, golfing, hiking trails, boat rentals, game fields, picnic areas, and a nature program.

**Narrow River** Not a state park or refuge, but a quiet, peaceful, silent place that few discover. The river (real name Pettaquamscutt) begins life as a tidal inlet, becomes a salt marsh, estuary, a fjordlike pond, and finally a river system, all of which are home to at least thirty species of birds and waterfowl. Best explored by kayak (see the listing for Narrow River Kayaks, under the heading Water Sports below).

## EAST

### *Aquidneck*

**Narragansett Bay Estuarine Research Reserve** (401-683-4236; 401-277-2771; Prudence Is.) This 5,000-acre reserve includes all of Hope Is. and most of Patience Is. (both served only by private boat) and sixty-one percent of Prudence Is. Perfect for shellfishing, hiking, and biking. On summer weekends, naturalists lead walks along the northern and southern tips of Prudence; beachcombing is a highlight. Call for schedule.

**Norman Bird Sanctuary** (401-846-2577; 583 Third Beach Rd., Middletown) Spy birds and other wildlife on 465 acres marked out by seven miles of trails. The reserve overlooks the sea and includes **Hanging Rock** — a natural wonder where Bishop Berkeley used to sit and meditate (see the section Culture for the listing Whitehall House). Habitats include hay fields, woodlands, and four craggy ridges of erosion-resistant rock. Nature study programs year-round and a "Birds and Breakfast" event in May. Trail fee: $4 adults, $1 children. Open daily in summer; closed Mon. in winter.

**Purgatory Chasm** Not a state park or refuge, but worth seeing. Where Paradise Ave. ends at Second Beach Rd. (also known as Purgatory Rd.), you'll see the Hanging Rock to your left and a small sign for Purgatory Chasm to the right. Park and follow the path to the sea; the chasm is a narrow cleft in the cliffs overlooking the ocean.

**Sachuest Point National Wildlife Refuge** (401-364-9124; follow Second Beach Rd. south to the right to land's end at Sachuest Pt.) Impossible to believe that Newport is just two promontories away. This 242-acre refuge offers a three-mile maze of hiking trails (like green tunnels in the summer) studded with wildflowers. Terrain includes salt marshes, grasslands, beaches, rocky cliffs, brushlands, and dunes — all resting areas for migratory birds. Visitor center. Free.

### East Bay

**Colt State Park** (401-253-7482; Hope St., Rte. 114, Bristol) This bayside park, on the site of the former 460-acre Colt estate and casino, has a fishing pier, boat launches, bicycle and walking trails through woods and along the water, a sculpture garden, playgrounds, a sixty-foot observation tower in a converted silo, and a scenic, rocky coast. $4.

**Touisset Marsh Wildlife Refuge** (401-984-5454; Barton Ave. and Touisset Rd.) A marsh site that's home to a variety of waterbirds. Managed by the Audubon Society of Rhode Island. $5.

### Sakonnet

**Ruecker National Wildlife Refuge** (401-624-2759; Seapowet Ave., Tiverton) This forty-eight-acre refuge offers hiking trails that wind through woodlands and an unforgettable salt marsh that's a habitat for herons, egrets, and osprey. Managed by the Audubon Society of Rhode Island. Free.

### TENNIS

See the section Lodging for inns, hotels, and B&Bs with tennis courts, which are often available to the public for a fee, or call individual Chambers of Commerce (see the section Tourist Information in Chapter Six, *Information)* for locations of public tennis courts.

## TOURS

A diverse range of tours by air, sea, land, and on foot are noted below. The boats listed here offer sight-seeing cruises with regularly scheduled departures (see the heading Sailing & Boating above for other sailing options).

### BY AIR

In the section Recreation in Chapter Three, *Newport,* see the heading Tours "By Air."

**Balloon Tours International** (401-423-9146; Jamestown, RI 02835).

### BY BOAT

**The Kayak Centre** (401-295-4400; 888-SEA KAYAK; E-mail: funn@kayakcentre. com; 9 Phillips St., Wickford, RI 02852) See the heading Water Sports below.

**Narragansett Bay Sailing Company** (401-789-3904; 103 Conch Rd., Narragansett, RI 02882) Regularly scheduled luncheon, twilight, and sunset cruises, plus special event outings aboard the *Legasea,* a fifty-six-foot schooner built as a replica of nineteenth-century traders. Departs from Conanicut Marina, Jamestown.

*Southland* (401-783-2954; Galilee Cruises, Inc., PO Box 522, Narragansett, RI 02882) Daily one hour and forty-five-minute tours of Galilee, Pt. Judith, and Jerusalem aboard this sixty-four-foot two-decker. Departs daily (early spring-fall) from State Pier 3, Galilee; 11:00 a.m., 1:00 p.m., 3:00 p.m., 5:00 p.m.

## WATER SPORTS

This section highlights sports in the water rather than on the water. Fans of **Kayaking, Parasailing, Scuba Diving, Snorkeling, Surfing, Waterskiing,** and **Windsurfing** will find what they're looking for. Lessons, sales, and rentals are readily available, on both sides of the bay.

**Divers** will be heartened to hear that pros consider Narragansett Bay to offer some of the best dives in New England. There are two excellent spots off Jamestown, both with ample parking (important when lugging gear). **Fort Wetherhill State Park** has two sheltered, southern coves and a rocky drop-off; look for flounder, tautog, eels, and squid. Nearby **Beaver Tail State Park** is also good, though there's less visibility underwater (it's more exposed); there's a rocky bottom, lots of seaweed, and fish.

**Surfers,** WBRU (95.5 FM) broadcasts daily surf reports at 8:35 a.m. The best surfing beaches are **Narragansett Town Beach** in Narragansett Pier and **Second Beach** in Middletown.

## WEST

### *Jamestown*

**Ocean State Scuba, Inc.** (401-423-1662; 800-933-DIVE; 23A Narragansett Ave.,

Jamestown, RI 02835) Diving rentals, sales, lessons, and boat dive charters. Also surf kayaking equipment — they call it "seagoing mountain biking."

### West Bay

Free surfing lessons are offered on **Narragansett Town Beach** from mid-June to Labor Day, Wednesdays, 12:00 noon (for more information, call The Watershed, 401-789-1954). The instructor's name is Peter Pan. If you wait for not-so-great weather, you might get an individual lesson.

**Anderson's Ski and Dive Center** (401-884-1310; 5865 Post Rd., Rte. 1, E. Greenwich, RI 02818) Free diving lessons, if you are at least 12 years old.

*There's no better way to explore Narragansett Bay's rocky coves than by kayak.*

Craig Hammell

**The Kayak Centre** (401-295-4400; 888-SEA KAYAK; E-mail: funn@kayakcen-tre.com; 9 Phillips St., Wickford, RI 02852) This is *the* kayak place in Rhode Is. In addition to kayak sales and rentals, plus a retail shop with clothing, books, videos, etc., the Centre offers guided harbor tours of Wickford Cove, group lessons, private instruction, a women's kayaking workshop, special clinics, and a host of kayak tours. The tours include a series of nighttime **Full Moon Paddles** from May-Sept., trips around Conanicut Is., tours of West Bay saltwater ponds, and an overnight sea-kayaking adventure to Block Is. (the latter costs $575, involves twelve miles of open-ocean kayaking, and includes a B&B stay). The Centre also owns a sailboat, the *Brandaris*, which serves as a floating B&B for open-ocean kayak trips.

**Narrow River Kayaks** (401-789-0334; 95 Middlebridge Rd., Narragansett, RI 02882) Nothing may be more appropriately described as idyllic than the Narrow River, a tidal inlet surrounded by salt marshes. Explore it by kayak or canoe; both sales and rentals available. May-Oct.

**Shark Watching** (401-884-9115; Narragansett/Pt. Judith) Listed here because there is no separate category for insane ideas. Capt. Charlie Donilon will take twelve people for ten hours on his thirty-foot boat *The Snapper*. Some thirty miles out, he baits the water and lowers you into a cage to get an up close and personal peek at the monsters.

**Warm Winds** (401-789-9040; 26 Kingstown Rd., Narragansett Pier, RI 02882) Bodyboarding center, plus athletic wear and bathing suits for men and women.

## EAST

### *Aquidneck*

**Island Divers** (401-841-9700; 999 W. Main Rd., Rte. 114, Middletown, RI 02842) Lessons and rentals year-round.

**Island Sports** (401-846-4421; 86 Aquidneck Ave., Middletown, RI 02842) They offer surfing, windsurfing, waterskiing, snorkeling, and boogieboard rentals, lessons, and sales. Also for sale are bicycles, in-line skates, and snowboards, plus active wear and limited volleyball and tennis equipment. Very hip and cool; calls itself "America's Oldest & Largest Windsurf Shop."

**Let's Go Diving** (401-848-0365; 717 Aquidneck Ave., Middletown, RI 02842) Scuba diving and snorkeling for beginners to advanced divers. Free transportation to and from dive site.

**Ocean State Dive Charters and Instructions** (401-683-3444; East Passage Yachting Center, Lagoon Rd., Portsmouth, RI 02871) Dive charters to RI, MA, CT, and NY; also night and lobster dives. Water pickup service available. All levels of dive instruction and certification.

**Redney's Surf Shop** (401-846-2280; 89 Aquidneck Ave., Middletown, RI 02842) Surfboard and boogieboard sales and rentals, plus beachwear for men and women. They have a surf condition hot line, call 401-841-5160.

### *East Bay*

**East Bay Dive Center, Inc.** (401-247-2420; 8 Church St., Warren, RI 02885) A complete diving facility with sales, service, rentals, and instruction.

### *Sakonnet*

**Sakonnet Boathouse and Kayak Touring Co.** (401-624-1440; 169 Riverside Dr., Tiverton, RI 02878) Kayaking instruction for all skill levels, plus tours of Seapowet salt marsh, Bristol Harbor, and Tiverton Harbor, as well as full-moon cruises.

### Seasonal Events

**Penguin Plunge** (Mackerel Cove Beach, Beaver Tail Rd., Jamestown) There are similar heart-stopping events in Newport and Boston, but this New Year's Day dip-in-freezing-cold-water draws the biggest crowd in New England. Human penguins are urged to dress in black-and-white (penguin style), except those who really want to make a splash; each year someone dresses as Batman, other nuts show up in diapers as Baby New Year, Elvis, etc. At noon, the 600-strong crowd rushes into the water, flaps around and gasps, then returns to waiting cars and hot towels. It's all to benefit the RI Special Olympics. Later in the day, if still alive, the "penguins" retire to the Narragansett Café for a big party.

**Surfing Championships** (401-789-3399) Eastern Surfing Association competitions for all ages at First (Easton) Beach in Newport and Narragansett Town Beach in Narragansett Pier. Bodyboarding titles as well. Call for dates.

**Swim the Bay** (401-272-3540) Swimmers have been breaststroking their way from Newport to Jamestown for over twenty years now. Check-in is at 9:00 a.m., starting time is at 11:00 a.m. for this two-mile swim across the bay — you get lunch on the beach when you finish. Preregistration is mandatory. Mid-Aug.

## WHALE WATCHING

Don't miss the opportunity to go out and see the big fellas: humpbacks, fin whales, right whales (the rarest on the Atlantic seaboard), and tiny minke whales are all to be seen in Rhode Island waters — not to mention sharks, dolphins, sea turtles, and a host of birds. All whale-watching cruises leave from the Galilee docks in Narragansett (see the heading Sailing & Boat above under Charters, Rentals, Lessons for other listings) and take an average of five hours. The season runs from July through early September, and each trip costs approximately $30 per adult. No matter how hot it is on the mainland, be sure to take a sweater or windbreaker — temperatures will drop at sea. Also bring a camera, sunglasses, a hat or scarf, and sunscreen. Most boats provide food and beverages.

## GRAB BAG

A miscellany of fun things to do, many ideal for children.

## WEST

### *West Bay*

**Adventure Land** (401-789-0030; Pt. Judith Rd., Rte. 108, Narragansett) The only miniature golf course in RI with waterfalls, caves, and islands. Also bumper boats, batting cages, and a state-of-the-art go-cart track.

**Fiddlesticks** (401-295-1519; 1300 Ten Rod Rd., N. Kingstown) Two eighteen-hole miniature golf courses, a driving range, and baseball and softball batting cages.

**Frosty Drew Observatory** (401-364-9508; Ninigret Park, Rte. 1A, Charlestown) Not quite on the bay, but very close by. Pick a clear Fri. night and go see the stars — best time is when the moon is in its first quarter. For general astronomical news, call **Sky Hotline** (401-726-1328) for information on meteor showers, comets, whatever is up there.

**Kingston Balloon Company** (401-783-9386; Kingston) Kingston isn't a bay town, but this is too good to leave out. Flights start an hour before sundown for a balloon's eye view of the sunset over the bay. About $200 per person.

**Narragansett Ocean Club** (401-783-6120; 360 South Pier Rd., Narragansett Pier) Indoor roller skating with loud music and shrieks.

## EAST

### *Aquidneck*

**Ryan Family Amusement Center** (401-849-9990; 105 Chases Ln., Middletown; also 401-846-5774; 266 Thames St., Newport) Miniature golf, bowling (see the heading Bowling above), video games, and a sports pub.

### *East Bay*

**Ernie's American Karate Academy** (401-253-6409; 20 Gooding Ave., Bristol) Self-defense instruction in American-style karate; weight room, too.

# SHOPPING

**M**any years ago Lincoln Steffens said that Rhode Island was a state for sale — cheap. From consignment shops to boutiques to antique malls, you'll find scrimshaw, costume jewelry, hip clothing, bodyboards, T-shirts, and much more. And very little, alas, is cheap.

Beyond Newport — unquestionably the shopping mecca of the bay — shoppers shouldn't miss Wickford village in North Kingstown (here identified simply as Wickford), which has a high concentration of upscale boutiques. Further south is Narragansett Pier, once a resort to rival Newport, now Pier Marketplace: a 1960s whim of resort planning that's ultimately just an outdoor mall, with a cinema, restaurants, delis, pizza places, doughnut shops, hair-styling salons, T-shirt shops, and a host of small boutiques jostled together in cookie-cutter spaces. It may be shingled, but otherwise Pier Marketplace has effectively erased the village's link to the past.

On the other side of the bay, Tiverton Four Corners has the largest number of shops in the otherwise blissfully rural Sakonnet region. Also on the East Bay, Bristol is coming into its own with a growing number of antique shops and boutiques, run by a vibrant bunch of young, artistic entrepreneurs. Turning back to the West Bay, the same may be said of East Greenwich, which now boasts galleries, artists studios, lots of unusual boutiques, and a very fine antiques mall. Both places are alive and hopping and very, very upbeat. With its own antiques mall, Warren remains, though, the antiquing center of the East Bay.

## ANTIQUES

### WEST

#### *West Bay*

**Antique Boutique** (401-884-6767; 527 Main St., E. Greenwich) A collection of old and new bric-a-brac, plus jewelry and Christmas items. Another location at 5707 Post Rd., Rte. 1 has new wares only. Prices and quality are both good.

**Antique Common of East Greenwich, Inc.** (401-885-4300; fax 401-885-5657; 461 Main St., E. Greenwich) A swanky new multidealer (50+) and consignment complex on the second floor of an office building. A very attractive, very large space with a fine mix of quality antiques. Don't miss it.

**Apple Antiques** (401-295-8840; 8045 Post Rd., Rte. 1, N. Kingstown) A nice selection of furniture and small items, just down the road from Smith's Castle (see the section Culture).

**Country Squire Antiques** (401-885-1044; 86 Main St., E. Greenwich) A brisk turnover, flexible prices, and a good mix of furniture, curios, bottles, and lamps make this worth a look. A find: a five-piece canine cider set for $225.

**Hill and Harbor Antiques** (401-885-4990; 187 Main St., E. Greenwich) A packed-full place with some real antiques and some merely old merchandise.

**Lafayette Antiques** (401-295-2504; 814 Ten Rod Rd., N. Kingstown) Specializes in mirrors, estate jewelry, wrought-iron pieces, and chairs, though the big space accommodates much more.

**Mentor Antiques** (401-294-9412; 7512 Post Rd., Rte. 1, N. Kingstown) Look for all of the stone garden ornaments outside; English furnishings and more. A venerable dealer.

**Wickford Antique Centre** (401-295-2966; 16 Main St., Wickford) A big space with mostly small antiques and vintage clothing; around the corner is **Wickford Antique Centre II** (401-295-2966; 93 Brown St.), which concentrates on furniture and art.

### EAST

#### *Aquidneck*

**The Antique Lady** (401-683-3244; Benjamin Fish Common, 934 E. Main Rd., Rte. 138, Portsmouth) A selection of large and small antiques.

**Benjamin Fish House Antiques** (401-683-0099; Benjamin Fish Common, 934 E. Main Rd., Rte. 138, Portsmouth) A fine collection of furniture and small items, with some exceptional ship models, lanterns, and artwork. The house was built in 1793. Fair prices up and down the scale.

**Eagles Nest Antique Center** (401-683-3500; 3101 E. Main Rd., Rte. 138, Portsmouth) Over 100 dealers set up wares, including furniture, jewelry, silver, toys, etc.

**Stock and Trade Antiques Center** (401-683-4700; 2771 E. Main Rd., Rte. 138, Portsmouth) Antique furniture and collectibles.

### *East Bay*

*Alfred's Gifts & Antiques reflects Bristol's holiday spirit.*

Pamela Petro

**Alfred's Gifts & Antiques** (401-253-3465; 331 Hope St., Rte. 114, Bristol) Custom mahogany furniture, crystal, and fine china, plus Christmas ornaments. Check out **Alfred's Annex** down the street (297 Hope St.), which has mainly small items on consignment.

**The Center Chimney** (401-253-8010; 39 State St., Bristol) High-level, fairly expensive country antiques. Look for the old "Hotpoint" appliance sign atop the building.

**Dantiques** (401-253-1122; 679 Hope St., Rte. 114, Bristol) A shop with glassware, accessories, and furniture.

**Jesse/James Antiques** (401-253-2240; 44 State St., Bristol) Lots of chairs (they specialize in caning) and nice "smalls" from glassware to china to bric-a-brac.

**Joe's Antiques** (401-254-1520; 278 Hope St., Rte. 114, Bristol) Good prices, lots of stuff, ranging from junk to finds.

**Robin Jenkins Antiques** (401-254-8958; 278 Hope St., Rte. 114, Bristol) Elegantly displayed country antiques; there's a refined taste behind the hand-hewn wares.

**Stickney & Stickney** (401-254-0179; 295 Hope St., Rte. 114, Bristol) American and European garden and architectural antiques and accessories.

### *Sakonnet*

**The Cottage at Four Corners** (401-625-5814; 3848 Main Rd., Rte. 77, Tiverton Four Corners) A top-drawer gallery with matching prices. Antique furni-

---

### Warren Antiques

Warren has been described as "an architectural gem waiting to be polished." This means that rents are still affordable (the chic boutiques haven't arrived yet), and there are bargains to be found, especially in the realm of antiques. More antique dealers cluster in Warren than anywhere else in Rhode Island.

Many have set up shop in the **Warren Antiques Center** (401-245-5461; Main and Miller Streets.). Over 100 dealers and consigners are represented in this attractive old theatre building. There's great diversity in merchandise (very little junk) but not so much that it overwhelms. Smaller items are displayed in lovely old oak cases. There's a café in the lobby.

Other shops in town mostly cluster on Miller, Main, and Water Streets. The latter is a venerable old thoroughfare along the Warren River, home to the Nathaniel Porter Inn, Tav-Vino's, Bullocks, and the Wharf Tavern (see the section Dining), as well as the wharves and buildings of a working waterfront. **The Square Peg** (51 Miller Street) is the venerable, eclectic, antique paradise that started it all.

---

ture, prints, quilts, and small items are beautifully displayed along with fine art, Simon Pearce glassware, garden ornaments, and ironware.

**Peter's Attic** (401-625-5912; 3879 Main Rd., Rte. 77, Tiverton Four Corners) A comprehensive selection without sky-high prices, including lots of glassware and mirrors made from old window frames.

## BOOKS, CARDS, MUSIC

For more on books about the area or by Rhode Island authors, see the section Bibliography in Chapter Six, *Information.*

## WEST

### *West Bay*

**The Book Garden** (401-294-3285; 99 Brown St., Wickford) One-half of the store has a fine selection of secondhand books; the other half is a garden shop.

**Rookiemania** (401-789-3597; 12A Pier Marketplace, Narragansett Pier) Baseball cards and sports memorabilia, not a fly-by-night enterprise.

**Sound Wave** (401-749-9570; Salt Pond Plaza, Pt. Judith Rd., Rte. 108, Narragansett) The best selection of tapes and CDs around: imports, plus classical, jazz, rock, rap, reggae, you name it.

## EAST

### *Aquidneck*

**Island Books** (401-849-2665; Wyatt Sq., 575 E. Main Rd., Rte. 138, Middletown) This is one of the few serious, nonspecialty bookstores in the Newport and

Narragansett Bay area. The selection isn't huge, but it's well chosen from classics to the latest fiction titles, as well as best-sellers. Also children's books and a good display of local works.

**Little Red Lighthouse Children's Books** (401-683-4443; Benjamin Fish Common, 934 E. Main Rd., Rte. 138, Portsmouth) A very good children's bookshop, with up-to-date titles and classics.

## *East Bay*

**Be Here Now Bookstore** (401-253-4099; 227 Thames St., Bristol) Somewhat New Age, specializing in psychology, philosophy, and world religions. Closed Sun.

**Good Books** (401-254-0390; 495 Hope St., Rte. 114, Bristol) This is what Bristol needed: a good all-around bookstore, with extras like homemade chocolates, magazines, and a few gifts.

**Paper, Packaging & Panache** (401-253-3795; 418 Hope St., Rte. 114, Bristol) Creatively upscale cards, wrappings, and paper products.

## *Sakonnet*

**A&R Books & Collectibles** (401-624-8947; Tiverton) A nationally known mail-order dealer in baseball books and cards and sports art. No retail shop, call for an appointment.

## CHILDREN

## WEST

## *West Bay*

**Juggles** (401-885-4578; East Greenwich Marketplace, 5600 Main St., Rte. 1, E. Greenwich) Children's toys. Another location is called **The Toy Cellar,** 7 Main St., Wickford.

**Little Ben's** (401-782-2773; Pier Marketplace, Narragansett Pier) Fine children's clothing from sizes newborn to six.

**Teddy Bearskins** (401-295-0282; 17 Brown St., Wickford) A great children's clothing store, infants through preteens.

## EAST

## *Aquidneck*

**The Walrus and the Carpenter Toy Store** (401-849-0012; Eastgate Center, 909 E. Main Rd., Rte. 138, Middletown) Don't miss this one — toys for every child and some adults as well. There's a terrific collection of unusual rubber stamps, plus books and a full range of toy horses.

### *East Bay*

**The Toy Shop** (401-253-8982; 450 Hope St., Rte. 114, Bristol) Just what the name says: a bright, fun place.

### *Sakonnet*

**Little Purls** (401-625-5990; Mill Pond Shops, 3964 Main Rd., Rte. 77, Tiverton Four Corners) Top-of-the-line children's clothing.

**The Toy Mill** (401-624-6188; 3845 E. Main Rd., Rte. 77, Tiverton Four Corners) A high-quality shop with fun stuff.

## CLOTHING & ACCESSORIES

## WEST

### *West Bay*

**Canvasworks** (401-295-8080; 10 Main St., Wickford) Custom-made canvas bags and more.

**Cathy's Clothes** (401-295-7222; 1 W. Main St., Wickford) Contemporary, upscale clothes.

**Green Ink** (401-294-6266; 17 Brown St., Wickford) Elegant, interesting, and pricey contemporary women's clothes, shoes, and accessories.

**Hatworks of Wickford** (401-294-9268; 83 Brown St., Wickford) A veritable attic full of hats.

**Kane & Hawkins** (401-294-6014; 66 Brown St., Wickford) Nautical and beach apparel, plus Wickford and RI T-shirts and sweatshirts. This is that rare hybrid: an upmarket T-shirt shop.

**Village Reflections** (401-295-7802; 5 W. Main St., Wickford) Both classic and semifunky clothes and accessories for women. Interesting prints.

**Wickford Shoes** (401-294-8833; 14 Phillips St., Wickford) A shoe boutique with high-quality, costly, and mostly traditional wear.

**Wilson's of Wickford** (401-294-9514; 401-884-8090; 35 Brown St., Wickford) Classic (dare I say preppy?) men and women's clothing that's perfect for the Wickford scene.

## EAST

### *Aquidneck*

**Ma Goetzinger's** (401-683-9400; 2908 E. Main Rd., Rte. 138, Portsmouth) An excellent women's clothing and shoe shop with good quality contemporary and classic styles, all by itself on Rte. 138. Recommended, though prices are on the high side.

### East Bay

**Jamiel's Shoe World** (401-245-4389; 471 Main St., Rte. 114, Warren) Come here first if you're looking for shoes. It's an old-fashioned shoe store with new-fangled merchandise. How about a pair of suede Esprit sandals for $34 (regularly $42)? Also Nickels, Rockport, athletic shoes, and more.

### Sakonnet

**Pond Lilies** (401-624-2594; Mill Pond Shops, 3964 Main St., Rte. 77, Tiverton Four Corners) An above-average source for stylish women's clothing from dresses and sweaters to coats and jewelry.

**Sakonnet Purls** (401-624-9902; 3964 Main St., Rte. 77, Tiverton Four Corners) Order a custom-knit sweater, or choose from a fine variety of yarns to make your own. Needlework, too.

## CRAFT GALLERIES & STUDIOS

### WEST

### West Bay

**Tailored Crafts** (401-885-1756; 211 Main St., E. Greenwich) A small gallery with somewhat slick-and-trendy Native American crafts and southwestern jewelry.

**The Wickford Stone Carver** (401-295-8332; 550 Ten Rod Rd., N. Kingstown) A very cool studio of contemporary stone-carved sculpture by Stefan Bach, who became a master carver after a three-year apprenticeship in Germany. His specialty is European-style granite tombstones, though he does custom-design work as well. A find.

**Wild Goose Chase** (401-884-7688; 312 Main St., E. Greenwich) Hand-painted furniture that's neither cloy nor ultrahip, reminiscent of Pennsylvania Dutch work. Call artist Bertie Ducker for an appointment.

**Wrigley Designs Studio & Shop** (401-884-9886; 6 King St., E. Greenwich) Painted earthenware (custom tiles, tiled murals, and more) in bright, energetic, free-flowing designs. The most innovative and original crafts in town. Brenda, the owner/artist, is a pleasure to work with.

### EAST

### Aquidneck

**The Quilt Artisan** (401-846-2127; 800-736-4364; Aquidneck Green, 747 Aquidneck Ave., Middletown) New and antique quilts, plus quilting supplies and classes. Call for a workshop schedule.

## East Bay

*The colorful wares of local artists and craftspeople have added pizazz to the sidewalks of Bristol.*

Pamela Petro

**Boo Bracken** (401-253-0646; 301 Hope St., Rte. 114, Bristol) Hip and cool painted furniture and small handmade pieces by local artists.

## Sakonnet

**The Metalworks, Inc.** (401-624-4400; Main Rd., Rte. 77, Tiverton Four Corners) Heating and ventilation systems are created here, as are very nice copper and brass lanterns.

**Ridabock Handblown Glass** (401-624-8220; Main Rd., Rte. 77, Tiverton Four Corners) A glass gallery and studio; visitors are invited to watch the glassmakers work their craft.

**The Windmill** (401-624-1818; 3988 Main Rd., Rte. 77, Tiverton Four Corners) This little shed offers hand-painted and glazed ceramic tiles, plus Byzantine and modern-style mosaics. Order a custom-made address tile, or pick up a wrought-iron table with a mosaic-patterned top.

## GIFTS

## WEST

## Jamestown

**Jamestown Designs** (401-423-0344; 17 Narragansett Ave., Jamestown) Fine quality gifts, handcrafted jewelry, cards, and original and reproduction prints of island scenes. Look for delicate, hand-thrown stoneware by island potter Irene Parthenis; she calls her work "All Fired Up."

**R & R Gallery** (401-423-0730; 47 Conanicus Ave., Jamestown) A gift shop with less style than Jamestown Designs, but nice ship models.

## *West Bay*

**Askham & Telham, Inc.** (401-295-0891; 12 Main St., Wickford) High-quality, traditional gifts and home accessories; look for the lovely needlepoint pillows. Expensive.

**Different Drummer** (401-294-4867; 7 W. Main St., Wickford) A neat little shop with cards, jewelry, locally made gifts, rubber stamps, and T-shirts.

**G. Willakers Country Store** (401-295-2570; 500 Tower Hill Rd., junction Rts. 102 and 1, N. Kingstown) The clichéd country look: scented candles, calico lamp shades, Christmas stuff.

**The Green Door** (401-885-0510; 378 Main St., E. Greenwich) A top-quality, eclectic shop with vintage linens, quilts, glassware, tinware, and more; folk art and craft offerings, too.

**J.W. Graham** (401-295-0757; 26 Brown St., Wickford) Crafts and other handmade wares, principally for the home; more traditional than unusual.

**Lavender & Lace** (401-295-0313; 4 Brown St., Wickford) Real and retro Victoriana in the realm of home furnishings and gifts; a seriously feminine shop.

**Robin's Nest Gift Shoppe** (401-885-7717; 36 Main St., E. Greenwich) Country accessories, candles, and "Victorian" gifts. Much of the same selection is on hand down the street at **Gracefully Yours** (401-885-1010; 442 Main St.).

**Victorian Lady** (401-789-0222; Pier Marketplace, Narragansett Pier) Frilly things galore; a plus is that they sell Martha Murphy's, *The Bed & Breakfast Cookbook.*

**The World Store** (401-295-0081; 16 W. Main St., Wickford) From environmental gifts to fossils, books, ant farms, and Swiss Army knives. Like The Nature Company, but more unique.

## EAST

### *Aquidneck*

**The Old Almy House** (401-683-3737; 1016 E. Main Rd., Rte. 138, Portsmouth) This place goes on and on, with everything from country store provisions (penny candy and coffee beans) to candles, cookbooks, and gifts; **Caron & Co. Antiques** is upstairs and the **Christmas Fantasy** shop is at the back.

### *East Bay*

**Blithewold Gift Shop** (401-253-4130; 101 Ferry Rd., Bristol) See the section Culture for more on Blithewold Mansion; its gift shop has pretty things for the home and garden.

**Kate & Co.** (401-254-6114; 301 Hope St., Rte. 114, Bristol) An international selection of jewelry, housewares, and toiletries. One of a group of hip new shops on Hope St.

**Linden Place Gift Shop** (401-253-0309; 500 Hope St., Rte. 114, Bristol) See the section Culture for the historic home Linden Place; it supports one of the best gift shops in town, including pewter ware, local handcrafts, books, and nautical items.

**Sweetbrier** (401-253-1904; 317 Hope St., Rte. 114, Bristol) A highly floral boutique, with a mix of old and new accents for the home.

### *Sakonnet*

**Country Cabin** (401-624-2279; Mill Pond Shops, 3964 Main Rd., Rte. 77, Tiverton Four Corners) Country-style gifts and handmade items (including quilts), plus some antiques.

## HOUSE & GARDEN

## WEST

### *West Bay*

**The Aunt's Attic** (401-783-4569; 401-783-3470; 966 Boston Neck Rd., Rte. 1A, Narragansett) A terrific source for used furniture, household accessories, and antiques.

**Farrago** (401-885-6960; 101 Main St., E. Greenwich) A tiny shop with unusual household items and gifts.

**Isabella's** (401-294-8151; 10 Phillips St., Wickford) A terrific spot with a yen for the European (mostly Italian, Portuguese, and French), hand-painted dishes, and kitchenware. The prices are good, and the colors are bright; also has Italian foodstuffs and cooking oils.

**Joint Venture Woodworking** (401-295-5308; 2549 Boston Neck Rd., Rte. 1A, N. Kingstown) Custom-handcrafted furniture, sign carving, and architectural and marine mill work. More of a studio than a shop, but well worth stopping.

**Rocco's Used Furniture and Things** (401-295-5551; 2507 Boston Neck Rd., Rte. 1A, N. Kingstown) A junkyard with exceptional flair, decorated with everything from buoys to a Cinzano café table umbrella.

**The Shaker Shop** (401-294-7779; 16 W. Main St., Brown Street Bridge, Wickford) Handmade Shaker-style furniture and accessories. Beautiful and costly.

**Topiaries Unlimited** (401-294-6990; 30 W. Main St., Wickford) Unusual sculpted shrubs, plus potting supplies and flowers.

## EAST

### *Aquidneck*

**Art Reflextions, Inc.** (401-683-2300; 2922; E. Main Rd., Rte. 138, Portsmouth) Not only do they import Oriental rugs, they make them, too. Look for the big end-of-summer sale.

**The Christmas Tree Shop** (401-841-5100; Aquidneck Center, Rte. 138, Middletown) These shops started as a Cape Cod phenomenon but are expanding across southern New England. Despite the name, you can find everything here from French glassware to Barbie Doll clothes to brassware from India. Their slogan "Don't you just love a bargain?" is apt — these are very low prices. Christmas stuff, too.

### *Sakonnet*

**Artrageous** (401-624-8738; Mill Pond Shops, 3964 Main Rd., Rte. 77, Tiverton Four Corners) Solid oak hand-painted home furnishings for adults and children in both sophisticated and whimsical designs. Look for high chairs embellished with Pooh, dollhouses with original paintings by a local artist, and all manner of furniture. Commissions, too.

**Courtyards** (401-624-8682; 3980 Main Rd., Rte. 77, Tiverton Four Corners) They advertise "garden ornaments and artifacts." Outside, you'll find lots of sundials, birdbaths, and statuary; inside, look for crafts, jewelry, and dried herbs hanging from the ceiling.

## JEWELRY

## WEST

### *West Bay*

**Browne and Co.** (401-295-2420; 14 Main St., Wickford) A very fine jewelry shop (and a good bet if your watch battery dies), plus original Nantucket lightship baskets, scrimshaw, and antique clocks.

**Harbour Galleries** (401-884-6221; 253 Main St., E. Greenwich) Antique and estate jewelry sold in a ca. 1775 building.

## EAST

### *East Bay*

**Bargains Unlimited** (401-253-8215; 437 Hope St., Rte. 114, Bristol) Stand with your back to Hope St. and you'll think that you're in the garment district in New York City. The owners make the most of what you see: a glittering, sparkling, spangling treasure trove of costume jewelry, plus hair ornaments, scarves, and handbags. Ungentrified Bristol at its best.

## KITCHEN

## EAST

### *Aquidneck*

**Kitchen Pot Pourri** (401-847-5880; 42 W. Main Rd., Rte. 114, Middletown) All manner of kitchen supplies and accessories: china, pottery, stemware, cookbooks, coffeemakers, linens, you name it.

*Sakonnet*

**Stone Bridge Dishes** (401-635-4441; PO Box 218, Stone Church Rd., Little Compton) A superb kitchen shop just up the road from the Rhode Island Red Monument (see the section Culture, under the heading Monuments & Memorials). From garlic presses to Quimper pottery from France, this is the place. Copper weather vanes, too. Go early and have breakfast at The Barn (see the section Dining). UPS shipping.

## MARINE SUPPLY

### WEST

*Jamestown*

**Conanicut Marine Services, Inc.** (401-423-1556; 1 Ferry Wharf, Jamestown) This may be one of the most comprehensive ship stores in the world — from marine hardware to gear for every kind of weather imaginable, plus gifts, rafts, dinghies, and more. Also a full-service marina, repair shop, and boatyard.

*West Bay*

**Arnold's Boat Shop** (401-884-4272; Water St., E. Greenwich) Sales and repairs.

### EAST

*Aquidneck*

**Aquidneck Island Marine** (401-847-0101; 134 Aquidneck Ave., Middletown).
**Brilliant Strokes** (401-683-4434; 3 Maritime Dr. #6, Portsmouth) Yacht interiors and exteriors, and furniture, too. Varnishing experts.

*East Bay*

**Shannon Yachts** (401-253-2441; 19 Broad Common Rd., Bristol) Builders of twenty-eight-, thirty-eight-, and fifty-foot ocean and cruising yachts.
**Water Street Yacht Shop** (401-245-5511; 259 Water St., Warren).

*Sakonnet*

**Riverside Marine** (401-625-5181; 211 Riverside Dr., Tiverton) Get your rods, reels, lines, bait, soda, cigarettes, and gifts here; ramps $5 a day.
**Standish Boat Yard & Ship's Store** (401-624-4075; Main St., Rte. 77, Tiverton Four Corners) All the essentials for boats and their sailors.

## PHARMACIES & NEWSSTANDS

### WEST

*Jamestown*

**Baker's Pharmacy** (401-423-2800; 53 Narragansett Ave., Jamestown) Sunscreen, beach toys, magazines, newspapers, and more.

### EAST

*East Bay*

**Delekta Pharmacy** (401-245-6767; 496 Main St., Warren) A superb old-fashioned apothecary shop straight from the 1880s (see the section Food & Beverage Purveyors). Great smells and sights, including soaps, perfumes, and locally crafted items. It's a prescription center, too.

**Duffy's News** (401-253-9851; 467 Hope St., Rte. 114, Bristol) Newspapers, stationery, magazines, and the like.

**Main Street News** (401-245-1627; 504 Main St., Rte. 114, Warren) Pretty much what the name says.

## SOUVENIRS & NOVELTIES

### WEST

*Jamestown*

**Town Hall** (401-423-7200; 93 Narragansett Ave., Jamestown) The town sells the official Jamestown flag for $35. What better souvenir could you get?

*West Bay*

**Earnshaw Drug, Card & Gift Shop** (401-294-3662; 63 Brown St., Wickford) Okay, so they do prescriptions, too, but the emphasis here is on RI souvenirs.

## SPECIALTY

### WEST

*West Bay*

**Bagpiper Smoke Shop** (401-783-0555; 32A Pier Marketplace, Narragansett Pier) A smoke shop with Irish imports, flasks, and more.

**The Hour Glass** (401-295-8724; 800-585-8724; 15 W. Main St., Wickford) An excellent clock shop with kaleidoscopes, weather instruments, sundials, and other mechanical gems.

**Needle Designs** (401-267-0800; 31 W. Main St., Wickford) Custom embroidery, plus clothing, accessories, and gifts. There's another location in the Pier Marketplace complex in Narragansett.

**Pet Peeves** (401-295-5035; 3 Main St., Wickford) A fun shop with "gifts for pets and their people," including "Groucho Barks" cigars for dogs.

**Wickford Candle** (401-294-7792; 11 Brown St., Wickford) Handmade candles, including ultralong tapers that should create a stir.

**Yankee Saddler** (401-885-1910; East Greenwich Marketplace, 5600 Post Rd., Rte. 1, E. Greenwich) An all-horse store, featuring riding gear, toy horses, and memorabilia.

## EAST

### *Aquidneck*

**Arnold Art Centre** (401-846-3349; The Polo Center, 700 Aquidneck Ave., Middletown) There is another location at 210 Thames St., Newport, but the parking is easier here, and the staff is great; all of the art supplies that you'll need.

**Inflicting Ink Tattoo Studio** (401-683-5680; E. Main Rd., Rte. 138, Portsmouth) A very hip, contemporary place to make yourself into artwork.

### *East Bay*

**Don's Art Shop** (401-245-4583; 543 Main St., Rte. 114, Warren) Art and drafting supplies.

**Photo World** (401-253-2248; 433 Hope St., Rte. 114, Bristol) If you drop your camera at Blithewold Mansion or the Herreshoff Marine Museum (see the section Culture), this is where to have it fixed. Film and processing, too.

### *Sakonnet*

**Dog Portraits by Brooks Wall** (401-635-4225; 11 Goodrich Ln., Little Compton) Bring a photo and artist Brooks Wall will paint (in oil, acrylic, or watercolor) a portrait of your pooch.

**Four Winds, Inc.** (401-624-4549; 800-638-8943; 149 Nanaquaket Rd., Tiverton) Self-described as "Rhode Island's Premier Flag Company," they stock 332 flags and banners from all over the world, plus seasonal and historical flags as well. Or come with your own design.

## SPORTING GOODS

## EAST

### *Aquidneck*

**Aquidneck Island Sporting Goods** (401-847-7317; 796 Aquidneck Ave., Middletown) Clothing, footwear, and gear.

*East Bay*

**Gob Shop** (401-245-4800; 465 Main St., Rte. 114, Warren) Sporting goods, plus clothing and athletic footwear.

## VINTAGE CLOTHING & THRIFT SHOPS

### EAST

*Aquidneck*

**Corner Consignment Quality Clothing** (401-683-1771; 980 E. Main Rd., Rte. 138, Portsmouth) Exactly what the name suggests.

**Vintage to Vogue Consignment Boutique** (401-841-5109; 1120 Aquidneck Ave., Middletown).

*East Bay*

**Too Good To Be Through** (401-253-2199; 18 State St., Bristol) Classy women's consignments from casual to formal and bridal wear.

*Sakonnet*

**Abigail & Magnolia's Specialty Shop** (401-624-2636; 3851 Main Rd., Rte. 77, Tiverton Four Corners) Contemporary vintage clothing, plus furniture and collectibles.

# CHAPTER FIVE
# *A Last Great Place*
## BLOCK ISLAND

Subject to eroding winds, sea currents, and the great storms of the Atlantic, in geological time Block Island has only a transitory existence. All the more reason, then, that we pay special attention to this small island in the open ocean, named by The Nature Conservancy as one of the "Twelve Last Great Places in the Western Hemisphere" — an honor that it shares with the likes of the Amazon Rain Forest. Not bad for a little island off the littlest state.

Craig Hammell

*There are few better places for rocking chairs and contemplation than an open porch overlooking the sea, especially at The Surf hotel on Block Island.*

Block Island received this distinction for its individual character, which residents have strenuously sought to protect and preserve in the face of growing tourism: namely, an undulating, irregular topography that's part of a glacial moraine, including Cape Cod, Martha's Vineyard, and Nantucket, which on Block Island shelters a number of plant and animal species unique to the island (the little Block Island vole is one example).

In practical terms, the only two centers of commerce are Old Harbor, on the southeastern side of the island (where most ferries dock) and New Harbor, which thanks to Great Salt Pond essentially occupies the middle of the island (ferries from Long Island arrive here). In-season, Water Street in Old Harbor is thronged with tourists meandering in and out of restaurants and shops. Despite the constant buzz, the village is essentially only one street long and one street deep. Beyond it lies a quiet, green, sea-smelling island — a quirky and timeless place where people have seen fit to accommodate themselves to the land, rather than bending the land to them. As one resident put it, "We've got to have the open space, or where's the rain going to fall?"

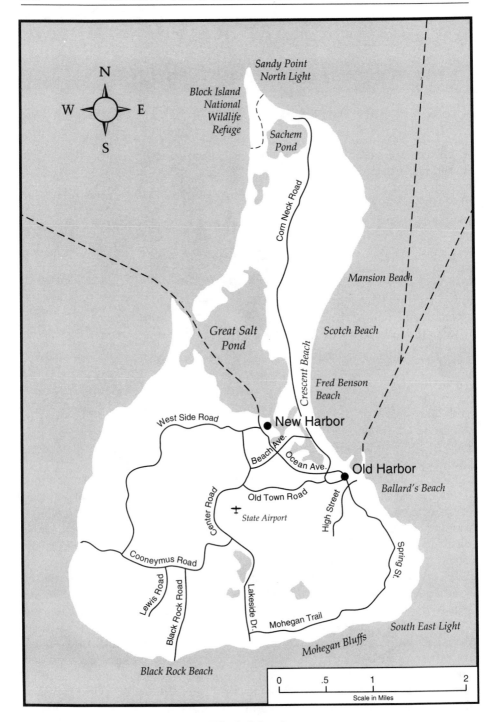

**Block Island**

# LODGING

To visit Block Island is to be romanced by its big old Victorian hotels, built ca. 1856 to 1910, when the island enjoyed its first heyday as a seaside resort. You don't have to stay in these beauties to enjoy their magnificent silhouettes — mansard roofs, turrets and towers, verandas wrapping around their exteriors like so much white-painted scaffolding — or to relax on their porches with an evening cocktail (many have restaurants open to the public). If your taste runs to smaller lodgings, visit the hotels but stay in an inn or bed-and-breakfast. Most inns on Block Island inhabit Victorian residences, and their decor evokes that period with a vengeance. As a rule, however, furnishings are simpler than on the mainland, as befits the casual, seaside environment.

Among the hotels and inns, there is an ever-growing number of bed-and-breakfasts on Block Island, a group of which has banded together under the name *Les Petites Maisons*, The Little Houses (call the Chamber of Commerce, 401-466-2982, for details). I've listed one of these "little houses" below — the thoroughly delightful Sasafrash, which was converted into a home from a Primitive Methodist church and have include two independent bed-and-breakfasts, both far from harbor crowds in less-visited parts of the island.

## LODGING NOTES

**Tax.** Most prices are quoted without the seven percent Rhode Island sales tax; to that add another five percent room (also called bed) tax. If the full twelve percent tax is included in the price, this is noted.

**Minimum stay.** Most establishments, large and small, have minimum-stay requirements (though they tend to be flexible if it's been raining all summer). Check first; it's usually two nights in season, though it can be up to six.

**When to book.** It's always a good idea to reserve early; holidays, such as the 4th of July, are often fully booked by January. Plan early.

**Refunds.** Make a point of asking about refund policies due to weather; for example, many inns expect guests to reach the island by ferry if flights are canceled (and vice versa).

**Reservation services.** The following services are free to folks trying to hunt down a room.

*Bed & Breakfast of Rhode Island* (401-849-1298; PO Box 3291, Newport, RI 02840) Covers the entire state.

*Block Island Chamber of Commerce* (401-466-2982; 800-383-BIRI; fax 401-466-5286; Drawer D, Block Island, RI 02807) Be sure to ask for Elva. She's patient, helpful, and brimming with knowledge about the island.

*Block Island Holidays, Inc.* (401-466-3137; 800-905-0590; PO Box 803, Block Island, RI 02807) Puts together package tours of the island.

*Block Island Reservation Center* (800-825-6254) Rents hotel rooms, suites, and apartments in Old Harbor.

## Rates

Rates are based on one night, double occupancy (most rooms are doubles) and reflect high-season prices (generally from Memorial Day to Labor Day). Off-season prices are often substantially lower. I've noted the few cases in which breakfast is not included or rooms do *not* have private baths.

### Lodging Price Code

| | |
|---|---|
| Inexpensive | Under $60 |
| Moderate | $60 to $120 |
| Expensive | $120 to $200 |
| Very Expensive | Over $200 |

### Credit Cards

| | |
|---|---|
| AE — American Express | DC — Diners Club |
| CB — Carte Blanche | MC — MasterCard |
| D — Discover | V — Visa |

## HOTELS

**THE ATLANTIC**
Innkeepers: Anne & Brad Marthens.
401-466-5883; 800-224-7422; fax 401-466-5678.
High St., Box 188 (Old Harbor), Block Island, RI 02807.
Open: Apr.–Oct.
Price: Expensive to Very Expensive.
Credit Cards: D, MC, V.
Smoking: No.
Handicap Access: No.
Restrictions: No pets.
Special Features: Tennis courts and croquet field.

One of the best places on the island for a fabulous view of stone-walled fields, Old Harbor, and the beaches beyond is the porch of The Atlantic. Perched high on a hill above the village, the 1879 hotel is one of the island's specialties: a big white clapboard building with a mansard roof and wraparound veranda. After being renovated a few years ago by new owners, it is also one of the island's most upscale lodgings; twenty-one guest rooms have telephones but no TVs, and many have sea views. The dining room is open to the public for dinner (see the section Dining), as is the veranda, where you can recline on wicker love seats and sip cocktails after 4:00 p.m. The llamas, emus, and their fellow beasts in the field below belong to the Hotel Manisses petting zoo.

**CHAMPLIN'S MARINA, MOTEL & RESORT**
Owner: Joe Grillo.
401-466-2641; 800-762-4521.
West Side Rd., PO Box J (New Harbor), Block Island, RI 02807.
Open: May–Columbus Day.

There is nothing else like Champlin's on the island. It's a self-contained resort, with its own pool, tennis courts, private beach, bicycle, car and moped rentals, cinema, restaurant, and dinner theatre; Aldo's (see the section Dining) even has a bakery annex out here. Guests come by car or boat; the marina has 225 slips. The twenty-eight rooms are motel style, with cable TV and deck (you can spec-

Price: Expensive to Very
  Expensive.
Credit Cards: AE, MC, V.
Smoking: Nonsmoking
  rooms available.
Handicap Access: Yes.
Restrictions: No pets.
Special Features: Pool,
  tennis courts,
  playground.

ify countryside or harbor view); efficiency suites are also available.

**THE HARBORSIDE**
Manager: Chris Sereno.
401-466-5504; 800-892-2022.
Water St., PO Box F (Old
  Harbor), Block Island, RI
  02807.
Open: May–Oct.
Price: Moderate to
  Expensive.
Credit Cards: AE, MC, V.
Smoking: Bar only.
Handicap Access: No.
Restrictions: No pets.

The Harborside's thirty-seven rooms aren't fancy. There's no air-conditioning, no TV, and no buffer from the noisy chatter outside. But there is real, old-island atmosphere here. The third-floor bathrooms are tucked under eaves, and the floorboards of the pleasant lobby list pleasantly northward; the building dates from 1887 and is on the National Register. Unlike The National, it's sister hotel down the street, lodging at The Harborside does include a full breakfast, served in its indoor/outdoor dining room — the only restaurant on the island with a salad bar (see the section Dining).

Craig Hammell

*Mountain bicycles meet high Victorian architecture at the Hotel Manisses on Block Island.*

**HOTEL MANISSES**
Owners: Joan Abrams &
  Rita Draper.
401-466-2063; 800-626-4773;
  fax 401-466-3162; E-mail:
  BIRESORTS@aol.com.

The Manisses is one of the best-known and most luxurious hotels on Block Is. Built in 1872, it's intensely Victorian, with a pagodalike central tower, front veranda hung with flowers, mansard roof, and sunny, wicker-filled parlor. Some of the seventeen guest rooms have Jacuzzis and — a nice

Spring St. (Old Harbor),
   Block Island, RI 02807.
Open: Mar.–Dec.
Price: Expensive to Very
   Expensive.
Credit Cards: AE, MC, V.
Smoking: Nonsmoking
   rooms available.
Handicap Access: No.
Restrictions: No pets, or
   children under 10.
Special Features: Animal
   farm.

touch — are named after shipwrecks. All are decorated with period antiques and include a complimentary decanter of brandy. A full breakfast is served across the street at The 1661 Inn. The Manisses dining room, one of the fanciest on the island, is open to the public for dinner (see the section Dining). Organized van tours of the island (some with picnic lunch) are offered to Manisses guests.

**THE NATIONAL HOTEL**
Manager: Chris Sereno.
401-466-2901; 800-225-2449;
   fax 401-466-5948.
Water St., Box 189 (Old
   Harbor), Block Island, RI
   02807.
Open: May–Oct.
Price: Moderate to Very
   Expensive.
Credit Cards: AE, MC, V.
Smoking: Bar only.
Handicap Access: One
   suite.
Restrictions: No pets.

The National Hotel porch, which looms above Water St. overlooking Old Harbor, is one of the most active spots on Block Is.; it's currently home to The Tap & Grille (see the section Dining). Until recently the hotel itself was in sore need of renovation; now the sister of The Harborside, another impressive old lodging down the street, help has come at last to the forty-five guest rooms that inhabit this venerable, 1888 structure. Rooms are now bright and attractive, with TV, telephone, and — for those facing the harbor — truly spectacular views. Room rate does not include breakfast. Those who crave quiet should think twice about The National, as the bar hops late into the night.

*The restrained charm of a guest room at The Spring House on Block Island reflects the island's easygoing style.*

Craig Hammell

**THE SPRING HOUSE**
Manager: David Houseman.
401-466-5844; 800-234-9263;
   fax 401-466-2633.

Set on a fifteen-acre promontory above the sea, The Spring House is the oldest of the island's grand Victorian hotels. The original structure, built

Spring St., PO Box 902 (Old Harbor), Block Island, RI 02807.
Open: May–October.
Price: Expensive to Very Expensive.
Credit Cards: AE, MC, V.
Smoking: Nonsmoking rooms available.
Handicap Access: No.
Restrictions: No pets.

in 1852, was revamped in 1870 to its present appearance: a white clapboard building with a superb wraparound porch, a red-shingled mansard roof, and a distinctive cupola. All forty-nine rooms — thirty-two in the main building and seventeen in a similar structure nearby — are furnished in simple, seaside style. To one side of the front entrance is a cavernous bar with clusters of upholstered love seats and chairs; to the other side is the lobby, a magnificent space with a fieldstone fireplace, open archways, and an air of just slightly faded elegance. Continental breakfast is served in the dining room on attractive, pink-clothed tables.

**THE SURF**
Owners: Ulric & Beatrice Cyr.
401-466-2241.
Dodge St., Box C (Old Harbor), Block Island, RI 02807.
Open: Mem. Day–Columbus Day.
Price: Moderate.
Credit Cards: MC, V.
Smoking: Rooms only.
Handicap Access: No.
Restrictions: No pets.
Special Features: Best porch on Block Is.

The porch of The Surf is supposedly the most-photographed spot in RI. Guests are tempted to lounge out there and rock the day away, gazing out over Old Harbor and Crescent Beach. The hotel itself, mostly built in 1876, is a local landmark and a gabled, shingled tribute to New England Victoriana. The lobby continues the theme with Tiffany lamps and comfortable antiques. The thirty-five rooms in the main building are smallish but charming with simple, old-fashioned decor; two other buildings house another twelve rooms. All have sinks and shared baths. A full breakfast is served in the tin-ceilinged dining room. Note that a six-day minimum is recommended in-season. Telephone and TV are in lobby only.

## INNS

**THE BARRINGTON INN**
Innkeepers: Joan & Howard Ballard.
401-466-5510;
fax 401-466-5880.
Beach and Ocean Aves., Box 397 (New Harbor), Block Island, RI 02807.
Open: Apr.–mid-Nov.
Price: Moderate to Expensive.
Credit Cards: D, MC, V.
Smoking: On decks and grounds only.
Handicap Access: No.

Set on a knoll at the cross of Beach and Ocean Aves., The Barrington Inn commands a view of the sweeping marshes and ponds that lead down to New Harbor and the sea. The six bedrooms in this 1886 farmhouse fill up quickly with repeat guests and are exceptionally light and airy. Three second-floor rooms open onto individual decks; another deck is off the dining room, where guests may elect to have their continental breakfast. Like many other island innkeepers, Joan provides a communal refrigerator, wineglasses, and hot and cold beverages for guests to enjoy throughout the day. There are two parlors, one

Restrictions: No pets, no children under 12 in main inn.

with TV and VCR; a nearby barn has been converted into two housekeeping apartments, where children are welcome.

**THE BELLEVUE HOUSE**
Owners: Neva Flaherty & Read Kingsbury.
401-466-2912.
High St., Box 1198 (Old Harbor), Block Island, RI 02807.
Open: Mid-May–Columbus Day.
Price: Moderate.
Credit Cards: MC, V.
Smoking: Not in rooms.
Handicap Access: 2 rooms.
Restrictions: No pets.

It looks like a farmhouse, set behind stone walls in a grassy meadow, but The Bellevue was actually built as an inn in 1882. Its freshly painted, gleaming blue clapboards speak for the owners' ongoing renovation work, though inside all of the things that really count have been well attended to. Five shared-bath guest rooms are of modest size but attractively furnished in cozy, easy-to-live-with antiques. An abundant continental breakfast is served in the kitchen, though guests may take a tray to the front porch and gaze at the ocean while they eat. Two cottages on the property rent weekly, as do two housekeeping apartments, three two-bedroom apartments, and two recently completed wheelchair-accessible rooms with private baths.

**THE BLUE DORY INN**
Owner: Ann Loedy.
401-466-5891; 800-992-7290.
Dodge St., PO Box 488 (Old Harbor), Block Island, RI 02807.
Open: Year-round.
Price: Moderate to Very Expensive.
Credit Cards: AE, D, MC, V.
Smoking: Discouraged.
Handicap Access: Minimal.
Restrictions: No pets in main inn.

There's something inherently nice about The Blue Dory — perhaps because it backs up to the beach, or maybe it's the cozy and compact quarters. Certainly it's the friendly atmosphere. Guests are welcome to use the kitchen (where continental breakfast is served), TV parlor, and outside shower; beach towels and chairs are also available on loan. Complimentary wine and cheese is served at 6:00 p.m., and later a plate of cookies is offered for dessert. Most of the eleven recently renovated guest rooms are smallish but decorated with clean, bright colors and comfortable antiques. In addition to the main building are four cottages: one rents weekly; another, the Tea House, served as a speakeasy during Prohibition; and three luxury suites with Jacuzzis. Both the Old Harbor ferry and Crescent Beach are an easy walk.

**GABLES INN & GABLES II**
Owners: Barbara & Stanley Nyzio.
401-466-2213.
Dodge St., PO Box 516 (Old

There are nineteen guest rooms between the Gables Inn & Gables II up the street, both built in the mid-nineteenth century. These charming, cozy rooms are decorated with antiques and Victorian print wallpaper, as are two lounges, one

Harbor), Block Island, RI 02807.
Open: May–Nov.
Price: Moderate.
Credit Cards: MC, V.
Smoking: No.
Handicap Access: No.
Restrictions: No pets.

with TV. Some have private baths, though most share. A pleasant front porch features rockers and hanging baskets. Barbara and Stanley also offer five efficiency apartments at the Gables II, plus a private cottage that tends to rent weekly in-season. Compliment Stanley on the continental breakfast pastries (he makes them himself), and be sure to have a chat with Barbara — she's fun and quite knowledgeable about the island. Beach supplies and bicycle rack are available.

### ROSE FARM INN
Owners: Robert & Judith Rose.
401-466-2021.
High St., Box E (Old Harbor), Block Island, RI 02807.
Open: May–Oct.
Price: Moderate to Expensive.
Credit Cards: AE, D, MC, V.
Smoking: Not in rooms.
Handicap Access: One room in modern extension.
Restrictions: No pets, or children under 12.

This turn-of-the-century farmhouse burrows deep into the rolling countryside and offers sweeping sea views. There are ten rooms in the main house and nine more in the Capt. Rose House, a serviceable extension. Only two of the nineteen guest rooms share a bath; others have private facilities, and deluxe rooms offer whirlpool and deck. The guest rooms are furnished with antiques and period replicas as is the parlor, which offers both TV and wet bar. A continental-plus breakfast is served on the attractive, enclosed front porch.

### SEA BREEZE INN
Owners: Bob & Mary Newhouse.
401-466-2275; 800-786-2276.
Spring St., Box 141 (Old Harbor), Block Island, RI 02807.
Open: Year-round.
Price: Moderate to Expensive.
Credit Cards: MC, V.
Smoking: Not encouraged.
Handicap Access: Limited.
Restrictions: No pets, or children under 5.

Hidden from Spring St. by tall pine trees, the Sea Breeze Inn is actually three smallish cottages, with a garden in between and nothing but the ocean behind. The rooms are simple and summery, decorated in fresh, clean-lined combinations of the old and new. A brass bed against a painted hardwood floor can be a welcome relief after all that Victoriana elsewhere on the island. Of ten guest rooms, breakfast is delivered in a picnic basket to those five rooms with private baths; guests in the other five rooms receive their morning meal at a communal table. Don't look for a TV or telephone, just a relaxed atmosphere, friendly hosts, and the sea.

### SHEFFIELD HOUSE
Innkeepers: Steve & Claire McQueeny.

A short trek uphill from Old Harbor, this Queen Anne was built in 1888 as a summer cottage, with a wraparound veranda (complete with comfy

401-466-2494; 800-466-8329;
fax 401-466-5067.
High St., PO Box C-2 (Old
Harbor), Block Island, RI
02807.
Open: Year-round.
Price: Moderate to
Expensive.
Credit Cards: AE, MC, V.
Smoking: No.
Handicap Access: Ramp
and first-floor room.
Restrictions: No pets or
children.

rocking chairs), patterned shingles, and a wonderful turret, all exceedingly well kept. In the summer, a lush, colorful flower bed dominates the front yard, while the backyard is given over to a perennial garden where guests are welcome to eat the continental breakfast. The inn's seven rooms are comfortably decorated with antiques, wicker, and family pieces; most have private baths. Extras include an outside shower in the back and a bicycle rack.

*Despite its farmhouse looks on the outside, rooms at The 1661 Inn are some of the most elegant on Block Island.*

Craig Hammell

### THE 1661 INN

Owners: Joan Abrams &
Rita Draper.
401-466-2421; 800-626-4773;
fax 401-466-3162; E-mail:
BIRESORTS@aol.com.
Spring St. (Old Harbor),
Block Island, RI 02807.
Open: Year-round.
Price: Expensive to Very
Expensive.
Credit Cards: AE, MC, V.
Smoking: Nonsmoking
rooms available.
Handicap Access: Yes.
Restrictions: No pets.

On the seaward side of Spring St. is The 1661 Inn, named for the year that Block Is. was purchased and settled by sixteen English families. The unpretentious exterior belies the lavishness inside. The nine sumptuous rooms in this mid-nineteenth-century, white clapboard house are decorated with a mix of antiques and colonial replicas; the most expensive suite has a private deck, endless ocean views, and a loft given over entirely to an enormous Jacuzzi. More rooms are located in a separate guest house and cottage. A fabulous breakfast/brunch is served in the sea view dining room and deck (see the section Dining), which is also open to the public for afternoon cocktails.

## THE WEATHER BUREAU INN

Owner: Brian Wright.
401-466-9977; 800-633-8624.
Ocean Ave., Box 577 (New Harbor), Block Island, RI 02807.
Open: Year-round.
Price: Expensive to Very Expensive.
Credit Cards: MC, V.
Smoking: No.
Handicap Access: No.
Restrictions: No pets, or children under 12.

This new inn is located in one of the landmark buildings on Block Is.: the former weather bureau station built in 1903 on a knoll overlooking the blue and green expanse of New Harbor. It's a white, stately, upright building that inspires confidence at a glance. Happily, guests will immediately discover that the confidence is warranted. Inside five guest rooms have lofty ceilings, original mahogany trim, glass transoms, and lovely old wainscoting (one also has a working fireplace). Antiques decorate the house, including the parlor, where wine and cheese are served in the evening, and the dining room, where guests meet to dine on gourmet breakfasts.

## BED & BREAKFASTS

### BEACH HOUSE B&B

Owner: Rosalie.
401-466-2929.
Corn Neck Rd. (Old Harbor), Block Island, RI 02807.
Open: Jul.–Aug.
Price: Expensive.
Credit Cards: No.
Smoking: No.
Handicap Access: No.
Restrictions: No pets. children under 12.

For people who love the beach — love it so much that they can't get close enough to the ocean — consider staying nowhere else on Block Is.; for those who value private baths and luxury above sand and a muscular sea breeze, don't consider Beach House at all. This 1885 home literally sits in the sand surrounded by sea grass at the head of Crescent Beach; a trail leads to Old Harbor in under two minutes. The house is still in the process of being renovated, and the exterior looks a little rough, but inside, the four guest rooms sum up everything good about seaside architecture and decoration. Light, bright, and sparely appointed in simple antiques, painted furniture, and lace curtains, the rooms are quintessentially *right*. Currently the rooms share two down-at-the-heel baths, though soon each will have its own bath. A full breakfast is included.

### McCOMBE'S B&B

Owners: Teri & Bill McCombe.
401-466-2684.
Old Town Rd., Box 261 (Center), Block Island, RI 02807.
Open: Mem. Day–mid-Sept.
Price: Moderate to Expensive.
Credit Cards: No.
Smoking: Porch only.

He's the chief of police, and she's the school art teacher; together they run a terrific B&B. There's only one guest room in this lovely, secluded spot, but it's a good one, with its own entrance and deck (recently extended) overlooking the back meadow, a private bath, and a queen-sized bed. The room is sizable, with a dining area complete with old ice-cream parlor furniture, white-washed wood, lace curtains, and Teri's own artwork. Every morning she'll deliver a gourmet continental breakfast to your door in an old picnic

Handicap Access: No.
Restrictions: No pets, or

hamper. It's perfect for a small family, two couples (the sofa pulls out), or as a great romantic getaway. In case it rains, there's color/cable TV. A nice touch is Teri's photo album of island attractions.

Craig Hammell

*A former Primitive Methodist Church, The Sasafrash on Block Island boasts a beautiful — and unusual — interior.*

**THE SASAFRASH**
Owners: Shirley &
 Sanford Kessler.
401-466-5486.
Center Rd., Box 1073
 (Center), Block Island,
 RI 02807.
Open: May–Oct.
Price: Moderate to
 Expensive.
Credit Cards: No.
Smoking: No.
Handicap Access: No.
Restrictions: No pets or
 children.
Special Features: Restored
 church.

It's impossible to express enough delight about the Sasafrash. It was built in 1907 as a Primitive Methodist Church, smack in the heart of Block Is. (where the old town center used to be, about a ten-minute walk to New Harbor). The Kesslers have restored the church and made it their home. Gothic arch, stained-glass windows complement their wonderful, eclectic collection of art and antiques — the view from the front door through to the rounded arch altar area is breathtaking. Three guest rooms are on the second floor, which extends like a choir loft over half of the living area below; a fourth room can be opened to make for two shared-bath quarters. All of the furniture is from the island, and the rooms are comfortable and bright, with unusual windows and angled walls. A full breakfast is served, followed later by wine and cheese in the afternoon. A back deck and an outside shower are also available.

**WILLOW GROVE**
Owners: Dan & Debbie
 Hart.
401-466-2896.

Dan and Debbie Hart's families have owned this fully restored, stately Victorian near the end of Corn Neck Rd. (close to Sachem Pond) for years. The Harts discovered that their home was a nine-

Corn Neck Rd. (The Neck), Block Island, RI 02807.
Open: Mem. Day–mid-Sept.
Price: Expensive.
Credit Cards: No.
Smoking: No.
Handicap Access: No.
Restrictions: No mopeds.

teenth-century boardinghouse called Willow Grove — hence the name. One antique-appointed guest room has a private bath and its own parlor, refrigerator, and separate entrance. Considering the beautiful, utterly peaceful setting, the lovely antiques, and Debbie's home-baked breakfast (her cooking has been written up in *Yankee Magazine*), it's not surprising that guests return year after year. Dan has a taxi service and will run you to and from the ferry.

# DINING

Those who have been around the Block a few times (sorry, island humor) offer the following recommendations when it comes to dining: if at all possible, BYOB and any edibles that you can carry. If your pack animal is a car, fill up the tank on the mainland — prices are half-again as high on the island. Groceries are high priced and limited here, as is liquor. Most inns have refrigerators at guests' disposal, and some have kitchens — take advantage of them. If you plan to cook fish, it's a good idea to purchase it in Galilee before you leave the mainland. It's very fresh there (home of the Rhode Island fishing fleet), and the prices are lower than those on Block Island. If that's not practical, buy your lobsters at the crack of dawn on New Harbor docks from returning lobstermen.

The rule for Block Island restaurants is simplicity. Even high-end, "fancy" places, of which there are only four — Atlantic Inn, The Spring House, Hotel Manisses, and Winfield's — don't go in for "fusion cuisine" or the intricate sauces that characterize gourmet restaurants in Newport; though because of the cost of importing ingredients, prices can be about the same. Grilled, super-fresh swordfish is the defining dish on the island.

Restaurants aside, my favorite Block Island dining experience is to take some newspapers and matches out to the beach at sunset, dig a hole, line it with rocks, put in some driftwood, and have a cookout — it's cheap, legal (though camping out is not), and fun. Load up a plastic bag with rocks for ballast and chill your wine or beer in the sea.

Following the restaurant listings is the section Food & Beverage Purveyors, which notes the best spots for quick meals, ice cream, frozen cappuccino, and the like.

The price range reflects the cost of a single dinner meal, including appetizer, entrée, dessert, and coffee or tea. Alcoholic beverages, tax, and tip are not included in the price scale.

## Dining Price Code

| | |
|---|---|
| Inexpensive | Up to $15 |
| Moderate | $15 to $25 |
| Expensive | $25 to $35 |
| Very Expensive | Over $35 |

## Credit Cards

| | |
|---|---|
| AE — American Express | DC — Diner's Club |
| CB — Carte Blanche | MC — MasterCard |
| D — Discover | V — Visa |

**ALDO'S ITALIAN SEAFOOD RESTAURANT**
401-466-5871.
Weldon's Way (Old Harbor), Block Island, RI 02807.
Open: Daily.
Price: Inexpensive to Moderate.
Cuisine: Italian.
Serving: L, D.
Credit Cards: AE, V.
Reservations: No.
Smoking: Sometimes.
Handicap Access: Yes.

Aldo's casual, family restaurant is the grand-daddy of island pizza joints. Whether you eat inside or out on the patio, try the chicken pasta andidmo (with broccoli and feta cheese) — it's plentiful and full of flavor. Baked ziti also scores, and the spinach pie and pizza are sound. Elva at the Chamber of Commerce says that the spaghetti and (giant) meatballs are one of the best bargains on the island. Everything is available for takeout. Don't overlook the homemade ice cream and baked goods at **Aldo's Bakery** next door.

**ATLANTIC INN**
401-466-5883; 800-224-7422.
High St. (Old Harbor), Block Island, RI 02807.
Open: Daily, Apr.–Oct.
Price: Expensive to Very Expensive.
Cuisine: Creative American.
Serving: D.
Credit Cards: D, MC, V.
Reservations: Recommended.
Smoking: No.
Handicap Access: No.

The Atlantic Inn is one of Block's grand old Victorian hotels, with a wraparound porch that affords a commanding view of the sea and the Hotel Manisses' herd of llamas, just down the hill. Under new management since 1994, the dining room now consistently prepares possibly the best meals on the island. The chef concentrates on local fish and rounds out the small, ever-changing menu with chicken, meat, and vegetarian options. Simplicity rules the kitchen: roasted striped bass is served over orzo salsa; roast chicken comes with red bliss potatoes and spaghetti squash; gnocci is sparingly prepared with kale, Gorgonzola cheese, and pine nuts. Desserts include plum crisp with ginger ice cream and a fine ricotta cheese tart with black current coulis. If you're not hungry for dinner, hors d'oeuvres and cocktails are available on the porch.

**BALLARD'S INN**
401-466-2231.
Water St. (Old Harbor),
  Block Island, RI 02807.
Open: Daily, May–Oct.
Price: Moderate.
Cuisine: American.
Serving: L, D.
Credit Cards: MC, V.
Reservations: No.
Smoking: Yes.
Handicap Access: Yes.

**E**very resort has one, and this is the one on Block Is.: a humongous, noisy, ultracasual seafood joint right on the water where children are welcome, the bar is always crowded, the food is not so great, and live music blares on weekends, while tipsy couples dance the night away. Lunch and dinner menus are the same; the food is standard (peel-and-eat shrimp, lobster, fish and chips, meatball sandwiches) but fairly priced. Ballard's has a hidden gem: a patio with café tables *right* on the beach, so close that the spray will curl your hair; there's nothing else like it on the island. Note that Ballard's also rents rooms and has its own marina, plus necessities like pay telephones and ATMs. A super location for those in a raucous mood.

**THE BEACHEAD**
401-466-2249.
Corn Neck Rd. (Old Harbor),
  Block Island, RI 02807.
Open: Daily, year-round.
Price: Inexpensive.
Cuisine: Burgers.
Serving: L, D.
Credit Cards: No.
Reservations: No.
Smoking: Yes.
Handicap Access: Yes.

**B**lock Islanders are in love with this place. The year-round lot gathers here to shoot pool, sit at the bar, talk about the weather, and down possibly the best burgers on the island. Beachy, right across from the Atlantic Ocean, it offers very good fish and deli sandwiches, chili, and a big chef salad. The clam chowder is served "Block Island style" in a clear broth with onions, potatoes, and local clams and is only available in-season — the mark of a wise cook.

**DEAD EYE DICK'S**
401-466-2654.
Payne's Dock (New Harbor),
  Block Island, RI 02807.
Open: weekends in May;
  closed Mon., mid-
  Jun.–Labor Day.
Price: Moderate to
  Expensive.
Cuisine: Seafood.
Serving: L, D.
Credit Cards: AE, MC. V.
Reservations: No.
Smoking: Smoking section.
Handicap Access: One step.

**D**ead Eye's is mobbed and noisy on summer weekends, and the wait can be long, but these few drawbacks are usually worth enduring for consistently decent food and a seat on the outdoor deck overlooking Payne's Dock, if you can get it. The menu features fresh fish spiffed up into entrées like grilled shrimp and andouille sausage, Maryland crab cakes, and grilled tuna in sun-dried tomato vinaigrette. Nothing too fancy — the inevitable grilled swordfish makes an appearance — but, except on rare off nights when things can get a little overcooked, the seafood is fresh and well prepared. Try the Maine raspberry cake; it's a longtime favorite.

**ELI'S**
401-466-5230.
Chapel St. (Old Harbor),
  Block Island, RI 02807.

**E**li's is unique on Block Is.: a tiny, storefront spot down a side street, it eschews fried fish (even grilled swordfish) to concentrate on creative pastas

Open: Year-round; closed
  Mon.–Wed., in winter.
Price: Moderate to
  Expensive.
Cuisine: Pasta.
Serving: D.
Credit Cards: MC, V.
Reservations: No.
Smoking: No.
Handicap Access: Yes.

that are as good as anything that you can get in Newport. Menu items change frequently, but feature classics like shrimp puttanesca and more adventurous options like duck ravioli with cashews, squash, and scallions in an apple cider-duck reduction. Specials, including veal chops, chicken breast, pork, and filet mignon, take the menu well beyond pasta. There's a nice casual feel to the place and a happily eclectic wine list. The drawback is that there's almost always a significant wait in-season, though all menu items are available to take out.

### ERNIE'S OLD HARBOR RESTAURANT

401-466-2473.
Water St. (Old Harbor),
  Block Island, RI 02807.
Open: Daily,
  May–Columbus Day.
Price: Inexpensive.
Cuisine: American.
Serving: B.
Credit Cards: AE, MC, V.
Smoking: No.
Handicap Access: Yes.

Since most lodging includes breakfast these days, not too many tourists discover Ernie's. But locals love this place, just a hop, skip, and jump from the Old Harbor ferry landing; a back deck overlooks the dock. The menu is extensive, from pancakes to eggs and oatmeal, and everything tastes good. Skip your B&B breakfast once to come here for a hearty meal and island gossip. Sometimes there's a wait, especially on weekends.

### FINN'S SEAFOOD RESTAURANT

401-466-2473.
Water St. (Old Harbor),
  Block Island, RI 02807.
Open: Daily, late
  May–Columbus Day.
Price: Moderate.
Cuisine: Seafood.
Serving: L, D.
Credit Cards: AE, MC, V.
Reservations: No.
Smoking: Outside only.
Handicap Access: Yes.

Finn's, the venerable seafood restaurant of Block Is., has it all, except for a view; its outdoor tables overlook the dock parking lot. The emphasis is on fresh fish (Finn's own fish market is next door), which is served every way imaginable. The best bet is the Fisherman's Platter, which includes a little bit of everything, either fried or broiled. There's also a raw bar, lobster in varying weights, even a superb bluefish pâté. In addition to complete dinners, you can also get sandwiches, burgers, and, of course, fish and chips. *Everything*, including the filet mignon, is available for takeout. Recommendation: stick with beer (the wine list is average at best) and fish; steaks are definitely not Finn's specialty. Save room for a slice of fresh pie.

### THE HARBORSIDE

401-466-5504; 800-892-2002.
Water St. (Old Harbor),
  Block Island, RI 02807.

This may be the first place that you see coming off the ferry at Old Harbor; the red-and-white striped café table umbrellas can't help but catch your eye. Breakfast and lunch menus offer stan-

Open: Daily, mid-May–late Sept.
Price: Moderate to Expensive.
Cuisine: American.
Serving: B, L, D.
Credit Cards: AE, MC, V.
Reservations: Suggested.
Smoking: Smoking section.
Handicap Access: No.

dard fare; dinner selections are straightforward and consistently good, if not memorable. The individual lobster bake is a favorite, as is the swordfish, and The Harborside boasts the only salad bar on Block Is. Interior dining rooms have attractive nautical antiques and uneven floorboards (the restaurant is within the 1887 hotel of the same name), but sit outside if you can — it's a great spot to watch the world go by. End with one of the most generous hot fudge sundaes around.

**HIGHVIEW INN EATERY**
401-466-5912.
Connecticut Ave. (Old Harbor), Block Island, RI 02807.
Open: Daily, May–Columbus Day.
Price: Moderate to Expensive.
Cuisine: American/ Caribbean.
Serving: D.
Credit Cards: MC, V.
Reservations: Yes.
Smoking: Upstairs lounge only.
Handicap Access: No.

The Highview dining room comes as something of a surprise and not just because of the delightful murals of island life that decorate the walls. The inn has a split personality: rooms are decidedly shabby, and the basement bar **Club Soda** (see the section Culture, under the heading Nightlife) is a cheerful dive, where you can get pub food when the restaurant isn't serving, yet the eatery is one of the best dining spots on the island. The young owners have put all of their efforts into the renovated Victorian dining room and a contemporary menu. The menu features fish, with swordfish and bouillabaisse as two of the specialties; Clams Islander (an appetizer) is really wonderful. There's also a well-rounded selection of poultry and meat items. A sophisticated wine list nicely complements the menu. Many islanders rank the Highview as one of their favorite restaurants. Note that smokers may eat dinner in the lounge.

**HOTEL MANISSES**
401-466-2421; 800-626-4773.
Spring St., PO Box 1 (Old Harbor), Block Island, RI 02807.
Open: Daily, in-season; Sat., only in winter.
Price: Expensive to Very Expensive.
Cuisine: Creative American.
Serving: D.
Credit Cards: AE, MC, V.
Reservations: Recommended.
Smoking: Outside only.
Handicap Access: No.

The dining room at the Hotel Manisses is one of the most elegant on Block Is., though the unofficial, island-wide policy of casual attire holds sway. Eat inside in the high Victorian dining room or outside on the back deck, overlooking the hotel's petting zoo. The menu, which treats seafood, fowl, and a few meat dishes with a light, nouvelle touch, rotates daily; sometimes the menu isn't made up until late afternoon when the fishing fleet comes in. Favorites range from baked-stuffed lobster and rack of lamb to more adventurous items like bluefish with Pernod, tomatoes, and mustard; word is that the kitchen has on and off nights. Appetizers also roam from the simple, steamed mussels to the provocative, apple-smoked quail. The Library Room and Top Shelf Bar offer a change of scene for desserts, liqueurs, flaming coffees, and fine cigars.

**MOHEGAN CAFÉ**
401-466-5911.
Water St. (Old Harbor),
    Block Island, RI 02807.
Open: Daily, in-season;
    Thurs.–Sun., Apr.–Nov.
Price: Inexpensive to
    Expensive.
Cuisine: American.
Serving: L, D.
Credit Cards: AE, MC, V.
Reservations: No.
Smoking: Smoking section.
Handicap Access: One step.

Located smack in the middle of Old Harbor village, Mohegan's is where you can watch ferries come and go from the café's big picture windows. But beware: locals warn that this spot has a reputation for "soaking the tourists on the fish," as one islander put it, so avoid the dinner specials. Better to order off the regular menu, which features Tex-Mex fare — the burrito is really top-notch — plus an international round of dishes from pad Thai to a veggie sushi roll, plus lobster and crab enchiladas, basil gnocchi, and prime rib. Everyone will be satisfied; no one will be awed. The desserts are rich and imaginative. The atmosphere is pleasantly plain and nautical.

**NATIONAL HOTEL TAP
& GRILLE**
401-466-2901.
Water St. (Old Harbor),
    Block Island, RI 02807.
Open: Daily, May–Oct.
Price: Moderate to
    Expensive.
Cuisine: American.
Serving: L, D.
Credit Cards: AE, MC, V.
Reservations: No.
Smoking: Outside only.
Handicap Access: No.

Like it's partner The Harborside, the National Hotel (see the section Lodging) is impossible to miss. It's hallowed porch overlooks Water St. and the harbor, and the building has been home to innumerable restaurants and bars over the years. The latest and most upscale incarnation, the Tap & Grille, bills itself as "Block Island's Only Steak House," so it's fitting that sirloins and rib eyes dominate the menu, rounded out by grilled seafood and predictable pastas. The food here doesn't have to be great — offer a great view from the most accessible porch on the island, and people will come — but it isn't bad. The luncheon salads are crisp and creative, and the grilled eggplant sandwich is a pleaser; the clam chowder, though, ranks as only ordinary. Live music on Fri.-Sun. nights.

**THE OAR**
401-466-8820.
Job's Hill, West Side Rd.
    (New Harbor), Block
    Island, RI 02807.
Open: Daily, Apr.–Nov.
Price: Inexpensive.
Cuisine: American.
Serving: B, L, D.
Credit Cards: AE, V, MC.

The Oar used to be a bar, no more, no less; but it was a bar with one of the best views on Block Is., with picture windows and a deck overlooking New Harbor. Now that it's been taken over by the owners of the Hotel Manisses, it's worth coming for more than the view. Don't get so enthralled by what's outside that you forget to look up — hundreds of oars dangle from the ceiling. The clam

*The Oar on Block Island lives up to its name.*

Craig Hammell

Reservations: No.
Smoking: Yes.
Handicap Access: No.

chowder is a winner, as is the crispy fried chicken, vegetarian chili, club sandwiches, and codfish and chips. There's also a nice range of beers and ales on tap. Locals recommend The Oar for breakfast; the lunch-dinner menu is offered from 12:00 noon-8:00 p.m., after which bar snacks are available until midnight. Occasional live music.

**SHARKEY'S**
401-466-9900.
Corn Neck Rd. (Old
   Harbor), Block Island, RI
   02807.
Open: Daily, year-round.
Price: Moderate to
   Expensive.
Cuisine: American.
Serving: L, D.
Credit Cards: MC, V.
Reservations: No.
Smoking: Bar only.
Handicap Access: Yes.

Forced to build new quarters when a plane crashed into its former digs a few years back, Sharkey's now occupies the island's slickest space. Choose to eat on an outdoor patio, inside under a vaulted ceiling, or at an eye-catching bar that occupies half of the room. Island opinion comes down in favor of what's basically good pub grub: burgers, sandwiches, and interesting beer selections (by comparison the wine list seems like an afterthought). The dinner menu is middle-of-the-road in offerings (steaks, chicken, fish) but consistently good in preparation.

**THE 1661 INN**
401-466-2421; 401-466-2063;
   800-626-4773.
Spring St. (Old Harbor),
   Block Island, RI 02807.
Open: Daily, May–Oct.
Price: Inexpensive to
   Moderate.

The daily brunch at The 1661 Inn, partner of the Hotel Manisses across the street, comes *highly* recommended as one of the best deals in town. Graze on a huge, creative breakfast buffet set up on a canopied deck that directly overlooks the Atlantic Ocean, which crashes rhythmically as you eat. The buffet includes eggs, waffles, hash browns, baked

Cuisine: American/
  International.
Serving: Brunch.
Credit Cards: AE, MC, V.
Reservations: No.
Smoking: Outside only.
Handicap Access: Yes.

beans, even smoked bluefish; more than enough to hold you well into the afternoon. (See the section Lodging for more on the inn.)

## THE SPRING HOUSE
401-466-5844.
Spring St. (Old Harbor),
  Block Island, RI 02807.
Open: Daily, mid-
  Jun.–Labor Day.
Price: Expensive to Very
  Expensive.
Cuisine: American.
Serving: L, D.
Credit Cards: AE, MC, V.
Reservations: Yes.
Smoking: Smoking section.
Handicap Access: No.

The Spring House, the oldest hotel on Block Is. (see the section Lodging) has an enchanting atmosphere earned by age and the dignity of its location on a knoll above the Atlantic. It's grandeur is a little worn, but that makes dining here a comfortable, rather than a stiff, experience. Better yet, the food is consistently good, simply prepared, and generous. The clam chowder is visibly full of potatoes, butter, and clams; the baked salmon in cracker crumbs and pesto is massive and perfectly cooked. The dinner menu features ribs, steaks, and grilled fish, with a honey-mustard veal chop as the signature dish. Desserts aren't as much of a focus as the extensive wine list. A pub menu is offered in the lounge, where a range of cigars and cognacs are also available, as well as on the porch — one of the best places on Block Is. to lounge and watch the ocean churn. An all-you-can-eat lunch barbecue is also served on the porch.

## WINFIELD'S
401-466-5856.
Corn Neck Rd. (Old
  Harbor), Block Island, RI
  02807.
Open: Daily, year-round.
Price: Expensive.
Cuisine: Creative American.
Serving: D.
Credit Cards: AE, MC, V.
Reservations: Yes, for 6 or
  more.
Smoking: No.
Handicap Access: One step.

Low, beamed ceilings, white tablecloths, and candlelight create a refined setting here, but dress is casual. The menu is creative with a good choice of pastas, fowl, red meat, and pork dishes. While the four-cheese penne is one of the best that I've had, a pork and shrimp curry missed the mark. Many, however, feel that Winfield's is one of the best eateries on Block Is. The restaurant is operated by the family that owns McGovern's Yellow Kittens nightclub next door (see the section Culture, under the heading Nightlife); on the other side of Kittens is a new outdoor venture called **The Deck,** which offers gyros and veggie roll-ups for lunch (among more traditional fare), plus straightforward grilled fish and meat dishes for dinner, including blackened tuna sashini, pork chops, and swordfish. If you're looking for less expensive, simple food, head to The Deck; for more nouvelle creations (and prices), try Winfield's.

# FOOD & BEVERAGE PURVEYORS

Note that starred listings (*) indicate a purveyor of local fame or of unusual or special merit.

## BAKERIES & COFFEEHOUSES

* **Aldo's Bakery & Ice Cream** (401-466-2198; Weldon's Way, Old Harbor) Next to the restaurant of the same name, the bakery offers fresh-baked breads, pies, pastries, and homemade ice cream.

**The French Connection** (401-466-2299; Water St., Old Harbor) This bakery in a row of shops under the National Hotel porch offers French pastries, plus breakfast items, sandwiches, and take-out desserts, even crème brûlée to go. All baking is done on the premises. Open May-late Oct.

**Juice 'N Java** (401-466-5220; Dodge St., Old Harbor) A comfortable coffeehouse with espresso, desserts, paperbacks, and regular old coffee.

**Portfolio Cafe & Gallery** (401-466-5455; Ocean Ave., Block Island Marketplace) In addition to excellent coffee, Portfolio also cooks up sandwiches, pastries, and stuffies (nickname for RI stuffed clams). Paintings and photographs on the walls are for sale. Open from early morning to late night.

## BARS

**The Albion Pub** (401-466-9990; Ocean Ave., Block Island Marketplace, Old Harbor) A total contrast to Mahogany Shoals (below), Albion's is upscale as opposed to unbuttoned in that easy, Jimmy Buffet kind of way. The Albion is the newest pub on Block Is.; look for a range of microbrewery beers.

* **Mahogany Shoals** (401-466-5572; Payne's Dock, New Harbor) This is such a wonderful — albeit tiny — spot that regulars wanted to keep it to themselves. No luck. It's in a tiny shack at the end of the pier behind the Mobile sign. It has good drink, good music (a house favorite is a tune about Bertha's Mussels in Baltimore), and great people. It's a plus that a T-shirt of "Bars of Block Island" doesn't picture it. Open 4:00 p.m.–1:00 a.m.

**Samuel Peckham Tavern** (401-466-5458; West Side Rd., New Harbor) Sam Peckham's is really much more than a bar; it serves steaks, ribs, chicken, and fish, as well as liquor. But since the place is so easygoing that you can get a full dinner at the bar, the tavern side of its nature wins out. It has a fine view overlooking New Harbor.

## FARM STANDS & MARKETS

**Block Island Farmer's Market** (401-466-2875) Held Wed., 9:00 a.m.–11:00 a.m. behind the Hotel Manisses and Sat. 9:00 a.m.–11:00 a.m. at Negus Park. A cornucopia of island produce, plus baked goods and crafts. Begins early Jun.

**Littlefield Bee Farm** (401-466-5364, fax 401-466-9978; Corn Neck Rd., Old Harbor) Walk the Clayhead Trail, then on the way back pick up fresh Block Is. honey, honey-mustard, beeswax candles, and gift baskets (the farm stand is opposite the beginning of the trail).

## FISH MARKETS

\* **Finn's Fish Market** (401-466-2102; Water St., Old Harbor) Pricey by off-island standards, Finn's nonetheless has the freshest lobster, fish, and clams that you'll find anywhere.

## GOURMET, DELI, GROCERY

**Block Island Depot** (401-466-2403; Ocean Ave., bet. Old and New Harbors) The island's natural and health foods shop.

**Block Island Grocery** (401-466-2949; Ocean Ave. bet. Old and New Harbors) Of the two grocery stores on the island, this is the one without liquor, though the produce here seems fresher. A deli counter is in the back.

\* **The Daily Market** (401-466-9908; Chapel St., Old Harbor) Calling itself "the island's organic greengrocer," this new spot is a welcome addition to island food shops. Besides fresh, organically grown vegetables, the market offers cheeses, prepared foods, condiments, fresh-baked pies, and sandwiches to go. Open year-round.

**Seaside Market** (401-466-5876; Water St., Old Harbor) This is the other minisupermarket on Block Is., but it sells liquor. Deli counter.

**The Wild Carrot** (401-466-5587; 30 Water St., Old Harbor) From fancy foods and baked goods to morning coffee, in the New Post Office Building.

## ICE CREAM & SWEETS

\* **The Ice Cream Place** (401-466-2145; Weldon's Way, Old Harbor) Flavors and concoctions are listed on an enormous chalkboard that takes forever to read. Great homemade peanut butter brownies and other goodies. Best ice cream and frozen yogurt on Block Is.

## SEASONAL FOOD FESTIVALS

**Block Island Pasta Cook-off** (401-466-2982) An all-you-can-eat opportunity to choose the best pasta on Block Is. Mid-May.

**Block Island Seafood Festival and Chowder Cook-Off** (401-466-2982; Harbor Baptist Church). Third weekend in Jun.

## TAKEOUT & CHEAP EATS

**Bethany's Airport Diner** (401-466-3100; State Airport, Center Rd.) One of the few places where Long Is. commuters mix with Block Is. locals. Serves breakfast fare, omelettes, burgers, and sandwiches. Stop here if you've biked all the way up the hill from Old Town Rd.

**Cappizzano's** (401-466-2829; Dodge St. and Corn Neck Rd., Old Harbor) Regular and gourmet pizzas, calzones, and grinders, plus nightly pasta specials. Serves beer and wine. Breakfast (5:30 a.m.–11:00 a.m.) leans to baked goods rather than bacon and eggs. Open Apr.–Nov.

**Froozies** (401-466-2230; Water St., Old Harbor, back porch of The National Hotel) A juice bar specializing in exotic frozen fruit smoothies. Also veggie sandwiches on homemade bread.

**Old Harbor Take-Out** (401-466-2935; Water St., Old Harbor) Couldn't be any closer to the ferry dock if it tried. Surprisingly good fare — try the pita sandwiches (Chicken Athena is delicious), fried seafood, or burgers. There's also a breakfast menu, plus ice cream and frozen yogurt. Fresh Block Is. blackberries on the sundaes are a nice touch.

**Payne's Dock** (401-466-5572; Payne's Dock, New Harbor) Slightly off the beaten path, most folks come here by accident. For under $4, the fried shrimp is a steal. Great chowder, clam cakes, hot dogs, ice cream, and homemade doughnuts until 6:00 p.m. Open Jul. 4–Labor Day.

**Rebecca's Seafood** (401-466-5411; Water St., Old Harbor) Owned by a fisherman, it's no surprise that the clam cakes here are fabulous. Also top-notch curlicue fries, plus chowder, burgers, sandwiches, even seafood dinners. Highly recommended for breakfast as well. Open May-Nov., 7:00 a.m.–2:00 a.m.

**Water Street Cafe** (401-466-5540; Water St., Old Harbor) An "alfresco only" spot where you pick up your order from a take-out window and eat at café tables overlooking the harbor. A small menu offers white Block Is. chowder (an award winner), fried clams, and seafood salad roll, plus burgers, clubs, tuna melt, etc. Will pack take-out boxes for "beach or ferry." Open late Jun.-Labor Day.

# CULTURE

## ARCHITECTURE

**B**lock Island is the East Coast's ode to Victoriana. Its homes are an architectural diary of the late nineteenth century, written in beams, clapboards, wooden shingles, and stone.

Until the government built a breakwater at Old Harbor in the mid-1870s, Block Island was a quiet farming and fishing community of simple, shingled farmhouses dotting its hilly landscape. Once Old Harbor was built, the island became fashionable for it's "unspoiled" nature, with visitors arriving to "take the waters" at The Spring House and other hotels built during the great Victorian boom years (actually The Spring House was built in 1852, prior to the harbor). After World War I, Block Island fell out of favor until the cycle of popularity and construction in the late twentieth century repeated itself exactly 100 years after its original heyday.

The chief result of this cycle is that the island's Victorian buildings appear now like so many wooden sleeping beauties, reawakened over the past twenty years through renovation and restoration, mirrored even in contemporary construction. Of all the late nineteenth-century buildings, the most immediately noticeable are the hotels: great, white clapboard affairs with wraparound porches and soaring, mansard roofs imported from Second Empire France. These cavernous structures don't so much provide shelter as loosely wrap their wooden frames around the island's sea-heavy air, relying on simple wainscoting and open windows to blend interior space with exterior landscape.

The hotels were soon joined by beach cottages, built by islanders and off-islanders alike in the picturesque styles popular on the mainland. There are Italianate villas and Second Empire cottages, Queen Anne, Gothic, and shingle-style beach houses. Look closely at the shingled skin of The Surf hotel, reproduced on hundreds of island homes and the wraparound porch and proud turret of Bit o' Heaven, a private cottage on a bluff above Black Rock Beach — however mighty, all are rendered in wood, Block Island's age-old building material.

It is a tribute to their builders that these wooden structures are not only standing, but still lived in, which is why, incidentally, there is no heading Historic Buildings & Sites in this chapter. The island's homes are too busy being used to be set aside as museums, which makes for a wonderful continuity in Block Island's building environment. While The Surf hotel may have gingerbread porch brackets and a multigabled roof, its gray shingles nonetheless hark back to the island's earliest farmsteads and outbuildings, built long before the Victorian boom. And in the early 1980s, when Robert Venturi started playing around with postmodernism, one of his first homes was a little shingled beach cottage off Corn Neck Road.

In 1952, a Harvard study proposed tearing down the existing architecture of Block Island and rebuilding it as an international-style resort — a world of elongated steel I beams and glass walls. Recognizing that change is not always for the better, the island's buildings held their own against innovation. In fact, today the entire Old Harbor district is listed on the National Register of Historic Places. For more about Block Island architecture and history, take a trip to the **Block Island Historical Society** (401-466-2481; Old Town Road, Old Harbor).

## CINEMA

**Empire Theatre** (401-466-2555; Water St., Old Harbor) Seasonal movies, plus snacks and a video game room.

**Oceanwest Theatre** (401-466-2971; Champlin's Marina, Motel & Resort, New Harbor) First-run movies, plus live entertainment from cabaret acts to children's shows. May-Sept.

## FINE ART GALLERIES

**Art Constructions** (401-466-2924; 800-419-3228; Corn Neck Rd., Crescent Beach) Sculptures, drawings, and paintings by the well-known Peruvian artist Ceopacatty.

**Crescent Pond and Coastal Design Galleries** (401-466-2033; Corn Neck Rd., The Neck) Rotating exhibitions showcase the work of well-known local artists, including Gretchen Dow Simpson, whose paintings of Block Is. have been featured on the cover of *The New Yorker*. Also nineteenth-century seascapes, nautical antiques, and painted furniture.

**Eisenhaur Gallery** (401-466-2422; Water St., New Post Office Building, Old Harbor) Shows the work of young, local painters and sculptors. Also sponsors painting classes and painting excursions on Block Is. and to the Southwest.

**Encore Gallery** (401-466-2275; Water St., New Post Office Building, Old Harbor) Very contemporary work by artists who live at least part of the year on Block Is. Abstract and minimalist oils, marble sculpture, and collages.

**Jessie Edward's Studio** (401-466-5314; Water St., New Post Office Building, Old Harbor) Shows the paintings of Jessie Edwards; closed Tues. to paint.

**Malcolm Greenaway Galleries** (401-466-2122; 401-466-5331; 800-840-5331; Water St., Old Harbor) Greenaway is the premiere photographer on Block Is. Purchase one of his cibachrome prints, or go down to Chapel St. to buy discounted prints at the **Block Island Glass & Greenaway Gallery II** (see the section Shopping, under the heading Craft Galleries & Studios).

**Mixed Media Art and Design Studio** (401-466-2910; Water St., New Post Office Building, Old Harbor) A variety of contemporary work by local artists.

**Ruseau Watercolors** (401-466-3123; 800-515-9904; Ocean Ave., bet. Old and New Harbors) Island scenes by John Ruseau, a professor of art at the University of Virginia. Originals and limited-edition prints are both fairly priced.

**Sea Breeze Gallery** (401-466-5870; Water St., New Post Office Building, Old Harbor) A creative co-op of artists who show paintings, contemporary rustic furniture, ceramics, sculpture, glass jewelry, and Moroccan rugs. Most artists live on Block Is.

**Spring Street Gallery** (401-466-5374; Spring St., Old Harbor) A cooperative gallery showing the work of island artists and craftspeople in a wide range of media from watercolors to stained glass, wood carvings, hand knits, even honey.

## GARDEN TOURS

**Block Island House & Garden Tour** (401-466-2982) Held every Aug., the tour offers a window on the island under cultivation — quite a contrast to the tangle of wild bayberry that has its way elsewhere. Also superb vernacular architecture.

## LIBRARIES

Consider spending a rainy day — at least part of it — in the library. For books on Block Island, check in the section Bibliography, under the heading Books to Borrow in Chapter Six, *Information*. Livermore's *History of Block Island, Rhode Island*, for instance, is well worth a glance, and a library thumbing is much easier, and cheaper, than carrying the tome home.

**Island Free Library** (401-466-3233; Dodge St., Old Harbor) Open daily, except Mon.

## LIGHTHOUSES

*The 1875 Southeast Light is the stuff of Block Island legend. Not only does it occupy a dramatic position atop Mohegan Bluffs and boast the strongest beacon in New England, but in 1993, the lighthouse was moved inland from the eroding cliff face at a cost of nearly 2 million dollars. Block Islanders believe every penny was worth it.*

Craig Hammell

Of all of Rhode Island's lighthouses, the **Southeast Light,** perched atop Block Island's towering Mohegan Bluffs, is decidedly the most glamorous. Until recently, it was also the most precarious. On August 14, 1993, the *Block Island Times* ran the simple headline "It Moved!" — referring to the Southeast Light's well-engineered trip 245 feet backward from the face of the eroding bluffs. It took islanders ten years to raise the nearly $2 million dollars required to save the Victorian landmark; one resident said that losing the beacon would be like losing the moon. The cliffs were crumbling so quickly that if it hadn't been moved in 1993, within several years the Southeast Light would have wound up a heap of red brick rubble on the beach, 204 feet below.

Its beauty notwithstanding, the Southeast Light was saved in order to provide dramatic rescues of its own. The island's longtime nickname is "The Stumbling Block," in honor of the fact that of the 1,000 or so nautical disasters that have taken place off the New England coast in the past two centuries, half have occurred within range of Block Island. (Legend has it that some of these were the work of "moon-cussers" — wreckers who used lanterns to lure ships into reefs, so they could pilfer the cargo.)

**North Light** (401-466-3200; Sandy Point, end of Corn Neck Rd.) Built in 1867, the North Light is the fourth lighthouse to occupy this position since 1829. Its beacon was automated by the Coast Guard in 1989 after a sixteen-year period of darkness. The first floor of the lighthouse now serves as a natural and historical maritime interpretive center. Open daily, late Jun.-Labor Day; weekends in the spring and fall.

**Palatine Light** This isn't quite a lighthouse, but according to some the Palatine Light is what can happen when lighthouses don't exist but should. On December 27, 1738, the *Princess Augusta,* loaded with emigrants from the Palatine area of Germany, sank off Sandy Point. Many passengers, near starvation, were brought to the island where some recovered and many more died. Local lore holds that on the anniversary of the disaster a ghostly ship sails ablaze on the horizon, which islanders remember as "The Palatine."

**Southeast Light** (401-466-5009; Mohegan Bluffs, off Spring St.) At 201 feet above sea level, this is the highest lighthouse in New England, with the most powerful beacon on the East Coast. The Southeast Light was built in the Gothic Revival style in 1873 at a cost of $70,000. Its hand-ground French lens is so powerful that if it stops rotating, refracting sunlight can ignite fires thirty-five miles away on the mainland. The grounds are open daily; tower tours by the Southeast Light Foundation are conducted in-season.

## MONUMENTS & MEMORIALS

**Block Island Cemetery** (West Side Rd., New Harbor) A quiet spot with a fabulous view of the North Light. The old, lichen-crusted headstones hold surprising appeal.

**Isaac's Corner** (intersection of Center Rd., Lakeside Dr., and Cooneymus Rd., West Side) The corner is named for Isaac Church, the last island-born Native American, who died in 1886. Just to the east is a Native American burial ground; the headstones are set closely together due to the custom of burying the dead in an upright position.

**Settler's Rock** (northern tip of Corn Neck Rd.) This sand-swept bronze plaque lists the names of the sixteen families (you'll find the same surnames in the current telephone directory), who arrived at this spot in April 1661 to establish the first white settlement on the island.

## MUSEUMS

**BLOCK ISLAND HISTORICAL SOCIETY**
401-466-2481.
Old Town Rd. (Old Harbor), Block Island, RI 02807.
Open: Daily, 10:00 a.m.–5:00 p.m., Mem. Day–Columbus Day.
Admission: $2.

Let yourself be lured inside by the Block Is. "double-ender" out front. Because the island had no natural harbor until breakwaters were built in the 1870s, fishermen used like-ended boats that could be easily hauled up onto the beach. Exhibits are a window on island life in the past.

## MUSIC

**Annual Barbershop Quartet Concert** (401-466-2982; Block Island School Gymnasium, High St., Old Harbor) They definitely know how to sing barbershop on Block Is.; they've been holding this event for over thirty years.

**Jazz & Blues Festival** (401-466-2982; The Spring House, Spring St., Old Harbor) The island's sixth annual jazz festival will take place in 1998 on the magnificent grounds of The Spring House.

## NIGHTLIFE

On a July or August weekend, Block Island can rock, though compared to Newport it's a pretty tame scene. The only clubs are in Old Harbor, but as for the rest of the island, nightlife means going outside and staring up at the summer constellations.

**Captain Nick's Rock & Roll Bar** (401-486-2000; Ocean Ave., Old Harbor) Live rock and roll rebounds between two floors, patio, deck, outside bar, and vast, interior bar. This is the largest club on Block Is.; I once burned my foot through a hole in my sneaker, twisting the night away.

**Club Soda** (401-466-5397; Connecticut Ave., Old Harbor) A strange dive bar under the Highview Inn Eatery, outfitted with barber's and dentist's chairs, pool tables, and an island-wide mural. Wed. is "open night talent-or-not night."

**McGovern's Yellow Kittens** (401-466-5855; Corn Neck Rd., Old Harbor) In addition to live bands throughout the summer, plus reggae on Sun. afternoons, Kittens is outfitted with pool tables, Ping-Pong, pinball, etc. The island's oldest nightclub, it can get raucous.

## SEASONAL EVENTS

**Annual Arts and Crafts Guild Fair** (401-466-2982; Esta's Park, Water St., Old Harbor) Local artists flaunt their stuff at this nearly twenty-year-old event.

## THEATER

**Ocean West Dinner Theatre** (401-466-2971, Champlin's Marina, Motel & Resort, New Harbor) A seasonal dinner theatre and late-night cabaret at Champlin's Marina (see the section Lodging). It's a cheap taxi fare from anywhere on the island.

# RECREATION

## BEACHES

**B**lock Island is washed by a sea so clean, so clear, so startlingly fresh that swimming is more like a purification rite than a simple dip in the ocean. If that sounds like hyperbole, find a beach and get wet yourself; the vigor of the open Atlantic has to be felt to be believed. Happily, beaches on Block Island aren't hard to find, from the classic, sandy sweep of Crescent Beach on the island's eastern neck to sheltered coves on the southwestern coast, reminiscent of Cornwall. Take your pick. Swimming is fairly safe all over Block Island, but because this is the open ocean the undertow is strong, and attention must be paid to underwater rocks, but for the northern tip called Sandy Point. Riptides here create very unstable seas, and many swimmers have been swept away. *Warning: Do not swim at Sandy Point. Ever.*

**Ballard's Beach** (Old Harbor) Just south of the ferry landing at Old Harbor, the beach is right next to the big, noisy restaurant and inn of the same name; it's sandy and good for fishing. 2,640 feet long.

**Black Rock Beach** (West Side) Walk or bicycle down the dirt lane (Black Rock Rd.) off Cooneymus Rd. past an atmospheric old beach cottage called Bit o' Heaven. Keep going until you reach a spot to clamber down the cliffs, then you're all alone with the surf and sand. It's magnificent here, but isolated; be careful of hidden rocks when swimming. Bring your dog, and stay all day. 2,640 feet long.

**Cooneymus Beach** (West Side) Just a thin strip of sand at the end of Cooneymus Rd. on the southwestern side of the island, this beach is more a place to hide than to revel in romantic scenery (see Black Rock Beach) or to survey an immense vista of sand and surf (see Crescent Beach); be careful of the powerful tides.

**Crescent Beach** (Corn Neck Rd.) This great, sandy swatch runs along the northeastern shoreline of Block Is., beginning in Old Harbor and encompassing Fred Benson Town Beach, as well as **Scotch Beach** and **Mansion Beach** (the latter is the northernmost). The sand is clean and white, and the water is clear and cold. Park at the Fred Benson Town Beach lot, or walk; it's easier to head down Corn Neck Rd. than to walk in the sand, and chances are someone will give you a lift. Mansion Beach is my personal favorite; the quarter-mile dirt road (a right off Corn Neck Rd.) is marked by a hedge of spruce trees and is one of the nicest beaches in RI. The beach is named for an ornate, eighteen-room Italian villa and Palladian bathhouse that once loomed behind the dunes; built in 1888, it was destroyed by fire in 1963. 13,200 feet long (two and a half miles).

**Fred Benson Town Beach** (Corn Neck Rd.) Formerly called Block Island State Beach, this is the state-owned patch in the middle of Crescent Beach (see above). Bathhouse, full cabana service, lifeguard; 200 parking spaces; free.

**West Beach** (West Beach Rd., off Corn Neck Rd.) An unusual, practically unknown beach with a light surf (good for young children) and low dunes; it's more like Cape Cod Bay than Block Is. To the south is a bird sanctuary; to the north you can follow the dunes all the way to the North Light.

## BICYCLING

*Cyclists round Block Island's one tiny rotary as Rebecca looks on; the Rebecca statue was erected at the end of the last century by an island temperance club.*

Craig Hammell

The ideal way to see Block Island is by bicycle. At three miles wide by seven miles long, the island is the perfect size for bicycle-speed exploration. Feet take too long; cars go too fast, are too intrusive, too noisy, too dirty. Cruising by pedal power, you can smell the salt air and privet hedges, hear the frogs in freshwater ponds, nose down dirt lanes to deserted beaches, and stop on a dime to photograph the farmhouse that you caught in the corner of your eye.

Here's the drawback: there are hills on Block Island. While some stretches are deceptively flat, the island's center and west side rises and falls like a choppy sea; Corn Neck Road, for instance, is a pleasure northbound but is uphill much of the way back to Old Harbor. Cycling from Old Harbor southwest on Spring Street toward the Southeast Light is particularly difficult. Consider when choosing a bicycle or moped that mopeds are intensely disliked by most islanders — they frighten wildlife, scare pedestrians, chew up the landscape (and thus are no longer permitted on dirt roads), and keep the island's lone doctor busy all summer. If you're not in shape to cycle, however, mopeds are the next best thing. Whichever you choose, make every effort to explore beyond Old Harbor; this is an exceptionally beautiful island.

## BICYCLE & MOPED RENTALS

Note that bicycle rentals generally cost between $10 to $15 per day (though there are hour and weekly rates as well); mopeds run between $30 to $60 per day and must be returned by dusk. Moped helmets and eye-protective gear are required by law.

**Beach Rose Bicycles** (401-466-2946; Roslyn Rd., Old Harbor) Mountain bicycles. Look for discount coupons.

**Block Island Bike & Car Rental** (401-466-2297; Ocean Ave., New Harbor).

**Block Island Boat Basin** (401-466-2631, West Side Rd., New Harbor) Bicycle, moped, and car rentals.

**Esta's Bicycle Rental** (401-466-5011; Chapel St., Old Harbor).

**Island Bike and Moped** (401-466-2700; Chapel St., Old Harbor) A full range of bicycles, beach cruisers, tandems, tag-alongs, and mint mopeds.

**The Moped Man** (401-466-5011; Old Harbor ferry landing) Mopeds, mountain bicycles, child seats, and safety gear. Look for discount coupons.

**Old Harbor Bike Shop** (401-466-2029; Old Harbor ferry landing) If you come off the ferry, turn left immediately, and these will be the first bicycles, mopeds, jeeps, cars, and vans that you'll find for rent. Tandems, child seats, and tag-alongs are also available.

**Seacrest Inn Bicycle Rentals** (401-466-2882; High St., Old Harbor) Bicycles only.

## SUGGESTED ROUTES

**The Neck** Cycle all the way out Corn Neck Rd. (about four and a half miles one way from Old Harbor) to the North Light. You'll pass stands of pine trees, old farmhouses, and lichen-encrusted stone walls; at the end is Settler's Rock and an expanse of marshland tipped by the granite tower of the lighthouse. Sorry, it's uphill on the way back.

**Southwest and Center** A linkage of roads forms an ad hoc ring road around the southern half of the island. Follow West Side Rd. out of New Harbor and all around the western coast; it leads into Cooneymus Rd., Lakeside Dr., and Mohegan Trail, which passes the Southeast Light and Mohegan Bluffs, and finally into Spring St. and down to Old Harbor. Or go the other way around and begin at Spring St. and head southwest. The benefit of going the other way is that the hills are less fierce, and when you reach Mohegan Bluffs, there's a breathtaking, panoramic vista due east (at night the lights of the mainland look like a necklace in the sea).

## BIRD-WATCHING

**B**lock Island lies twelve miles off the coast of Rhode Island, in the direct path of the Atlantic Flyway. During the spring and fall, it provides a stopover (a food and fuel respite) to over 175 species of songbirds, shorebirds, and waterfowl — even the endangered peregrine falcon.

The birding event of the year is the **Block Island Bird Count,** sponsored by the Audubon Society and held during the first week of October. In the past, binoculared birders have spied up to 141 species of migrating birds (that's the record). Vans ferry groups from one end of the island to the other, hoping to catch sight of the white ibis, semipalmated sandpiper, lesser black-backed gull, and others. For information, call 401-231-6444.

Throughout the year good spots for birding include the following: the thickets of bayberry, blackberry, and chokeberry that thrive in Rodman's Hollow; the Lewis-Dickens sanctuary at the southwest corner of the island (look for the rare grasshopper sparrow); Mohegan Bluffs, where kestrels and merlins ride warm updraughts rising from the sea; and the salt marshes that fringe the island (for example, off Spring Steet, just below The Spring House), where herons and egrets loiter.

## CAMPING

**T**here is no camping permitted on Block Island.

## FISHING

*A nineteenth-century fishing fleet on Block Island.*

Courtesy Block Island Historical Society

**S**ome of the best fishing grounds in Rhode Island lie about 100 feet off Block Island, where small bait fish get "balled up" in the current, sending blues and stripers into a perpetual feeding frenzy. It's not difficult to hook either by surf casting from island beaches; one of the best of these is Charlestown Beach, with its own jetty, off West Side Road just west of New Harbor.

You can't miss at New Harbor (aka Great Salt Pond), especially along the channel that leads out to sea; look to hook tautog, mackerel, fluke, and flounder. Ask around the island for other popular hot spots as well. See below for rowboat rentals, as well as deep-sea charters. There are also over 300 freshwater ponds on Block Island, which hold large-mouth bass, pickerel, perch, and panfish. Before hooking into any freshwater fish, however, pick up a license at the Town Hall (401-466-3200).

### RENTALS, BAIT, TACKLE

**Oceans & Ponds/ The Orvis Store** (401-466-5131; Ocean Ave., bet. Old and New Harbors) Surf and fly rod, plus kayak and canoe sales and rentals; they also organize fly/spin inshore fishing trips with guides.

**Twin Maples** (401-466-5547; Beach Ave., New Harbor) Bait and tackle, plus rowboat rentals for New Harbor (Great Salt Pond). These guys know where the fish are running all around the island; ask nicely, and they may let you know, too. (Come early in the morning, and you can also pick up a fresh lobster.)

### SEASONAL EVENTS

**Block Island Billfish Tournament** (401-466-2982; Block Island Boat Basin) Late Jul.

## HIKING & WALKING

*On the west side of the island especially, dirt paths beckon hikers and cyclists to the sea.*

Craig Hammell

**B**lock Island offers ideal terrain for hiking. Hills that are steep on bicycles yield more easily to calves. Even better, without traveling footsore miles, you can disappear from the maddening crowd at Old or New Harbor in less than a ten-minute march and can find yourself in a green, quiet world of seascape, stone wall-hemmed fields and thickets of bayberry. Because even in the summer there's little traffic on interior roadways, hiking along the road-sides themselves isn't a bad idea. If you want to probe further into the island's mysteries, however, consider the following options.

The **Nature Conservancy** (401-331-7110), the **Block Island Conservancy** (401-466-2129; Ocean Ave., New Harbor), and the **Block Island Resident's Association** co-sponsor a series of guided nature walks from late June to mid-September. Each walk has a designated meeting point and takes about one and a half hours. Call the Chamber of Commerce (401-466-2982) for more information. Self-guided trails include the following:

**Clayhead Nature Trail** (off upper Corn Neck Rd.; look for parking area) This superb coastal trail, also called **Bluestone,** begins at Corn Neck Rd. and heads east to the cliffs, then turns north all the way to Settler's Rock (see the section Culture, under the heading Monuments & Memorials) at Sandy Point. A network of secondary paths, known as **The Maze,** offers scenic views and scores of seabirds. These trails are privately owned, but the public is welcome to hike them for free.

**The Greenway** (starting point at Nathan Mott Park, off Center Rd. opposite the airport) This is The Nature Conservancy-maintained, twelve-mile network of trails that leads from midisland to the southern coast, featuring old stone walls, dense copses, and stunning sea vistas. Its primary purpose is to provide a corridor for wildlife migration, but the terrain and views are so compelling that it's become a refuge for hikers, too. A highlight is **Rodman's Hollow,** a glacial ravine, sheltering a cornucopia of plant and animal life. Trailheads dot the network; the Rodman's Hollow access is off Black Rock Rd, off Cooneymus Rd.

SEASONAL EVENTS

**Block Island Chamber of Commerce Triathalon** (401-466-2982) A grueling event that combines a short swim across a channel, a six-mile beach run, and a biking course: total fifteen miles. Early Aug.

**Run Around the Block** (401-466-2982) A 15K-run around the island.

## HORSEBACK RIDING

**Rustic Rides** (401-466-5060; PO Box 842, West Side Rd., New Harbor) Tim and Eve McCabe offer guided trail rides on the beach and horse-drawn carriage rides on the beach and elsewhere, plus pony rides for children. An unusual, and appropriately romantic, way to explore Block Is. year-round.

## SAILING & BOATING

Like Newport, Block Island is a sailor's haven, but as practiced in the waters off Block Island, the sport is more casual and chummy, less about prestige and money than it is in Newport. The big event here is **Block Island Race Week,** which began in 1965 with a good idea and a couple of entries, and today has become the largest sailing event on the East Coast. Over 5,000 people wash up on the little island in over 300 sleek racing machines to compete in a score of different events, the highlight of which is the midweek "Round the Island Race." By night, there's a happy, noisy, carnival atmosphere; by day, it looks like a rainbow has been ironed flat and stretched across the horizon: 360-degree views of brilliantly colored sails. For more information, call the Storm Trysail Club, 401-846-1983 or 914-834-8857. Held the last week in June.

For information about kayaking, see the heading Water Sports below.

## CHARTERS, LESSONS, RENTALS

**G. Willie Makit Charters** (401-466-5151; Dorries Cove Rd., Weock Is.) A charter with a great name: inshore trips for bass, blues, cod, fluke, and pollack (maximum six passengers, four or eight hours); offshore trips for tuna, shark, and marlin (four passengers, six or ten hours). Capt. Billy Gould offers the only on-island charter.

**Block Island Club** (401-466-5939; PO Box 147, Corn Neck Rd., Old Harbor) Sailing, windsurfing, swimming, tennis, and children's activities. They offer one-, two-, and three-week memberships.

## MARINAS

The following marinas offer public docking slips and/or moorings, predominantly in New Harbor. The harbor, also called Great Salt Pond (a channel to the sea was dredged in 1894), supports around 2,000 boats in midsummer. It's vital to call for a reservation; there are about 500 slips available on the island. The inner harbor is known as the Hog Pen. Note that a $.50 landing fee is charged every person over twelve years old.

**Block Island Boat Basin** (401-466-2631; 401-466-3361; PO Box 412, Job's Hill, New Harbor) 110 slips. A huge range of amenities, including The Oar, a recently gussied-up bar (see the section Dining). Transient dockage; channel 9.

**Champlin's Marina** (401-466-2641; 800-762-4541; New Harbor) 250 slips. It's part of a large resort complex, so there's lots here, from tennis courts to a bakery. Transient dockage; channel 68.

**Old Harbor Dock** (401-466-3235; Old Harbor) 40 slips. Right in the heart of things, but moorings in Old Harbor can get crowded. Transient dockage; channel 12.

**Payne's Dock** (401-466-5572; New Harbor) 75 slips. Try Dead Eye Dick's, the restaurant on the dock (see the section Dining). Transient dockage.

**Smuggler's Cove Marina** (401-466-2828; Hog Pen, New Harbor) 14 slips. Transient dockage.

**Town Moorings** (401-466-3204; New Harbor) 90 moorings. On a first-come, first-served basis. Transient dockage; channel 12.

## TENNIS

**Atlantic Inn** (401-466-5883; High St., Old Harbor) Four courts free to guests; hourly rentals to the public.

**Block Island Club** (401-466-5939; Corn Neck Rd., The Neck) Two courts available for rental.

**Champlin's Marina, Motel & Resort** (401-466-2641; West Side Rd., New Harbor) Two courts free to guests; hourly rentals to the public.

## TOURS

### BY BOAT

**Around-the-Island** (401-466-2164) Circumnavigate Block Is. in a motorboat; open daily in-season, 9:00 a.m., 12:00 noon, 3:00 p.m., 6:00 p.m.

**Harbor Cruises** (401-466-1835; New Harbor) Hourly cruises around New Harbor.

**Ocean Trolley** (401-466-2337; Block Island Boat Basin, New Harbor) In addition to private charters, the *Ocean Trolley* leaves the Boat Basin for regular tours at 10:30 a.m., 12:30 p.m., 3:30 p.m., 6:30 p.m.

**White Rose Charters** (401-789-0181; Narragansett) Here's the deal: you board the boat on the mainland in Narragansett, sail to Block Is., and anchor for the night. It's boat-and-breakfast, with time on the island included.

### ON LAND

**Cruise the Island** (401-466-2234) Motor tours of Block Is.

**Rice Bus Charter** (401-466-5472; fax 401-466-5418) Guides drive you around the island, pointing out natural and historic highlights.

**Rose Limo** (401-466-2189) Sight-seeing tours.

## WATER SPORTS

This section highlights sports in the water rather than on the water. Fans of **Kayaking, Parasailing, Scuba Diving, Snorkeling, Surfing,** and **Windsurfing** will find what they're looking for. Lessons, sales, and rentals are readily available.

**Block Island Club** (see the heading Sailing & Boating above).

**Block Island Parasail** (401-466-2474; Old Harbor Dock) The Parasail people's slogan is "Stay dry while you fly!" You take off and land from the boat's deck and en route gaze upon the northeastern coastline of the island from midair. Tandem rides, too. This is also the place to rent jet boats.

**Island Outfitters** (401-466-5502; Ocean Ave., bet. Old and New Harbors) This is *the* place for rentals and sales of scuba diving gear, wet suits, and snorkling and spearfishing equipment. Also organizes dive charters; PADI certification diving courses.

**Island Sport Shop** (401-466-5001; Weldon's Way, Old Harbor) Surfboard rentals and sales.

**Ocean Kayak** (401-466-7717; Town Beach, Corn Neck Rd., The Neck) Kayak rentals.

**Oceans & Ponds/The Orvis Store** (401-466-5502; Ocean Ave, bet. Old and New Harbors) Canoe and kayak rentals and sales.

## WILDLIFE REFUGES

Some of the highest preservation accolades on the East Coast go to Block Island, named by The Nature Conservancy as "One of the Twelve Last Great Places in the Western Hemisphere." The long-standing efforts of islanders to conserve open space and to resist the temptations of tourism have been rewarded: the island remains home to forty rare and endangered species, including some unique to Block Island. It used to call itself "The Bermuda of the North" — now it's become "Nature's Treasure on the Sea." (See the headings Bird-Watching and Hiking & Walking above.)

**Block Island National Wildlife Refuge** (401-364-9124; Corn Neck Rd., The Neck) This is a forty-seven-acre refuge of sandy beaches and rolling dunes at the tip of The Neck, on the western shore of Sachem Pond. Look for herons, woodcock, osprey, cowbirds, and many other migratory birds. In the summer, it's a haven for tiger swallowtails, swallowtails, and cabbage butterflies. No facilities; free.

**Mohegan Bluffs** (off Mohegan Trail on the southeast side of the island) These aren't part of a refuge or park system, but are simply magnificent sea cliffs; at nearly 200 towering feet, they're the highest in New England. The view is spectacular, and the nearest landfall is Africa. A famous Native American battle took place here nearly five centuries ago between the Manisseeans and the invading Mohegans; the Mohegans lost and were pitched from the bluffs that still bear their name.

# SHOPPING

## ANTIQUES

**Crescent Pond and Coastal Design Galleries** (401-466-2033; Corn Neck Rd., The Neck) Nautical antiques. (See the section Culture, under the heading Fine Art Galleries for additional information.)

**The Island Exchange** (401-466-2093; Ocean Ave., bet. Old and New Harbors) Revolving collection of antiques and used everything from housewares to furniture and tools. Open daily in the summer; weekends off-season.

*Relaxation and the sea are two of Block Island's most precious resources.*

Craig Hammell

**Lazy Fish** (401-466-2990; Water St., Old Harbor) Antiques, contemporary photographs, and more.

## BOOKS, CARDS, MUSIC

**Book Nook** (401-466-2993; Water St., Old Harbor) Beach reading stuff: paperbacks, magazines, newspapers. It's a good idea to reserve ahead for Sunday's the *New York Times*.

**Island Book Exchange** (401-466-5456; Old Town Rd., Midisland) Marked-down used books, collectibles, Christmas ornaments, etc.

**Island Bound** (401-466-8878; Water St., New Post Office Building, Old Harbor) The biggest bookstore on Block Is. Offers best-sellers in paperback and hardback; specializes in Block Is. information, sailing, and boating.

**Ship to Shore Bookstore** (401-466-5198; Water St., Old Harbor) Small shop specializing in New England and nautical books, plus some first editions and children's books.

## CHILDREN

**No Kidding** (401-466-2777; Dodge St., Old Harbor) Cool children's clothes, often with nautical motifs.

## CLOTHING & ACCESSORIES

**The Boatworks** (401-466-2033; corner Corn Neck Rd. and Beach Ave., The Neck) Classic, beach clothing, clogs, and sandals, plus hammocks, Adirondack chairs, beach umbrellas, and more.

**Été** (401-466-2925; Dodge St., Old Harbor) Hip and cool clothes to let folks know that you went to Block Is.

**Island Clothing Company** (401-466-5190; Water St., Old Harbor) Fashionable, comfortable clothes in understated colors; outdoor and indoor wear, plus discrete island T-shirts.

**Madhatter** (401-466-5264; Chapel Cottage, Chapel St., Old Harbor) Hats for men, women, and children; despite the name, nothing too wild.

**Oceans & Ponds/The Orvis Store** (401-466-5131; Ocean Ave., New Harbor) Orvis is America's oldest mail-order company. Here you can get all manner of outdoor gear without paying for postage: Timberland hiking boots, Orvis jackets, Nautica swimwear, lots of Gortex, and much more. Also eclectic merchandise like weather instruments, Caribbean spices, and the official, hand-sewn Block Is. flag. Fishing charters and canoe and kayak rentals, too.

**On Island** (401-466-5496; Weldon's Way, Old Harbor) Trendy flax linen clothing, jewelry, plus cool, locally designed Block Is. T-shirts.

**The Shoreline** (401-466-2541; Water St., Old Harbor) Great outdoor and casual clothing for women and men (Putumayo, Patagonia, and more). Another location is on Ocean Ave., New Harbor (401-466-5800).

**Strings & Things** (401-466-5666; Water St., Old Harbor) More contemporary clothes, plus neat stuff and beaded jewelry (also beads for stringing, should you run into a patch of bad weather).

**Wave** (401-466-8822; Water St., Old Harbor) Hip clothing, sunglasses, and T-shirts.

## CRAFT GALLERIES & STUDIOS

**Block Island Blue Pottery** (401-466-2945; Dodge St., Old Harbor) Attractive baking dishes, mugs, bowls, and more, displayed in a ca. 1790 home.

**Block Island Glass & Greenaway Gallery II** (401-466-5331; 401-466-2122; 800-840-5331; Chapel St., Old Harbor) A kind of seaside "factory outlet" for work by New Hampshire artist Chris Baker Salmon, who specializes in clear and colored glass goblets, candlesticks, bowls, and vases. Also an outlet for discount photos, posters, and lithos from the Malcom Greenaway Galleries (see the section Culture, under the heading Fine Art Galleries).

**The Red Herring** (401-466-2540; Water St., Old Harbor) Handcrafted items and home accessories from around the island and the country, selected with a sure eye, plus jewelry and a few antiques.

**Watercolors** (401-466-2538; Dodge St., Old Harbor) All handcrafted gifts and jewelry, including pottery by local RISD graduates, tile work tables, sea glass vases, and more.

## GIFTS

**Archipelago** (401-466-8920; Water St., Old Harbor) Handcrafted imports from clothing and jewelry to teakwood furniture.

**Green Thumb Country Store, Ltd.** (401-466-8844; Corn Neck Rd., Old Harbor) A new venture trying to look old and folksy: T-shirts, candy, clothes, cooking utensils, etc.

**Sandpiper** (401-466-2722; Water St., Old Harbor) An "everything" shop for tourists: Block Is. photos, cards, gifts, jewelry, clothes, you name it.

**Scarlet Begonia** (401-466-5024; Dodge St., Old Harbor) Home-oriented gifts from around the world, including pottery, table linens, quilts, etc.

**Sheila's of Block Island** (401-466-2377; Dodge St., Old Harbor) A gift shop for those who like cute bric-a-brac and candle-scented air.

**The Spindrift** (401-466-2596; Dodge St. and Corn Neck Rd., Old Harbor) Gifts, jewelry, and clothes of a funky / whimsical nature.

## JEWELRY

**Island Dreams** (401-466-2301; Chapel St., Old Harbor) Gold, silver, and gemstone jewelry, plus bric-a-brac.

**Jennifer's Jewelry** (401-466-2744; Dodge St., Old Harbor) Costume and fine jewelry, Chinese and Japanese pearls, scrimshaw, estate items, and Block Is. designs.

## MARINE SUPPLY

**Block Island Boat Basin** (401-466-2631; West Side Rd., New Harbor) A general store for boats, with everything from clothing to paperbacks, ice, marine hardware, plus eighty-five slips. Car and bicycle rentals, too.

**Block Island Marine** (401-466-2028; High St., New Harbor) Nautical hardware and more.

## PHARMACIES

**Block Island Pharmacy** (401-466-5825; High St., Old Harbor) Prescriptions and such, plus a large video library, paperbacks, magazines, camera supplies, TV and VCR rentals, and a fax machine.

## PHOTOGRAPHY

**Photo Dog** (401-466-5858; Chapel St., Old Harbor) Film, batteries, and disposable cameras, plus color, black-and-white, and same-day processing.

## SOUVENIRS & NOVELTIES

**Star Department Store** (401-466-5541; Water St., Old Harbor) A wonderful place to wander around; the old wooden floor creaks as you browse. It has Block Is. souvenirs, T-shirts and sweatshirts, saltwater taffy, film, beach toys, and sportswear, including Woolrich and Jansport.

## SPECIALTY

**Allegro Gifts** (http://www.allegro-gifts.com) Here's a virtual gift shop for those taking a virtual trip to Block Is.; log on and order Block Is. clothing, hats, backpacks, etc. The logo — an image of the island on a spiderweb background (Block Is. on the Web, get it?) — is a little eerie.

**Block Island Historical Society Shop** (401-466-2481; Ocean Ave., Old Harbor) Don't miss the small museum or the shop, which sells exclusive reprints of old postcards, plus great T-shirts, etc.

## SPORTING GOODS

**Block Island Kite Co.** (401-466-2033; Corn Neck Rd. and Beach Ave., The Neck) Every kind of kite imaginable, plus snorkel gear and boogieboards; rentals available, too.

**Island Sport Shop** (401-466-5001; Weldon's Way, Old Harbor) Surf, cycle, fitness, and more.

## VIDEO RENTALS

**Block Island Pharmacy** (see the heading Pharmacies above).
**Esta's Movie Rentals** (401-466-2652; Water and Chapel Sts., Old Harbor).

# CHAPTER SIX
## *The Nitty-Gritty*
## INFORMATION

Craig Hammell

*An edible guest of honor is displayed to admirers at Kempenaar's annual July 4th Public Clambake.*

This compact reference source will come in handy for planning a trip or in midvacation. It covers the following:

# AREA CODE, ZIP CODES, TOWN HALLS

The area code for all of Rhode Island, with few exceptions, is **401**. Zip codes and town hall telephone numbers are listed below. Note that the official name for Block Island is New Shoreham.

| Town Halls | Telephone | Zip Code |
|---|---|---|
| Block Island | 401-466-3200 | 02807 |
| Bristol | 401-253-7000 | 02809 |
| E. Greenwich | 401-886-8665 | 02818 |
| Jamestown | 401-423-7220 | 02835 |
| Little Compton | 401-635-4400 | 02837 |
| Adamsville | | 02801 |
| Middletown | 401-849-2898 | 02842 |
| Narragansett | 401-789-1044 | 02882 |
| Newport | 401-846-9600 | 02840 |
| N. Kingstown | 401-294-3331 | 02852 |
| Portsmouth | 401-683-3255 | 02871 |
| Prudence Island | | 02872 |
| Tiverton | 401-624-4277 | 02878 |
| Warren | 401-245-7340 | 02885 |

# BANKS

The following banks are well represented in the Narragansett Bay area. All are members of international ATM networks, which are noted below.

| Bank | Telephone | ATM Networks |
|---|---|---|
| Bank of Newport | 401-273-6620 or 800-234-8586 | Cirrus, Yankee 24 |
| Citizens Bank | 401-849-6444 or 800-922-9999 | Cirrus, Yankee 24 |
| Fleet Bank | 401-846-7400 or 800-445-4542 | Cirrus, NYCE |
| Hospital Trust | 401-847-2280 or 800-662-5086 | NYCE, Yankee 24, Plus |
| Shawmut Bank of RI | 800-742-9688 | Cirrus, NYCE, Yankee 24 |
| The Washington Trust Company | 401-466-7710 (Block Is.) 401-782-1000 (Narragst.) | Cirrus, Yankee 24, Plus |

## BIBLIOGRAPHY

The following books represent the tip of a great literary iceberg of what's been written about Newport and Narragansett Bay. The Newport Library's Newport Room is a great place to start reading.

### *Books You Can Buy*

### ART, ARCHITECTURE, PHOTO ESSAY

*The Artistic Heritage of Newport and the Narragansett Bay.* Exhibition Catalogue, William Vareika Fine Arts, 1990. Full-color illustrations, $5.95 pb. The exhibition was held to benefit Save the Bay. Everyone benefits from this charming catalogue.

Guinness, Desmond and Julius Sadler. *Newport Preserved: The Architecture of the 18th Century.* NY: Viking Press, 1982. 152 pp., illustrations. The story behind the conservation and restoration of Newport's colonial heritage.

Mulvaugh, Jane and Mark Weber. *Newport Houses.* NY: Rizzoli, 1989. 220 pp., color photos. The domestic architecture of Newport, from colonial clapboards to the mansions. Introduction by Robert Stern.

*Newport Mansions: The Gilded Age.* Foremost Pubs., 1982. A photo extravaganza by photographer Richard Cheek. Text by Tom Gannon.

Smith, Clyde H. *Coastal Rhode Island.* Foremost Books, 1987. 128 pp., $35. A stunning, all-photo coffee table book that shows off the beauty of the bay.

Turbeville, Deborah. *Newport Remembered.* NY: Harry Abrams, Publishers, 1994. $20. Soft-focus, sepia- and pastel-shaded photographs of the Newport mansions and their grounds by a well-known fashion photographer. Text by Louis Auchincloss.

Welch, Wally. *The Lighthouses of Rhode Island.* Apopka, FL: Lighthouse Publications, 1987. 34 pp. Full-color booklet, with descriptions of all of the lighthouses in the state.

### AUTOBIOGRAPHY, BIOGRAPHY, REMINISCENCE, TRAVEL LITERATURE

Botkin, B.A., ed. *A Treasury of New England Folklore.* NY: American Legacy Press, 1989. 618 pp. Reminiscences, legends, ghost stories, and other tales of New England, state by state.

Cantwell, Mary Lee. *American Girl.* 1992. Lyrical, funny memoir of growing up in "the country of the blue-eyed" in Bristol, RI.

Gavan, Terence. *The Barons of Newport.* Newport, RI: Pineapple Publications, 1988. 88 pp., photos, $7.50. Chatty history of the Gilded Age gang.

James, Henry. *Collected Travel Writings, Great Britain and America: English Hours, The American Scene, Other Travels.* The Library of America, 1993. $35. This thick (846-page) collection is a treasure trove for James fans; his "America:

Early Travel Writings" are splendid, vividly observed, and acutely analyzed — Newport in particular. This is travel literature at its finest.

McEntee, Grace Hall. *Where Storms Are Beautiful*. Pastoral Publishers, 1993. 167 pp., $12.95. Tales of a teacher who lives on Prudence Island and commutes to the mainland by fishing boat.

O'Connor, Lucy, ed. *Jonnycakes and Cream*. 1993. Forty-five oral histories of Little Compton, RI, supplemented by news clippings, photos, and poems by area residents.

## COOKBOOKS

Hammersmith Farm. *The Hammersmith Farm Cookbook*. 1990. 242 pp. Illustrated recipes from Jackie O's childhood home.

Murphy, Martha. *The Bed & Breakfast Cookbook: Great American B&Bs and Their Recipes from All 50 States*. Owings Mills, MD: Stemmer House Publications, Inc., 1991. A great cookbook and guide from a Narragansett B&B owner.

_____. *A New England Fish Tale*. Harry Holt Publishers. 270 pp., $25. Murphy's latest book collects 100 seafood recipes, developed by the author or regional chefs, from all over New England and intersperses them with stories and tales and a century's worth of black-and-white photographs. Makes a terrific gift.

*Rhode Island Menu*. Cranston, RI, 1995. $14.95. A collection of international recipes from RI restaurants.

Riess, Shirley F. *Newport Cooks and Collects*. 1996. Preservation Society of Newport County, 1996. A collection of residents' favorite recipes.

Shernam, Barbara. *The Island Cookbook*. Favorite Recipes Press, 1993. 199 pp., $14.95. Highlights the cuisine of Block Island, Newport, Jamestown, Prudence, Nantucket, and Martha's Vineyard.

The Society for the Propagation of the Jonnycake Tradition, eds. *The Jonnycake Cookbook*. 1972. $7. Many ways to cook and serve Rhode Island's favorite food.

## FICTION

Casey, John. *Spartina*. NY: Alfred A. Knopf, Inc., 1989. This story of a Rhode Island fisherman won the National Book Award in 1989.

Flook, Maria. *Open Water*. Ecco Publications, 1995. 327 pp., $10.40 pb. A disturbing yet comic tale set in Newport.

Rice, Luanne. *Blue Moon*. Viking, 1993. A novel about a troubled family in the fictional fishing village of Mount Hope, RI.

Wilder, Thornton. *Theophilus North*. Carroll & Graf Publishers, Inc., 1973. Amusing tale of a young man who sorts out the woes of his rich patrons in 1920s Newport. Also made into a film called *Mr. North*.

Wolff, Geoffrey. *Providence.* Penguin Books, 1986. A fast-paced crime novel set in Providence, though the characters roam around Narragansett Bay.

## HISTORY

Conley, Patrick T. *An Album of Rhode Island History, 1636-1986.* Virginia Beach, VA: The Donning Company, Pubs., 1992. 288 pp., photos, $29.95. Illustrated history of the state; great early photos and prints.

Hale, Stuart O. *Narragansett Bay: A Friend's Perspective.* Rhode Island Sea Grant, URI, 1988 (second edition). 130 pp., illustrations, $12.95 pb. Social history of the bay.

*Images of America Series.* Dover, NH: Acadia Publishers, an imprint of Chalford Publishers, 1996. $16.99. Each book in this series is a compilation of old photographs of a specific town or region; those in the Narragansett Bay area include Bristol, Warren, Portsmouth, Newport, and Aquidneck Island.

Jefferys, C.P.B. *Newport: A Short History.* Newport Historical Society, 1992. 101 pp., $9.95.

Madden, Sue. *Jamestown Affairs.* Jamestown, RI: West Ferry Press, an imprint of Seagrant Publications, 1996. $18. A collection of newspaper articles on Jamestown, printed between 1992-1995.

McLoughlin, William, G. *Rhode Island: A History.* The States and the Nation Series, American Association for State and Local History, NY: W.W. Norton & Co., 1986. 240 pp., $9.95. Intelligent and readable paperback covering RI events and ideas.

Quinn, Alonzo W. *Rhode Island Geology for the Non-Geologist.* Providence, RI Department of Natural Resources, 1976. 63 pp., photos, and illustrations. Concise, understandable history of RI geology.

Sharp, Eleyne Austen. *Haunted Newport.* Newport, RI: Austen Sharp Publishing, 1996. 64 pp., $9.95.

## RECREATION

*Bird Walks in Rhode Island: Exploring the Ocean State's Best Sanctuaries.* Woodstock, VT: Backcountry Publications, 1992. 144 pp., $9.95 pb.

McCabe, Catherine O. *Cyclist's Guide to Block Island.* Booklet with three island tours.

Stone, Howard. *Short Bike Rides in Rhode Island.* Chester, CT: Globe Pequot Press, 1988 (third edition). 241 pp., illustrations, and maps. A terrific resource for bicycle touring in the Ocean State.

Weber, Ken. *Walks & Rambles in Rhode Island: A Guide to the Natural and Historic Wonders of the Ocean State.* Woodstock, VT: Backcountry Publications, 1996 (second edition, third printing). 166 pp., maps, photos. Forty self-guided walking tours throughout RI. Also see his *More Walks & Rambles in Rhode Island,* 1992.

## TRAVEL GUIDES

Gannon, Tom. *Newport, Rhode Island: A Guide to the City by the Sea.* Woodstock, VT: Countryman Press, 1992 (second edition). 174 pp., illustrations.

Gavan, Terence. *Exploring Newport.* Newport, RI: Pineapple Publications, 1992. 111 pp., $8.95. A guide to Newport's historic attractions, planned as a series of walking tours. Restaurant and lodging information included.

Meras, Phyllis and Tom Gannon. *Rhode Island, An Explorer's Guide.* Woodstock, VT: Countryman Press, 1995. 294 pp., photos. A thorough guide that goes beyond the Newport and Narragansett Bay area.

## BLOCK ISLAND

Berrigan, Daniel. *Block Island.* Unicorn Press, 1985. 102 pp.

Ritchie, Ethel. *Block Island Lore and Legends.* Block Island, RI: F. Norman Associates, 1956. 93 pp., illustrations. An indispensable glimpse of island folklore.

Wilkinson, Chilton. *Saltbound: A Block Island Winter.* NY: Methuen, 1980. 263 pp., illustrations. Life "on-island" throughout the seasons.

## CLIMATE, WEATHER, WHAT TO WEAR

Despite meteorologists' tag for Rhode Island weather — "humid continental" — it's never as hot and muggy here in the summer as in New Jersey or Washington D.C., nor does it stay bitterly cold in the winter for very long. The average mean temperature is 50° F, with January logging in as the coldest month (28° F) and July as the hottest (72°F).

There is one factor that belies these seemingly moderate temperatures, however, and that is wind. Block Island especially, but the bay towns as well, can be extraordinarily windy places; expect everything from gentle breezes to hurricane-force blows, and note that it's always cooler and windier offshore — so especially if sailing or boating is in your plans, bring a waterproof windbreaker and wear light layers beneath it.

Casual is the one adjective that describes dress in and around Newport. There's literally no place on Block Island that won't let you in the front door in jeans (even the spiffiest restaurants), and the same is true for most of Newport's eateries, though there are a few exceptions (the White Horse Tavern and the Inn at Castle Hill require jackets and ties). Comfortable walking shoes are a necessity, with soles that can negotiate cobblestones. Sunglasses are also necessary since the glare factor is high here, with reflected sunlight off the sea.

## WEATHER INFORMATION

**Rhode Island** (401-976-1212).

**New England** (401-976-6666).

# DISABLED SERVICES

Most state facilities in Rhode Island, such as parks and campgrounds, offer access for the physically impaired. See the Lodging and Dining sections in Chapters Three, Four, and Five for information on individual establishments. The following organizations can provide more detailed information on disabled services in the Narragansett Bay area.

**Deaf Interpreters** (800-525-0770).
**Information for the Handicapped: Tips on Tape** (401-831-1131).
**Rhode Island Governor's Commission on the Handicapped** (401-277-3731).
**Rhode Island Relay** (800-RI-55555).

# EMERGENCY NUMBERS

| Town | Ambulance | Fire | Police |
|---|---|---|---|
| Block Island / New Shoreham | 911 | 401-466-3220 | 401-466-3220 |
| Bristol | 911 or 401-253-6611 | 401-253-6900 | 401-253-6611 |
| E. Greenwich | 911 | 401-884-4211 | 401-884-2244 |
| Jamestown | 911 | 401-423-1313 | 401-423-1212 |
| Little Compton | 401-635-2323 | 401-635-2323 | 401-635-2311 |
| Middletown | 911 | 401-847-3636 | 401-846-1104 |
| Narragansett | 911 | 401-789-1011 | 401-789-1011 |
| Newport | 911 or 401-846-2211 | 401-846-2211 | 401-847-1212 |
| N. Kingstown | 911 or 401-294-3344 | 401-294-3344 | 401-294-3311 |
| Portsmouth | 911 | 401-683-1155 | 401-683-2422 |
| Tiverton | 401-624-4242 | 401-624-4242 | 401-624-3222 |
| Warren | 911 or 401-245-3411 | 401-245-3411 | 401-245-1311 |

# HOSPITALS

The following hospitals provide emergency room services.

Newport Hospital (401-846-6400; Friendship St., Newport, RI).
Rhode Island Hospital (401-277-4000; 593 Eddy St., Providence, RI).
Roger Williams Hospital (401-456-2000; 825 Chalkstone Ave., Providence, RI).
South County Hospital (401-782-8000; 100 Kenyon Ave., Wakefield, RI).
Westerly Hospital (401-596-6000; 25 Wells St., Westerly, RI).
Women and Infants Hospital (401-274-1100; 101 Dudley St., Providence, RI).

# MEDIA

The following publications are but a selection of what's available. In the summer, especially, a host of free weekly and monthly magazines flourish, such as *Ocean State Traveler*, all of which contain up-to-date reviews and information on seasonal events. An indispensable source of information statewide is the *Rhode Island Monthly* (401-421-2552) Rhode Island Monthly Communications, 95 Chestnut Street, Providence, Rhode Island 02903. Every year the June issue offers a Beach and Summer Guide, and the August issue rounds up the "Best and Worst of the Ocean State."

## PUBLICATIONS

*The Block Island Times* (401-466-2222; 401-466-5533; PO Box 278, Block Is., RI 02807).
*Bristol Phoenix* (East Bay Newspapers; 401-253-6000; One Bradford, Bristol, RI 02809).
*East Greenwich Magazine* (401-885-3447; 655 Main St., E. Greenwich, RI 02818).
*Jamestown Press* (401-423-3200; 42 Narragansett Ave., Jamestown, RI 02835).
*Narragansett Times* (401-789-9744; 187 Main St., Wakefield, RI 02880).
*Newport Daily News* (401-849-3300; 101 Malbone Rd., Newport, RI 02840).
*Providence Journal-Bulletin* (East Bay offices; 401-846-0600; 28 Pelham St., Newport, RI 02840; 401-245-8600; 529 Main St., Rte. 114, Warren, RI 02885) The largest paper in the state. Restaurant reviews appear on Friday.
*Sakonnet Times* (401-683-1000; 2829 E. Main Rd., Rte. 138, Portsmouth, RI 02871) Covers Little Compton, Tiverton, and Portsmouth.
*The Standard-Times* (401-294-4576; 13 W. Main St., N. Kingstown, RI 02852) "Jamestown's Hometown Newspaper."
*Warren Times-Gazette* (401-245-6002; 72 Child St., Warren, RI 02885).

## RADIO

WELH-FM 88.1; Providence; Alternative, urban rock.
WRIU-FM 90.3; URI; Most eclectic mix of music in the state, from reggae and gospel to folk and funk.
WXIN-FM 90.7; Providence; Top 40, heavy metal, alternative rock.

**WDOM-FM** 91.3; Providence; Classical, jazz, rock.
**WPRO-FM** 92.3; Providence; Chewing-gummy top 40.
**WSNE-FM** 93.3; Providence; Adult contemporary.
**WHJY-FM** 94.1; Providence; Hard rock, loud DJs.
**WBRU-FM** 95.5; Brown University; Cutting-edge (and some album) rock.
**WVBI-FM** 95.9; Block Island; Classical.
**WERI-FM** 99.3; Block Island and South County; Soft rock and local information.
**WDGE-FM** 99.7; Providence; Modern and alternative rock.
**WWBB-FM** 101.5; Providence; Oldies.
**WWRX-FM** 103.7; Providence; Classic rock and Imus in the Morning.
**WWLI-FM** 105.1; Providence; Adult contemporary.
**WWKX-FM** 106.3; Providence; Top 40 and dance.

## POST OFFICES

| Town | Address | Telephone |
|---|---|---|
| Block Island | Dodge St. | 401-466-7733 |
| Bristol | 515 Hope St., Rte. 114 | 401-253-6100 |
| E. Greenwich | 176 First Ave. | 401-884-2610 |
| Jamestown | 75 Narragansett Ave. | 401-423-0330 |
| Little Compton | 2 Meeting House Ln. | 401-635-2332 |
| Middletown | Commercial Ave. | 401-846-1283 |
| Newport | Fed. Bldg., Thames St. | 401-847-2329 |
|  | Broadway Sta., 195 Broadway | 401-846-0444 |
| N. Kingstown | 234 W. Main St. | 401-294-4641 |
| Portsmouth | 95 Chase Rd. | 401-683-1320 |
| Tiverton | 600 Main St., Rte. 77 | 401-624-4772 |
| Warren | 53 Child St. | 401-245-5039 |

## PUBLIC REST ROOMS

This list contains possibly the most crucial information in *The Newport & Narragansett Bay Book.*

**Block Island:** Chamber of Commerce building in parking lot at Old Harbor ferry landing; New Harbor dock; Library; Police Dept.; Town Hall.
**Bristol:** Colt State Park.
**E. Greenwich:** Town Hall (125 Main St.); open Mon.-Fri., 8:30 a.m.-4:30 p.m.

**Jamestown:** Recreation Center on Conanicus Ave. (rest rooms in separate structure facing Union St.); seasonal.

**Little Compton:** Town Hall (40 Commons).

**Middletown:** None.

**Narragansett:** In the Pier Marketplace complex next to the Public Library, corner of Kingstown Rd. and Caswell; seasonal.

**Newport:** Newport Gateway Convention & Visitors' Bureau, 23 America's Cup Ave.; Cardines Field (during ball games only), corner of America's Cup Ave. and Broadway; Mary St. parking lot; Ft. Adams; Breton Point State Park; Easton Beach; Wellington Ave. at King's Park.

**N. Kingstown:** Located between Brown St. and Wickford Harbor.

**Portsmouth:** Sandy Point Beach Bathhouse; seasonal.

**Tiverton:** Grinnell and Fogland Beaches; seasonal.

**Warren:** Town Beach; seasonal. Hugh Cole Pavilion at the playground on Hugh Cole Rd., off Child St.; seasonal.

## ROAD SERVICES

The number to remember is **800-AAA-HELP: AAA** 24-Hour Emergency Road Service Hot Line. If you're looking for information rather than immediate assistance, try one of these regional offices.

**AAA Narragansett** (401-789-3000; 14 Woodruff Ave., Narragansett, RI 02882).

**AAA Newport** (401-841-5000; 99 E. Main Rd., Rte. 138, Middletown, RI 02842).

**AAA Providence** (401-272-7000; 55 Dorrance Ave., Providence, RI 02903).

**AAA Warwick** (401-736-0001; 501 Centerville Rd., Warwick, RI 02887) The main office for Rhode Island.

## TOURIST INFORMATION

### CHAMBERS OF COMMERCE

**Block Island Chamber of Commerce** (401-466-2982; Drawer D, Block Is., RI 02807) Be sure to ask for Elva. She's patient, helpful, and brimming with knowledge about the island.

**Bristol County Chamber of Commerce** (401-245-0750; PO Box 250, Warren, RI 02885).

**Narragansett Chamber of Commerce** (401-783-7121; PO Box 742, Narragansett, RI 02882).

**Newport County Chamber of Commerce** (401-847-1600; PO Box 237, Newport, RI 02840).

**North Kingstown Chamber of Commerce** (401-295-5566; PO Box 454, N. Kingstown, RI 02852).

## FISHING & HUNTING REGULATIONS

For questions about fishing or shellfishing, hunting, boating restrictions, or coastal resources, contact the **Rhode Island Department of Environmental Management** (401-789-3094) and in particular, the **Division of Fish and Wildlife** (401-277-3075).

## REGIONAL ORGANIZATIONS

**Block Island Tourism Council** (401-466-5200; 800-383-BIRI; PO Box 356, Block Is., RI 02807).
**Newport Gateway Convention & Visitors' Bureau** (401-849-8048; 800-548-4662; 23 America's Cup Ave., Newport, RI 02840) An essential stop: they have a reservation service and plenty of resource material on Newport and Aquidneck.
**South County Tourism Council, Inc.** (401-789-4422; 800-548-4662; PO Box 651, Narragansett, RI 02882).

## TRAVELER'S AID

**Newport Council for International Visitors** (401-846-0222; 401-846-5314; PO Box 3032, Newport, RI 02840).
**Traveler's Aid Society of Rhode Island** (401-521-2255; 177 Union St., Providence, RI 02903).

## VISITOR INFORMATION

**Rhode Island Tourism Division Office of Economic Development** (401-277-2601; 800-556-2484; 7 Jackson Walkway, Providence, RI 02903) For statewide information, the free *Rhode Island Visitor's Guide* is published every Apr. and is an excellent resource for attractions and seasonal events.
**Rhode Island Welcome Center** (401-539-3031; bet. exits 2 and 3 on Rte. 95 near the CT border) Open daily year-round; lots of brochures, plus human assistance.

# IF TIME IS SHORT

The following suggestions include attractions so well known that if you don't see them, you'll be scorned by friends and family, as well as a few little-known spots that are personal favorites. I've also included some suggestions across the budget board for both lodging and restaurants. Finally, don't forget to take a look at the sections Food & Beverage Purveyors in Chapters Three, Four, and Five; the starred entries are especially worth a look.

### In Newport

For Gilded Age glamour, try the **Elm Tree Cottage** (401-849-1610; 800-882-3356; 336 Gibbs Avenue) or **The Ivy Lodge** (401-849-6865; 12 Clay Street). For sheer *authenticity* and a stupendous view, go to the **Sanford-Covell Villa Marina** (401-847-0206; 72 Washington Street) — my favorite inn in Newport. Two quiet, eighteenth-century B&Bs are the **Elliott Boss House** (401-849-9425; 20 Second Street) and the **Culpeper House B&B** (401-846-4011; 30 Second Street), and for lighthouse fans, try the **Rose Island Lighthouse** (401-847-4242).

A unique dining choice is **Cheeky Monkey Cafe** (401-845-9494; 14 Perry Mill Wharf), which offers "British Colonial Cuisine." For a pull-out-the-stops meal go to the **Castle Hill Inn and Resort** (401-849-3800; Ocean Drive), a shingle-style mansion on its own peninsula off Ocean Drive. The **Marina Grille** (401-841-0999; Goat Island South), which occupies the tip of Goat Island, has an unparalleled vista of the city; eat elsewhere.

When it comes to the mansions, for my money **Marble House** (401-847-1000; Bellevue Avenue) is the one to visit. It's nearly as lavish as The Breakers, but its gilt and alabaster add up to more than conspicuous consumption. Also don't miss: **Ten Mile Drive** (aka **Ocean Drive),** either by car or bicycle; the magnificent **Cliff Walk,** which offers a view of both the sea and the mansions; the **International Tennis Hall of Fame** (401-849-3990; 194 Bellevue Avenue), originally the Newport Casino and first site of the U.S. Open; and the **International Yacht Restoration School** (401-849-3060; Thames Street), where you can watch the old beauties being brought back to life.

### On the shores of Narragansett Bay

On the West Bay, Narragansett offers some gems of B&Bs: **The Old Clerk House** (401-783-8008; 49 Narragansett Avenue, Narragansett Pier) is genteel and private; **Murphy's B&B** (401-789-1824; 43 South Pier Road, Narragansett Pier) offers superb breakfasts; and **Historic Home B&B** (401-789-7746; 144 Gibson Avenue, Narragansett Pier) occupies an 1884 gabled stone cottage. On the East Bay, the **Inn at Shadow Lawn** (401-847-0902; 800-352-2750, 120 Miantonomi Avenue, Middletown) has common rooms worthy of the mansions; the **Nathaniel Porter Inn** (401-245-6622; 125 Water Street, Warren) is an affordable historic charmer with a fine restaurant. I'd recommend any of the fine B&Bs in **Bristol,** and for something completely different, try **White Cap Cabins** (401-683-0476; Vanderbilt Lane, off Route 138, Portsmouth): an utterly private spot on the edge of the bay.

When it comes to food, *the* place not to miss on the West Bay is **Chez Pascal** (401-782-6020; 944 Boston Neck Road, Route 1A, Narragansett) for scrupulously authentic French food. On the East Bay, **Sea Shai** (401-849-5100; 747 Aquidneck Avenue, Middletown) offers fantastic Japanese cuisine. Try the **Sea Fare Inn** (401-683-0577; 3352 East Main Road, Portsmouth) for a really special meal, and the **Commons Lunch** (401-635-4388; The Commons, Little Compton) for down-home New England cooking.

On the West Bay, don't miss **Wickford,** a village of historic homes, shops, and galleries, backed by an elegant harbor; while there, check out **The Kayak Centre** (401-295-4400; 9 Phillips Street, Wickford). Cyclists should visit **Jamestown** and make a circuit of the island, finishing at **Beaver Tail State Park** at the southern tip. History and architecture buffs should visit **Casey Farm** (401-295-1030; Boston Neck Road, Route 1A, North Kingstown), a rare eighteenth-century *northern* plantation house. On the East Bay, highlights include the following: **Green Animals Topiary Gardens** (401-847-1000; Cory's Lane, off Route 114, Portsmouth); the **Herreshoff Marine Museum** (401-253-5000; 7 Burnside Street, Bristol); the **Commons Burial Ground** in Little Compton; **Sachuest Point** in Middletown; and **Goosewing Beach** in Little Compton — easily the most idyllic, if hidden, beach in Rhode Island.

## On Block Island

**The Spring House** (401-466-5844; 800-234-9263; Spring Street, Old Harbor) is the oldest hotel on Block Island, with a wide veranda facing the sea. The **Sea Breeze Inn** (401-466-2275; 800-786-2274; Spring Street, Old Harbor) is simply decorated and satisfying. **The Sasafrash** (401-466-5486; Center Road, Center) was once a former Primitive Methodist Church. And the **Beach House B&B** (401-466-2929; Corn Neck Road, Old Harbor) is for those who want to stay *right smack* on the ocean.

Regarding food, simplicity is the rule on Block Island, in both upscale dining rooms and simple fish joints. The best of the latter is **Finn's Seafood Restaurant** (401-466-2473; Water Street, Old Harbor ferry landing); the best of the former is (arguably) the **Highview Inn Eatery** (401-466-5912; Connecticut Avenue, Old Harbor). For breakfast, try **The 1661 Inn** (401-466-2421; 800-626-4773; Spring Street, Old Harbor), which offers a massive buffet in-season. Also try **Mahagony Shoals** (401-466-5572; New Harbor), a tiny, low-key bar on Payne's Dock.

**Crescent Beach** is the cleanest, widest, and grandest in all Rhode Island. Of its designated stretches, the northernmost, called **Mansion Beach,** is the most private. Don't miss **Mohegan Bluffs,** the highest sea cliffs in New England, and the **Southeast Light** (401-466-5009), which perches on top of them. Best of all, tour the western side of the island by bicycle and head down Black Rock Road, off Cooneymus Road, to **Black Rock Beach** — it looks like a secluded spot in Cornwall.

# Index

# LODGING BY PRICE CODE

## DINING BY PRICE CODE

# DINING BY CUISINE

# About the Author

Marguerite Harrison

Pamela Petro has lived in Rhode Island for eleven (nonconsecutive) years, including her undergraduate days at Brown University. She's a frequent contributor to the *New York Times* Travel and Arts Sections as well as a host of other publications, including *Islands, The Atlantic Monthly,* and *Four Seasons Magazine.* She is the author of *Travels in an Old Tongue: Touring the World Speaking Welsh,* a book of travel literature published in 1997 by HarperCollins U.K.